Implementing Azure: Putting Modern DevOps to Use

Transform your software deployment process with Microsoft Azure

Florian Klaffenbach
Oliver Michalski
Markus Klein
Mohamed Wali
Namit Tanasseri
Rahul Rai

BIRMINGHAM - MUMBAI

Implementing Azure: Putting Modern DevOps to Use

First published: January 2019

Production reference: 1290119

Published by Packt Publishing Ltd.
Livery Place
35 Livery Street
Birmingham
B3 2PB, UK.

ISBN 978-1-78883-393-6

www.packtpub.com

`mapt.io`

Mapt is an online digital library that gives you full access to over 5,000 books and videos, as well as industry leading tools to help you plan your personal development and advance your career. For more information, please visit our website.

Why subscribe?

- Spend less time learning and more time coding with practical eBooks and Videos from over 4,000 industry professionals

- Improve your learning with Skill Plans built especially for you

- Get a free eBook or video every month

- Mapt is fully searchable

- Copy and paste, print, and bookmark content

Packt.com

Did you know that Packt offers eBook versions of every book published, with PDF and ePub files available? You can upgrade to the eBook version at `www.packt.com` and as a print book customer, you are entitled to a discount on the eBook copy. Get in touch with us at `customercare@packtpub.com` for more details.

At `www.packt.com`, you can also read a collection of free technical articles, sign up for a range of free newsletters, and receive exclusive discounts and offers on Packt books and eBooks.

Contributors

About the authors

Florian Klaffenbach is working as a technology solutions professional at Microsoft. He is a well-known expert in hybrid cloud scenarios, cloud connectivity, and cloud environment optimization. Before he started working with Microsoft, he worked in several companies in different roles, such as the technical community manager and solution expert at Dell, and solutions architect at CGI Germany.

Oliver Michalski started in 1999 with his IT carrier as a Web Developer. Now, he is a Senior Software Engineer for Microsoft .NET and an SOA Architect. He also works as an Independent Enterprise Consultant in the field Microsoft Azure. When he started in 2011 with Microsoft Azure, there was no Azure Community on the German market. Therefore, Oliver founded the Azure Community Germany (ACD). Oliver is Chairman of the Azure Community Germany, and since April 2016 and July 2017, he has been a Microsoft Most Valuable Professional for Microsoft Azure. Oliver is author (co-author) of Implementing Azure Solutions and Implementing Azure Cloud Design Patterns, both available from Packt Publishing.

Markus Klein works as a technology solution specialist at Microsoft Germany, and specialize in Azure and Hybrid Azure scenarios. He is passionate about the Microsoft technology for more than 20 years, starting with System Center, Service Provider Foundation, KATAL, Azure Pack, Azure, and Azure Stack. Before joining Microsoft, he worked as an architect at Microsoft Cloud Partners. In 2007, he founded a cloud community and was the co-founder of some Azure meetups. Before he joined Microsoft, he was recognized as an MVP in cloud and datacenter management for seven years. He supports the community and is a regular blogger and speaker at conferences in Europe and abroad.

Mohamed Wali is a cloud DevOps engineer based in Amsterdam who has been working with Microsoft technologies for around seven years. He has been working with Azure since 2013. In July 2014, Mohamed became recognized as the youngest Microsoft MVP in the world. He has already authored and co-authored multiple books about Microsoft Azure. He shares his knowledge and expertise through blogging, authoring books, and speaking at events.

Namit Tanasseri is a certified Microsoft cloud solutions architect with an experience of more than 11 years. He started his career as a software development engineer with Microsoft Research and Development Center in 2005. During the first five years of his career, he had opportunities to work with major Microsoft product groups, such as Microsoft Office and Windows. During this time, he strengthened his knowledge of agile software development methodologies and processes. He also earned a patent during this tenure. As a technology consultant with Microsoft, Namit worked with Microsoft Azure Services for four years. Namit is a subject matter expert in Microsoft Azure and actively contributes to the Microsoft cloud community, while delivering top quality solutions for Microsoft customers. Namit also led the Windows Azure community in Microsoft Services India. Namit currently serves as a Microsoft cloud solutions architect from Sydney, Australia, and works on large and medium-sized enterprise engagements.

Rahul Rai is a technology consultant based in Sydney, Australia with over nine years of professional experience. He has been at the forefront of cloud consulting for government organizations and businesses around the world. Rahul has been working on Microsoft Azure since the service was in its infancy, delivering an ITSM tool built for and on Azure in 2008. Since then, Rahul has played the roles of a developer, a consultant, and an architect for enterprises ranging from small start-ups to multinational corporations. He worked for over five years with Microsoft Services with diverse teams to deliver innovative solutions on Microsoft Azure. In Microsoft, Rahul was a subject matter expert in Microsoft cloud technologies. Rahul has also worked as a cloud solution architect for Microsoft, for which he worked closely with some established Microsoft partners to drive joint customer transformations to cloud-based architectures.

Packt is searching for authors like you

If you're interested in becoming an author for Packt, please visit authors.packtpub.com and apply today. We have worked with thousands of developers and tech professionals, just like you, to help them share their insight with the global tech community. You can make a general application, apply for a specific hot topic that we are recruiting an author for, or submit your own idea.

Table of Contents

Preface

This Learning Path helps you understand microservices architecture and leverage various services of Microsoft Azure Service Fabric to build, deploy, and maintain highly scalable enterprise-grade applications. You will learn to select an appropriate Azure backend structure for your solutions and work with its toolkit and managed apps to share your solutions with its service catalog. As you progress through the Learning Path, you will study Azure Cloud Services, Azure-managed Kubernetes, and Azure Container Services deployment techniques. To apply all that you've understood, you will build an end-to-end Azure system in scalable, decoupled tiers for an industrial bakery with three business domains. Toward the end of this Learning Path, you will build another scalable architecture using Azure Service Bus topics to send orders between decoupled business domains with scalable worker roles processing these orders.

By the end of this Learning Path, you will be comfortable in using development, deployment, and maintenance processes to build robust cloud solutions on Azure.

This Learning Path includes content from the following Packt products:

- Implementing Azure Solutions - Second Edition by Florian Klaffenbach, Oliver Michalski, Markus Klein
- Learn Microsoft Azure by Mohamed Wali
- Microservices with Azure by Namit Tanasseri and Rahul Rai

Who this book is for

If you are an IT system architect, network admin, or a DevOps engineer who wants to implement Azure solutions for your organization, this Learning Path is for you. Basic knowledge of the Azure Cloud platform will be beneficial.

What this book covers

Chapter 1, *Getting Started with Azure Implementation*, will help you understand how the basic services of Azure make up the core of an application running in Azure. We will also give the reader an idea as to how Azure influences Microsoft's products and product strategy. We will explain the different Cloud Models and Multi Cloud strategies in conjunction with Microsoft Azure too.

Chapter 2, *Azure Resource Manager and Tools*, describes the Azure Resource Manager (ARM) concept, the ARM Tools Instrumentation and how it works. We show: Working with the Azure Portal and working with Azure PowerShell. Last, we will also describe the differences between classic deployment and ARM.

Chapter 3, *Deploying and Synchronizing Azure Active Directory*, will describe how to deploy Azure Active Directory, how to secure it for the next following steps and give some best practice advises when using Azure Active Directory together with other Microsoft Services like Office 365. Within the chapter we will describe how Azure Active Directory Synchronization could be implemented. We will give best practices which Synchronization method is the best for different environments. We will also explain how to secure and filter which accounts and attributes are synced.

Chapter 4, *Implementing Azure Networks*,in this chapter you will learn how to deploy and configure virtual networks in Azure and will get some best practice advises about working with subnets and network splitting. We will also provide an overview about routing in Azure and Network Devices in Azure.

Chapter 5, *Implementing Azure Storage*, in this chapter, you will get to know how to implement storage accounts in azure, the differences between accounts and give a brief overview about the different usage scenarios.

Chapter 6, *Implementing Azure-Managed Kubernetes and Azure Container Service*, will describe the general concept behind containers in Azure work, the need to have Kubernetes as an orchestrator, how AKS works and where Azure Managed Instances make sense, how they are created, deployed and managed.

Chapter 7, *Azure Hybrid Data Center Services,* will give the reader an overview how to implement Azure Hybrid Data Center Services using Azure Stack.

Chapter 8, *Azure Web Apps Basics,* covers one of Azure App Service, its different types, and how to work with them.

Chapter 9, *Managing Azure Web Apps,* covers some of the highly available solutions for Azure Web Apps in this chapter.

Chapter 10, *Basics of Azure SQL Database,* explores the Azure SQL Database, its types, and how to deploy it in Azure.

Chapter 11, *Managing Azure SQL Database,* covers other Azure SQL Database types and explains how to provide a highly available solution for them.

Chapter 12, *Microservices 2013– Getting to Know the Buzzword,* lays the foundation of concepts of Microservices and explores the scenarios, where Microservices are best suited for your application.

Chapter 13, *Understanding Azure Service Fabric,* explains the basic concepts and architecture of Azure Service Fabric.

Chapter 14, *Hands-on with Service Fabric – Guest Executables,* talks about building and deploying applications as Guest Executables on a Service Fabric cluster.

Chapter 15, *Hands on with Service Fabric – Reliable Services,* explains the concept of Reliable Services programming model for building Microservices hosted on Service Fabric.

Chapter 16, *Reliable Actors,* introduces Actor programming model on Service Fabric and the ways to build and deploy actors on a Service Fabric cluster.

Chapter 17, *Microservices Architecture Patterns Motivation,* provides an overview of the motivation behind driving Microservices architectural patterns. The chapter also talks about the classification of the patterns that are discussed in this book.

Chapter 18, *Microservices Architectural Patterns,* introduces a catalog of design patterns categorized by its application. Each design pattern explains the problem and the proven solution for that problem. The pattern concludes with considerations that should be taken while applying the pattern and the use cases where the pattern can be applied.

Chapter 19, *Securing and Managing Your Microservices*, will guide you on securing your Microservices deployment on a Service Fabric cluster.

Chapter 20, *Diagnostics and Monitoring*, covers how to set up diagnostics and monitoring in your Service Fabric application. You will also learn how to use Service Fabric Explorer to monitor the cluster.

Chapter 21, *Continuous Integration and Continuous Deployment*, takes you through the process of deploying your Microservices application on a Service Fabric cluster using Visual Studio Team Services.

Chapter 22, *Serverless Microservices*, helps you understand the concept of Serverless Computing and building Microservices using Azure functions.

To get the most out of this book

A basic knowledge of virtualization, networks, web development, databases, and active directory is required to get the most out of this book.

Download the example code files

You can download the example code files for this book from your account at www.packt.com. If you purchased this book elsewhere, you can visit www.packt.com/support and register to have the files emailed directly to you.

You can download the code files by following these steps:

1. Log in or register at www.packt.com.
2. Select the **SUPPORT** tab.
3. Click on **Code Downloads & Errata**.
4. Enter the name of the book in the **Search** box and follow the onscreen instructions.

Once the file is downloaded, please make sure that you unzip or extract the folder using the latest version of:

- WinRAR/7-Zip for Windows
- Zipeg/iZip/UnRarX for Mac
- 7-Zip/PeaZip for Linux

The code bundle for the book is also hosted on GitHub at `https://github.com/PacktPublishing/Implementing-Azure-Putting-Modern-DevOps-to-Use`. In case there's an update to the code, it will be updated on the existing GitHub repository.

We also have other code bundles from our rich catalog of books and videos available at `https://github.com/PacktPublishing/`. Check them out!

Conventions used

There are a number of text conventions used throughout this book.

`CodeInText`: Indicates code words in text, database table names, folder names, filenames, file extensions, pathnames, dummy URLs, user input, and Twitter handles. Here is an example: "In the search bar, write `storage account`."

Bold: Indicates a new term, an important word, or words that you see onscreen. For example, words in menus or dialog boxes appear in the text like this. Here is an example: "If you need something different, click on the **DOWNLOADS** link in the header for all possible downloads: "

 Warnings or important notes appear like this.

 Tips and tricks appear like this.

Get in touch

Feedback from our readers is always welcome.

General feedback: If you have questions about any aspect of this book, mention the book title in the subject of your message and email us at `customercare@packtpub.com`.

Errata: Although we have taken every care to ensure the accuracy of our content, mistakes do happen. If you have found a mistake in this book, we would be grateful if you would report this to us. Please visit www.packt.com/submit-errata, selecting your book, clicking on the Errata Submission Form link, and entering the details.

Piracy: If you come across any illegal copies of our works in any form on the Internet, we would be grateful if you would provide us with the location address or website name. Please contact us at copyright@packt.com with a link to the material.

If you are interested in becoming an author: If there is a topic that you have expertise in and you are interested in either writing or contributing to a book, please visit authors.packtpub.com.

Reviews

Please leave a review. Once you have read and used this book, why not leave a review on the site that you purchased it from? Potential readers can then see and use your unbiased opinion to make purchase decisions, we at Packt can understand what you think about our products, and our authors can see your feedback on their book. Thank you!

For more information about Packt, please visit packt.com.

Getting Started with Azure Implementation

Cloud services have come a long way in the last 5 to 10 years. Cloud was and still is one of the biggest trends in **Information Technology** (**IT**), with new topics still to be discovered.

In the early 2000s, cloud computing wasn't a widely phrase, but the concept, as well as data centers with massive computing power, already existed. Later in that decade, the word **cloud** became a buzzword for nearly anything that was not tangible or online. But the real rise of cloud computing with all its different service models happened before, when big IT companies started their cloud offerings. That was Amazon, Google, and Microsoft in particular. As these cloud offerings developed, they enabled companies from start ups to Fortune 500s to use cloud services, from web services to virtual machines, with billing exact to the minute.

In this chapter, we'll explore the following topics:

- Cloud service models
- Cloud deployment models
- Cloud characteristics
- Multi-cloud characteristics and models
- An overview of Azure services

Technical requirements

To start with Microsoft Azure and cloud services, you need an active Azure subscription and an Azure tenant, which will be obtained with the subscription. There are different ways to order such an subscription.

The following list provides a few options:

- Microsoft MSDN subscription
- Microsoft Azure free trial
- Microsoft Azure pass
- Microsoft **Enterprise Agreement (EA)** with Azure commitment
- Microsoft Azure cloud solution provider
- Microsoft Azure in open licensing
- Microsoft BizSpark program

Service models

Cloud computing is a new trend model for enabling workloads that use resources from a normally huge resource pool that is operated by a cloud service provider. These resources include servers, storage, network resources, applications, services, or even functions. These can be rapidly deployed, operated, and automated with little effort and the prices are calculated on a per-minute basis. This cloud model is composed of five essential characteristics, three service models, and four deployment models.

Cloud offerings are mainly categorized into the following service models:

- **Infrastructure as a Service (IaaS)**: This describes a model where the cloud provider enables the consumer to create and configure resources from the computing layer upwards, without any need to care or know about the hardware layer. That includes virtual machines, networks, appliances, and lots of other infrastructure-related resources and services. The most popular IaaS resources in Azure contain virtual machines, virtual networks (internal and external), container services, and storage.
- **Platform as a Service (PaaS)**: This gives the consumer an environment from the operating system upwards. So, the consumer is not responsible for the underlying IaaS infrastructure. Examples are operating systems, databases, or development frameworks. Microsoft Azure contains many PaaS resources such as SQL databases, Azure app services, or cloud services.

- **Software as a Service (SaaS)**: This is the model with the lowest level of control and required management. A SaaS application is reachable from multiple clients and consumers, and the owning consumer doesn't have any control over the backend, except for some application-related management tasks. Examples of SaaS applications are Office 365, Visual Studio Online, the Outlook website, OneDrive, and even the Amazon website itself is a SaaS application with Amazon as its own consumer.

A comparison of service model responsibilities is shown in the following diagram:

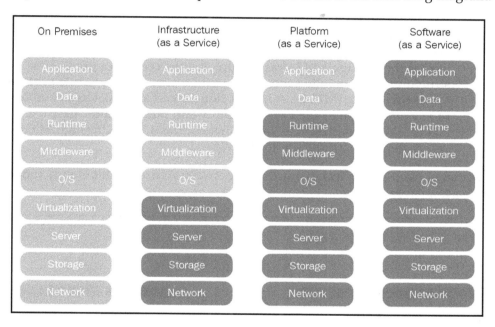

Deployment models

There are also a number of deployment models for cloud computing that need to be discussed. These deployment models cover nearly all common cloud computing provider scenarios. They describe the group of consumers that are able to use the services of the cloud service, rather than the institution or the underlying infrastructure:

- **Public cloud**: A public cloud describes a cloud computing offer that can be accessed by the public. This includes individuals as well as companies. Examples of a public cloud are Microsoft Azure and Amazon AWS.

- **Community cloud**: A community cloud is only accessible by a specified group. These are, for example, connected by location, an organization membership, or by reasons of compliance. Examples of a community cloud are Microsoft Azure Germany (location) or Microsoft Azure Government (organization and compliance) for US government authorities.
- **Private cloud**: A private cloud describes an environment/infrastructure built and operated by a single organization for internal use. These offers are specifically designed for the different units in the organization. Examples are Microsoft **Windows Azure Pack** (**WAP**) or Microsoft Azure Stack, as well as OpenStack, if they are used for internal deployments.
- **Hybrid cloud**: The hybrid cloud combines the private and public clouds. It is defined as a private cloud environment at the consumer's premises, as well as the public cloud infrastructure that the consumer uses. These structures are generally connected by site-to-site VPNs or **Multiprotocol Label Switching** (**MPLS**). A hybrid cloud could also exist as a combination of any other models, such as community and public clouds. Examples are Azure VMs connected to an on-premises infrastructure through Microsoft Azure ExpressRoute or site-to-site VPN.

The following diagram depicts a comparison between Azure (public cloud) and Azure Pack (private cloud):

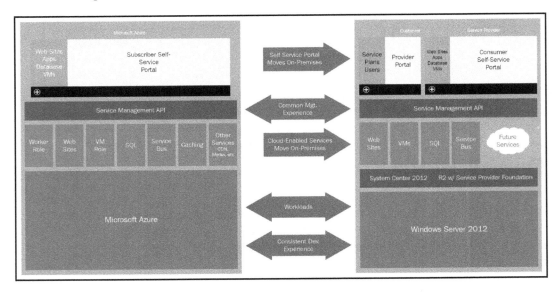

In the summer of 2017, Microsoft released the new version of the private cloud adoption from Azure Resource Manager. The new version is named **Azure Stack** and will sooner or later be equal to the Azure Resource Manager framework.

Cloud characteristics

Microsoft Azure is one of the biggest cloud service providers worldwide, offering a wide range of services from IaaS to PaaS to SaaS. It fulfills all of the characteristics that the **National Institute of Standards and Technology** (**NIST**) describes for cloud computing. These are as follows:

- **On-demand self-service**: This means an automated deployment of resources that a consumer orders through an interface such as a consumer portal.
- **Broad network access**: Providing availability of cloud services through a standardized network interface that is, at best, accessible by several endpoint devices.
- **Resource pooling**: This means that the automated assignment and reassignment of diverse resources from various resource pools for individual customers is possible.
- **Rapid elasticity**: It is also known as rapid scaling and describes the ability to scale resources in a massive way. The automatic and fast assignment and reassignment of resources, and rapid up and down scaling of single instances, are keywords when talking about rapid elasticity. The adjustment of web server resources depending on the demand is an example of rapid elasticity.
- **Measured service**: All data usage for consumer resources is monitored and reported, to be available for consumers and the cloud provider. This is one of the requirements for minute-based billing.

Multi-cloud characteristics and models

When defining multi-cloud, you need first to be aware of what a cloud service is. At this stage of this book, you already had some insight into cloud computing and cloud models and characteristics. Now, you should be able to identify the cloud services you already use in your company and that you might use in the future.

Multi-cloud means you or your company are using not only the services of one cloud provider, but different solutions from different cloud providers. That could be an example of using Microsoft Office 365 for business collaboration, Salesforce for CRM, and AWS Area 52 for GeoDNS and GeoIP, or even OpenStack or Azure Stack as your private cloud solution within your data center or co-location.

The following diagram shows a schematic definition of a person or company between multiple cloud providers:

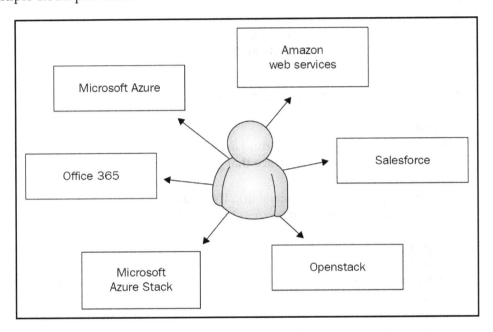

Why use multiple cloud providers and not only one that fits all? There are different reasons why someone chooses a multi-cloud solution. Let me explain the most common reasons in the field:

- **Redundancy**: You don't want to build up your environment on only one cloud provider because one can fail, as happened with AWS in the past. So, you want to keep the business running with the services of another cloud provider. That's mostly a reason when using IaaS or PaaS. Redundancy is mostly not possible with SaaS if the cloud provider does not support hybrid environments.

- **The solution does not fit my needs**: Mostly when choosing a cloud solution, you see whether it fits your need. You mostly look to features such as data center location or performance. Sometimes, a cloud solution from my preferred provider does not fit those needs, so I need to choose another cloud provider with its solution. Often, you see that in Microsoft Dynamics CRM Online versus Salesforce, or your preferred provider does not offer a data center in South Africa. So, you may switch from AWS to Microsoft Azure for that reason.

- **The cloud provider does not offer the service I need**: Often, cloud providers are strong in one field and less so in others. This means they don't offer the services you may want; for example, you use Salesforce and want to have a unified single sign-on solution with Facebook, Twitter, or Instagram for your marketing teams. That's a service Salesforce does not offer at the moment, which means you may want to include Microsoft Azure **Active Directory (AD)** in your environment to achieve your goal.

- **Your departments use a cloud service as shadow IT**: I have seen shadow IT in nearly every company in the last 12 years of my work experience. It means a department uses a solution outside of the IT controlled area or solution field, managing the application itself without IT knowing of it. Often, it happens that those solutions become business critical and C-level management forces IT to take over the solution and support it. In times of easily accessible cloud solutions, this issue increased dramatically. Their are mostly two reasons for shadow IT:
  - IT departments aren't fast enough to deploy an appropriate on-premises solution
  - The user thinks, *Okay I only need a credit card? Let's try.*

The key elements to building and performing a successful multi-cloud solution is to build a uniform solution between all of the cloud providers. Those solutions are based on a uniform **Identity and Access Management (IAM)**, network, and application infrastructure.

Within this field, you might see two flavors of multi-cloud.

Cloud brokering

With cloud brokering, you migrate your workload depending on the price and needs from one cloud provider to another. That can be on a day-to-day or more frequent basis.

This brokering was the first intention of businesses to save money with the cloud, but in practice, brokering only works with very simple IaaS or very standardized PaaS solutions. Most of the more complex workloads, such as Microsoft Exchange, SAP, and Oracle depend on drivers and you always have different hypervisor solutions between your cloud providers. In addition to that, IaaS workloads are very costly compared with solutions built on PaaS. So, looking down and ahead the timeline, the second multi-cloud model has become more common—**best of breed**.

Best of breed

Best of breed means you choose your cloud provider and a solution that fits for your needs and business requirements, or that is the market leader in a special area, for example, artificial intelligence, **Network as a Service** (**NaaS**), collaboration software, or data center distribution. Mostly, that means you will always end up with three or more cloud providers integrated with each other.

Microsoft Azure

When Windows Azure came online for the general public in February 2010, there were only database services, websites, and virtual machine hosting available. Over time, Microsoft constantly added features and new services to Azure, and, as there were more and more offerings for Linux and other non-Windows services, Microsoft decided in April 2014 to rename Windows Azure to Microsoft Azure. This supported Microsoft's commitment to transform itself into a services company, which means that, in order to be successful, you have to offer as many services as possible to as many clients as possible. Since then, Microsoft has constantly improved and released new services. Additionally, it constantly builds and expands data centers all over the world.

 Service updates happen very frequently. That is the reason why you need to keep yourself informed. For example, the database offering you are using could have improved storage or performance capabilities. Information sources are the official Microsoft Azure blog and the Azure Twitter channel. Furthermore, information can be found on the websites of several Azure MVPs.

Azure services overview

Azure offers many services in its cloud computing platform. These services include the following:

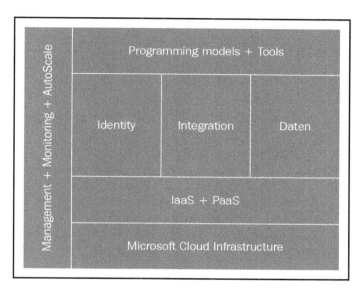

The service categories, differentiated between platform services and infrastructure services.

The platform services are as follows:

- **Management**: These services include the management portal, the marketplace with the services gallery, and the components to automate things in Azure.
- **Compute services**: Compute services are Azure cloud services that are basically PaaS offerings for developers to quickly build and deploy highly scalable applications. The service fabric and Azure RemoteApp are also in this category.
- **Security**: This contains all of the services that provide identity in Azure, such as Azure AD, multi-factor authentication, and the key vault, which is a safe place for your certificates.
- **Integration**: The integration services include interface services such as BizTalk and Azure Service Bus, but also message helpers such as storage queues.

- **Media and CDN**: These are basically two services. One is the CDN, which makes it possible to build your own content delivery network based on Azure. The other is media services that make it very easy to use and process different media with the help of Azure.
- **Web and mobile**: These include all of the services that assist in creating apps or backend services for the web and mobiles, for example, web apps and API apps.
- **Developer services**: These are cloud-based development tools for version control, collaboration, and other development-related tasks. The Azure SDK is a part of the developer services.
- **Data**: The data services contain all of the different database types that you can deploy in Azure (SQL, DocumentDB, MongoDB, Table storage, and so on) and diverse tools to configure them.
- **Analytics and IoT**: As the name suggests, analytics services are tools to analyze and process data. This offers a broad range of possibilities, from machine learning to stream analytics. These can, but don't have to, build on certain data services. The **Internet of Things** (**IoT**) services include the fundamental tools needed to work with devices used for the IoT, such as the Raspberry Pi 2.
- **Hybrid operations**: This category sums up all of the remaining services that could not clearly be categorized. These include backup, monitoring, and disaster recovery, as well as many others.

The infrastructure services are as follows:

- **Operating system and server compute**: This category consists of compute containers. It includes virtual machine containers and, additionally, container services, which are quite new to the product range.
- **Storage**: Storage services are the two main storage types—**BLOB** and **file storage**. They have different pricing tiers depending on the speed and latency of the storage ordered.
- **Networking**: This category consists of basic networking resources. Examples are load balancer, ExpressRoute, and VPN gateways.

The important thing is to remember that we are talking about a rapidly changing and very agile cloud computing platform. After this chapter, if you have not already done so, you should start using Azure by experimenting, exploring, and implementing your solutions while reading the correlating chapters.

For testing purposes, you should use the **Azure Free Trial**
(`https://azure.microsoft.com/en-in/offers/ms-azr-0044p/`), **Visual Studio Dev Essentials** (`https://www.visualstudio.com/dev-essentials/`), or the included Azure amount from an MSDN subscription.

Azure basics

In the following section, we will take a look at the basic Microsoft Azure key concepts. This should provide an overview and an idea of how to use Azure.

Azure Resource Manager (ARM)

In the previous major version of Azure, a deployment backend model called **Azure Service Manager** (ASM) was used. With higher demand on scaling, and being more flexible and standardized, a new model called **ARM** was introduced and is now the standard way of using Azure.

This includes a new portal, a new way of looking at things as resources, and a standardized API that every tool, including the Azure portal, that interacts with Azure uses.

With this API and architectural changes, it's possible to use such things as ARM templates for any size of deployment. ARM templates are written in **JavaScript Object Notation (JSON)** and are a convenient way to define one or more resources and their relationship to another programmatically. This structure is then deployed to a resource group. With this deployment model, it's possible to define dependencies between resources, as well as being able to deploy the exact same architecture again and again. The next section will dive a little deeper into resources.

Resources

Azure resources are the key to every service offering in Azure. Resources are the smallest building blocks and represent a single technical entity, such as a VM, a network interface card, a storage account, a database, or a website. When deploying a web app, a resource called **app service** will be deployed along with a service plan for billing.

When deploying a virtual machine from an Azure Marketplace template, a VM resource will be created as well as a storage account resource holding the virtual hard disks, a public IP Address resource for initial access to the VM, a network interface card, and a virtual network resource.

Every resource has to be deployed to one specific **resource group**. A resource group can hold multiple resources, while a single resource can only exist in one resource group. Resource groups also can't contain another resource group, which leads to a single layer of containers regarding resources.

One resource group can contain all resources of a deployment or multiple resources of different deployments. There are no strong recommendations on structuring resource groups, but it's recommended to organize either the resources of one project/enrollment/deployment in separate resource groups or distribute resources based on their purpose (networking, storage, and so on) to resource groups.

Azure regions

Azure as a global cloud platform provides multiple regions to deploy resources to. One region consists of at least one highly available data center or data center complex. At the time of writing, 54 regions are distributed all over the world and include community clouds, so-called sovereign regions.

Microsoft also divides its regions into geopolitical zones, which can be found at the following URL: `https://azure.microsoft.com/en-us/global-infrastructure/regions/`.

These sovereign clouds where built by Microsoft to fit customer or governmental needs, such as for special compliance and/or data privacy laws. At the moment, the following sovereign clouds are available:

- Microsoft Azure US **Department of Defense (DoD)**
- Microsoft Azure US Government
- Microsoft Azure China
- Microsoft Cloud Germany

Microsoft Cloud Germany is also special among the sovereign clouds. Because of customer demands, Microsoft built up Microsoft Cloud Germany differently. Microsoft does not operate the cloud in Germany itself; they use a data trustee to operate the cloud for them.

Microsoft Azure staff and all Microsoft employees are not allowed to enter the data centers or lay hands on the servers or framework. Everything is operated by the trustee, starting with hardware maintenance up to updates of the framework.

 Fun fact: Before Microsoft moved into its data center in Berlin, I used to be allowed to walk straight through the data center with a guide to reach my peer, who is a regional director of the data center provider. Since Microsoft moved into the data center, I can no longer use the shortcut and need to walk around the outside of the building to reach the office of my buddy. So, Microsoft is very serious with their policies.

Regions can also have an impact on the performance and availability of some resources. Some services may not be, or are only partially, available in a specific region.

The costs of offered services also vary by region. For reduced latency, it's recommended to choose a region next to the physical location of the consumer. It might also be important to see which legal requirements must be met. This could, for example, result in a deployment only in EU regions, or even regions in specific countries:

- **Available Azure regions**: https://azure.microsoft.com/en-us/regions/
- **Lists all the services available in specific regions**: https://azure.microsoft.com/en-us/regions/services/

Microsoft data center and backbone

Microsoft operates two types of following data centers:

- The first type is the production data center, where Microsoft calculates all workloads of its customers and stores all the data.
- The second type is the edge or delivery site. Those sites connect all Microsoft Cloud services to the internet and Microsoft's customers. Edge sites come in two stages of expansion. The smallest one allows Microsoft public direct peering through the internet. With the second stage of expansion, Microsoft allows customers and providers to establish a private connection to the Microsoft backbone using the Microsoft Azure ExpressRoute service.

The following diagram shows a schematic of the Microsoft data center structure:

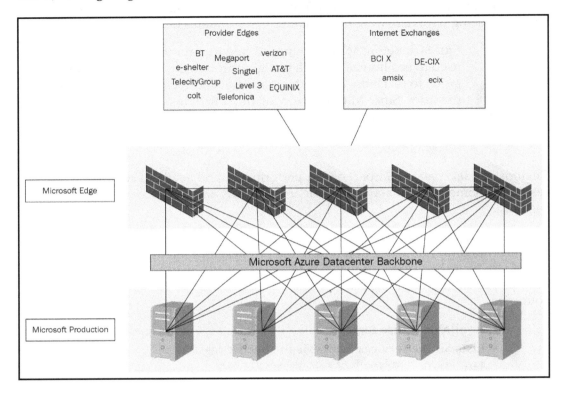

Edge and production sites are connected through the Microsoft backbone. Currently Microsoft owns and operates the second largest and fastest full meshed provider backbone of the world.. Microsoft also owns and operates own see cables such as the MAREA cable from Bilbao (Spain) to Virginia (US).

This map shows the current Microsoft Azure backbone with the new MAREA cable:

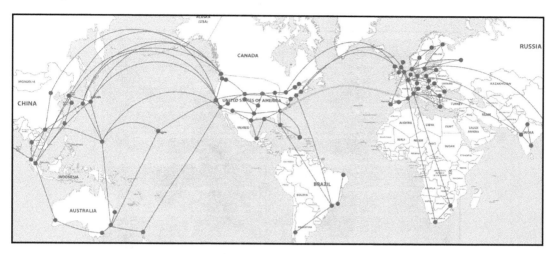

 Fun fact: *What was the hardest thing for the Microsoft backbone teams when building the MAREA cable?* To create and get the purchase order for the submarine approved because of Microsoft processes.

While building its backbone, Microsoft acts differently to the other cloud providers. Microsoft builds its own dark fibre cables or leases dark fibre cables and operates the whole backbone itself. Microsoft runs a fully software-defined network and infrastructure for its backbone, using firewall appliances built for **network function virtualization**.

If you ever have the chance to see a server rack that connects the Microsoft backbone or represents a Microsoft Edge site, it will probably look like this:

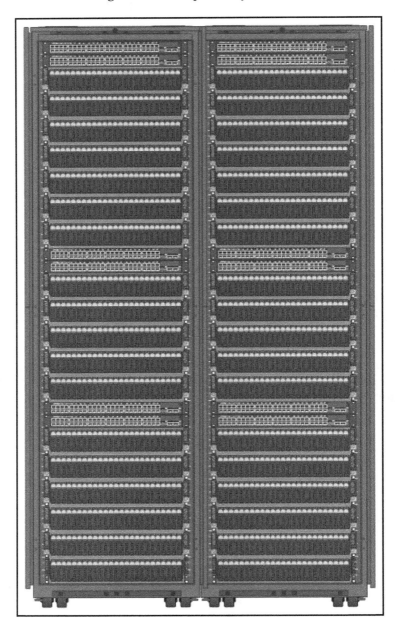

If you want to know more about Microsoft regarding data center equipment and software defined, I highly recommend you consult open source and open compute projects. Microsoft is investing highly in these and is very open in the following projects:

- **Microsoft cloud servers:**
    - **Open cloud server platform**: https://www.opencompute.org/projects/server
    - **ARM-based cloud server project olympus**: https://www.opencompute.org/wiki/Server/ProjectOlympus
- **Microsoft network cards for backbone and cloud services:**
    - **Smart NIC**: https://www.opencompute.org/wiki/Server/Mezz
- **Microsoft networking and switch software**:
    - **Project SONiC**: https://azure.microsoft.com/de-de/blog/sonic-the-networking-switch-software-that-powers-the-microsoft-global-cloud/

 Microsoft also makes heavy use of **Field Programmable Gateway Arrays (FPGAs)**, to make Azure as flexible as possible and adjust the hardware layer as much as possible to the needs of their workloads. If you really want to become an insider in this technology, I would high recommend the session, *Inside Microsoft's FPGA-Based Configurable Cloud,* by Mark Russinovich, CTO of Azure. You can find the session here: https://www.youtube.com/watch?v=v_4Ap1bjwgs.

Azure portal

The Azure portal is a web application and the most straightforward way to view and manage most Azure resources. The Azure portal can also be used for identity management, to view billing information, and to create custom dashboards for often used resources to get a quick overview of some deployments.

Although it's easy to start with using and deploying services and resources, it's highly recommended to use some Azure automation technologies for larger and production environments. The Azure portal is located at https://portal.azure.com.

Azure automation

Azure automation is a service and a resource, as well as an Azure concept in the context of cloud computing.

It's very important to see automation as an essential concept when it comes to cloud computing. Automation is one of the key technologies to reduce operational costs and will also provide a consistent and replicable state. It also lays the foundation of any rapid deployment plans.

As Azure uses a lot of automation internally, Microsoft decided to make some of that technology available as a resource called **automation account**.

Azure automation tools

Azure provides several ways of interacting and automating things. The two main ways to interact with Azure besides the portal are Azure PowerShell and the Azure **Command-Line Interface (CLI)**.

Both are basically just wrappers around the Azure API to enable everyone not familiar with RESTful APIs, but familiar with their specific scripting language, to use and automate Azure. The Azure PowerShell module provides cmdlet for managing Azure services and resources through the Azure API. Azure PowerShell cmdlet are used to handle account management and environment management, including creating, updating, and deleting resources. These cmdlet work completely the same on Azure, Azure Pack, and the Azure Stack, Microsoft's private cloud offerings.

Azure PowerShell is open source and maintained by Microsoft. The project is available on GitHub at the following link: https://github.com/Azure/azure-powershell. The Azure CLI is a tool that you can use to create, manage, and remove Azure resources from the command-line. The Azure CLI was created for administrators and operators that are not that experienced with Microsoft technologies, but with other server technologies, such as Unix or Linux. The Azure CLI is an open source project as well, and is available for Linux, macOS, and Windows here: https://github.com/Azure/azure-cli.

REST APIs

All Azure services, including the Azure Management Portal, provide their own REST APIs for their functionality. They can, therefore, be accessed by any application that RESTful services can process.

In order for software developers to write applications in the programming language of their choice, Microsoft offers wrapper classes for the REST APIs.

These are available as an Azure SDK for numerous programming languages (for example, .NET, Java, and Node.js) here at `https://github.com/Azure`.

Summary

In this chapter, we learned about cloud models and what cloud in general means. We now know how Microsoft fits into that ecosystem with its cloud services and their strategy. We also gained some very important insights into Azure and Microsoft regarding their data centers and backbone.

2
Azure Resource Manager and Tools

The Azure platform consists primarily of three parts—**Azure execution model**, which denotes the areas where you can provide your services and applications in the cloud; **Azure Building Blocks**; and **Azure Data Services**, which refers to services that extend the platform to common capabilities and functionalities.

I could actually forgo the description of the platform, because most users only get to see these three parts, but there are still more. Many other services are working under the hood of the platform and ensure its ongoing operation. These services include, for example, **Azure Traffic Manager**, **Azure Load Balancer**, and **Azure Resource Manager** (**ARM**). All of these services can be customized using various interfaces for your personal needs.

In this chapter, I'll introduce you to ARM in detail, and we will explore the following topics:

- ARM and Azure resource groups
- Azure resource tags
- Azure resource locks
- Working with ARM templates
- Creating your own ARM template

Technical requirements

For running containers in a cloud environment, no specific installations are required, as you only need the following:

- A computer with an internet browser
- An Azure subscription (if not available, a trial could work too, at `https://azure.microsoft.com/en-us/free/`)
- The code in this chapter can be found here:
  `https://github.com/PacktPublishing/Implementing-Azure-Putting-Modern-DevOps-to-Use`

Understanding ARM

With the classic Azure system management, you could previously manage only one resource on the Azure platform at the same time. But what about more complex applications, as are common today? The infrastructure of today's applications typically consists of several components—a virtual machine, a storage account, a virtual network, a web app, a database, a database server, or a third-party service. To manage such complex applications, with the first preview of the Azure Management Portal 3.0, the concept of resource groups was introduced.

You now no longer see your components as separate entities, but as related and interdependent parts of a single entity. So, you will be able to manage all the resources of your application simultaneously. As an instrument for this type of management, ARM (and ARM tools) was introduced.

Enough of the preliminary remarks. Let's take a look at ARM in detail with the following diagram:

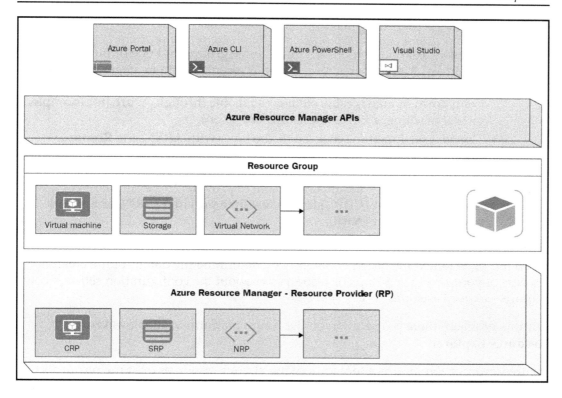

As you can see in the preceding diagram, ARM can be accessed through a variety of different technologies and interfaces. These access options include the following:

- The traditional way, through the Azure portal (version 3.0 and newer)
- The script-based way, through Azure PowerShell (look for PowerShell modules with the AzureRM prefix) or through the Azure **Command-Line Interface (CLI)** (cross-platform CLI)
- For developers, through Visual Studio
- For developers, there are also SDKs available (.**NET** and some other programming languages) and, as with all Azure services, an extensive RESTful API

Let's go through the preceding diagram:

- It consists of one or more Azure resource groups and one or more Azure resources. An Azure resource group is a container (a management unit), that all of the resources of your Azure solution contain. The Azure resource is any form of manageable element available through Azure (for example, a virtual machine, a virtual network, and so on).
- The next section of the diagram is the layer with ARM—the **Resource Provider** (**RP**). A resource provider is an internal interface to the platform and offers you numerous operations to handle the resources you need. Each resource type has its own resource provider, for example, a **compute resource provider** (**CRP**), **storage resource provider** (**SRP**), or **network resource provider** (**NRP**).

Not shown in the diagram is the template functionality of the ARM. With a so-called ARM template (a text file based on JSON) you determine the details of the creation process of your resource groups or resources or about the configuration settings you require. *Confused about the variety of items?*

For this problem, there is a solution on the Azure platform available—**Azure Resource Explorer**.

Azure Resource Explorer is a tool for looking at your resources or at the resources of the Azure platform. By using this tool, you can see how the resources are structured and it enables you to view the properties of resources.

How can I find the Azure Resource Explorer? Follow these steps:

1. Open your Azure Management Portal at `https://portal.azure.com`.
2. In the portal, click on the **All services** option, as shown in the following screenshot:

3. In the list of services, search for **Resource Explorer**, and then click the **Resource Explorer** button:

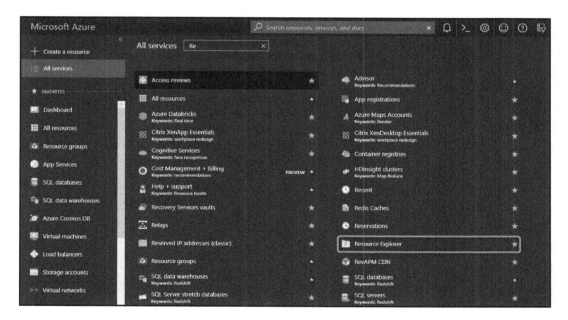

4. In the **Resource Explorer** tab, you can find the following two nodes:

- **Providers**: A list of all available resource providers from the Azure platform itself
- **Subscriptions**: A list of resource groups, resources, and resource providers used by yourself:

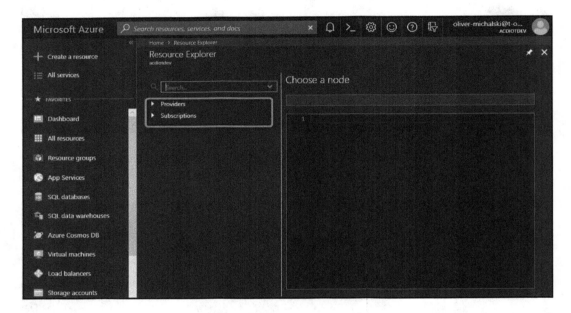

5. By clicking the nodes, you can see the information you want:
   - In the first example for the **Providers** section, note the following:

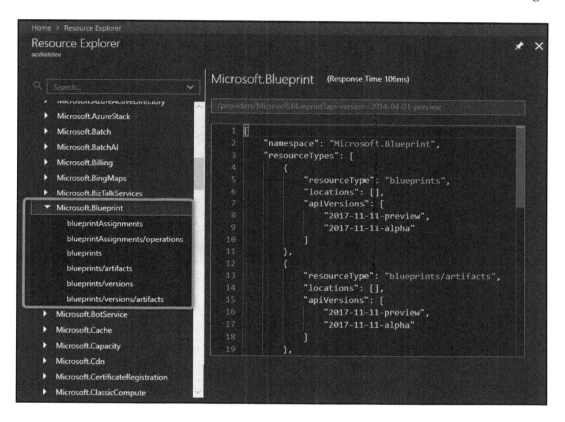

- In the second example for the **Subscriptions** section, note the following:

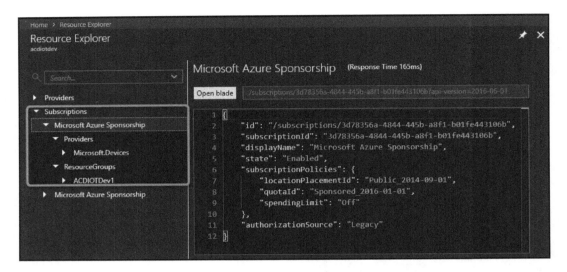

Functionalities provided by ARM

In this section, I would like to give you a brief overview of the functionalities of ARM. The list, however, is only a selection and is limited to the most frequently used features. You will find detailed information on the use of the features in the following sections of this chapter.

Let's take a look at the functionalities:

- There's a access control with Azure **role-based access control** (**RBAC**).
- There's logical organization of all the resources of a subscription, with Azure resource tags (for example, for each project and tenant).
- There's improved cost control. You can view the costs for the whole group or for a group of resources with the same tag.

- There's the use of ARM templates:
  - As a deployment template, in the provision of individual solutions on the Azure platform (the most popular example is deploying a SharePoint server farm).
  - As a resource provider template, for the implementation of measures (for example, configuration) within the resource groups.
- By using templates, you have the ability to define dependencies between resources, so that they are provided in the correct order.
- Through the use of templates, you have the possibility to repeatedly and securely provide your application and resources throughout the entire life cycle, and this always in the same form.
- You can modify the templates (JSON data files) to your own needs and even create your own templates.

Working with ARM

We now know that ARM serves as the technical base for the provision of resources. *How are we going to continue?* First, we will deal with the basic workflows in ARM. Then, in the second part, we will look at working with templates.

Before we begin, I want to introduce some very important facts that are crucial for all workflows:

- All of the resources in your resource group have the same life cycle. You will deploy, update, and delete them at the same time.
- Each resource can only exist in one resource group.
- You can add or remove a resource to a resource group at any time. You can also move a resource from one resource group to another.
- A resource group can contain resources that exist in different locations.
- A resource can interact with a resource in another resource group when the two resources are related, but do not share the same life cycle (for example, a web app connecting to a database).

OK, let's start with the first workflow.

Creating an Azure resource group

The creation of an Azure resource group workflow is the first in a series of basic workflows, but also the most important. *Why?* A resource group is the central element of the ARM concept. Without an existing resource group, nothing works, and I mean not only individual services, but your complete Azure subscription. To create a resource group, perform the following steps:

1. Open your Azure portal at `https://portal.azure.com`.
2. In the portal, click on the **Resource groups** blade, as shown in the following screenshot:

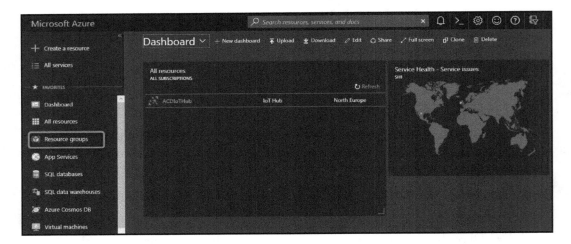

3. On the **Resource groups** blade, click on the **Add** option:

4. On the **Resource groups** blade, type the following values. After that, click on the **Create** button:

- **Resource group name**: `acdppbook`, as used in the following screenshot (or the name of your choice).
- **Subscription**: Use the default subscription.
- **Resource group location**: Select your preferred location:

5. As soon as the resource group has been created, you can find it in the list:

Adding a resource to a resource group

We have just learned how to create an Azure resource group. Now, we'll fill the new resource group with life and add a resource. To complete this process, the Azure platform has a total of two possible approaches. I will now introduce you to them one by one.

For all approaches, I will show the necessary work steps for the example of adding an Azure storage account. But, note that the description of the procedure applies also to all other resource types in the same or slightly modified form.

First approach – adding a storage account to your resource group

To add a storage account to your resource group, perform the following steps:

1. Open your Azure portal at `https://portal.azure.com`.
2. In the portal, click on **Create a resource | Storage | Storage account - blob, file, table, queue**, as shown in the following screenshot:

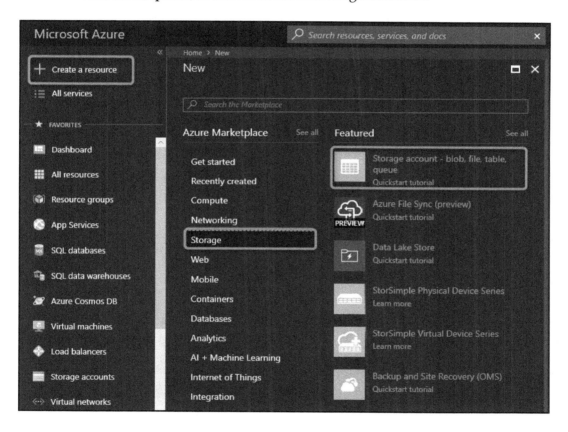

3. On the **Create storage account** blade, type a unique name for the storage account you are creating in the **Name** textbox. If the name is unique, you will see a green tick:

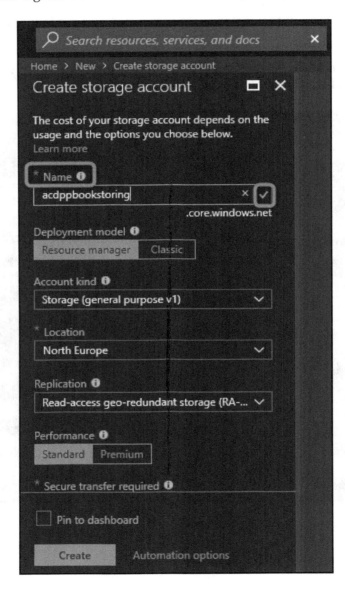

4. In the **Location** list, select the same location you have been using for the resource group:

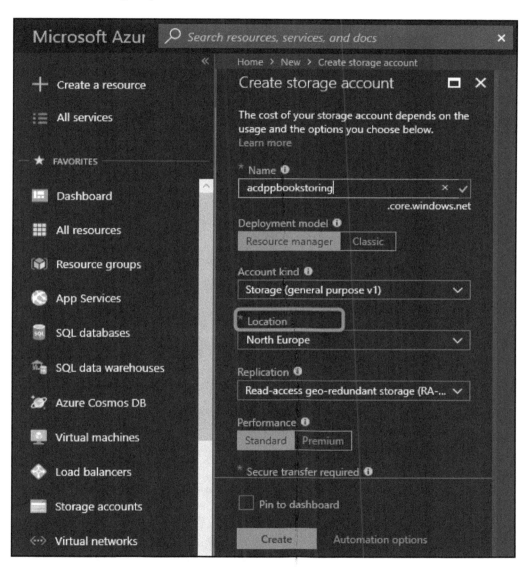

5. In the **Resource group** blade, click the **Use existing** checkbox, then search for and select `acdppbook` in the drop-down list, and then click on the **Create** button, as shown in the following screenshot:

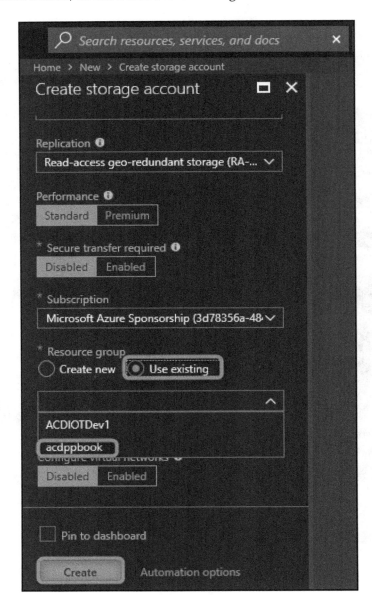

Second approach – adding a storage account to your resource group

The first approach is the default path for adding Azure resources and usually suffices in most cases. There is a second possibility available, which is also applicable for all types of Azure resources but was originally intended for offers from third-party companies, through the Azure Marketplace. Let's have a look:

1. In the portal, click on the **Resource groups** blade:

2. On the **Resource groups** blade, click on the `acdppbook` name field:

3. On the **Resource groups** dashboard, click on the **Add** option:

4. Now, the Azure Marketplace opens. Select a resource and create it, as described in the previous section:

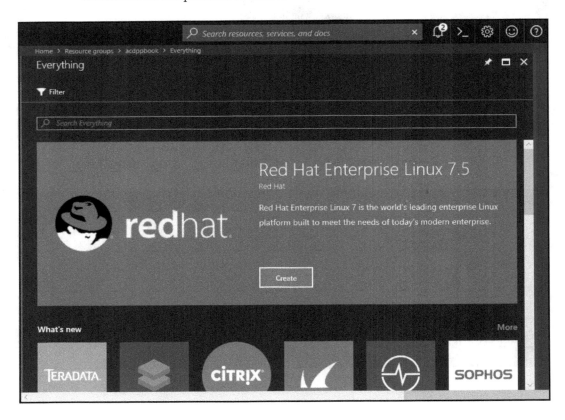

Tagging in ARM

We have just learned how to create a resource group and how to add a resource. *What we are still missing?* We still need a way to organize our resources logically, for example, for the calculation of cost or for a targeted tracking.

ARM offers a solution for this—**Azure resource tags**. Resource tags are any key/value pairs that appear useful for describing a resource.

Let's see an example:

Key	Value
Department	Management
Project	PPBook
Tenant	ACD

Once you have defined a resource tag, you can use this as a filter in Azure PowerShell or in the Azure Billing APIs (Azure Usage API and Azure RateCard API). Up to 15 tags can be defined per resource.

I will show you the necessary work steps on the example of tagging an Azure storage account, but note that the description of the procedure applies to all other resource types in the same form:

1. Open your Azure portal at `https://portal.azure.com`.
2. In the portal, click on **Resource groups,** and then click on the **Resource groups** blade, then the `acdppbook` name:

3. In the navigation section on the **Resource groups** dashboard, click on the **Tags** section:

4. Open the **Tags** blade. In the **Name** field, type Name, and then in the **Value** field, type ppbook. After this, click on the **Save** button:

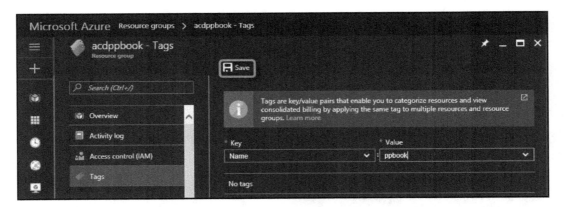

5. Go back to the **Resource groups** dashboard. In the resource grid, select the `acdppbookstoring` row, and then click the **...** button, as shown in the following screenshot:

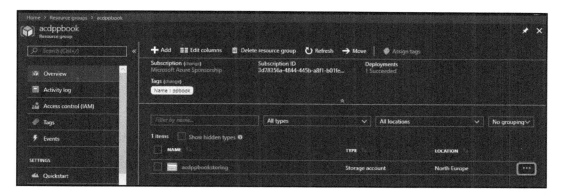

6. In the navigation section of the **Resource groups** dashboard (`acdppbookstoring`), click the **Tags** section. In the **Name** field, type `Name` again, and then in the **Value** field, type `ppbook`. Click on the **Save** button, as shown in the following screenshot:

7. In the portal, click on **All services**, and then click on **Tags**, as shown in the following screenshot:

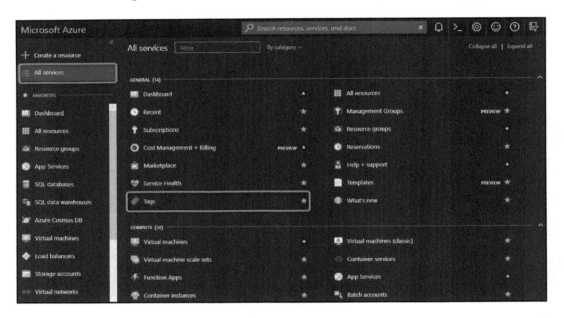

8. In the **Tags** blade, search the row for your tag, Name : ppbook, and then click the ... field. Now, you can see all of the resources that are associated with the tag, shown as follows:

Locking Azure resources

Now you know how to organize your resources, but for working with those resources, there is still another functionality that is important, which I will introduce now.

Azure resource locks

What does this mean? As an administrator, you may need to lock a resource group or resource to prevent other users from accidentally deleting or modifying critical resources. ARM offers a mechanism with two levels (`CanNotDelete` or `ReadOnly`) to be able to make appropriate settings.

Let's take a look at this:

1. In the portal, click on **Resource groups,** and then click on the **Resource groups** blade, then the `acdppbook` name, as shown in the following screenshot:

2. In the navigation section on the **Resource groups** dashboard, click on the **Locks** button, then click on the **Locks** blade, followed by clicking on the **Add** button:

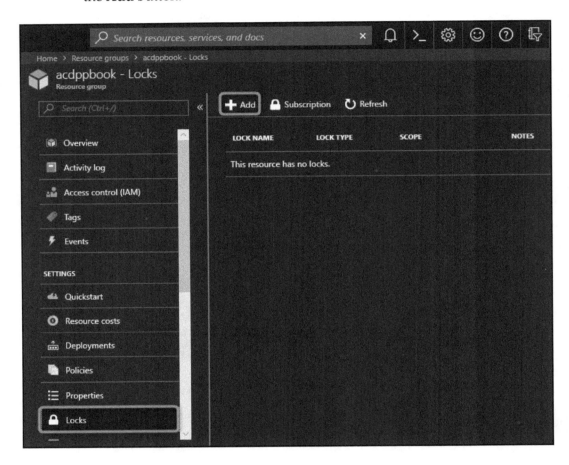

3. Now, type `ppbookdemo` in the **Lock name** field, select a lock type, and click on the **OK** button:

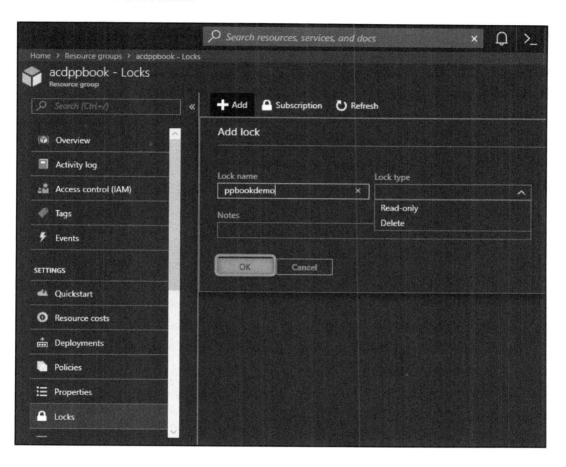

4. Your first lock is ready, as shown in the following screenshot:

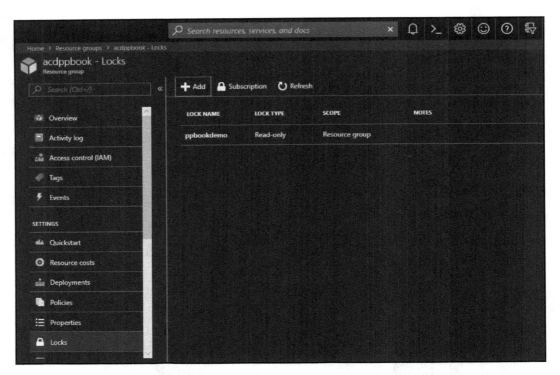

 Attention! In my example, I have put **Read-only** as a lock type on resource groups. This lock is automatically inherited to all subordinate resources. This has the consequence, however, that the functionality of individual resource types is no longer guaranteed.

For example, no keys can be retrieved for a storage account (this is a read and write operation). The operation is, however, mandatory for access:

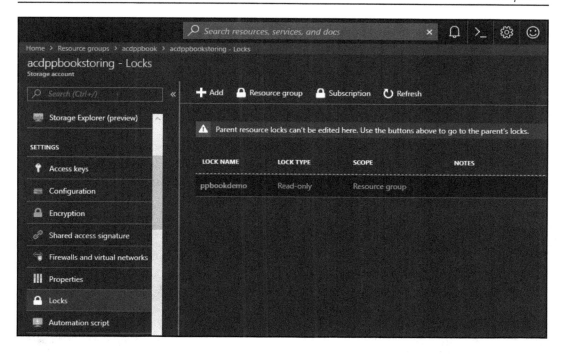

Working with ARM templates

Now, we come to the more advanced section of the explanations on the subject of working with ARM. The content of this section is also divided into two parts:

- In the first part, we consider the issue from the view of an IT professional. IT professionals are less interested in developing their own templates but want to reuse their existing deployments in template form. The corresponding feature in ARM is to export a deployment as an ARM template. This feature allows you to create templates of your deployment and download the templates to secure them in a source code repository, modifying your templates and of course the redeployment.
- The second part (from the perspective of the developer) is easier to explain. This section deals with the topic of authoring an ARM template.

Exporting a deployment as an ARM template (for IT pros)

Do you often realize demos or customer projects and always roll out the same basic configuration in Azure? If so, the following procedure could make the work easier in future:

1. Open your Azure Management Portal at `https://portal.azure.com`.
2. In the portal, click on **Resource groups,** and then click on the **Resource groups** blade, then the `acdppbook` name, as shown in the following screenshot:

Now, we will export our deployment to an ARM template.

Example 1 – exporting a resource group to an ARM template

The first example is about the export of a complete resource group, that is, a resource container and any number of other resources. To export a resource group, perform the following steps:

1. In the navigation section of the **Resource groups** dashboard, click on **Automation script**, as shown in the following screenshot:

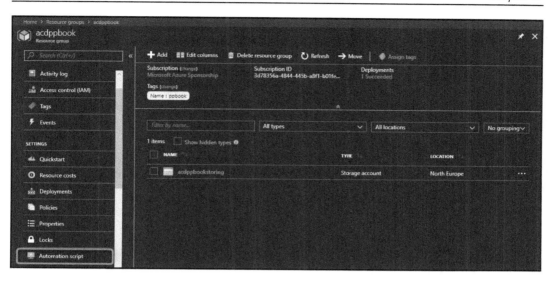

2. Now you can see the resource group template. Click on the **Download** button to save the template on your local site and to finalize your work:

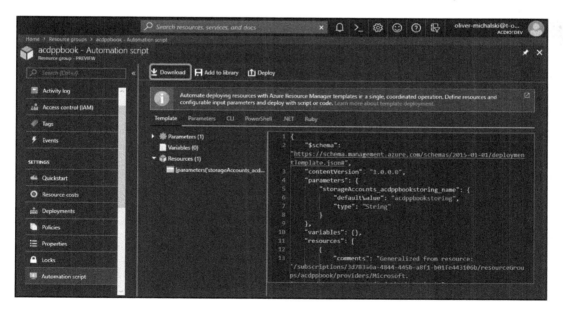

3. Alternatively, you also have the option to save your template directly on the Azure platform. Press the **Add to library** button for that:

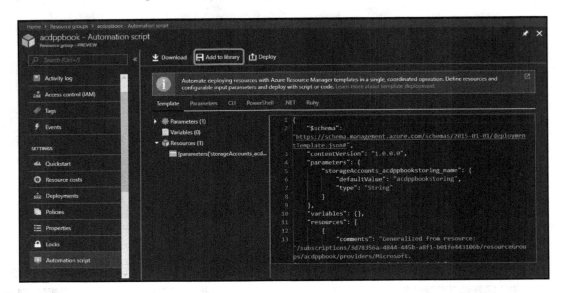

4. Now, open the **Save template** blade. Here, you must type in a value for the **Name** and the **Description** of the template, then click the **Save** button:

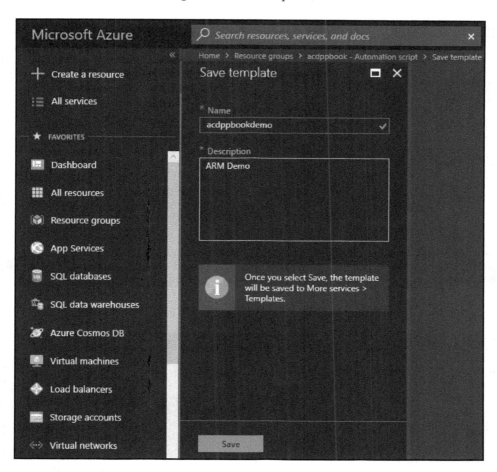

5. If you want to find your template within the Azure platform, click the **All services** list and then the **Templates** option:

6. Open the **Templates** blade with a list of all available templates:

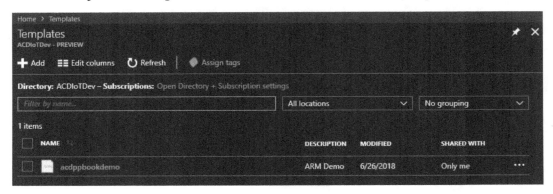

7. Let's go back to the **Automation script** blade. In addition to the template in the JSON data format, special scripts (or classes) are also provided for **Azure CLI**, **Azure PowerShell**, **.NET**, or **Ruby**. You will see this by pressing one of the links in the navigation area. These scripts help you to deploy the template:

 Not all resource types support the export `template` function. If your resource group only contains a storage account, a virtual machine, or a virtual network, you will not see an error. However, if you have created other resource types, you may see an error stating that there is a problem with the export.

Example 2 – exporting a resource (classic) to an ARM template

In the second example, we want to export a single resource (app, database, and so on), in the so-called classical way. This means that only the most recent version of the resource is exportable. To export a resource in this way, perform the following steps:

1. Go back to the **Resource groups** dashboard for `acdppbook`. In the resource grid, select the `acdppbookstoring` row, and then click the ... field, as shown in the following screenshot:

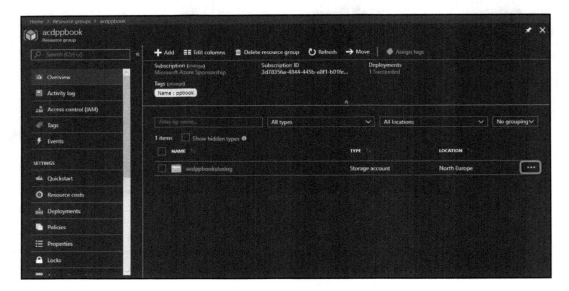

2. In the **Resource groups** dashboard, click on **Automation script** in the
   SETTINGS area. Now, you can see your template:

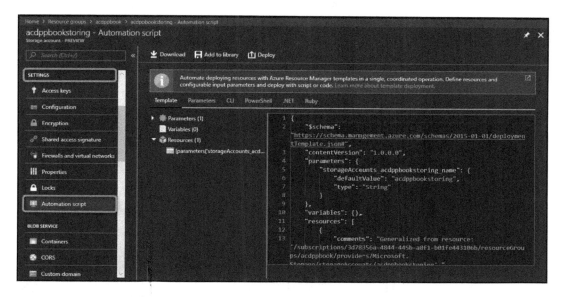

3. Click on **Download** or **Add to library** to save your template, and to finalize
   your work.

Modifying an ARM template

We have finished the topic of exporting to an ARM template. Now the question arises—*what is missing?* As I said earlier, the feature supports the ability to redeploy and modify templates. We shall take a look now:

1. Go back to the **Automation script** view. Click on **Deploy**, as shown in the following screenshot:

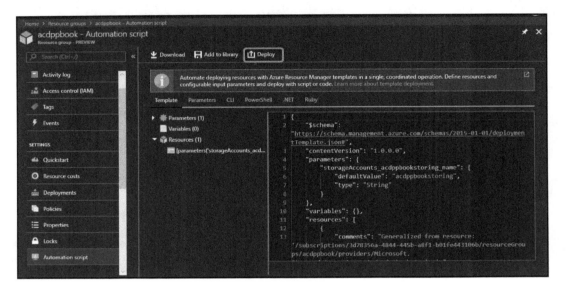

2. Next, the **Custom deployment** blade opens. Note that this is the same environment as used for the Azure Marketplace's template deployment offer, but this time, there is one resource available. To start the working process, you must press the **Edit template** button:

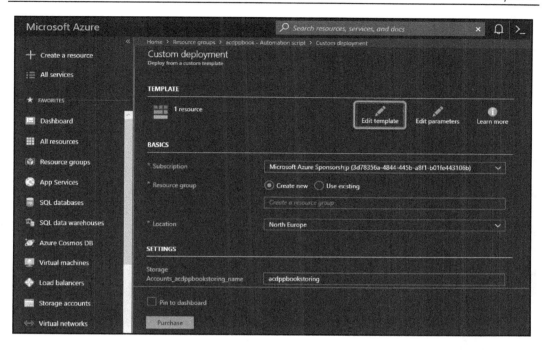

3. The next window is the **Edit template** view. Here, you can edit your template directly in the text:

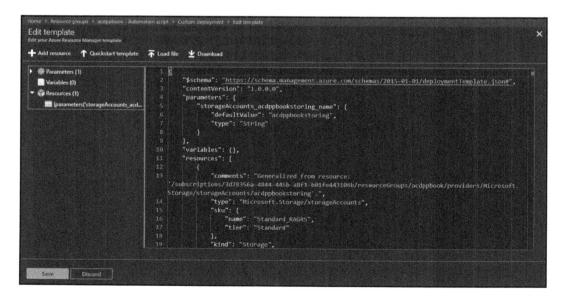

4. You can add another resource to your template (for example, a virtual network to a virtual machine). Click on the **Add resource** button and then select the desired resource from the list:

5. You can also take a **Quickstart template** as a reference for your work. Click on the **Quickstart template** button and then select the desired template from the list:

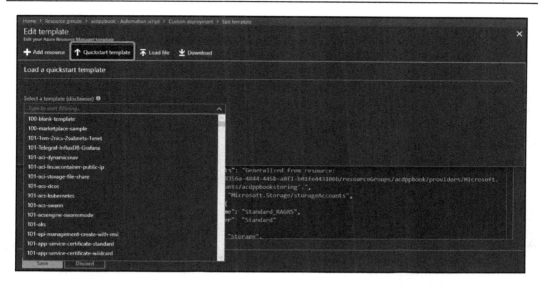

 Azure Quickstart templates are a collection of ARM community templates (with solutions for many workloads), and you can find them at `https://github.com/Azure/azure-quickstart-templates`.

6. When everything is OK, press the **Save** button:

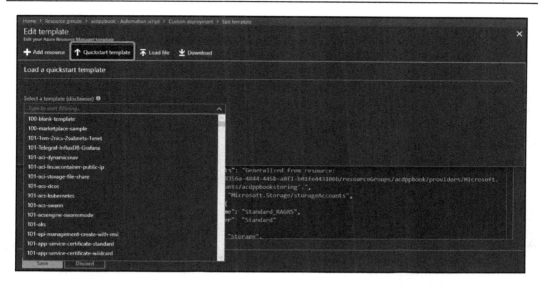

7. We are back in the **Custom deployment** blade. Here, you have to make a few final entries. First, define a resource group and a location, as shown in the following screenshot:

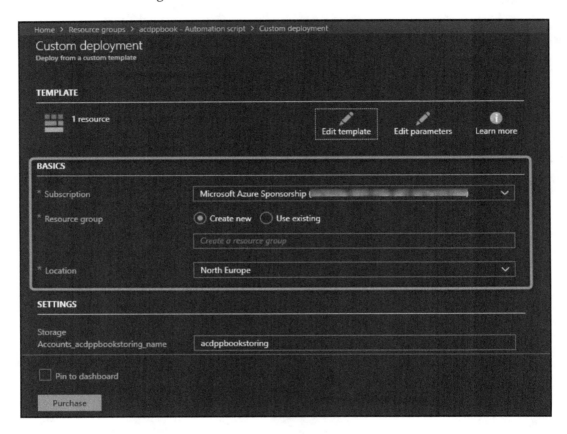

8. In the **SETTINGS** section, you must type a new name for your resource:

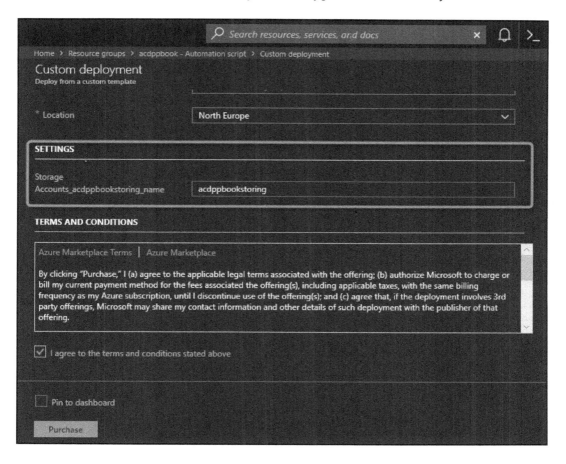

9. Finally, you must accept the **Azure Marketplace Terms**, and then press the **Purchase** button:

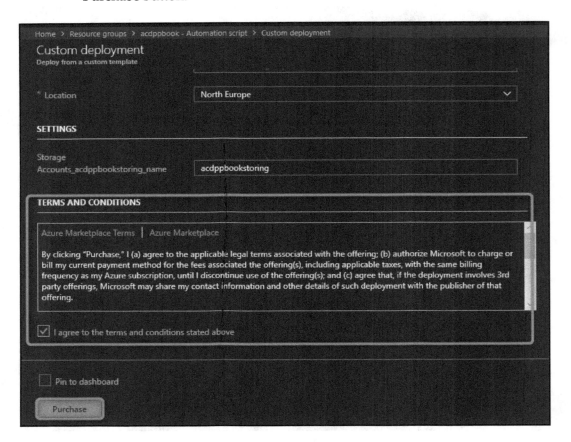

 Pressing the **Purchase** button is not really a purchase.

Authoring an ARM template

Before you can create a template, some planning tasks are required:

- What are the types of resources to be provided?
- What are the locations of resources?
- What is the version of the resource provider API used to deploy resources?
- Must some resources be provided for other resources?
- What values should be passed during the deployment, and what values would you define directly in the template?
- Do you need to return values from the deployment?

Once you have answered these questions, you can get started. OK, at least theoretically, you can start. Before you can start, we should clarify the software requirements.

Because a JSON data file is an XML-based text file, you really need only a simple text editor (for example, Notepad). I recommend you still use Visual Studio (with an excellent JSON editor).

To prevent unnecessary expense, the **Visual Studio Community Edition** or **Visual Studio Code** is completely sufficient for our purposes.

Formerly, another alternative was still available—**Azure Resource Manager Template Visualizer (ArmViz)**. With ArmViz, you can create templates with graphical means or in an editor. However, ArmViz has a weakness—it's an open source project and only available outside the platform. *Formerly?* Unfortunately, yes—the team is currently working on version 2.0 of the ArmViz tool, which does not work 100%. If you still want to try out ArmViz, you will find the tool at http://armviz.io.

Creating your own ARM template (for developers)

To create an ARM template, perform the following steps:

1. Open your Visual Studio. First, click on the **File** button, then click on **New** and the **Project...** link, as shown in the following screenshot:

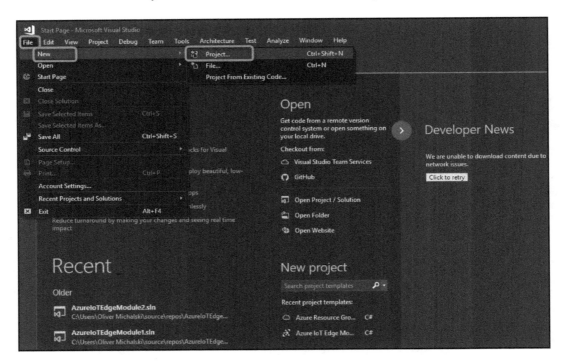

2. The selection dialog opens with the available project templates. The required template, **Azure Resource Group**, can be found in the **Cloud** area:

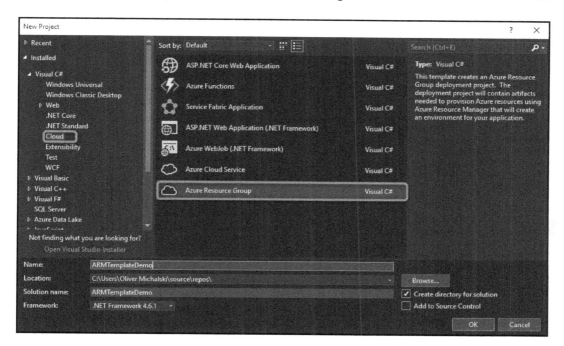

 If you use an older version of Visual Studio and do not find the entry there, you have probably forgotten to install the Azure SDK and Azure VS tooling.

3. If everything is clear, specify a project name, for example, ARMTemplateDemo, and press the **OK** button.

4. Now, another selection dialog opens, this time with a list of available Azure templates. For our demo, we need **Blank Template**. Select the entry and press the **OK** button:

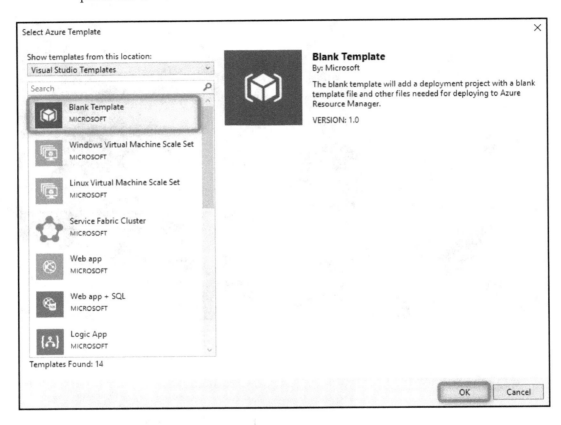

5. Wait briefly until the project has been loaded. You should now see the following screen:

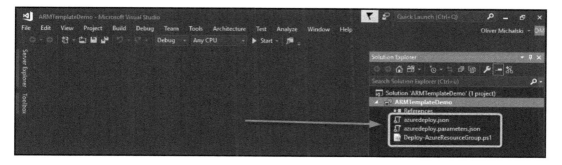

The project consists of the following three artifacts:

- `azuredeploy.json`: This is the template for your own ARM template
- `azuredeploy.parameters.json`: This is used as a store for all the required parameter values
- `Deploy.AzureResourceGroup.ps1`: This is a PowerShell script that will help you to perform the final deployment

 You can change the `azuredeploy` name in any way you like, but the extensions `.json` and `.parameters.json` extensions must be maintained.

Let's have a deeper look:

I would like to start with the `azuredeploy.json` file. Please click on the corresponding entry in the Solution Explorer. Now, you should see the following screen:

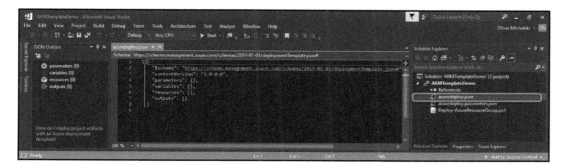

In the middle area of the Visual Studio IDE (the editor window) the following code block is now given:

```
{
    "$schema": "http://schema.management.azure.com/schemas/2015-01-
01/deploymentTemplate.json#",
    "contentVersion": "1.0.0.0",
    "parameters": {},
    "variables": {},
    "resources": [],
    "outputs": {}
}
```

This code is the simplest form of an ARM template, but I should like to point out that, in this form, the template is not valid and cannot be executed.

Here is the reason: some of these fields are required and others are optional. The following table shows whether a field should be filled in:

Field	Required
$schema	Yes
contentVersion	Yes
parameters	No
variables	No
resources	Yes
output	No

As you can see, the $schema, contentVersion, and resources fields need to be filled in. For the $schema and contentVersion fields, you can continue to use the pre-enclosed values, so you must add at least one resource.

Now, let's add a resource. Once again, I chose a storage account as the resource type. The relevant section in the azuredeploy.json file looks like this:

```
"resources": [
    {
        "type": "Microsoft.Storage/storageAccounts",
        "name": "[parameters('storageAccountName')]",
        "apiVersion": "2015-06-15",
        "location": "[resourceGroup().location]",
        "properties": {
```

```
        "accountType": "Standard_LRS"
      }
    }
  ]
```

There's one thing I need to point out: the use of parameters is not necessary, but without parameters, your template would always deploy the same resources with the same names, locations, and properties.

In order to avoid this situation, in the presented code segment, a parameter for the resource name is used.

For the parameters, we have to provide the corresponding definition. The relevant section in the azuredeploy.json file looks like this:

```
"parameters": {
    "storageAccountName": {
      "type": "string",
      "metadata": {
        "description": "Storage Account Name"
      }
    }
}
```

The template is now ready, valid, and executable. The complete code for our azuredeploy.json sample file looks like this:

```
{
  "$schema":
"https://schema.management.azure.com/schemas/2015-01-01/deploymentTemp
late.json#",
  "contentVersion": "1.0.0.0",
  "parameters": {
    "storageAccountName": {
      "type": "string",
      "metadata": {
        "description": "Storage Account Name"
      }
    }
  },
  "resources": [
    {
      "type": "Microsoft.Storage/storageAccounts",
      "name": "[parameters('storageAccountName')]",
      "apiVersion": "2015-06-15",
      "location": "[resourceGroup().location]",
      "properties": {
```

```
          "accountType": "Standard_LRS"
        }
      }
    ]
  }
```

The next step in our tour is the `azuredeploy.parameters.json` file. Please click on the corresponding entry in the Solution Explorer. Now, you should see the following screen:

Parameters are automatically adopted during the entire processing of the `azuredeploy. json` file, but can also be inserted manually (for example, to define default values).

The last step in our tour is the `Deploy.AzureResourceGroup.ps1` file. Please click on the corresponding entry in the Solution Explorer. Now, you should see the following screen:

Again, all settings during the entire processing of the `azuredeploy. json` file are automatically taken over and can be manually inserted.

Summary

In this chapter, we learned all about ARM, and therefore the basics for implementing Azure solutions.

In the first part of this chapter, we saw how to create an Azure resource group, how to add resources to this group, and last but not least, how to organize the work with the resources in this group.

The second part of this chapter followed detailed information on ARM templates, divided into two areas for developers and IT professionals.

3
Deploying and Synchronizing Azure Active Directory

As the quantity of cloud services increases, identity management and security, as well as access policies within cloud environments and cloud services, are becoming even more essential.

The Microsoft central instance for identity management for all Microsoft cloud services is Azure **Active Directory** (**AD**). Every subscription, contract, security policy, or identity Microsoft provides for their cloud services is based on Azure AD, which is also called Microsoft Tenant.

In this chapter, you will learn the basics of Azure AD, and how you implement Azure AD and hybrid Azure AD when connecting to **Active Directory Domain Services** (**AD DS**).

We are going to explore the following topics:

- Azure AD overview
- Azure AD subscription options
- Azure AD deployment
- Azure AD user and subscription management
- How to deploy Azure AD hybrid identities with AD DS
- Azure AD hybrid high availability and non-high availability deployments

Azure AD

Azure AD is a multi-tenant cloud directory and identity management service developed by Microsoft. Azure AD also includes a full suite of identity management capabilities, including the following:

- Multi-factor authentication
- Device registration
- Self-service password management
- Self-service group management
- Privileged account management
- Role-based access control
- Application usage monitoring
- Rich auditing
- Security monitoring and alerting

Azure AD can be integrated with an existing Windows Server AD, giving organizations the ability to leverage their existing on-premises identities to manage access to cloud-based SaaS applications. An organization is also able to easily implement **single sign-on (SSO)** and **multi-factor authentication (MFA)** through Azure AD without adding third-party software into its environment.

After this chapter, you will know how to set up Azure AD and Azure Connect. You will also be able to design a highly available infrastructure for identity replication.

The following diagram describes the general structure of Azure AD in a hybrid deployment with AD DS:

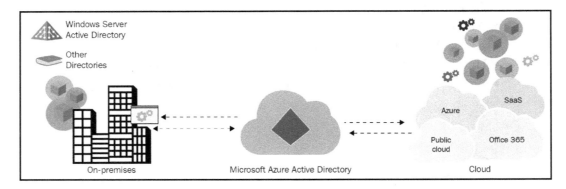

Customers using different Microsoft services, such as Office 365, CRM Online, or Intune, are already using Azure AD for their service. You can easily identify whether you use Azure AD if you have a username such as `user@domain.onmicrosoft.com`. Other top-level-domains, such as `.de` or `.cn`, are also possible if you are using Microsoft Cloud Germany or Azure China.

Azure AD is a multi-tenant, geo-distributed, high availability service running in every Microsoft datacenter around the world. Microsoft has implemented automated failover with a minimum of two copies of your Azure directory service in other regional or global datacenters.

Your directory is running in your primary datacenter, but is regularly replicated into another two in your region. If you only have two Azure datacenters in your region, as in Europe, a copy will be distributed to another datacenter in another region:

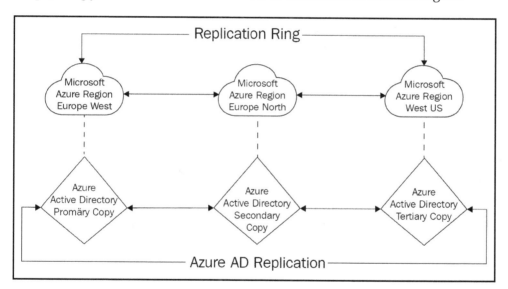

In regular cases, Microsoft prefers to synchronize Azure AD only within a geopolitical region, such as the European Union or United States. In some cases, where no third region is available, Microsoft replicates a copy outside the geopolitical region. For Europe, that was the case until regions in France became available. Since France has been online and generally available, the replication of Azure AD only runs in regions within the EU.

Azure AD options

There are currently four electable options for Azure AD with different features to use.

Azure AD free

Azure AD free supports common features such as these:

- Up to 5,00,000 directory objects, which could be users, devices, applications, or groups
- User/group management (add/update/delete), user-based provisioning, and device registration
- SSO for up to ten applications per user
- Self-service password changes for cloud users
- Connect and sync with on-premises AD DS
- Up to three basic security and usage reports

Azure AD basic

This supports all the common features from free Azure AD and more, such as:

- Same features—free and additional group-based access management/provisioning
- Self-service password reset for cloud users
- Company branding (logon pages/access panel customization)
- Application proxy
- Service level agreement of 99.9%

Azure AD premium P1

Supports common features from free and basic Azure AD, such as:

- Group-based access management/provisioning
- Self-service password resets for cloud users
- Company branding (logon pages/access panel customization)
- Application proxy
- Service level agreement of 99.9%

Premium features also include:

- Self-service group and app management/self-service application additions/dynamic groups
- Self-service password reset/change/unlock with on-premises write-back
- MFA (cloud and on-premises MFA server)
- **Microsoft Identity Manager** (**MIM**) CAL plus MIM server
- Cloud app discovery
- Connect health
- Automatic password rollover for group accounts

Since Q3/2016, Microsoft has also allowed customers to use the Azure AD P2 plan, which includes all the capabilities in Azure AD premium P1 as well as new identity protection and privileged identity management capabilities. This was an important step for Microsoft to extend its offering for Windows 10 and Windows Server 2016/19 device management with Azure AD.

Currently, Azure AD enables Windows 10 customers to join a device to Azure AD, implement SSO for desktops, use a Microsoft passport for Azure AD, and have a central administrator BitLocker recovery.

Depending on what you plan to do with your Azure environment, you should choose the right Azure AD option.

Deploying a custom Azure AD

To understand how you deploy Azure AD, you need to understand that Azure AD is directly connected to your Azure subscription. So, the Azure account subscription administrator is always the first service administrator for your Azure environment. There can only be one account administrator per Azure subscription. The account administrator is the only one who can manage Azure AD and subscription connections. If you lose your administrator credentials or lose access to the administrator account, you can no longer manage your subscription.

You should therefore plan who will create your subscription and which account is the account administrator. To create a subscription, the subscription administrator must have a Microsoft account formerly known as a Live ID or Microsoft account, or an Azure AD account. This can be created, for example, through Office 365 before adding Azure agreements and subscription payments, or could be an account created and synchronized through the AD DS to Azure. What you shouldn't do is to use a personal account for an employee to function as an account administrator and global Azure administrator. If there is any change with that employee, you could lose Azure AD access. In any case, you should work with group accounts or service accounts, so that a minimum of two people are able to access the subscription.

Normally, an Azure AD is created when you create an Azure subscription or you subscribe to a Microsoft cloud service such as Office 365. As an Azure account administrator, you can create a new Azure AD and change your Azure subscription to the new Azure AD.

Let's begin by creating an Azure AD:

1. First you need to log in to `https://portal.azure.com/#create/Microsoft.AzureActiveDirectory`.

With effect from January 2018, Microsoft only offers one portal, `https://manage.windowsazure.com`, since the old deployment engine based on **Microsoft Service Manager** was discontinued. The modern portal, `https://portal.microsoft.com`, which is based on the Microsoft resource manager engine (ARM), is the primary and preferred portal.

2. With the new portal, creating an Azure AD becomes quite easy:
    - Select a display name
    - Select your tenant/Azure AD name
    - Select the country where you are legally based

- Click on the **Create** button:

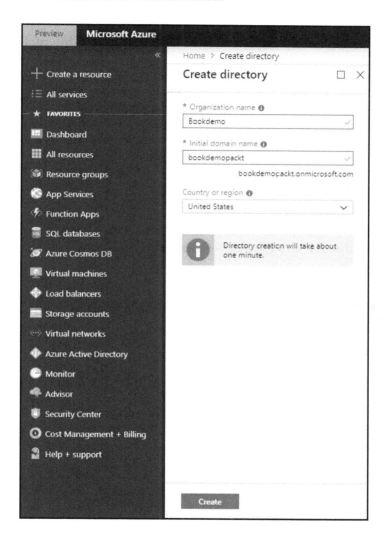

 Azure AD B2C is a cloud identity management solution for your consumer-facing web and mobile applications. You can find more information in the Azure documentation at `https://docs.microsoft.com/en-us/azure/active-directory-b2c/active-directory-b2c-overview`.

3. The process will take about a minute, and at the end you'll be navigated to your newly created tenant.

 The regular way an Azure AD is created is a bit different. Normally, the Azure AD is created by your license or subscription seller, for example, COMPAREX, SoftwareONE, or Ingram Micro. They will create the subscription for you when ordering an Azure subscription, an online **Enterprise Agreement** (**EA**), or other Microsoft 365 services. EA customers are normally only allowed to have one Azure AD; if you need to have more than one Azure AD, you need to extend your EA with an additional contract. This contract will allow you to use EA subscriptions in a multi-tenant environment.

To make identity management between Microsoft 365 services, Azure, and other identity services consistent, you should use one tenant for all your users and only split between production and the **dev/test** Azure AD and so on.

Adding accounts and groups to Azure AD

First, you need to understand what accounts can be added to Azure AD. Basically, there are two types of account:

- **Cloud accounts**: Accounts that are created through Azure AD or other Microsoft cloud services, such as Office 365.
- **Hybrid accounts**: Accounts that are created and located in on-premises Microsoft AD DS. Those accounts are deployed through a the Azure AD Connect and synchronization tool.

To create cloud accounts, you have several options. Most Azure AD users start with Office 365 and do not natively add users through Azure. If you've used Office 365 before, that would be the simplest for you.

The example shown in the following screenshot guides you through how to add a user from the Office 365 preview portal through `https://portal.office.com`:

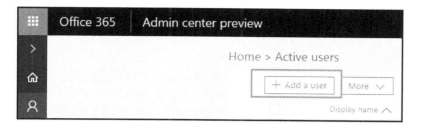

Alternatively, to create new users in Azure AD through the Azure portal, you need to follow these steps:

1. Browse to `https://portal.azure.com`.
2. Click on the **More services** option on the sidebar:

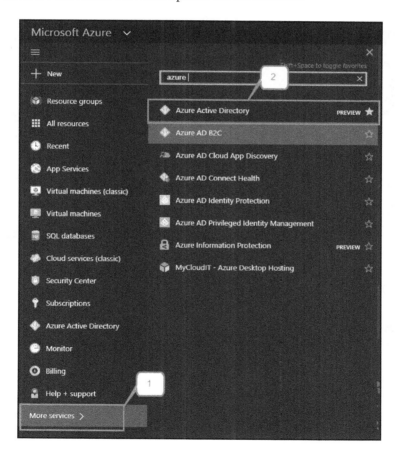

3. The new Azure AD interface does not yet have all features enabled. Currently, it is not possible to create new Azure active directories, but you can perform most user and application operations.

4. In addition to the new portal, Microsoft also extended user management to the Azure AD management portal. At the time of writing this book, the new user and group management is still in preview, so changes are still possible. To add or change user accounts, you now have different options. The first one would be to open user and group management through the Azure AD interface:

5. The next step is look for **Users and groups** with Microsoft resources:

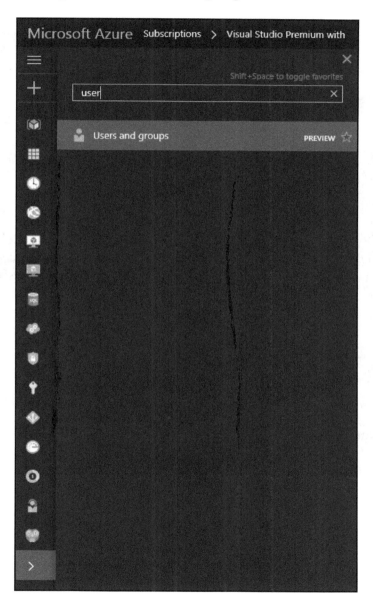

6. Both ways will bring you to the same blade, with options to create users and groups as shown in the following screenshot:

7. To add a user in the new UI, you click on the **All users** section, as shown in the following screenshot:

8. There, you click on the **+Add** button and follow the instructions shown in the following screenshot:

9. The blade will ask you to provide a username, as shown here:

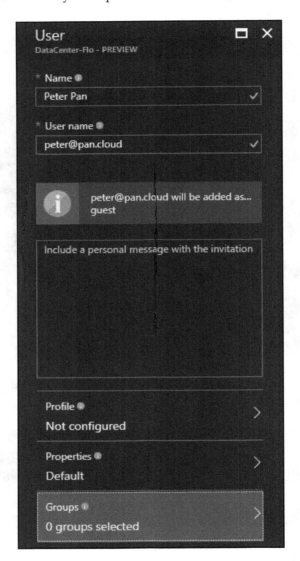

 Be aware that with Azure AD free without Office 365, the username must be an email or a Microsoft account (formerly a Microsoft Live account) to be able to receive the invitation from Azure AD.

10. While creating the user, you have different options for pre-staging information about the user, including the **First name**, **Last name**, **Job title**, or **Department** fields as shown in the following screenshot:

11. With a synced AD DS and other joined services, you can change the **Source of Authority** option:

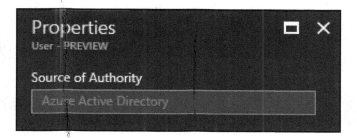

12. You can also join the account directly to Azure AD groups during creation:

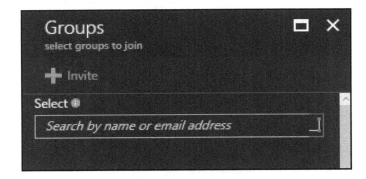

13. The new UI for Azure AD includes a new option to join users as account admins (formerly known as co-administrators). To do this, change the administrator rights of the user by clicking on the relevant user to open the user blade:

14. Then, click on the **Directory role** section to open the role options:

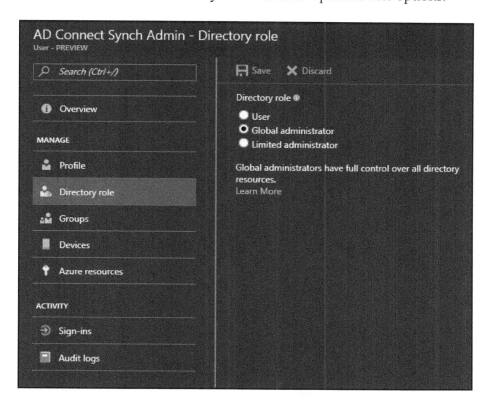

15. Not every user needs to be global administrator to be able to fulfill their job. Mostly, one or more of the options of a limited administrator should be enough:

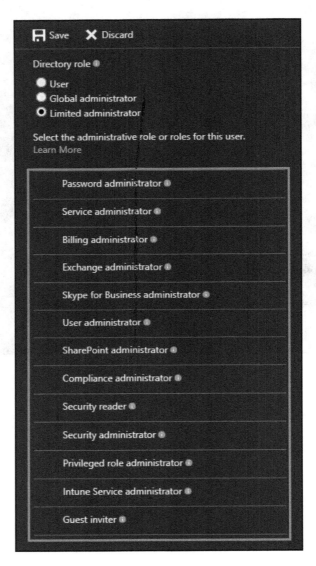

16. After you add the user to their admin role, you need to go to the **Subscriptions** section in the Azure resources:

17. There, you select subscriptions for which the user should be the co-administrator:

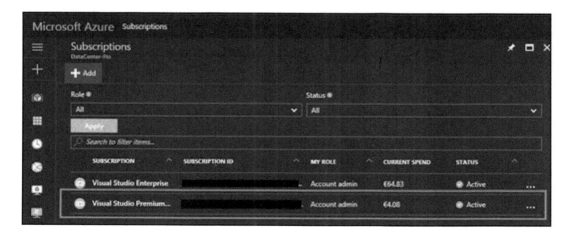

18. In the following blade, click on the **Access control (IAM)** section and then on the **+Add** button:

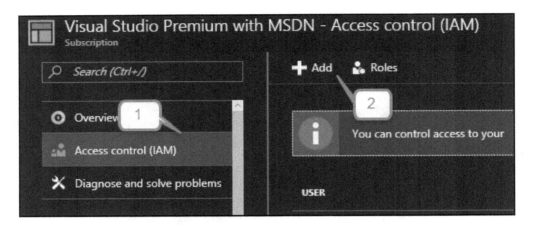

19. Now, select a role for the user. To make them a co-administrator, we need to give them **Owner** rights:

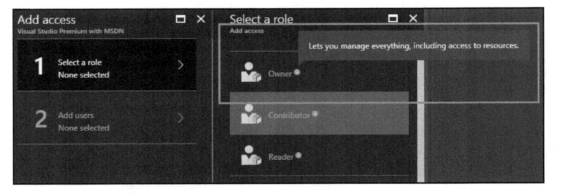

As an owner, they have full access to the subscription resources, which will enable them to do all operations that need to be done on a subscription. As a reader, they can see billing and resources for a subscription but can't change things inside the subscription. That is the option most billing tools such as **Microsoft Cloudyn / Azure Cost Management, Cloud Cruiser**, or **Azure Costs** need to create their statistics.

20. The user is now able to manage the subscription. Next, select the user or group that should have the permissions. This user can now manage the subscription.

 You can also invite Microsoft accounts to your subscription without creating a user first. When it comes to best practice or how it would be done in the field, you wouldn't add any single accounts into the subscription. You should give permission for the subscription or resource to a group, and then add users to the group.

The other option to create new users and groups is to sync them through AD DS from your connected on-premises Windows Server AD DS. To do this, you'll need an additional tool named **Azure AD Connect**.

 From a security and compliance perspective, never synchronize the administration account to Azure AD. Leave that account for on-premises AD DS only and create cloud-only accounts in Azure AD for administrative work in Azure or Microsoft 365 Services.

Azure AD Connect will integrate your on-premises directories with Azure AD. This allows you to provide a common identity for your users for Office 365, Azure, and SaaS applications integrated with Azure AD:

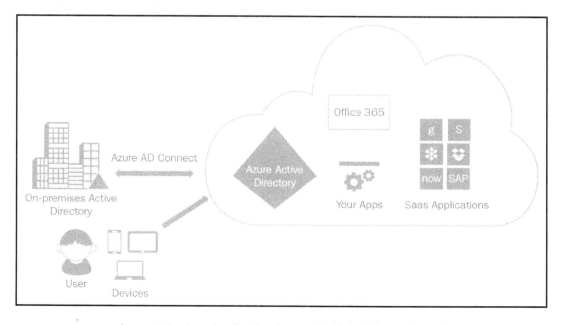

Image source: https://azure.microsoft.com/en-us/documentation/articles/active-directory-aadconnect/

Azure AD Connect is the central tool with which to implement hybrid identities in Azure, and enables you to license your software or implement identity and access management tools such as SSO, MFS, or **Active Directory Rights Management Services** (**AD RMS**).

Azure AD Connect brings five programs with different purposes:

- **Azure AD Connect**: This is a configuration tool with an integrated and detailed wizard to configure Azure AD and on-premises AD DS synchronization.
- **Synchronization rules editor**: This is a basic tool to configure and customize synchronizations between Azure AD and on-premises AD DS:

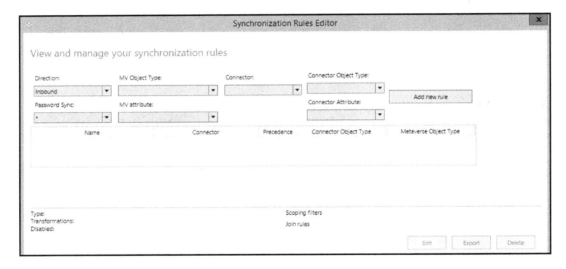

- **Synchronization service**: The synchronization service is a tool to basically monitor and log synchronization between Azure AD and on-premises AD DS. You can supervise the synchronization process:

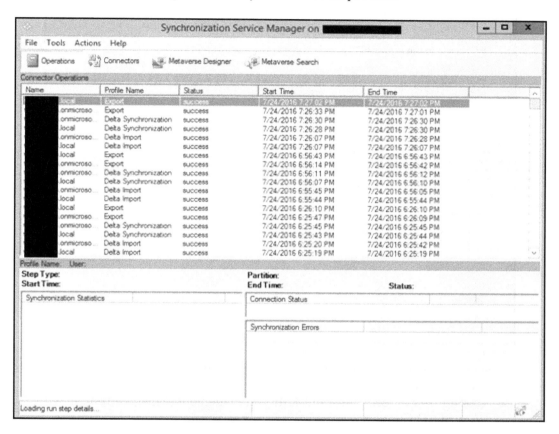

- **Synchronization service key manager**: Helps you manage security keys to encrypt data transferred between Azure AD and on-premises AD DS:

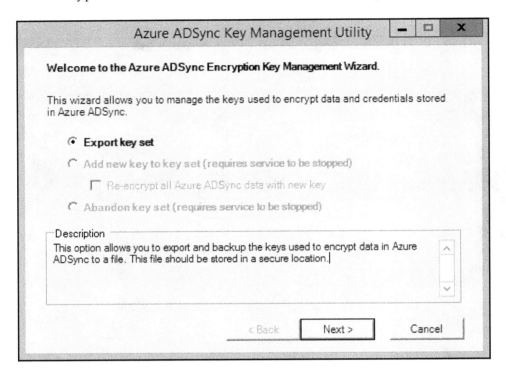

- **Synchronization Service Web Service Configuration Manager**: This came with version 1.1.189.0 of Azure AD Connect in June 2016. It is used to configure Microsoft Account Entity Management (MIM) endpoints with Azure AD Connect:

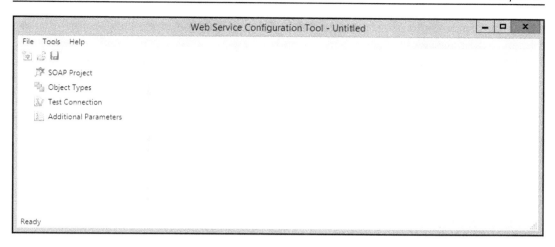

 Azure AD Connect and all its components are freely available and can be downloaded from Microsoft: `https://www.microsoft.com/en-us/download/details.aspx?id=47594`.

You can deploy Azure AD Connect in three different ways for users. Each method provides different integration levels and is more or less dependent on your Azure AD subscription level:

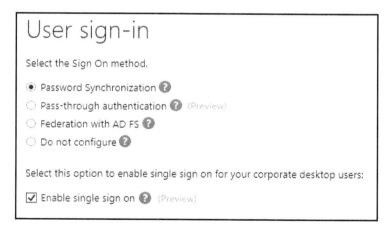

The first solution is to use the **Password Synchronization** option. This option transfers user passwords as hashed values to the cloud. This option is also the one that enables a basic SSO option for your users to Azure AD-based applications in your organization. This password synchronization is only based on user account and password replication. So, changes within Azure AD will take some time or be manual. This option is also only practical for small environments with fewer than 300 users. For larger environments, you would have too much replication traffic and too many changes within Azure AD, which would take too long. As an example, a replication of around 4,000 users could take up to 12 hours before it is visible in the Azure AD:

 To choose the right sign in option for your organization, please refer a very detailed guide on that topic here: `https://blogs.msdn.microsoft.com/samueld/2017/06/13/choosing-the-right-sign-in-option-to-connect-to-azure-ad-office-365/`.

- The following screenshot shows you the tooltip you get when you hover over the question mark for the **Password Synchronization** option:

> **PASSWORD SYNCHRONIZATION**
>
> This option allows your users to sign in to the cloud using the same passwords that they use on-premises.
> Password synchronization does not store or send clear text passwords.
>
> Learn more

- The second option is to select the new **Pass-through authentication** option. With this option, your AD Connect and Azure AD will not store any identity data, and they will send all requests directly to your environment. The following screenshot shows you the tooltip you get when you hover over the question mark for **Pass-through authentication**:

> **PASS-THROUGH AUTHENTICATION**
>
> Pass-through authentication enables Azure Active Directory to authenticate users using your on-premises identity infrastructure.
>
> Learn more

- The third and most complex solution is to implement **Active Directory Federation Services (AD FS)** with Azure AD, in the interface named federation with AD FS. That will enable full SSO and add MFA. The organizations and implementations. If you want to implement AD FS, you need also to have public and **private key infrastructure (PKI)** and certificates from a trusted agency in place. For AD FS, you need good response times so you might need to upgrade your internet access and/or Wide Area Network connectivity. The following screenshot shows you the tooltip you get when you hover over the question mark for **Federation with AD FS**:

SINGLE SIGN ON

This option allows your users to do federated sign in using AD FS.
While logged in to the corporate network, your users can access cloud resources without entering their passwords again.

Learn more

- The fourth and easiest way is to not configure user sign-in. This option enables only license and user replication from local to cloud and vice versa. There is no option to replicate passwords, and your users will not be able to sign in or use Azure AD resources. Users would be able to use, for example, Office 365 or the Azure remote app. The following screenshot shows you the tooltip you get when you hover over the question mark for **Do not configure**:

DO NOT CONFIGURE

This option allows your users to do federated sign in using a solution not managed by this wizard.
While logged in to the corporate network, your users can access cloud resources without entering their passwords again.

Learn more

- With the new enhancements in Windows 10 and with Azure AD, you can now also configure SSO directly from your on-premises Windows systems. To enable this feature, you need to check the **Enable single sign on** checkbox:

Single sign on

This option enables users on the corporate network to get a single sign on experience when accessing cloud services from their domain joined desktop machines.

Learn more

Installing Azure AD Connect – prerequisites

For those who haven't worked with AD FS before, federations offer a standardized service that allows the secure sharing of identity information between trusted business partners (known as a **federation**) across an extranet. When a user needs to access a web application from one of its federation partners, the user's own organization is responsible for authenticating the user and providing identity information in the form of *claims* to the partner that hosts the web application. The hosting partner uses its trust policy to map incoming claims to claims that are understood by its web application, which uses these claims to make authorization decisions. So basically, Azure AD and Microsoft become your business partner in AD FS.

From a planning perspective, the following prerequisites must be in place:

- An Azure subscription or an Azure trial subscription; this is only required for accessing the Azure Portal and not for using Azure AD Connect. If you are using Azure PowerShell or Office 365, you do not need an Azure subscription to use Azure AD Connect.
- An Azure AD global administrator account for the Azure AD tenant you wish to integrate with.
- An AD **Domain Controller** (**DC**) or member server with Windows Server 2008 or newer (see the following table for the appropriate sizing for that machine).

The DC or member server you will be using as the Azure AD Connect machine in your environment must meet the following minimum specifications:

Number of objects in AD	CPU	Memory	Hard drive size
Fewer than 10,000	1.6 GHz	4 GB	70 GB
10,000 to 50,000	1.6 GHz	4 GB	70 GB
50,000 to 100,000	1.6 GHz	16 GB	100 GB
For 100,000 or more objects, the full version of SQL Server is required; otherwise, a Windows internal database or SQL Express can be used			
100,000 to 300,000	1.6 GHz	32 GB	300 GB
300,000 to 600,000	1.6 GHz	32 GB	450 GB
More than 600,000	1.6 GHz	32 GB	500 GB

First, before you start the installation of AD Connect, you need to configure two user accounts. The first one should be a service account with enterprise administrator rights, or for sub-domains with domain administrator rights within your on-premises AD DS. The other one must be a global administrator in Azure AD.

The following screenshot shows the **User** settings you need for the Azure AD `synch` administrator:

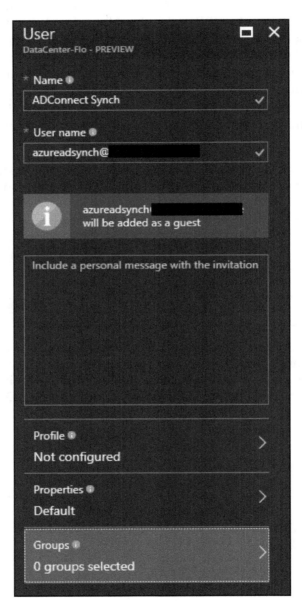

These two accounts will perform actions on both directories. So, the on-premises user won't have access to Azure AD, and the Azure AD admin won't have access to the on-premises AD:

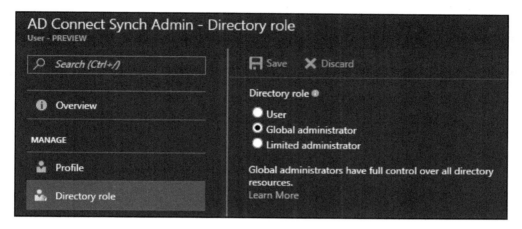

The following diagram shows you the basic workflow behind communication between Azure AD, AD Connect, and on-premises AD DS:

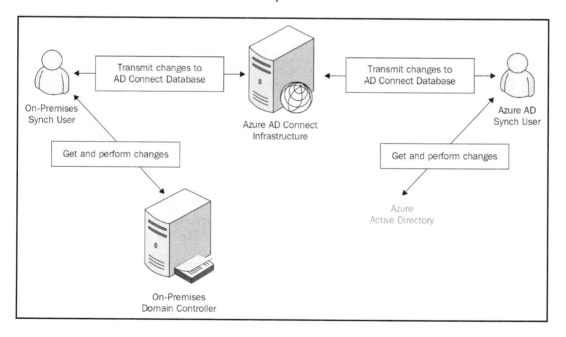

After you choose which type of user sign-on you want to use for your Azure AD users implementation, the wizard changes and adds or removes configuration options. For the AD FS implementation, you need to perform some more steps to get the federation running. For the AD FS implementation, you will need at least one AD FS Server and one AD FS Proxy additionally, as well as additional service accounts. The connection will work automatically, based on **Windows Remote Management (WinRM)**. As explained earlier, the Azure AD will authenticate against your on-premises AD FS implementation.

The following diagram reflects the more complex environment:

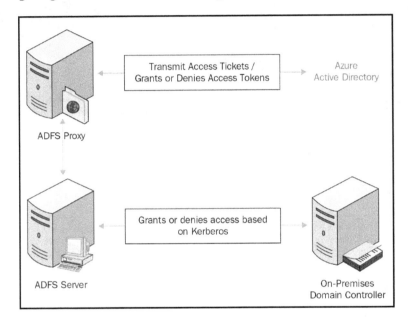

Installing a basic Azure AD Connect environment

As an example, I will show you how to implement Azure AD Connect with password synchronization. The other options for the setup are similar:

1. First you need to download **Azure AD Connect**. In the setup, you will have to configure synchronization but you can redo your setup by looking for **Azure AD Connect** in the Windows Start menu:

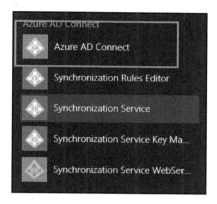

Be aware your AD Connect Server must be joined to the on-premises AD domain.

2. Accept the license terms and click on the **Continue** button as shown in the following screenshot:

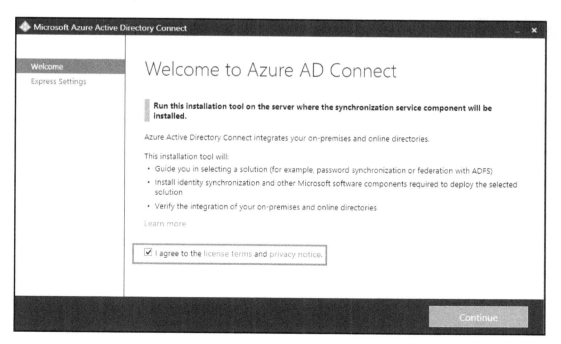

3. Click on the **Customize** button to continue:

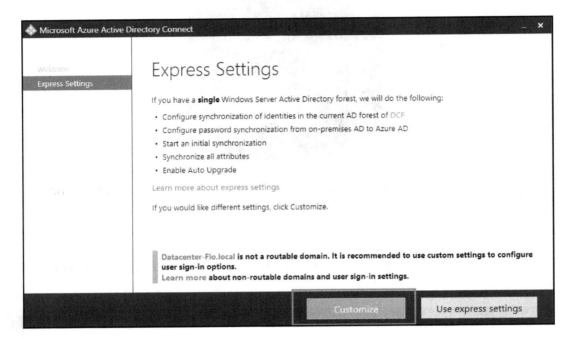

4. Choose the **Password Synchronization** option and click on the **Next** button:

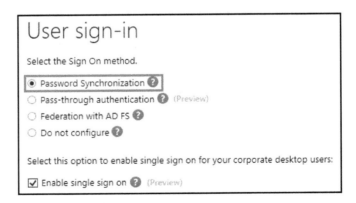

5. In the next window, enter the credentials for your Azure AD `synch` account:

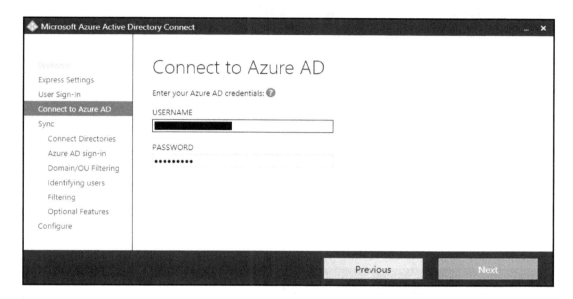

6. On many websites, and also in Microsoft documentation, you will find terms such as **DirSync** and **Azure AD Sync**. Both have no longer been supported since Azure AD Connect reached a production state. Visit this website for more information: `http://blog.azureandbeyond.com/2017/04/06/dirsync-azu re-ad-sync-end-of-support/?fb_action_ids=1199177306847421&fb_action_types=news.publ ishes`.

7. Next, you need to add your on-premises administrator account:

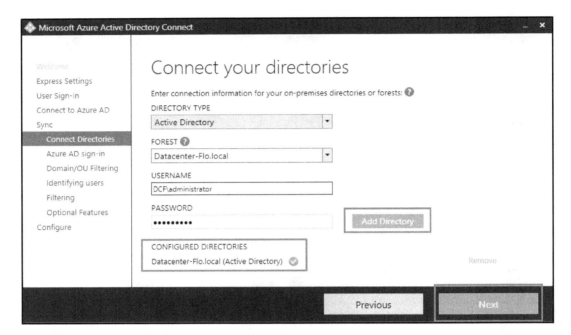

 For multi-domain forest AD infrastructures, your on-premises administrator account needs to be an enterprise administrator. If you only have a single domain forest, you can use a regular domain admin.

8. For the next step, you need to select the attribute in your on-premises domain that identifies the **User Principal Name** (**UPN**) in the Azure AD.

 The UPN is an internet-style login name for a user based on the internet standard RFC 822.

9. Microsoft's best practice is to select the principal user name of your on-premises domain. This isn't the best option in all scenarios:

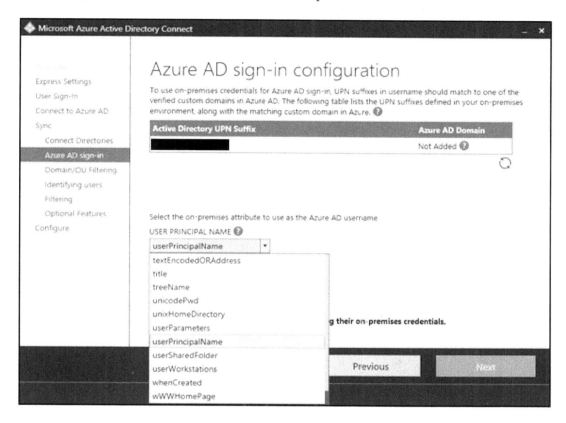

Just from the field, it is not always helpful to choose the principal user. Depending on the domain, sometimes it is better to choose the email instead of the principal user name in Azure AD. That's because the primary email in a synced scenario is always the login name. So, if your login name is `@company.onmicrosoft.com`, the primary email will become this domain too.

10. The following diagram shows you an example of a decision path: when to choose UPN and when an email address. It's very basic but helps in most cases:

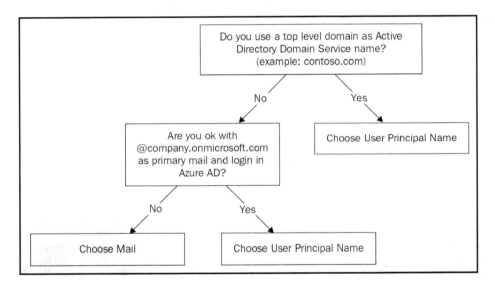

11. After you select which attribute will be your identifier, you need to set the AD filter. It isn't recommended to parse the whole AD DS for synchronization, because that would take a lot of time, unless you have a large on-premises AD. For faster synchronization, it is recommended to select only a subset of the on-premises AD objects; for example, select only the **organizational units** (**OUs**) that contain requested objects:

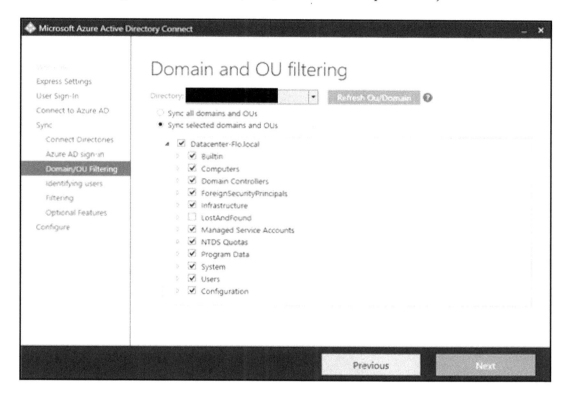

12. Now, choose how your users should be identified over your domain. Depending on your decision, you now select the principal user name or email:

13. Afterwards, configure the filter for your accounts. You can either synchronize all users and devices or use a filter group. Here, the best way is to have specified groups for your users. From a security and resource perspective, you shouldn't select all users; otherwise, you would sync unnecessary or possibly restricted accounts to Azure AD:

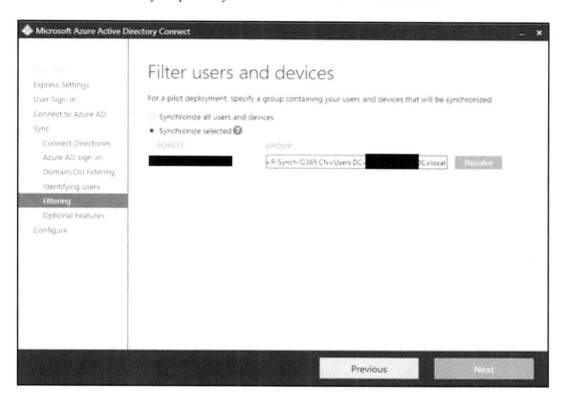

14. In the next steps, choose which features you want to have synced in addition to the attributes:

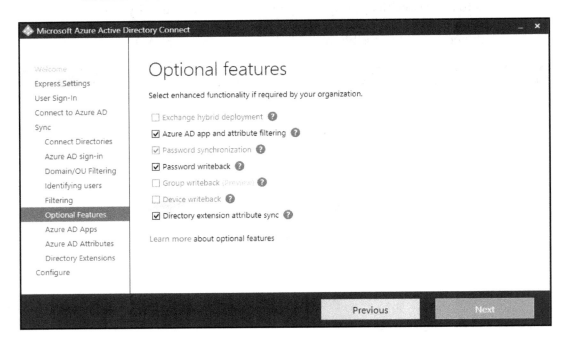

Some, such as the **Exchange hybrid deployment** and **Device writeback** options, are only available with certain AD extensions, or with additional subscriptions such as Azure AD premium or mobile device management such as Intune. Best field practice is to at least sync the **Azure AD app and attribute filtering** option. That will enable you to sync allowed apps and license attributes between Azure AD and AD, which is, for example, necessary if you license your Microsoft Office in your Terminal server environment with the Office 365 E3 or E5 plans. If you do not choose to enable the feature, it may be possible that some applications will not appear to be licensed. Office 365 installed on a **Citrix Terminal Server** is a good example of that. Without synchronization, Citrix does not know about the license details and the user receives an Office licensing login every time they start their Office applications on the Terminal Server.

If you are running a Microsoft Exchange within your AD DS, enable the **Exchange hybrid deployment** checkbox. There are certain little challenges with configuring it afterwards. One of common one is broken Exchange mail routing for users who had an Exchange Online mailbox without an on-premises connection before.

15. In the next few windows, you can decide which Azure AD apps will be synced:

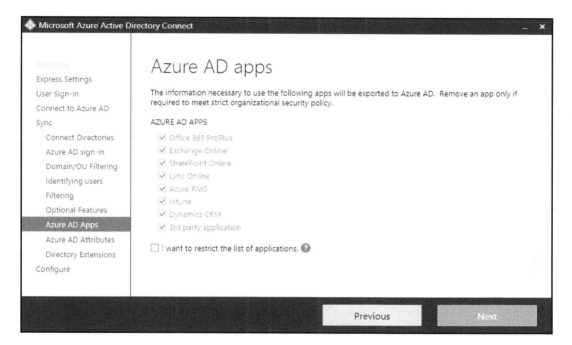

16. Afterward, you can limit the attributes from AD that will be transferred to Azure AD. Microsoft does not recommend limiting attributes:

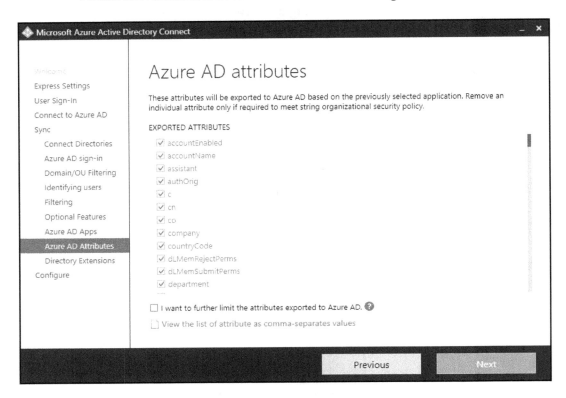

17. Now, you can select which directory extension attributes from your on-premises environment are transferred to Azure AD. This is important for certain applications running in the cloud. In this walk-through, we will not select any attributes:

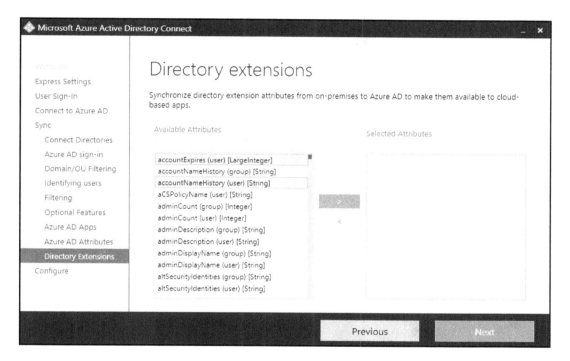

18. Once you've run through these steps, you can complete the installation. Outside a migration scenario, or as long as you don't want to enable high availability for Azure AD Connect, you can start synchronization. Otherwise, you should stage your installation first and start the first synchronization afterward:

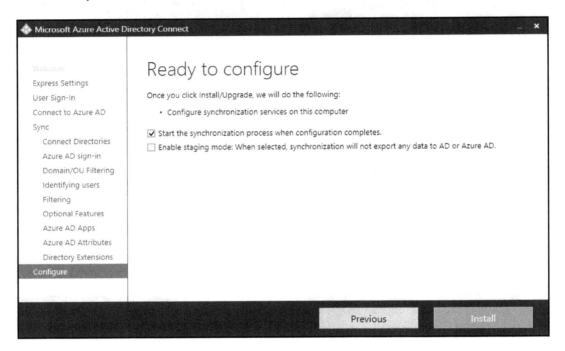

19. To disable staging mode, you need to start Azure AD Connect from the Start menu again. It will act like a regular Azure AD Connect, except that the second wizard option is to disable staging mode:

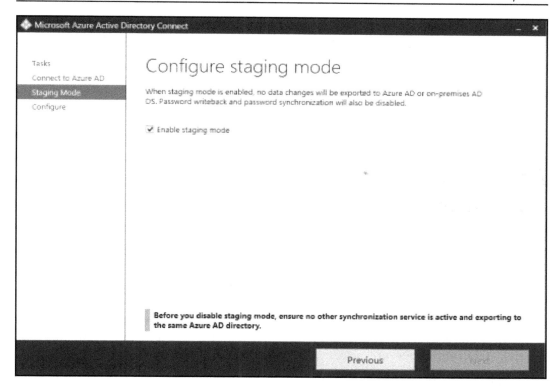

You have now implemented a simple, SSO-enabled Azure AD and AD synchronization. After you've started synchronization, Azure AD Connect will replicate changes every hour between Azure AD and AD.

You can trigger synchronization manually by using either of the following PowerShell commands:

- With `Start-ADSyncSyncCycle -PolicyType Delta`, you sync all changes since the last sync.
- With `Start-ADSyncSyncCycle -PolicyType Initial`, you perform a full sync with all the settings you have configured in Azure AD Connect. It's likely to be what you would do when you start a sync *after* installation.

From a common practice and security standpoint, you should not sync any on-premises domain administrator accounts in Azure AD, and shouldn't give the personal Azure AD account of your IT people any admin rights in Azure AD. Each time, you should create cloud-only accounts for your admins, which also only serve as admin accounts in Azure AD. That protects both directory from capturing if any of the admins is corrupted.

Azure AD Connect highly available infrastructure

Now you know how to set up a basic AD synchronization without considering the availability infrastructure, we'll look at how you can achieve Azure AD synchronization in a high availability environment.

The first thing you should know is that the Azure AD Connect tool cannot be clustered, so you need to use *staged mode* to implement it in passive mode. In the case of a failure, you have three days to recover the AD Connect Server. This can be either done through recovering from backup redeployment or switching to the staged, passive AD Connect Server.

So, for placement in either high availability or non-high availability infrastructures, it is recommended that you place systems that are involved in the synchronization of Azure VMs. This is so that you do not transfer as much data through the open internet, thus improves the performance of communication and identity token exchanges between Microsoft Cloud Services. More details about these concepts will be given in the next chapter about Azure networking.

In our high-availability scenario, every active and primary source of synchronization is placed into Azure and configured with either **Availability Zones (AZs)** or **sets**. A connection to on-premises is done through a **virtual private network (VPN)** or **Multiprotocol Label Switching (MPLS)** connection.

So, to have a user and password synchronization option in a high-availability environment, we need the following system:

- Two AD DCs with global catalog and DNS
- Two Azure AD Connect servers, one in active and one in staged mode

For the DCs and database servers, both will automatically fail-over if one system fails. For the Azure AD Connect server, you need to disable staged mode and perform the fail-over manually.

Looking at a more complex scenario, if you want to implement a high availability AD FS infrastructure, some additional systems are needed:

- Two AD DCs with global catalog and DNS
- Two Azure AD Connect servers, one in active and one in staged mode
- Two AD federation servers
- Two AD federation proxies

Such an infrastructure could look like the following architectural schema:

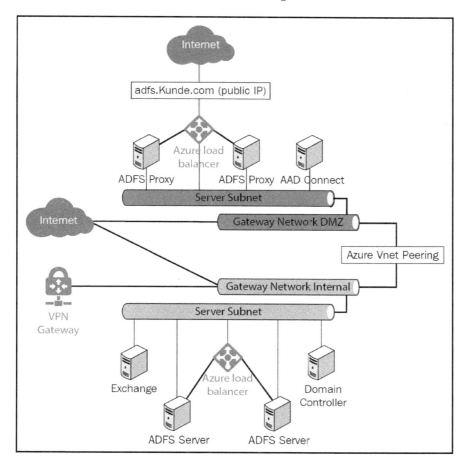

Microsoft recently published a very good guide deploying AD FS in Azure. You can find the guide through the following link: `https://docs.microsoft.com/en-us/azure/active-directory/connect/active-directory-aadconnect-azure-adfs`.

Azure AD conditional access

At this point, I want to give some credit to a very important child service of Azure AD. Azure AD conditional access is a very simple way to control and secure access to resources in the cloud and on premises. Azure AD conditional access is a premium feature in Azure AD. You can grade access, for example, by the following conditions:

- **Group membership**: Access based on group membership
- **Location**: Block controls when a user is not on a trusted network, or trigger MFA
- **Device platform**: Use the device platform (iOS, Android, Windows versions) to apply a policy
- **Device-enabled**: Device state (enabled or disabled) is validated during device policy evaluation
- **Sign-in and user risk**: Azure AD Identity Protection for conditional access risk policies

 Azure AD conditional access is, for example, the only option to disable access for Azure through the public internet or based on network policies. Even private connections, such as Microsoft ExpressRoute, do not allow limiting access through a network. They always depend on conditional access through Azure AD.

The following screenshot shows you the overview page for Azure AD conditional access:

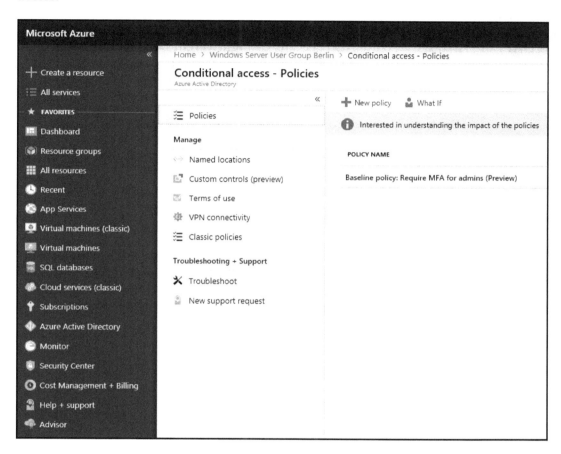

I would also recommend you consult the documentation to get a deeper look into the capabilities of this service: `https://docs.microsoft.com/en-us/azure/active-directory/conditional-access/overview`.

Azure AD DS

Another service I want to give some credit to is Azure AD DS. This service builds a bridge to services that depend on AD DS or **Lightweight Directory Access Protocol (LDAP)** and Azure AD. Azure AD DS is an AD **Lightweight Directory Services (LDS)**deployed over Azure AD. It allows read access through common AD DS calls and can handle normal domain identity and access. In the majority of use cases, Azure AD DS can replace a classic AD DS.

For the deployment and more, consult the documentation for this service: https://docs.microsoft.com/en-us/azure/active-directory-domain-services/active-directory-ds-overview.

Summary

You have learned how Azure AD works and what features each subscription level of Azure AD offers you. You are now also familiar with creating users in Azure AD and syncing them with your on-premises AD. You also saw other options for user sign-in with AD FS and how to make your Azure hybrid environment highly available.

Implementing Azure Networks

4

Just as you plan the network in your data center or company, you need to do it in Azure also. Networking is essential in Azure and if you do not plan it right you could force outages or bottlenecks for deployed services.

Depending on what you plan with Azure, you should put some effort in planning your network and connections into Azure.

Within this chapter, you will learn the basics about Azure networking, how to implement Azure networking, and how to decide which WAN and connectivity solution you should use.

We are going to explore the following topics:

- Azure virtual networks
- Azure virtual network gateways
- Azure local gateways
- Azure site-to-site and point-to-site VPN
- Azure ExpressRoute
- Azure virtual WAN
- Azure Firewall
- Azure DDoS
- Azure connections and routes
- Azure DNS
- Azure application gateway

We will also set up a basic network configuration during this chapter.

Azure networking limits

Microsoft offers a wide range of capabilities when it comes to networking in and to Azure. That makes a network solution very flexible but also complex. You have many options to achieve your goal, but to do so you need to keep some limitations in mind. Behind the following link, you can find those Azure limitations: `https://docs.microsoft.com/en-us/azure/azure-subscription-service-limits`.

Azure networking components

To start with Azure networking, you need to know and understand the components which are needed to set up an Azure solution.

Let us start from the easiest part to the more difficult ones.

Azure virtual networks (VNet)

An Azure VNet is a logical isolated network for your services connected to your subscription in Azure. You have full control about the IP address blocks, DNS settings, security policies, and route tables within this network. You can also split your VNet into subnet and launch Azure IaaS virtual machines and cloud services within these subnets. By using Azure virtual gateways and WAN solutions, you can also connect your virtual networks to the internet or your on-premises environment.

When you look for Azure VNet in Azure, you basically search for the network and you should see the symbol shown in the following screenshot:

Normally you're setting up a network like you do in your on-premises network. You create a network with an IP range such as 10.0.0.0/15 and split it up into different subnetworks. Every Azure VNet has at least a minimum of two subnets. The first is the **gateway subnet**, which is basically a router network where every internal network router for the other Azure VNet subnetworks is in. We personally prefer to use the first subnet of the Azure VNet as the gateway subnet but you can choose any subnet you like. The only thing you need to know is that the gateway subnet needs a minimum of /29 CIDR IPs. I normally recommend /24 CIDR. You would never use it but it's logical and you can follow up with a /24 CIDR subnet design. The second one is the network for your services or servers depending on your own design, normally it is /24 CIDR.

 As of September 2016, Azure started to support IPv6 to be used in Azure. The deployment and support of IPv6 is still in progress while writing the book.

The following diagram shows you an example for a network configuration:

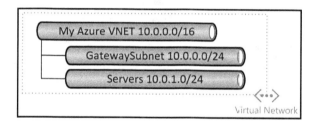

All subnetworks are fully routed to each other. That is not the best situation in most of the cases. One example is when you need a **Frontend** and a **Backend** network in Azure, as shown in the following diagram:

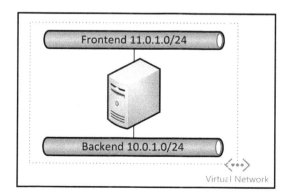

Currently there are only two ways to resolve that issue:

- The first one is to create two subnetworks and put a virtual machine with two network adapters in both networks and route within the virtual machine and prevent default routing with configuration of route filters
- The other way is to implement custom routes and send packages for the frontend network into the either of your other Azure or on premises networks

There is a great *nice to know* within the VNet setting. Under **MONITORING**, you can see a detailed networking diagram of your Azure network.

The following screenshot shows an example of a **Diagram**:

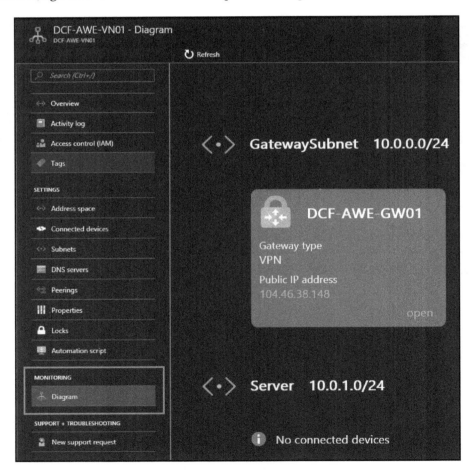

VNet peering and global VNet peering

There is also an option to connect different Azure VNet works in the same and between Azure region. This option is called Azure VNet peering for VNetworks in the same Azure region and global VNet peering for inter region peering. VNet peering for Azure virtual network lets you directly link two virtual networks via private IPs. VNet peering routes packets between virtual networks through the internal Azure backbone network. There is no Azure gateway between these networks. This allows a low-latency, high-bandwidth connection between virtual machines in the virtual networks.

VNet peering also allows transit through the peered virtual networks, so a network virtual appliance or a VPN gateway in one virtual network can be used by a virtual machine in another peered virtual network. Peering works across virtual networks in different subscriptions. So you are able to connect, for example, subscriptions paid by different departments or subscription owners. Later in this chapter, I will show you how to set up VNet peering.

 As of September 2016, Microsoft allows VNet peering between **Azure Resource Manager** (**ARM**) environments and **Azure Service Manager** (**ASM**) environments. That enables customers to migrate from ASM to ARM more easily.

VNet service endpoints

VNet service endpoints are an extension of a virtual network private address space and a VNet to connect to Azure PaaS services through a direct connection through the Azure backbone to those services. Those private connections and endpoints allow services, virtual machines or users to secure critical and access Azure PaaS service resources only from a virtual network. Traffic from a VNet to the Azure service remains on the Microsoft Azure backbone network at any time, even if the communication between the endpoint and VNet is established through public IPs.

Currently VNet endpoints are GA for following services:

- **Azure Storage**: Generally available in all Azure regions
- **Azure SQL Database**: Generally available in all Azure regions
- **Azure Database for PostgreSQL server**: Generally available in Azure regions where database service is available
- **Azure Database for MySQL server**: Generally available in Azure regions where database service is available

- **Azure Cosmos DB**: Generally available in all Azure public cloud regions
- **Azure Key Vault**: Generally available in all Azure public cloud regions

Following services are currently in preview:

- **Azure SQL Data Warehouse**: Available in preview in all Azure public cloud regions
- **Azure Service Bus**: Available in preview
- **Azure Event Hubs**: Available in preview
- **Azure Data Lake Store Gen 1**: Available in preview

Azure VPN gateways

Azure VPN gateways are basically your core routers and firewalls within your Azure environment.

An Azure gateway can serve different purposes:

- Internet gateway
- Site-to-site VPN gateway
- Point-to-site VPN gateway
- ExpressRoute gateway
- VNet-to-VNet gateway

 We won't be able to cover the deployments of point-to-site VPN gateways in this book but you can find a detailed guide in the Microsoft documentation at `https://azure.microsoft.com/en-us/documentation/articles/vpn-gateway-howto-point-to-site-rm-ps/`.

The following screenshot shows the Azure service you need to look for when you want to implement an Azure VPN gateway:

Every VNet can have at least one VPN gateway. VPN gateways are available in different service offerings with different features and available services.

The following table shows a short summary:

	VPN gateway throughput	VPN gateway max IPSEC tunnels	Active-Active VPN	ExpressRoute gateway throughput	VPN gateway and ExpressRoute coexist	Zone redundant
Standard	100 Mbps	10	No	1000 Mbps	Yes	No
High Performance	200 Mbps	30	Yes	2000 Mbps	Yes	No
Ultra High Performance	200 Mbps	30	Yes	9000 Mbps	Yes	No
VpnGw1	650 Mbps	30	Yes	No	No	No
VpnGw1AZ	650 Mbps	30	Yes	No	No	Yes
VpnGw2	1 Gbps	30	Yes	No	No	No
VpnGw2AZ	1 Gbps	30	Yes	No	No	Yes
VpnGw3	1,25 Gbps	30	Yes	No	No	No
VpnGw3AZ	1,25 Gbps	30	Yes	No	No	Yes
ErGw1AZ	No	No	No	1000 Mbps	Yes	Yes with separated VPN gateway
ErGw2AZ	No	No	No	2000 Mbps	Yes	Yes with separated VPN gateway
ErGw3AZ	No	No	No	9000 Mbps	Yes	Yes with separated VPN gateway

Since Ignite 2018, Microsoft extended his offering around network gateways. The address customer needs regarding better SLAs on gateways, they started to offer Zone-redundant virtual network gateways for ExpressRoute and VPN. Those gateways are placed into different Azure data center with separated power supply, cooling and datacenter environments. That prevents those gateways from datacenter outages and failures. Those Gateways are marked with AZ within der SKU Friendly Name.

The following diagram shows how the basic **VPN gateway** is connected to your Azure network:

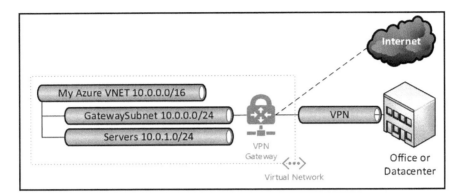

With the standard or performance gateway it would look like the following diagram:

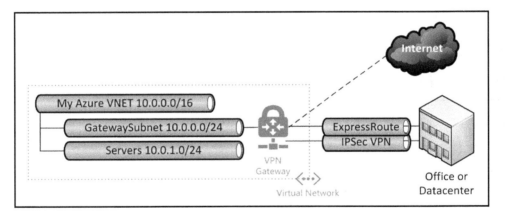

When you start the setup of a gateway, you need to decide what kind of gateway you want to deploy. The basic offering can be deployed via Azure GUI; for the other offerings, you need to do some PowerShell. The following screenshot shows the GUI version:

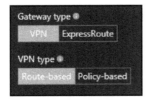

Depending on your WAN solution, you choose either **VPN** or **ExpressRoute**. For **ExpressRoute**, you need an MPLS solution in place. I will explain that later. For the **VPN** solution, you need to decide between a **Route-based** or **Policy-based** VPN, which means you need to decide if you want to enable dynamic routing with IPSEC IKEv2 or static IPSEC IKEv1.

The decision as to which VPN type you need must be done based on your on-premises VPN device. Not every device can speak **Route-based** VPN. Microsoft has published a list of supported devices. You can see them here at
`https://azure.microsoft.com/en-us/documentation/articles/vpn-gateway-about -vpn-devices/`.

There are also some more additional requirements you need to think of when choosing your VPN gateway in Azure. The following table shows you those provided by Microsoft:

	Policy-based basic VPN gateway	Route-based basic VPN gateway	Route-based standard VPN gateway	Route-based high performance VPN gateway
Site-to-site connectivity (S2S)	Policy-based VPN configuration	Route-based VPN configuration	Route-based VPN configuration	Route-based VPN configuration
Point-to-site connectivity (P2S)	Not supported	Supported (can coexist with S2S)	Supported (can coexist with S2S)	Supported (can coexist with S2S)
Authentication method	Pre-shared key	Pre-shared key for S2S connectivity, certificates for P2S connectivity	Pre-shared key for S2S connectivity, certificates for P2S connectivity	Pre-shared key for S2S connectivity, certificates for P2S connectivity
Maximum number of S2S connections	1	10	10	30
Maximum number of P2S connections	Not supported	128	128	128
Active routing support	Not supported	Not supported	Supported	Supported

In summary, you can basically have the following gateway configurations:

- The policy-based basic **VPN Gateway** with site-to-site VPN is shown in the following diagram:

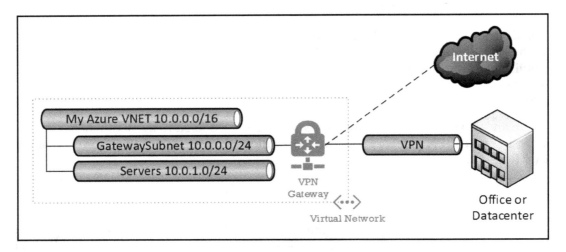

Looking on the current WAN developments and most of the customer infrastructures, a policy-based VPN gateway should only be used if there is absolutely no other option. Most enterprise grade Firewalls are able to work with route-based VPN. Otherwise you can switch to a virtual network device in Azure. Behind the following link you will find a list of devices with information about their available VPN options. `https://docs.microsoft.com/en-us/azure/vpn-gateway/vpn-gateway-about-vpn-devices`.

- Route-based standard **VPN gateway** with **ExpressRoute** shown in the following diagram:

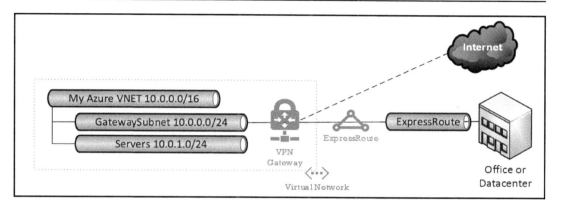

- Route-based basic **VPN Gateway** with a **Site 2 Site VPN** and **Point 2 Site VPN** or a **Route-based** standard or performance **VPN gateway** with a **Site 2 Site VPN** and **Point 2 Site VPN** in shown in the following diagram:

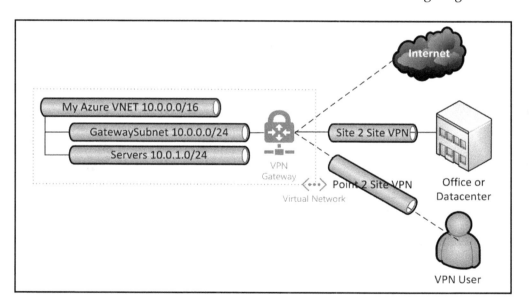

- Route-based standard or performance **VPN gateway** with **Site to Site** or **ExpressRoute** in shown in the following diagram:

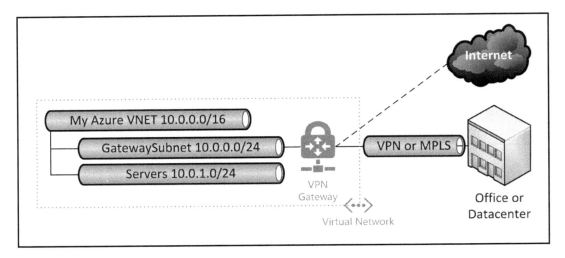

- Route-based standard or performance **VPN gateway** with a site-to-site VPN and **ExpressRoute**:

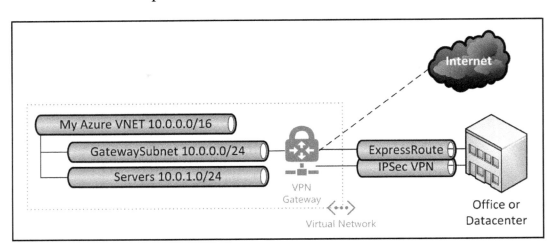

Later in the chapter, you will learn how to configure a VPN gateway with ExpressRoute and a basic VPN with a site-to-site VPN and how to upgrade that VPN to standard or performance. You will also learn what you need to do to implement a point-to-site VPN.

Azure local gateway

Local network gateways represent the configuration of your local firewall environment. Within a local network gateway, you configure the public IP of your firewall device as well as the IP spaces you manage within a local environment. The following screenshot shows the Azure service you need to look for when you want to implement an Azure local network gateway:

The following screenshot shows you how to configure a local network gateway:

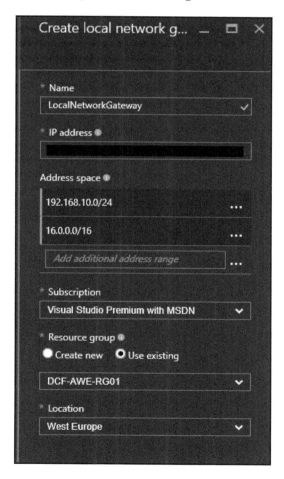

Currently, it is not possible to work with DNS entries or dynamic public IPs. Azure is also not supporting IPv6 within the environment as a local network gateway at the present time. So you definitely need a public IPv4 IP for your production environment. That may change in the near future when the IPv6 deployment is moving on in Azure.

 There is an option to work with dynamic public IPs but I only recommend that for test environments or home labs. You can use a dynamic DNS provider such as DynDNS to collect your changing IP address. Afterwards, you can recreate your Azure local gateway with the newly obtained IP. MVP Florent Appointaire wrote a little script for the Azure Resource Manager to configure to help you with that; please refer to https://gallery.technet.microsoft.com/Update-AzureRM-S2S-VPN-c46cc39e.

Azure virtual WAN

Azure virtual WAN is a networking solution based on SD-WAN that provides an automated branch-to-branch connectivity through the Azure backbone network. Virtual WAN allows to connect and configure branch devices to communicate with the Azure SD-WAN hub. This can be done manually, for not supported devices or by using preferred partner devices, where the configuration can be done automatically.

 A list of supported devices, partner, and locations can be found here. https://docs.microsoft.com/en-us/azure/virtual-wan/virtual-wan-locations-partners.

Using Microsoft partner devices allows to simplification of connectivity and configuration management. The Azure WAN built-in dashboard helps instant troubleshooting insights and gives you a way to get an overview about large-scale connectivity networks.

SD-WAN is an acronym for software-defined networking abstraction layer for **wide area networks (WAN)**. An SD-WAN makes the management and operation of a WAN more simple by decoupling (separating) the WAN hardware from its control mechanism like MPLS, DSL, or even mobile protocols like LTE. This concept of SD-WAN is similar to software-defined networking implementation where virtualization technology improves data center management and operation. SD-WAN is meant to be the future of performant and cost efficient wide area networks.

The following drawing shows a schematic overview about the implementation Azure:

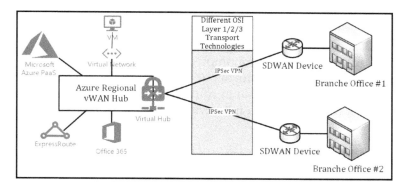

 Because Azure vWAN is a very new service and still partly in preview. It is highly recommended to follow the documentation to stay on track about the capabilities and changes. `https://docs.microsoft.com/en-us/azure/virtual-wan/virtual-wan-about`.

Please be aware, even if Microsoft delivers you a very powerful backbone, you still need good last mile providers. Those providers should have a very good latency to Azure and a lot of peering's with Microsoft within the area you want to use them.

 Please be careful, not every big provider also has a good local network. Often they need to lease line from local MAN providers or especially in the international business from other providers. That makes those providers very expensive, less performant, and a bad choice for a good cloud connectivity.

Azure ExpressRoute

When we are talking about ExpressRoute, we are talking about a common **Internet Service Provider** (**ISP**) technology called **Multi Protocol Label Switching** (**MPLS**) or ISP IP VPN.

MPLS is a type of data-carrying technique for telecommunications networks that directs data from one network to the next based on short path labels rather than long network addresses. This technology avoids long and complex routing tables. The labels identify virtual links between distant nodes. MPLS can encapsulate packets of various network protocols; that's why it is named multiprotocol. MPLS supports nearly all common access technologies, including T1/E1, ATM, frame relay, and dark fiber connects, into points of presence or DSL.

The routing within those networks is based on **Border Gateway Protocol** (**BGP**) routing. BGP is a standardized gateway protocol designed to exchange routing and reachability information among autonomous systems on the Internet. The protocol is often classified as a **path vector** protocol but is sometimes also classed as a **distance-vector routing** protocol. The BGP makes routing decisions based on paths, network policies, or rule sets configured by a network provider and makes core routing decisions.

Normally you see MPLS when connecting a range of offices or data centers with very complex routing or mashed networks between the network sites. MPLS also does not terminate **Quality of Service** (**QoS**) settings at the gateway; all settings can be transported from network site to network site. The following diagram shows an example for such a mashed environment:

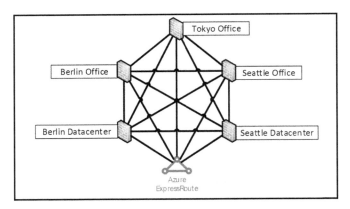

Microsoft offers with ExpressRoute the option to connect your Azure and Office 365 environment directly to your MPLS network.

When you configure, you will be able to configure the different peering's. The three peering types are:

- **Private peering**: Azure compute services, namely virtual machines and cloud services that are deployed within a virtual network can be connected through the private peering domain. The private peering domain is considered to be a trusted extension of your core network into Microsoft Azure. You can set up bidirectional connectivity between your network and Azure virtual networks.

- **Microsoft peering**: Services such as Azure Storage, SQL databases, and websites are offered on public IP addresses. You can privately connect to services hosted on public IP addresses, including VIPs of your cloud services, through the public peering routing domain. You can connect the public peering domain to your DMZ and connect to all Azure services on their public IP addresses from your WAN without having to connect through the Internet. It also connects to all other Microsoft online services (such as Office 365 or Dynamics CRM). You can enable bi-directional connectivity between your WAN and Microsoft cloud services through the Microsoft peering routing domain.

 Because of the different deployment and distribution strategy from Azure and Microsoft 365 Services, it is not recommended to use ExpressRoute for Microsoft 365. You should only use ExpressRoute for Azure Services and/or as your global MPLS backbone interconnect.

The following diagram shows the basic schema on the Microsoft site:

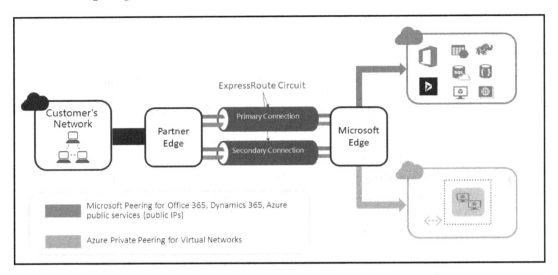

Source: https://azure.microsoft.com/en-us/documentation/articles/expressroute-introduction/

What basically happens is that your ISP connects your network to the network of Microsoft. Those connections happen at most of the **Point of Presence (PoP), Meet Me Locations** or **Private Network Interconnect** hubs all over the globe. The following diagram shows how this happens within the Azure data center:

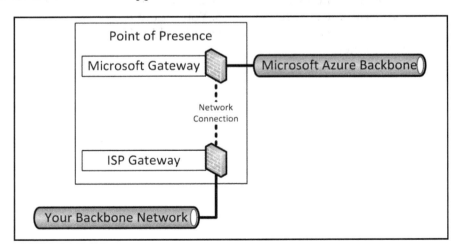

To find information about the Azure PoPs and peering partners, you can visit the Azure documentation website at `https://azure.microsoft.com/en-us/documentation/articles/expressroute-locations-providers/`.

Microsoft also started to maintain a list of direct through ISPs, those ISP who leverage Equinix, Interxion, e-shelter, and so on, to connect to Azure ExpressRoute. The list can be found in the Azure Documentation visiting following website `https://docs.microsoft.com/en-us/azure/expressroute/expressroute-locations-providers#a-namec1partnersaconnectivity-through-service-providers-not-listed`.

Another point Microsoft also started is to name certified and qualified Solution Integrator for ExpressRoute which support customers with planning, deploying and maintaining ExpressRoute in a customer environment. Microsoft maintains the list of those Partners on their Azure documentation website `https://docs.microsoft.com/en-us/azure/expressroute/expressroute-locations-providers#expressroute-system-integrators`.

Microsoft offers ExpressRoute in the following two service levels: **Standard SLA** and **Premium SLA**. As described next, the premium offering expands the standard offering in the following limits:

- Increased routing table limit from 4K routes to 10K routes for private peering.
- Increased number of VNets that can be connected to the ExpressRoute circuit (default is 10).
- Global connectivity over the Microsoft core network. You will now be able to link a VNet in one geopolitical region with an ExpressRoute circuit in another region. Example: You can link a VNet created in Europe West to an ExpressRoute circuit created in Silicon Valley.
- Connectivity to Office 365 services and CRM Online.

Depending on the bought ExpressRoute service level there are different limitations:

Resource	Default limit
ExpressRoute circuits per subscription	10
ExpressRoute circuits per region per subscription for ARM	10
Maximum number of routes for Azure private peering with ExpressRoute standard	4,000

Maximum number of routes for Azure private peering with ExpressRoute premium add-on	10,000
Maximum number of routes for Azure public peering with ExpressRoute standard	200
Maximum number of routes for Azure public peering with ExpressRoute premium add-on	200
Maximum number of routes for Azure Microsoft peering with ExpressRoute standard	200
Maximum number of routes for Azure Microsoft peering with ExpressRoute premium add-on	200

Depending on the ISP and network location, Microsoft offers the following bandwidths and connections:

Circuit size	Number of VNet links for standard	Number of VNet links with premium add-on
50 Mbps	10	20
100 Mbps	10	25
200 Mbps	10	25
500 Mbps	10	40
1 Gbps	10	50
2 Gbps	10	60
5 Gbps	10	75
10 Gbps	10	100

ExpressRoute is highly recommended for enterprise environments which need a guarantee for latency and bandwidth for their Azure environment.

Microsoft will also enable a high performance ExpressRoute circuit. The high performance ExpressRoute will enable customers to throughput 10 Gbps from the WAN directly to their VM's.

An Azure ExpressRoute circuit is represented in the Azure portal with the following symbol:

Later on in the chapter, I will explain how to deploy an ExpressRoute circuit.

Route filter

When Microsoft peering is configured on your ExpressRoute circuit, the Microsoft edge routers establish a pair of BGP sessions with the customer or provider edge routers. In the first place no routes are advertised to a customer network. To enable route advertisements to those networks, a route filter must be associated. A route filter lets identify services a customer want to consume through your ExpressRoute circuit's Microsoft peering. It is essentially a white list of all the BGP community values that should be announced. Once a route filter resource is defined and attached to an ExpressRoute circuit, all prefixes that map to the BGP community values are advertised to the customer network.

ExpressRoute Direct

ExpressRoute Direct provides the ability to connect directly into Microsoft's global network at peering locations across the world. ExpressRoute Direct provides a redundant 100 Gbps connectivity, which supports active/active connectivity and scalability.

 While writing the book, ExpressRoute Direct is in public preview.

ExpressRoute Global Reach

With **ExpressRoute Global Reach**, customers are able to link ExpressRoute circuits together to make a private backbone network between your on-premises networks via the Microsoft global backbone. With that, Microsoft becomes the global backbone provider of the customer.

That enables customers to always choose the best local MPLS or WAN provider in their area, link them to an ExpressRoute and afterwards link the ExpressRoutes together to build a global Backbone Network.

The following diagram shows a schematic overview:

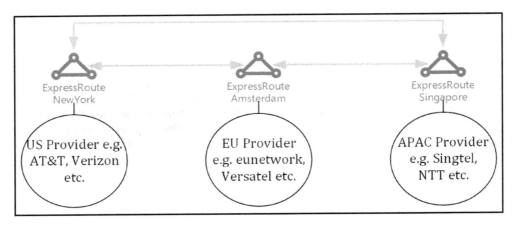

With ExpressRoute Global Reach, Customers get the option to always choose, the best and cost efficient local provider to connect to Azure. Customer gain also flexibility when choosing providers and are able to easily exchange providers or built cheap WAN Networks of their own. It also an option for smaller ISPs and Network providers because they can now use ExpressRoute to use Microsoft cables through the Atlantic and pacific instead of renting expensive dark fiber of their own.

ExpressRoute Global Reach is currently available in following regions:

- Australia
- France
- Hong Kong
- Ireland
- Japan
- Netherlands
- United Kingdom
- United States

Microsoft is currently working to make more regions available. With ExpressRoute Global Reach, Microsoft becomes the second largest telecom provider on the globe and therefore they are a some government regulations and restrictions which need to be cleared first. Afterwards Microsoft will bring the service into those regions first.

Azure connections

Azure connections are the *wire* between the internal VNet gateway and your Azure VPN gateway or ExpressRoute circuit. With these connections, you can establish the tunnel through the Azure network and establish the connection to your on-premises environment or other VNets.

You can find the Azure connections by searching for **Connections**, as shown in the following screenshot :

An Azure connection offers the options shown in the following screenshot:

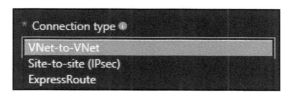

Later on in the chapter, we will use Azure connections to build up a connection between virtual network and MPLS gateways.

Azure route

With routes in Azure, you can change the default *any to any* routing within Azure to meet your needs.

The following screenshot shows the Azure service you need to look for when you want to implement an Azure route:

With routes, you can basically redirect traffic from one subnet to another location. The following screenshot shows the current offerings of that Azure service:

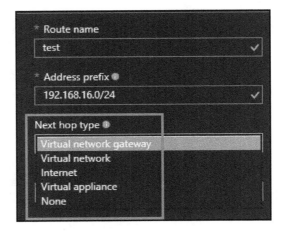

Within the setup part of this chapter, I will explain how to configure a custom route:

- **Virtual network gateway**: The traffic will be forwarded to another Azure gateway. This option can be used if you maybe want to send traffic via another gateway or route to its target. Or you have redirected all traffic to a Virtual Appliance and want specific traffic to bypass the appliance.
- **Virtual network**: Transfers traffic directly into another VNet. That could be used to transfer traffic from one VNet to another which can't be reached directly.
- **Internet**: Traffic will be send directly into the Internet.
- **Virtual appliance**: The traffic will be sent to a third-party virtual network device hosted in your Azure environment. That can be a Barracuda Next Generation Firewall or a Cisco Nexus device, for example.
- **None**: Traffic will be dropped and will not be routed.

Azure Firewall

Azure Firewall is a managed, cloud-based OSI Layer 3 to 7 network security service that protects customer Azure VNet resources. It is a fully stateful firewall as a service with implemented high availability and unrestricted scalability in the cloud.

Customers can centrally create, enforce, and log application and network connectivity policies across subscriptions and virtual networks within one Tenant. Azure Firewall uses a static public IP address for a VNet resources, that allows outside firewalls to identify traffic originating from a VNet. The service is fully integrated within the Azure Monitoring services like Azure Monitor, that works as an interface and platform for logging and analytics.

Azure third-party network devices

Some vendors such as Cisco, Barracuda, or F5 offer VPN and network devices such as firewalls or load balancers as Azure virtual appliances via the Azure marketplace. Those devices can be directly integrated in your Azure infrastructure.

If you want to use one of these devices, you can look after them in the Azure marketplace and deploy them out like regular virtual machines.

The following screenshot shows an example search for `barracuda`:

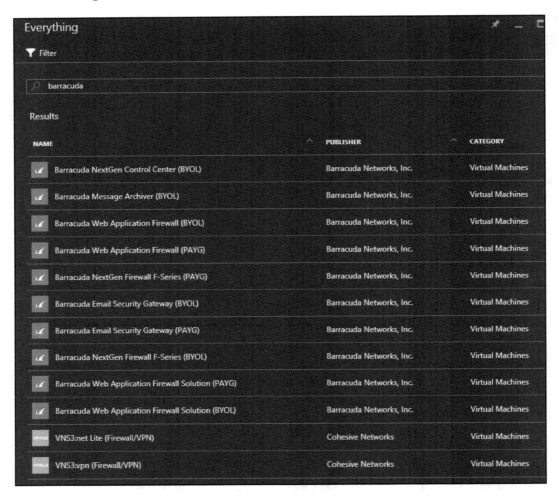

To integrate one of these devices into your environment, you need to implement Azure routes to pass traffic to the third-party devices, as shown in the next diagram.

Normally there is no need to implement a third-party device because the Microsoft standard services offer approximately 80% of all services that are needed by most customers. Sometimes there are cases where you need to implement special systems such as a load balancer in Azure. Under certain circumstances, your target application has to use a load balancer feature that is not supported by the Azure load balancer.

The following diagram shows another case where you have the requirements for additional data encryption on a transfer level. In that case you implement a VPN Tunnel or other encryption technology within an **ExpressRoute** and Azure VPN gateway. The following diagram is based on the Barracuda Next Generation Firewall design:

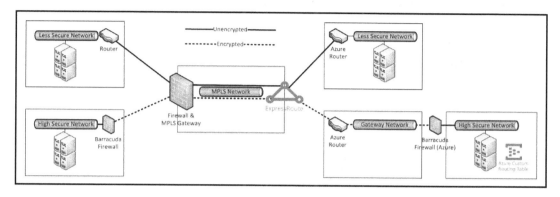

One thing you need to be aware of is that most of the third-party network solutions need an additional license and have some additional costs which might be not covered by you Microsoft Azure Subscription. So please read the introduction page of the product carefully.

Normally you should see information as shown in the following screenshot:

In the text, there should be additional information, as shown in the example screenshot :

- This Barracuda NextGen Control Center is licensed using the Bring-Your-Own-License (BYOL) model. Fill out the evaluation form to receive a 30-day evaluation license or purchase one of the licenses depending on your requirement.

Azure load balancer

The Azure load balancer is a layer 4 (TCP, UDP) load balancer which distributes incoming traffic among healthy instances of a service or among virtual machines in Azure. You can compare it with well-known load balancers such as Citrix Netscaler, Microsoft TMG, or Windows server load balancer.

The Azure Resource Manager load balancer can distribute traffic that works with public IPs and Azure DNS entry. The following diagram shows the basic load balancing mechanism:

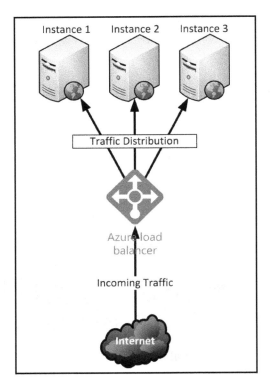

The feature list of an Azure load balancer is shown in the following sections.

Hash-based distribution

The load balancer uses a hash-based distribution algorithm. By default, it uses a 5-tuple hash to map traffic to available services and servers. It provides stickiness only within a transport session. Packets in the same TCP or UDP session will be directed to the same instance behind the load balancer. When the sender site closes, and reopens the session or starts a new session from the same source IP, the source port changes. This may result in a redirection of the traffic to a different data center and load balancer endpoint.

Port forwarding

The load balancer gives you control over how inbound communication is managed. This communication can include traffic that's initiated from Internet hosts or virtual machines in other cloud services or virtual networks.

An input endpoint listens on a public port and forwards traffic to an internal port. You can map the same ports for an internal or external endpoint or use a different port for them.

You can use port forwarding to redirect traffic from an incoming port to another port your server listens to. For example, your endpoint listens to port 443 and you have a web application on the server listening to port 8443. You can configure the endpoint to redirect the traffic from port 80 to port 8443 on the server.

Automatic reconfiguration

The load balancer instantly reconfigures itself when you scale instances up or down. That happens, for example, when you add or remove new servers or instances into the same load balancer set.

Service monitoring

The load balancer can probe the health of the various server instances. When a probe fails to respond, the load balancer stops sending new connections to the unhealthy instances. Three types of probes are currently supported:

- **Guest agent probe (on PaaS VMs only)**: The load balancer utilizes the Azure guest agent inside the virtual machine. The guest agent listens and responds with an HTTP 200 response only when the instance is ready and healthy. If the agent fails to respond with an HTTP 200 response, the load balancer marks the instance as unresponsive and stops sending traffic to that instance. The load balancer will continue to ping the instance until it responds again or the instance is removed from the load balancer set. Attention: If you are running a website, the code is typically running the process w3wp.exe. This processes are not monitored by the guest agent so the load balancer will never informed when the instance fails.
- **HTTP custom probe**: This probe overrides the default (guest agent) probe. You can use it to create your own custom logic for your application to determine the health of the role instance. As an example, the HTTP probe could login to a page and changes some values as a result of the logic. If the when fine without issues, the probe is good, otherwise it will generate an alert. The load balancer will regularly probe your endpoint (every 15 seconds, by default).
- **TCP custom probe**: This probe relies on successful TCP session establishment to a defined probe port.

Source NAT

All outbound traffic to the Internet comes from your instances and services that go through **source NAT (SNAT)**. The VMs and services use the same **virtual IP (VIP)** address as the incoming traffic. SNAT provides different benefits:

- It enables upgrade and disaster recovery of services, since the VIP can be dynamically mapped to another instance of the service.
- It reduces the access control list easier. ACLs expressed in terms of VIPs do not change as services scale up, down, or get redeployed.

The load balancer configuration supports full NAT for UDP. Full NAT is a type of NAT where the port allows inbound connections from any external host.

To learn more about the Azure network load balancer, you should visit the Microsoft MSDN source at `https://azure.microsoft.com/en-us/documentation/articles/load-balancer-overview/`.

Azure Application Gateways and Web Application Firewall

The Azure application gateway is another form of load balancing in Azure. Application load balancing enables Azure customers to create routing rules for network traffic based on HTTP protocols like for publishing websites on the same IP address.

Application gateways currently support layer-7 application delivery for the following application-based load balancing algorithms:

- HTTP load balancing
- Cookie-based session affinity
- **Secure Sockets Layer** (**SSL**) offload
- URL-based content routing
- Multi-site routing

Application gateways currently offer the sizes **small**, **medium**, and **large**.

You can create up to 50 application gateways per subscription. Each application gateway can have up to 10 instances each, which makes up to 500 instances depending on the gateway site.

Please note that the small size is only for testing purpose and shouldn't be used in production.

Every gateway has a limited throughput performance. The following table shows the performance per gateway:

Back-end page response	Small	Medium	Large
6 K	7.5 Mbps	13 Mbps	50 Mbps
100 K	35 Mbps	100 Mbps	200 Mbps

The Azure application gateway is represented in the Azure portal with the symbol shown in the following screenshot:

We will not cover Azure application gateways further in this book, but to get more information, you can access the Azure application gateway documentation at `https://azure.microsoft.com/en-us/documentation/articles/application-gateway-introduction/`.

Web Application Firewall

Web Application Firewall (**WAF**) is an operation mode of application gateway that provides centralized protection of customer web applications from most common exploits and vulnerabilities.

WAF is based on rules from the OWASP core rule sets 3.0 or 2.2.9, which can also be customized. It automatically updates it self to include protection against new vulnerabilities and exploits, without any additional configuration.

Following features are currently included in the service:

- SQL injection protection
- Cross site scripting protection
- Common Web Attacks Protection like command injection, HTTP request smuggling, HTTP response splitting, or remote file inclusion attack
- Protection against HTTP protocol violations
- Protection against HTTP protocol anomalies like missing host user-agent and accept headers
- Prevention against bots, crawlers, and scanners
- Detection of common application misconfigurations (that is, Apache, IIS, and so on.)

Azure Traffic Manager

Like the application gateway or the load balancer, the **Traffic Manager** is a mechanism to distribute incoming traffic among different Azure data centers. Unlike the load balancing of the other Azure balancers, the Traffic Manager works based on distribution via DNS entries, which means you deploy an DNS Name for the traffic manager. The clients connect directly to the endpoint for the application which has the best response time for his location. Traffic manager is mostly used as a frontend for content delivery networks or applications distributed over different Azure regions. The following table summarizes the differences between all three load balancers:

Service	Azure load balancer	Application gateway	Traffic Manager
Technology	Transport level (OSI layer 4)	Application level (OSI layer 7)	DNS level
Application protocols supported	Any	HTTP and HTTPS	Any (An HTTP/S endpoint is required for endpoint monitoring)
Endpoints	Azure VMs and cloud services role instances	Any Azure internal IP address or public internet IP address	Azure VMs, cloud services, Azure web apps and external endpoints
VNet support	Can be used for both Internet facing and internal (VNet) applications	Can be used for both Internet facing and internal (VNet) applications	Only supports Internet-facing applications
Endpoint monitoring	Supported via probes	Supported via probes	Supported via HTTP/HTTPS GET request

The Azure Traffic Manager is symbolized with the following item in the Azure portal:

Azure DNS

With Azure DNS, you can host your DNS domains in Azure and manage your DNS records using the same credentials you use for other Azure services. So Azure DNS offers basically the same services as GoDaddy or United Domains and other DNS providers.

Azure DDoS

Distributed Denial of Service (DDoS) attacks are some of the largest availability and security concerns global IT is facing at that time and while moving their applications to the cloud. A DDoS attacker attempts to exhaust an application's resources as long and as high with the result to make the application unavailable to legitimate users. DDoS attacks can be targeted at any endpoint that is publicly reachable through the internet or even if the attacker was able to corrupt a private network, from private network resources of bigger networks.

Azure DDoS protection together with application design by best practices will provide a defense against DDoS attacks. With Azure DDoS protection provides the following service tiers are available:

- **Basic**: Automatically enabled as part of the Azure platform and services. In includes Always-on traffic monitoring and real-time mitigation of common network-level attacks it provide the same defenses utilized by Microsoft's online services like Office 365, Outlook.com, Xbox, Azure SQL. The entire scale and resources of Azure's global network can be used to distribute and mitigate attack traffic across regions and with that, protect customers and workload against attacks. Protection is either available for IPv4 and IPv6 Azure public IP addresses.
- **Standard**: Provides additional mitigation capabilities over the Basic service tier that are tuned specifically to Azure virtual network resources. It enables customers to customize and optimize their DDoS protection to their Workloads within the VNet.

Setting up Azure networks

Let us start deploying our Azure network infrastructure. We will start from the basics and then go up with different external and internal connections. All steps we do are also possible to do via PowerShell but we will stay with the Portal GUI within this guide.

Setting up Azure VNet

The following are the steps to set up Azure VNet:

1. First of all, we navigate in our **Resource group** and use **Add** to open the Azure marketplace:

2. In the next step, we look for `virtual network` within the Azure marketplace and click **Virtual network**:

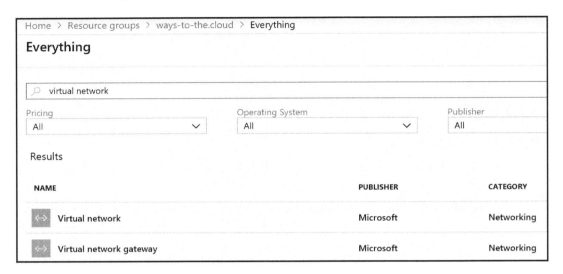

3. In the Azure blade afterwards you need to decide between Resource Manager and Classic. You should only choose **Resource Manager**. The Classic is based on the old **Azure Service Manager** (**ASM**) environment and has certain limitation. Microsoft is currently migrating all services left in ASM. After the migration Microsoft will some when remove ASM and all resources deployed within it:

4. In the next interface, we need to configure the network details:
   - **Name**: The name of your Azure network.
   - **Address space**: The IP address range you want to use within your Azure environment.
   - **Subnet Name**: The name of your first subnet that could be either the gateway subnet or another one. We will stay with our server network for now and add the gateway network later.
   - **Subnet Address range**: The IP range of the subnet you want to use.

- **DDoS protection**: You can enable DDoS standard for the VNet.
- **Service endpoints**: You can enable service endpoints for that VNet
- **Firewall**: You can enable Azure firewall for the VNet.

The rest should be predefined by your resource group:

5. After the creation, the **Virtual Network (VNet)**, should be listed in your resource group. You maybe need to click on **Refresh**:

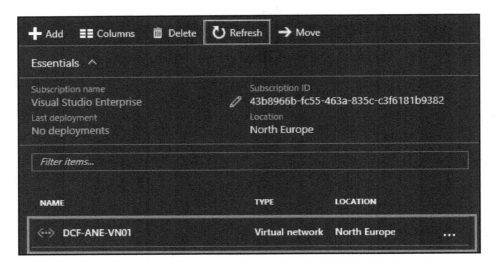

6. Now we will add our gateway subnet. Therefore, we select the VNet to open the settings:

7. Yet we want to add the gateway subnet. Click on **Subnets** to open the subnet blade:

8. Afterwards you select the **+ Gateway subnet** button and another blade with the creation details will open:

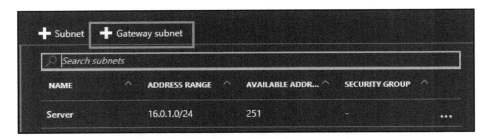

9. Within that blade, you need to define the subnet mask that the gateway uses. As explained earlier, we need a minimum of /29 CIDR addresses:

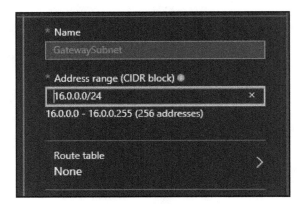

10. After clicking **OK**, the gateway subnet will be deployed in Azure. If you want to add more subnetworks, you can use the **Subnet** button:

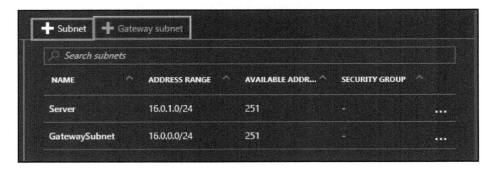

11. In the VNet settings, there is another option that could come in handy. Azure deploys every system with DHCP and by default configures Microsoft DNS servers as default DNS to the virtual machine. In most scenarios, you will need to change this setting to your own DNS server. Therefore, you can do this manually within the VM or change the default configuration within your Azure VNet. To do so, you need to select the **DNS servers** option in the **SETTINGS**:

12. There you have a switch which changes between **Azure DNS** and **Custom DNS**:

13. We need to change it to **Custom DNS** and then we can add our DNS servers and **Save** the change:

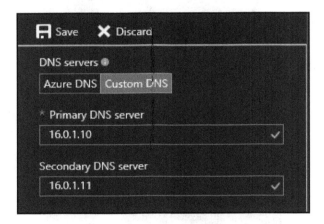

14. Now every system within that VNet will use the **Custom DNS** server settings.

Setting up Azure virtual network site-to-site VPN

After we have deployed our network, we can now start to deploy our VPN gateway. At first we deploy a site-to-site VPN to one of your sites. We will use the Azure portal to deploy the gateway and later update it via PowerShell.

Configuring local network gateway

Network gateway follow the given steps:

1. To configure the local network gateway follow the given steps: at first we need to deploy the local network gateway. Therefore, we click **+Add** in our resource group and search after `Local network gateway` in the Azure marketplace:

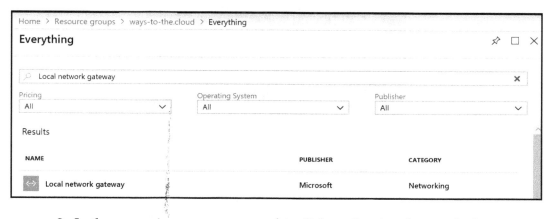

2. In the upcoming menu, you need to click on **Create**, afterwards the set up for the local gateway configuration appears:

    - **Name**: The name of your Azure local gateway
    - **IP address**: The public IPv4 address of your local firewall or router device

- **Address space**: The IP ranges you use behind your local firewall and router device

3. That's all from for the local network gateway. Now we go on with the configuration of our VPN gateway in Azure.

Configuring Azure virtual network gateway

To configure the virtual network gateway, follow the given steps:

1. At first, we need to deploy the virtual network gateway. Therefore, we click **Add** in our resource group and search after `virtual network gateway` in the Azure marketplace:

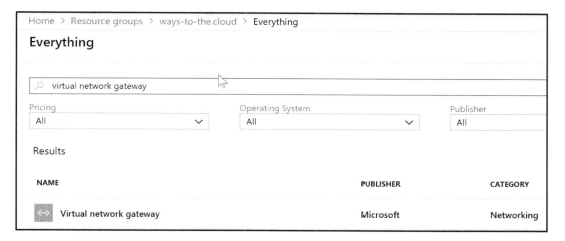

2. After changing to the next blade, you need to configure your gateway. Therefore, you need to proceed as follows:

- **Name**: Set the name of the virtual network gateway.
- **Gateway type**: You need to choose between VPN and ExpressRoute. In our case we choose VPN.
- **VPN type**: Now you need to decide between **Route-based** and **Policy-based**, it is recommended to use **Route-based** if possible.
- **SKU**: Choose your gateway size, you can also enable active/active mode.
- **Virtual network**: Connect the virtual network gateway to a specific virtual network.
- **Public IP address**: Create a public IP for the gateway. You can also create BGP if necessary .
- **Subscription**: Choose a subscription you want to deploy into.
- **Location**: Choose an Azure region to deploy to. The region must be the same than the virtual network.

Which type of VPN you can use is based on your on-premises firewall. The following table shows the configuration you need to do on your on-premises firewall. IKE phase 1 setup:

Property	Policy-based	Route-based and standard or high performance VPN gateway
IKE version	IKEv1	IKEv2
Diffie-Hellman group	Group 2 (1024 bit)	Group 2 (1024 bit)
Authentication method	Pre-shared Key	Pre-shared Key
Encryption algorithms	AES256 AES128 3DES	AES256 3DES
Hashing algorithm	SHA1(SHA128)	SHA1(SHA128), SHA2 (SHA256)
Phase 1 **Security Association** (**SA**) lifetime (time)	28,800 seconds	10,800 seconds

IKE phase 2 setup:

Property	Policy-based	Route-based and standard or high performance VPN gateway
IKE version	IKEv1	IKEv2
Hashing algorithm	SHA1(SHA128)	SHA1(SHA128)
Phase 2 SA lifetime (time)	3,600 seconds	3,600 seconds
Phase 2 SA lifetime (throughput)	102,400,000 KB	-
IPSEC SA encryption and authentication offers (in the order of preference)	1. ESP-AES256 2. ESP-AES128 3. ESP-3DES 4. N/A	See Route-based gateway IPSEC SA offers
Perfect forward secrecy (PFS)	No	No (*)
Dead Peer Detection	Not supported	Supported

Microsoft maintains a list of test and supported VPN devices which can be used by customers. You can find the list of devices and more information about the VPN setup at https://azure.microsoft.com/en-us/documentation/articles/vpn-gateway-about-vpn-devices/.
If you don't have any of these devices or you didn't want to use a Windows server as VPN gateway, there is also the option to use free firewall solutions such as pfSense. Bart Decker wrote a great blog about the topic. You can find the blog at http://www.hybrid-cloudblog.com/pfsense-azure-hybrid-cloud/.

3. To finish the setup, we click **Create**. Now it will take around 45 minutes until our gateway is deployed.

In some cases and with some firewall for example, Cisco ASA you need to do some PowerShell to reconfigure the VPN policies to match the vendor specific configuration. The PowerShell commands can be found here. https://docs.microsoft.com/en-us/azure/vpn-gateway/vpn-gateway-ipsecikepolicy-rm-powershell#a-name-paramsapart-2---supported-cryptographic-algorithms--key-strengths.

4. After the deployment is finished, we have created an Azure virtual network gateway as with the SKU *basic*. If you want to upgrade the gateway to standard or performance, you only need to run following PowerShell script against your Azure environment:

```
Resize-AzureVNetGateway -GatewaySKU <gatewaysize>
  -VnetName <gatewayname>
```

5. PowerShell command example to resize to high performance gateway:

```
Resize-AzureVNetGateway -GatewaySKU HighPerformance
  -VnetName DCF-ANE-GW01
```

6. PowerShell command example to resize to standard gateway :

```
Resize-AzureVNetGateway -GatewaySKU Standard -VnetName
  DCF-ANE-GW01
```

7. The same works also with downsizing a gateway:

```
Resize-AzureVNetGateway -GatewaySKU Basic -VnetName
  DCF-ANE-GW01
```

8. Besides the PowerShell way of resizing the gateway, Microsoft started to include the feature into the portal GUI. Therefor you need to navigate to the **Gateway** and open the detail blade:

9. Within the detail blade you go to **Configuration** and change the **SKU**. Afterwards you need to save the new SKU. Please be aware that the change of the SKU will take again up to 45 minutes:

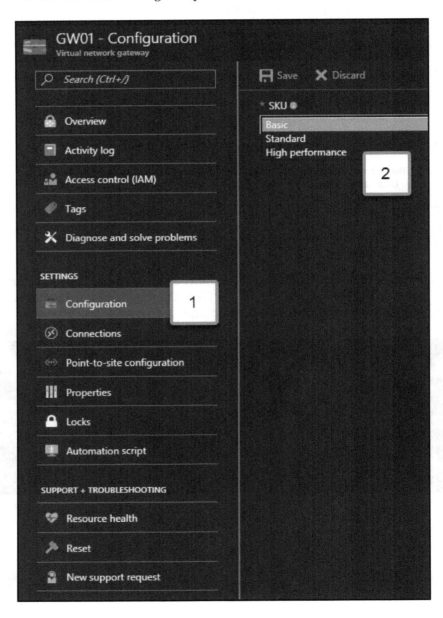

Configuring connection between local and virtual network gateways

1. Now we need to establish a connection between gateways and enable the routing: Please go back to your resource group and click **Add** again. Now we look for **Connection** in the marketplace. Then select **Connection**:

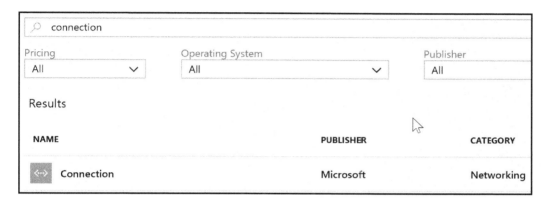

2. Now change the **Connection type** to **Site-to-site (IPsec)**:

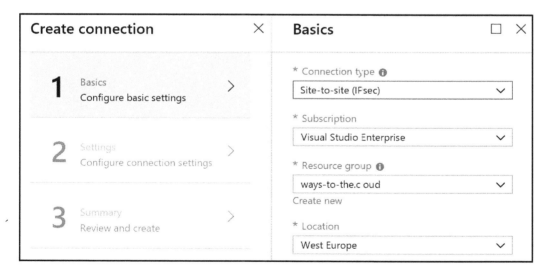

3. In the **Settings** phase, we first select the Azure **Virtual network gateway**, **Local network gateway**, **Connection name** and **Shared key**:

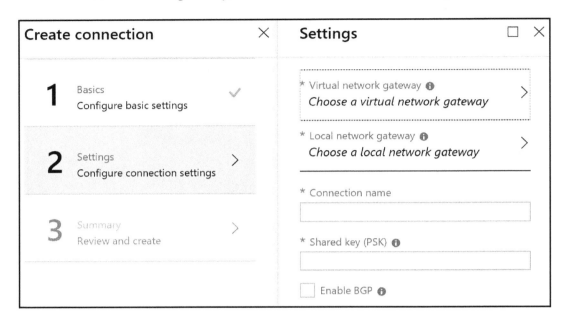

4. To check if the connection is deployed and working fine, you need to leverage the connection item in your resource group:

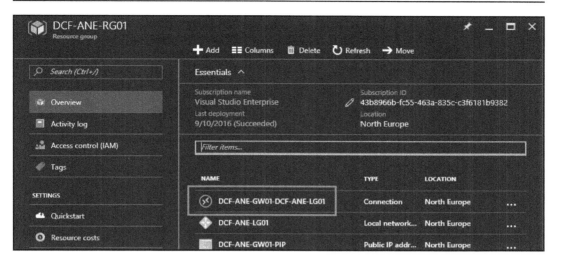

5. There is an **Overview** within the detail blade of the connection. When the connection is successful the **Status** will change to **Successful**:

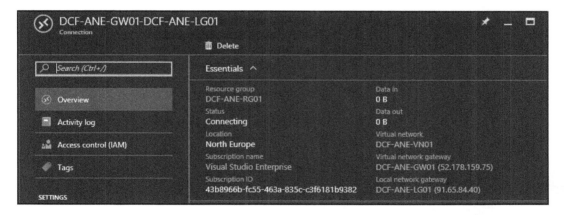

In most of the cases when the Status of the connection is not changing to connected, there are misconfiguration on the on premises Firewall or Network device. Mostly it's because there are different configurations of timeouts or encryption. For most of the VPN Devices you can find configuration guides on within the Azure documentation. `https://docs.microsoft.com/en-us/azure/vpn-gateway/vpn-gateway-about-vpngateways`. If you still have issues, please contact the support of your VPN device manufacturer.

6. If you want to connect multiple sites to one Azure environment, you need to configure the Azure **Virtual network gateway** as a **Route-based** VPN and create a **Local network gateway** for each on-premises site. Then you create a connection for each site link. The following diagram illustrates the count of connections that need to be set up:

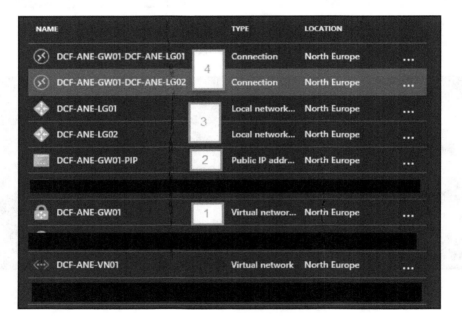

You need at least one route-based **Virtual network** gateway (**1**), one **Public IP address** for the gateway (**2**), two **Local network** gateways (**3**) and two **Connections** between **Virtual network** and **Local network** gateway (**4**).

7. Now you have deployed a site-to-site tunnel to your on-premises environment.

As of September 2016, Microsoft started to support active/active site-to-site VPN tunnels with high performance virtual network gateway. Therefore, you need to configure two local network gateways: VNets and VPN gateways.

Setting up Azure virtual network with MPLS and ExpressRoute

For enterprise customers, a regular VPN connection may not be enough. Most of those customers will want to deploy an ExpressRoute connection. In the next part of the chapter, we will go through an ExpressRoute deployment.

First of all, to deploy ExpressRoute, you need some prerequisites. You need a contract with an ISP who connects your office to an MPLS network. That's a thing Microsoft cannot do for you at the moment.

The future goal of Microsoft and other Cloud Providers is, that you can deploy and order even ISP connections for your on premises location via Cloud Provider Portals and it's deployed on demand. In most countries that is some kind of science fiction because it requires a full supported and over all available software defined WAN in-depended from ISP infrastructures.

After you have signed the contract, you need to evaluate the peering location, the peering partner, and the bandwidth with your ISP. You will need this information during the ExpressRoute deployment.

As soon as you have this information, you can start with the deployment.

Configuring Azure virtual network gateway

We need to configure an Azure virtual network gateway as an ExpressRoute gateway. The following screenshot shows an example:

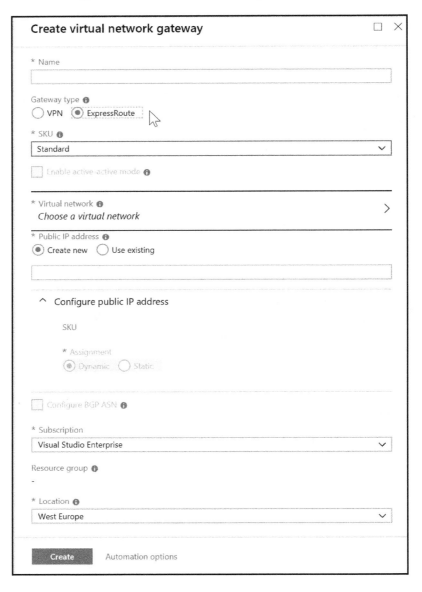

Configuring Azure ExpressRoute circuit

1. During the installation process of the gateway, you can proceed and install the ExpressRoute circuit. To do so: You need to go back to your Resource group and click **Add** again. From the marketplace, we select the **ExpressRoute**:

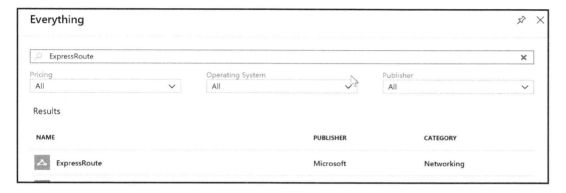

2. In the next blade, we set up our ExpressRoute circuit. Now we need the information your ISP gave you:

   - **Circuit name**: The name of your ExpressRoute circuit.
   - **Provider**: The provider you or your ISP uses for the peering with Microsoft Azure.
   - **Peering location**: The edge gateway location your provider peers with Microsoft.
   - **Bandwidth**: The bandwidth you ordered from your ISP.
   - **SKU**: Select the service level for your ExpressRoute.
   - **Billing model**: Select your billing. With **Metered** you will pay per download. With **Unlimited** you have a flat rate for your network traffic.

- **Allow classic operations**: Enables your Azure Service Manager deployment model environment to use the ExpressRoute too.

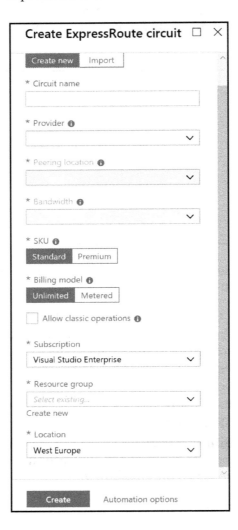

Please be aware that the billing for your Azure ExpressRoute will start as soon as you click **Create**. To reduce unnecessary deployment costs, you should do that together with your service provider during a live activation session for both sites of the service.

3. After you have created the ExpressRoute circuit, you need to provide the **Service key** to your provider. The **Service key** will identify your Azure **Subscription** against its deployment and it can then create the connection to your environment.

4. You can find the **Service key** within the settings of the ExpressRoute circuit after it is completely deployed:

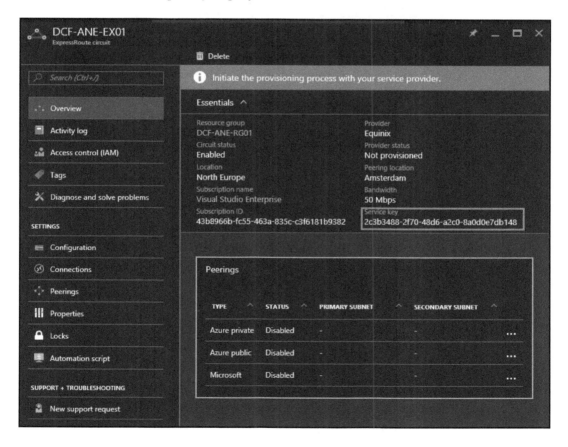

5. After the **Provider** status has changed to **Provisioned**, you can configure the Azure peering's:

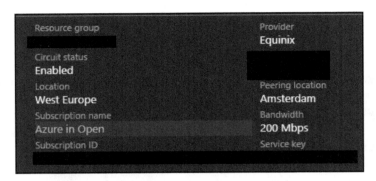

6. To configure the peering's in Azure, you need additional information from your ISP. You need the **Peer ASN**, **Primary subnet**, **Secondary subnet**, **VLAN ID**, and for Microsoft peering, the **Advertised public prefixes**:

7. To configure the peering, click on the peering type you want to configure:

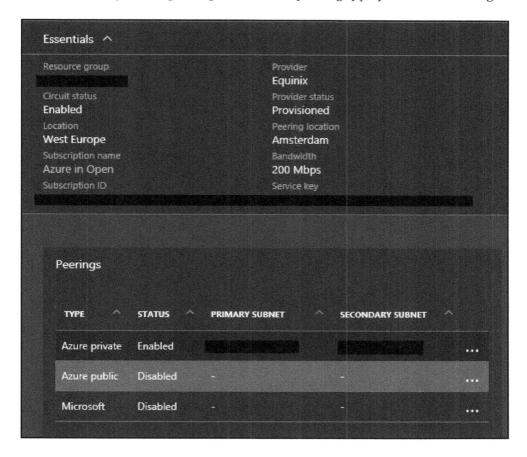

8. Within the upcoming blade, you configure the information you've got from your ISP:

9. In Azure you don't need to do additional routing. As soon as you establish the connection, Azure will directly configure the BGP settings.
10. After you have configured the peering's, you need to create a connection between the ExpressRoute circuit and the Azure virtual network gateway, like you already did for VPN in the previous guide.

Setting up Azure VNet peering

Now let's look at how you implement the new VNet peering. As already mentioned, you can use VNet peering to configure a connection between VNets in the same Azure region via the Azure backbone.

We will look at the configuration for VNet peering of VNets with different subscriptions. That's the most difficult scenario and you normally would use it to pair networks within different company subscriptions or with subscriptions from other companies.

Preparing the deployment

The following are the steps to prepare the deployment:

1. First you need two subscriptions and both subscriptions need a VNet in the same Azure region. The following screenshot shows you an example:

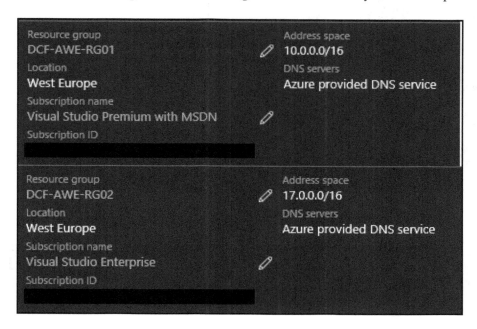

2. Both need to use different IP subnetwork address ranges. In my case, I use `10.0.0.0/16` for **subnet A** and `17.0.0.0/16` for **subnet B**.

3. Before we start, we need to get the **Resource ID** of our partner VNet. You can find your resource IDs by navigating to the settings of your resource. You need to open the **Properties** to find the ID:

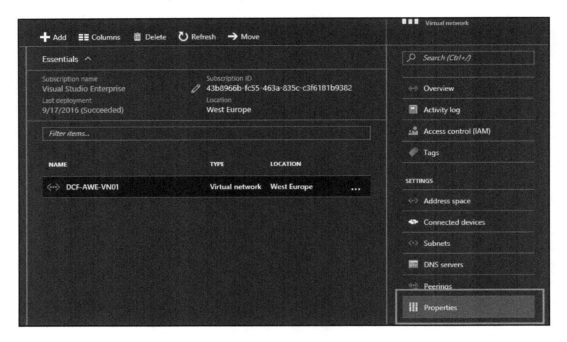

4. In the **Properties** blade, you will see the ID in the upper-right corner:

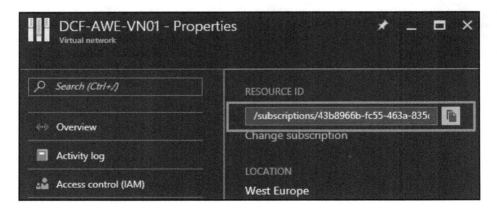

Configuring VNet peering

For configuring the VNet peering, perform the following steps:

1. After the VNets in both subscriptions are prepared, navigate to one of the **Virtual network** and in the **SETTINGS** you need to click on **Peerings**:

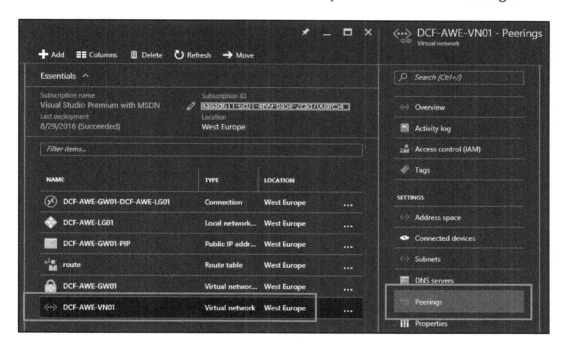

2. In the **Peerings** blade, click on **+Add**:

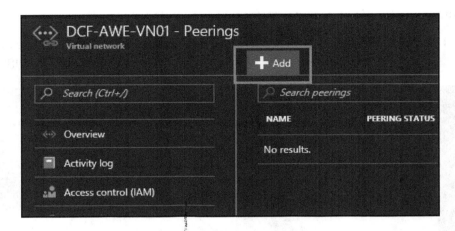

3. In the upcoming blade, you have the opportunity to create a new peering subnet in the existing **Subscription** and **Resource group**. In our current scenario, we need to select **I know my resource ID** to connect a VNet in another subscription:

4. Now you need the resource ID. You need to fill in the ID in the context field after the checkbox:

5. Now you can do some more settings if you need them for your scenario:

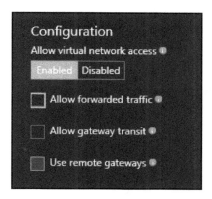

- **Allow virtual network access**: Allows the address space of the peer VNet to be included as part of the Virtual_network. In general the peered networks are linked to each other and become one big network.

- **Allow forwarded traffic**: Allows traffic not originated from the peered VNet to be accepted or dropped.
- **Allow gateway transit**: Allows the peer VNet to use your VNet gateway.
- **Use remote Gateways**: Uses your peer's VNet gateway. The peer VNet must have a gateway configured and a `AllowGatewayTransit` selected. You cannot use this option if you have a gateway configured.

6. After clicking **OK**, it will take a few minutes until the connection is established. After you have deployed the peering in the first subscription, you should see the status of the connection in the peering blade as **Initiated**:

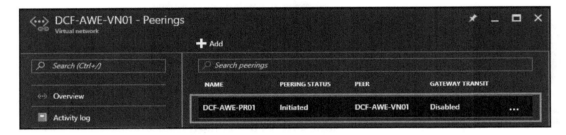

7. To set the **PEERING STATUS** of both networks as **Connected**, you need to repeat the steps mentioned previously in the other subscription too. Afterwards, you change the status in both subscriptions to **Connected** like shown in the following diagram for `DCF-AWE-PR02`:

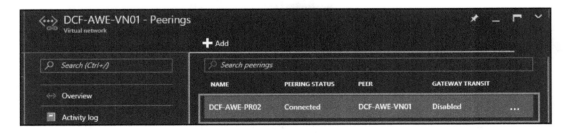

8. The same should happen for `DCF-AWE-PR01`:

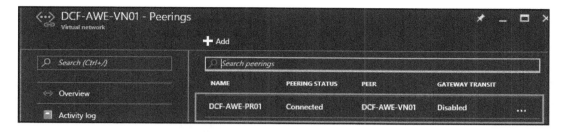

 Currently VNet peering is still in preview and under development. Microsoft will extend this service in the near future to support VNet peering with Microsoft Azure public services such as Storage or Azure SQL too.

Configuring custom routes

As you already know, Azure by default routes every traffic to its virtual network gateways. Azure also routes any traffic in any direction. If you want to change those default behaviors, you need to create custom routes:

1. First you need to look for the `Route table` within the Azure marketplace:

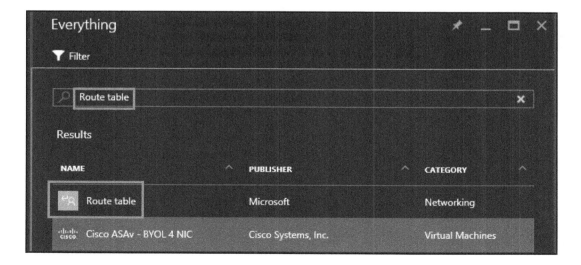

2. The only option in the enrollment process to give your route table a name. The rest will be done through **Route table** settings in the **Resource group**:

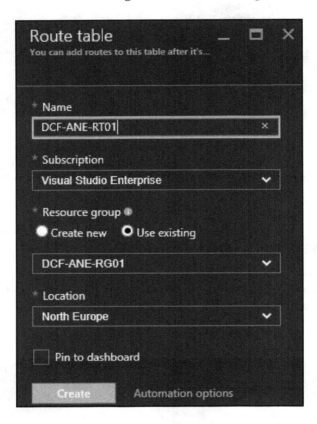

3. After you created the **Route table**, you need to go back to your resource group and select the route table you created:

4. The **Settings** blade opens. Here you click first on **Subnets** to open the detail blade to associate subnets to that routing table:

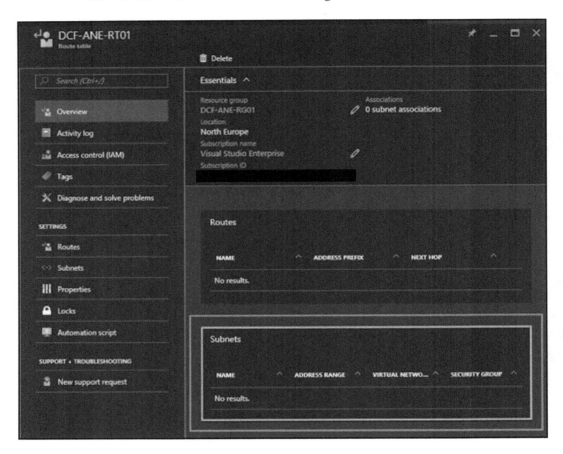

5. In the details blade, you click on **Associate** and add the Azure VNet where the route table should be applied to:

6. Then choose the subnet where you want to apply the table to and click **OK** to commit:

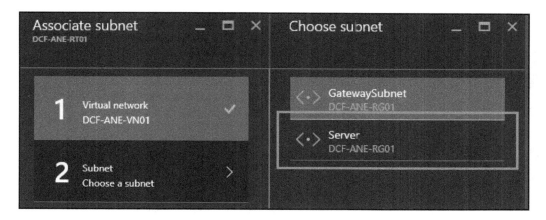

7. As soon as the subnet association is created, you need to configure the route. Click on **Routes** to open the detail blade:

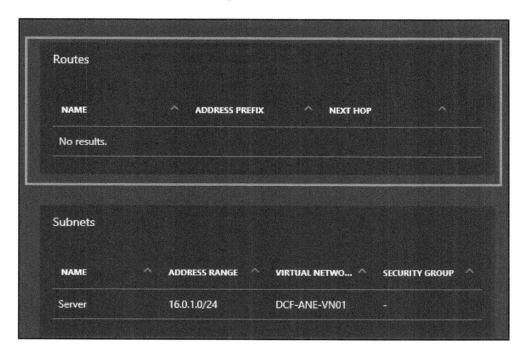

8. In the detail blade, click **Add** to configure the new route. In the upcoming blade, you select a **NAME** for your router, the **ADDRESS PREFIX**, the **NEXT HOP** type, and the address of the next hop:

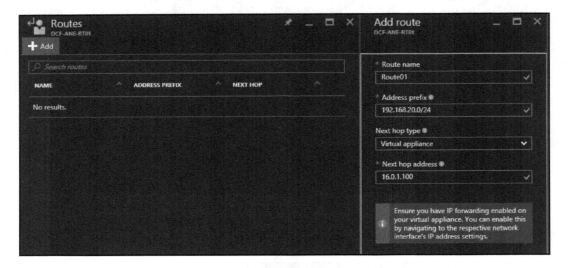

9. It will take a moment until the route will be applied to the subnet.

Common Azure network architectures

Looking at the networking scenarios, the most common one is to integrate Azure and Office 365 directly into your MPLS. Every connection from any location is transmitted via the MPLS network.

The following diagram shows a short abstract of such an environment:

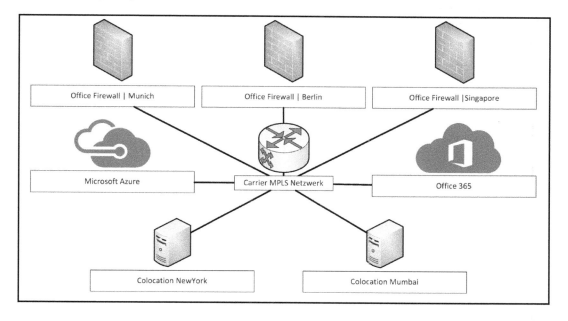

There are also options to use Azure as colocation and connect offices via a VPN. This option is often used by small or medium business companies. There every VPN connection terminates in Azure. Office 365 is reached via Internet from the Office directly:

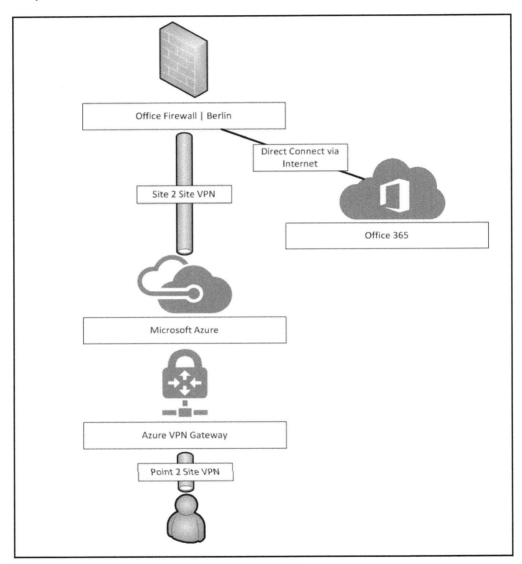

Another very common form of setting up WAN links to offices or other data centers is to have a primary link via ExpressRoute and a secondary link via a **Site 2 Site VPN** with BGP enabled. So your services stay available for your users even if your MPLS fails. You only have a performance impact but stay in production. The rerouting will happen automatically because of the enabled BGP:

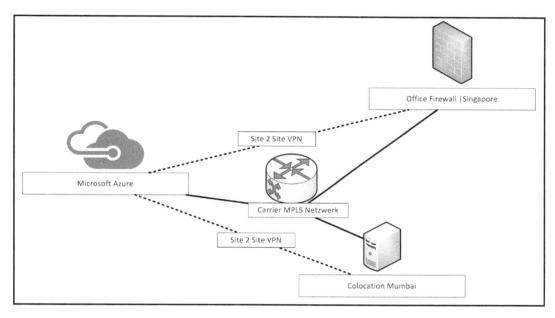

There are also common scenarios where Azure is used only for online services without any on-premises connection or where resources are resold to other customers or end users:

Summary

So let us summarize this chapter. Now you should have learned how networking in and with Azure works. You now know what basics need to be deployed and how to deploy external connections with VPN or MPLS. You also learned about common scenarios and how to change implemented Azure behaviors such as routing.

Implementing Azure Storage

5

Just like you plan the network in your datacenter or company, you need to do the same in Azure. Nearly every service in Azure is related to storage. Therefore, it has to be planned well. You should consider scalability, durability, and high availability depending on the scenario and target you try to achieve.

In this chapter, Azure Storage management is discussed. The key takeaways are how and when to implement and integrate the different Azure Storage types.

In this chapter, we will cover the following topics:

- Storage accounts
- Replication and redundancy
- Azure Storage services:
    - Blob
    - Table
    - Queue
    - File
- Exploring Azure Storage with Microsoft Azure Storage Explorer
- Premium storage accounts
- Pricing

This chapter does not cover deep backup, Azure site recovery, or StorSimple topics. We will set up some basic storage configurations in this chapter.

Storage accounts

Azure Storage implements the following four services:

- **Blob storage**: Blob storage stores unstructured object data, which can be text or binary data.
- **Table storage**: Structured datasets are stored in Table storage. Table storage is a NoSQL key attribute data store, enabling rapid development and fast access to data.
- **Queue storage**: In addition to providing reliable messaging for workflow processing, Queue storage makes communication between segments of cloud services available.
- **File storage**: Using the standard **Server Message Block** (**SMB**) protocol, file storage offers shared storage for legacy applications. Azure virtual machines and cloud services can share file data over application components using mounted shares. Utilizing the file service REST API, on-premise applications can obtain file data.

The Blob storage account

A general-purpose storage account provides entrance to Azure Storage services such as tables, queues, files, blobs, and Azure virtual machine disks, combined under a single account. The two performance tiers are as follows:

- **Standard storage performance tier**: The standard storage performance tier permits the customer to file tables, queues, files, blobs, and Azure virtual machine disks
- **Premium storage performance tier**: This currently exclusively supports Azure virtual machine disks

To store unstructured data as Blobs (objects), a Blob storage account is available in Azure Storage. Blob storage shares characteristics with existing general-purpose storage accounts. Similar to this are the durability, availability, scalability, and performance features. Microsoft recommends using Blob storage accounts for applications requiring entirely block or append Blob storage.

Blob storage accounts expose the Access Tier attribute, which can be specified in the process of account creation. It is possible to modify this later if needed. Two types of Access Tiers can be defined based on the data access pattern:

- **Hot access tier**: This tier designates that the objects in the storage account will be obtained on a frequent basis. This allows data storage at a lower access cost.
- **Cool access tier**: This tier indicates that the objects in the storage account will be less regularly accessed. This too allows data storage at a lower cost.
- **Archiving tier:** The archive tier is made for data that can work with several hours of retrieval latency and will remain in the archive for a minimum of 180 days. The archive tier is the most cost-effective opportunity for storage data, but access to that data is more expensive than in the hot or cool tiers.

It is permitted to switch between these tiers if there is a change in the usage pattern of data. It must be noted that changing the Access Tier can result in additional costs.

MSDN subscribers, for example, can get free monthly credits which can be used with Azure services, including Azure Storage.

The requirement to create a storage account is that you have an Azure subscription. The subscription gives the customer access to numerous Azure services. It is possible to create a free Azure account to get started. Once the consumer decides to acquire a subscription plan, it is possible to choose from a variation of purchase alternatives. A single customer can create up to 100 storage accounts with an individual subscription.

As there are several differences in pricing for the two account types, in a Blob storage account, the Access Tier (hot, cold) also indicates the billing model. The **service level agreement (SLA)** for both is nonetheless the same.

In the example, we will choose a general-purpose storage account. The next configurable field, besides standard and premium storage, is the replication setting. To be able to know which one we need, it's important to first understand the different replication redundancy settings. You will find more detailed information about the available redundancy options later in the chapter.

General-purpose storage v1 account

The general-purpose storage account is very universal. It can contain storage services of any type available. That includes blobs (of course, also virtual machine disks based on blobs), files, queues, and tables in a storage account. On creation, there are two available performance settings available. The first available performance option is the standard option. This type of storage account holds queues, tables, blobs, and files.

The second option is the premium one. This is only capable of storing Azure virtual machine disks. For more information about this, see the *Premium storage accounts* section later in this chapter.

General-purpose storage v2 accounts

General-purpose storage v2 accounts have some of the same features as the v1 version, but they combine them with the tiering options of Blob storage accounts. In addition to that, v2 accounts also offer Geo Redundancy Storage for data stored in that account. V1 accounts only offer **Read Access Geo Redundant Storage (RA-GRS)**.

Geo Redundancy Services enable customers to access and write data from different locations. Azure will take care of data and replication. So, there is no longer any need to replicate data or files through virtual machines or other external services.

Azure File Sync/Storage Sync services

Azure File Sync is an Azure service that enables customers to centralize file shares in Azure files, while keeping the flexibility, performance, and compatibility of a local file server. Azure File Sync enables Windows Servers to perform a quick cache of an Azure file share. Any protocol that's available on Windows Server to access data locally, including SMB, NFS and FTPS, can be used. Those caches have no limit and customers can have as many local file server caches as they need.

To use Azure File Sync, you need at least Windows Server 2012 R2 or later and PowerShell 5.1 installed on the server. Azure File Sync supports also **cloud tiering**, ACL replication between cloud and on-premise, as well as the integration of Azure AD identity management.

Azure Data Lake

Azure Data Lake Storage is a set of capabilities built for big data analytics, on top of Azure Blob storage. It enables customers to interface with data using both file system and object storage paradigms. This makes Data Lake Storage the cloud-based multi-modal storage service, allowing applications to extract analytics value from all customer's available data.

Replication and redundancy

In order to guarantee stability and high availability, the customer's data in Azure Storage is replicated constantly. The customer may choose between two replication options: either storage within the same datacenter or to a second datacenter. Replication guards the user's data; in the case of hardware failures, the application is preserved. The use of a second datacenter provides security in the case of a catastrophic failure in the location of the primary datacenter. The process of replication warrants that the customer's storage account meets the SLA for storage.

There are four replication options between which the user can choose when creating an Azure Storage account.

Locally redundant storage (LRS)

LRS means that the data is held three times in a datacenter in a region. The LRS manages three copies of the customer's data to protect it from hardware failures. LRS does not protect workloads from the failure of a whole datacenter; it only replicates data within an Azure Storage scale Unit from about 1,000 physical machines.

Zone-redundant storage (ZRS)

ZRS stores three copies of the customer's data as well as the LRS. The difference is that the data is guarded in two to three facilities. These facilities can be located in different regions. This concept provides more enhanced durability than LRS. The user profits from durability within a region.

Geo-redundant storage (GRS)

An even higher durability can be achieved with GRS. GRS manages six copies of the user's data. The first three copies are replicated in the primary region. Additionally, another three copies are maintained in a secondary region that is located remotely from the primary region. This concept provides an even higher level of durability. This means that Azure Storage will failover to the secondary region if a failure in the primary region should occur.

Read-access geo-redundant storage (RA-GRS)

Replication to a secondary geographic location is provided with RA-GRS. The customer holds read access to the data, maintained in the secondary location. Access from the primary and the secondary region is possible. RA-GRS is the default option for your storage account on creation.

The following is an overview of the redundancy options in Azure Storage:

Replication strategy	LRS	ZRS	GRS	RA-GRS
Data is replicated across multiple datacenters	No	Yes	Yes	Yes
Data can be read from the secondary location as well as from the primary location	No	No	No	Yes
Number of copies of data maintained on separate nodes	3	3	6	6

Source: https://docs.microsoft.com/en-us/azure/storage/storage-redundancy

For our example, we select **Locally-redundant storage (LRS)**, as high durability is not necessary in our example. Let's look at the current settings:

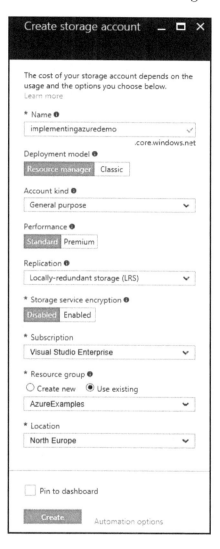

Storage account settings

In the example, an existing resource group is used to store the storage account resource. **North Europe** is used as deployment location as it's the nearest location and will probably have the least latency.

To achieve the same goal using PowerShell with the Azure PowerShell module, the following commands can be used:

```
New-AzureRmStorageAccount `
-ResourceGroupName 'AzureExamples' `
-Name 'implementingazuredemo' `
-Location 'northeurope' `
-SkuName 'Standard_LRS' `
-Kind 'Storage'
```

In the previous command, `ResourceGroupName` is the resource group that the storage account should be deployed to. The `Name` parameter is the planned name for the storage account, the `location` parameter is the Azure deployment region, and the `SkuName` parameter is a mix of the performance and replication settings from the Azure portal. This parameter can take the following values:

- `Standard_LRS`: Locally redundant storage
- `Standard_ZRS`: Zone-redundant storage
- `Standard_GRS`: Geo-redundant storage
- `Standard_RAGRS`: Read-access geo-redundant storage
- `Premium_LRS`: Premium locally redundant storage

Azure Storage services

As previously mentioned, the difference between Blob storage and general-purpose storage is to be found in the purpose for which they're used. While Blob storage stores unstructured data, the general-purpose account stores structured data. Azure differentiates between four types of storage—blob, queue, table, and file storage. It's important to understand the scopes, in order to be able to decide on a certain type of storage.

Blob storage services

For customers needing to store large sets of unstructured data, Blob storage offers an attractive and scalable answer. The types of data that can be retained in Blob storage are—documents, photos, music, videos, blogs, file backup, databases, images and text for web applications, big data, or configuration data for cloud applications.

Containers offer a useful way to assign security policies to sets of objects; each blob is assigned a container. A storage account can hold indefinite containers; a container may contain an indefinite number of blobs. The only restriction is the 500 TB capacity limit of the storage account.

There are three types of blobs:

- **Block blobs**: Block blobs are utilized for streaming and storing cloud objects. They are best used for storing documents, media files, backups, and so on.
- **Append blobs**: Block blobs are used for streaming and storing; append blobs fulfill the same task with the addition that they are optimized for append operations. Updating an append blob can only be done by adding a new block to the end. An append blob's field of application consists of logging, in which data has to be written to the end of the blob.
- **Page blobs (disks)**: The third type of blob is the page blob. In most cases, page blobs are used to store **Infrastructure as a Service (IaaS)** disks. They support random writes. This means that an Azure IaaS VM **virtual hard disk (VHD)** is stored as a page blob.

In the cases where downloading data over the wire to Blob storage is unrealistic, for example for large datasets, the customer is able to send a hard drive directly to Microsoft, where the data gets directly imported to or exported from the datacenter. In Azure, blobs are stored in containers. These containers are the upper most element that needs to be used to store files as blobs.

In Azure IaaS, there will be a VHDs container created when you deploy an image from the gallery. These containers hold the VHD files for the VMs as page blobs, and also hold status blobs as block blobs.

Azure Storage blobs have access types; those access types define how your blobs can be accessed publicly:

Type	Description
Private	If this type is selected, blobs can only be accessed by the account owner with the access key and no anonymous access is granted. In PowerShell, this option is referred to as off.
Blob	When this type is selected, only blobs can be accessed from the outside with read permissions.
Container	If this type is selected, the whole container content will be publicly available with read rights.

 Remember that these are access policies for the blob container only, and have no influence on the other containers or the storage account.

Table storage services

Table storage in Azure can be described as a NoSQL database. This basically means that the database has no schema and each value in a table has a typed property name. This property name can be used for filtering, sorting, and as selection criteria. There are multiple entities in a table that each consist of a collection of values and their property names. NoSQL, and thus also Azure Table storage, has much higher performance, scalability, and flexibility at a much lower, complexity.

Common usage scenarios for Table storage are databases or datasets for web applications, collections of metadata, or bigger collections, for example, addresses. As with the other Azure Storage services, the only limiting factor for Table storage is the size of your storage account, which means, there is no limit on the number of tables or entities in tables.

Since Table storage is fast to set up and access, the next demo will show the creation of a simple table. Often, Table (NoSQL) storage is much cheaper than traditional relational databases.

Queue storage services

Azure Queue enables messaging between different parts of applications. This is used in the development of highly scalable and flexible applications. Components of applications are often decoupled, to enable independent scalability for the individual parts. Queues are also used as an asynchronous method of communication between components that run on different locations (cloud, on-premises, desktop, mobile). It's also possible to build workflows and asynchronous tasks based on Azure Queues storage . One storage account has no limit on the number of queues, as well as the number of messages these contain. A single message can be up to 64 KB in size.

There are two different kinds of queues in Microsoft Azure:

- **Azure Queues:** This is a part of Azure Storage and the one that we are working with in this chapter
- **Service Bus queues**: This is a feature of Microsoft's Azure messaging infrastructure and has more advanced features for application development

According to Microsoft, Azure Storage queues should be used when your application must store over 80 GB of messages in a queue, where the messages have a lifetime shorter than 7 days. And, Service Bus queues should be used when you need more advanced features such as guaranteed **First-In, First-Out** (**FIFO**) ordered delivery, bigger handles, message receiving without polling, and so on.

For more information on how to choose the right queue solution, visit
https://docs.microsoft.com/en-us/azure/service-bus-messagin g/service-bus-azure-and-service-bus-queues-compared-contrasted.

File storage services

Currently, the most interesting type of storage for the IT professional is **Azure File storage**. File storage in Azure refers to cloud-based **Server Message Block** (**SMB**) or **Common Internet File System** (**CIFS**) such as that provided by traditional Windows or Samba fileservers. Like an SMB share, an Azure Storage share can be used from multiple computers and by multiple users simultaneously. The difference is that the users don't have to be connected to the company network anymore.

Azure file shares are commonly used for so called **lift-and-shift** migrations, where the on-premises app is basically copied to the cloud as-is. This is often fast and easy, but not always the most cost-efficient solution. Other scenarios are shares for diagnostics or debugging data, shared application files, or simply temporary storage:

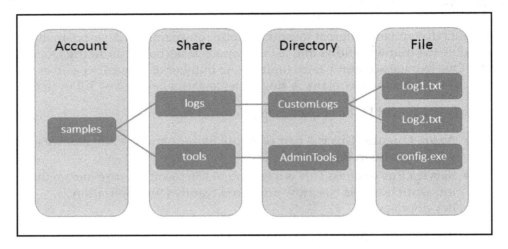

Levels of file storage (https://docs.microsoft.com/en-us/azure/storage/storage-dotnet-how-to-use-files)

In the preceding diagram, the different logical levels of Azure file storage are shown. Directories and files are optional. Therefore, it's enough to create a share and connect to it, to start working with file storage. But there are also several downsides to the current file share implementation. Currently, there are only two important downsides to consider:

- **Storage limit**: In addition to the 500 TB per storage account and the limit of 200 storage accounts per subscription, there are also limits on file shares. The maximum size of a file share is 5 TB and the maximum size per file in a file share is 1 TB. On the other hand, there is no limitation on the number of files in total, if you stick to the file and file share size.
- **Latency between location and Azure Storage:** Because we are still talking about SMB traffic, and with that a protocol which is not WAN-optimized, we are struggling with latencies. Normally, you say every latency above 16 ms is not feasible for an SMB share. To solve that issue, you should consider using Azure File Sync and keep a file server in your location.

The only ways to authenticate for file share access are access keys and **shared access signatures (SAS)**. An SAS is basically a link that can be generated if someone needs limited access to a storage resource. They can be limited by time and storage service type (queue, table, blob, file). Basic permissions such as read, write, delete, and so on can also be defined when generating an SAS. An SAS should be used for untrusted external staff, temporary development test, or for customers for tests.

At the time of writing, Microsoft has started to work on a premium version of Azure file shares. The following table shows the most significant changes to standard file shares:

Resource	Standard file share	Premium file share
Minimum size of a file share	(no minimum; pay as you go)	100 GB
Max IOPS per share	1000 IOPS	5120 IOPS baseline 15360 IOPS with burst
Target throughput for single file share	Up to 60 MiBps	Up to 612 MiBps(provisioned)

Access keys will be discussed in the next section.

 Microsoft released a tool for working with blob, file, and table storage called **AzCopy**. Its main purpose is to transfer data from and to Azure Storage. It can be found at `http://aka.ms/azcopy`.

Access keys

In Azure, storage Access keys are used to authenticate applications that use external or internal interfaces to interact with Azure Storage. Example interactions are a RESTful API call or a simple net use of an SMB share.

When a storage account is created, Azure generates two 512-bit access keys. These keys are very important to the security of the storage account, and for this reason they must be kept safe all the time. An SAS is also created based on the storage accounts access keys. That means that when the access key that a specific SAS is based on is regenerated, the SAS is invalid and has to be regenerated. The reason that there are two access keys in each storage account is mainly high availability. As it's recommended to regenerate access keys on a regular basis, keys should be rotated to avoid any downtime. Key regeneration does not influence access of your VMs to their VHDs.

The current access keys of a storage account can be found in the **Access keys** menu in a storage account:

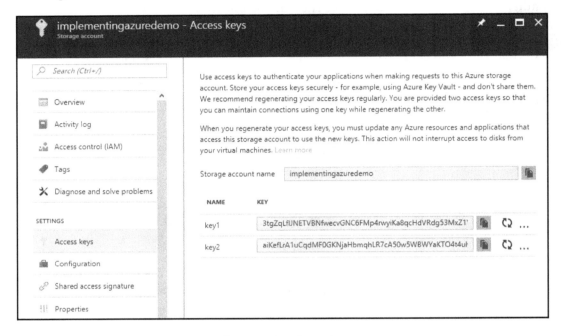

Storage account access key overview

They can also be received with PowerShell with the following command:

```
Get-AzureRmStorageAccount `
  -name $storageAccountName `
  -ResourceGroupName $resourceGroupName `
  | Get-AzureRmStorageAccountKey
```

To regenerate a storage key, the Regenerate button in the portal is used, as highlighted in the following screenshot:

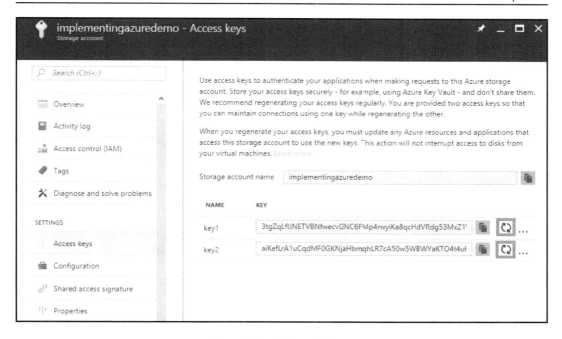

Regenerating keys with the marked buttons

To regenerate a key using PowerShell, the following **cmdlet** is used:

```
New-AzureRmStorageKey -ResourceGroupName "MyResourceGroup" -
AccountName "MyStorageAccount" -KeyName "key1"
```

Exploring Azure Storage with Azure Storage Explorer

Microsoft Azure Storage Explorer is a free, available graphical tool for managing Azure Storage without the portal or PowerShell. Azure Storage Explorer is still in preview and could have some bugs in some places. To start working with Azure Storage Explorer, it needs to be downloaded first. The current download link is http://storageexplorer.com/.

After downloading and installing Azure Storage Explorer, the following screenshot is shown:

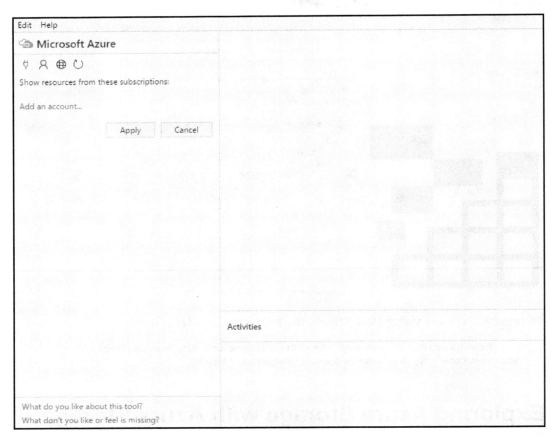

Storage explorer dashboard

First, a storage account needs to be connected. There are two ways in which one can connect to a storage account:

1. Add a Microsoft or company account. This is the easiest solution. Azure Storage Explorer asks for credentials for a Microsoft or company account that has an active subscription. After typing the username and password, Azure Storage Explorer lets you to select which subscriptions should be managed. By default, all are selected. After clicking on the **Apply** button, the setup is done, and Azure Storage nodes can be explored:

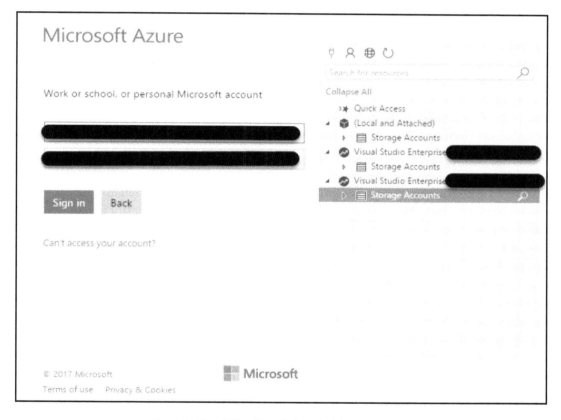

Azure login dialogue (left), and Storage Explorer subscriptions overview (right)

2. Add a connection string, SAS URI, or account. It's also possible to connect to your storage accounts by typing a storage account key or SAS:

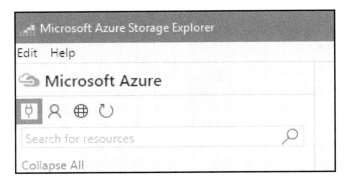

Connecting with URI, SAS, or the key button

The plug symbol as shown in the preceding screenshot opens a dialog that is used to connect to Azure Storage by SAS, access key, or connection string.

3. After connecting to the storage account, a node with the name of the added storage account appears in Azure Storage Explorer. Browsing through the **File Shares** section, the previously-created file share can be found:

The connected storage account node

Premium storage accounts

When it comes to performance, you can decide between standard or a premium storage account. For most workloads, standard accounts are more than suitable, but in some cases, more I/O-intensive applications need very fast storage. For this use case, the premium storage account was introduced. Premium storage is fully backed by SSD tiers and provides high-performance and low-latency storage.

Premium storage can currently only be used for virtual disks used in VMs (page blobs). The performance property can't be changed after storage account creation, but it's possible to migrate VMs from the standard to premium storage tier.

Depending on the machine size, it's possible to attach up to 64 disks to a VM (`Standard_GS5`). A `Standard_GS5`-sized machine supports up to 80,000 uncached **input/output operations per second** (**IOPS**) and 2,000 MBps disk throughput.

Microsoft examples of enterprise applications that may need premium storage are—Dynamics AX, Dynamics CRM, Exchange Server, SharePoint Farms, SAP Business Suite, SQL Server, Oracle, MongoDB, MySQL, and Redis.

Premium storage requirements

Premium storage supports DS-series, DSv2-series, GS-series, and Fs-series Azure virtual machines. Standard and premium VM disks can be attached to premium storage VMs. Premium storage disks cannot be used if the VM is not premium storage-compatible.

Pricing

The billing for Azure Storage usage depends on the used storage account. Also, storage costs are based on these determinants:

- **Location**: This describes the geographical region in which the account is based.
- **Storage capacity**: This refers to how much of the storage account is used to store data.

- **Account type**: Based on the usage of either the general-purpose storage account or the Blob storage account; the account type affects the billing. When using a Blob storage account, the access tier also defines the billing model for the account.
- **Storage transactions**: Transactions are all read and write operations to Azure Storage.
- **Replication scheme**: This describes the number of copies of your data and where they are stored.
- **Data egress**: This is the data that is transported out of an Azure region. This usually happens when the data is obtained by an application that is located in another region or in an on-premises location. If data egresses from Azure, charges apply.

 For more information on pricing, use the Azure pricing calculator, located at
`https://azure.microsoft.com/en-us/pricing/calculator/`.

How to deploy a storage account?

Now that we have learned so much about accounts and storage, let's deploy a storage account within our Azure subscription with the following steps:

1. Go to the Azure portal and navigate to the **All services** section as shown in the following screenshot:

2. Within the next blade, search for `storage` as shown in the following screenshot:

3. Click on the **Storage accounts** option to open new blade to add a storage account to your subscription. Click on the **+Add** button to continue:

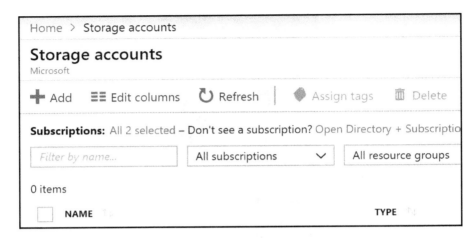

4. In the following blade, we will start with a basic storage configuration:
   - Select the subscription for your deployment
   - Select or create a resource group
   - Name the storage account
   - Select the region where you want to locate the storage account
   - Select your performance tier
   - Select your kind of storage account; in our example we will use a general purpose v2 account
   - Select the replication option

- Depending on your account type, you will have additional options such as the Access Tier, as shown in the following screenshot:

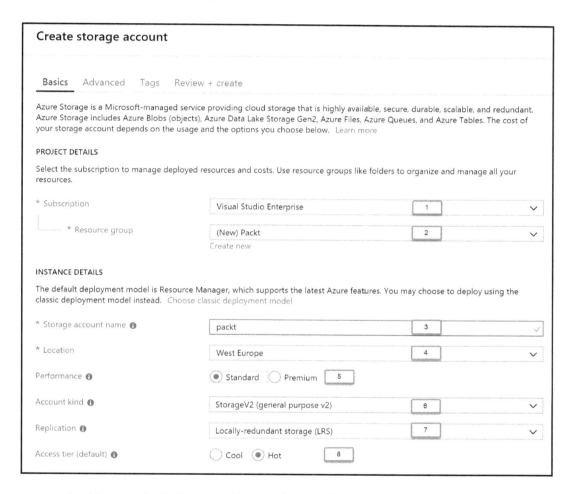

5. Afterward, click on the **Next: Advanced >** button to continue with the configuration:

6. Within the next blade, we configure additional security features, such as encryption, VNet access, or access to the namespace from Azure Data Lake Gen2:

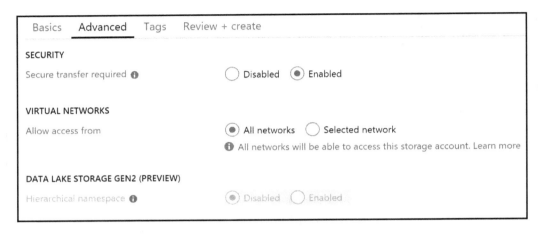

7. After configuring advanced settings, we only need to add some more tags, for example the cost center. To do that, click the **Next : Tags >** button:

8. As you already know, tags are very important in Azure. They help with automation, development, cost management, and even more. So, it is very important to use those tags and optimize Azure resource management:

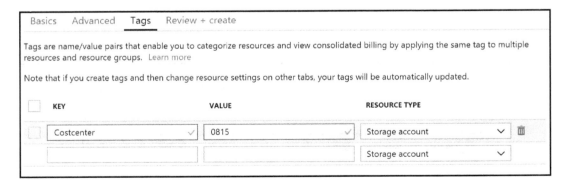

9. After setting the necessary tags, we only need to validate and review our configuration, and finally create the storage account. To do that, click on the **Next : Review + create >** button:

10. When you have passed the validation, you can click on the **Create** button and the deployment of the account will start:

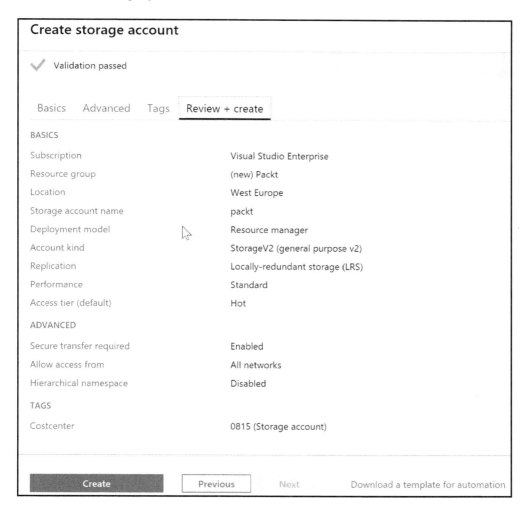

Microsoft has enhanced the portal experience in the Azure portal. You will now get a response showing the deployment status in the storage **Overview** blade. The status is shown here during deployment:

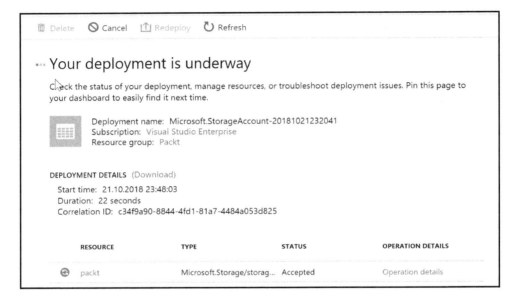

When the deployment is finished, the status will change and the portal will represent the completed deployment:

When you now go to the resource, you can create different types of storage service within that newly created storage account:

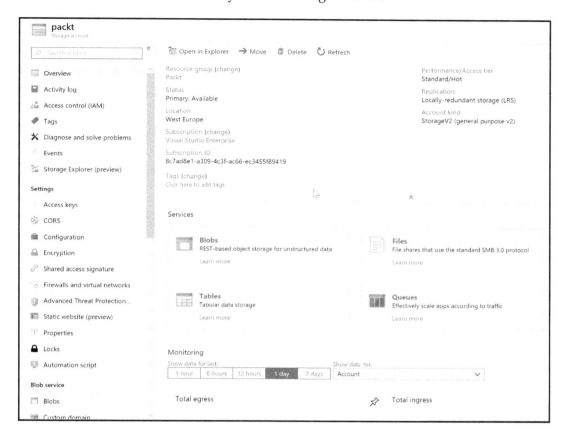

Lets create an Azure file share as an example:

1. Click on the **Files** section as shown in the following screenshot:

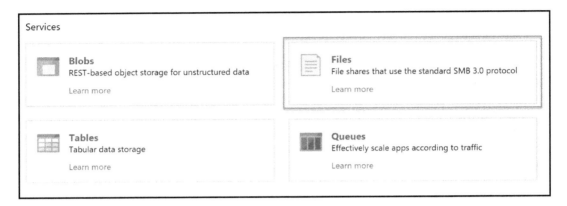

2. In the next blade, click on the **+ File share** button:

3. Now, create a name for the file share and set a quota; remember, the current limit for a share is 5 TB. Afterward, click on the **Create** button:

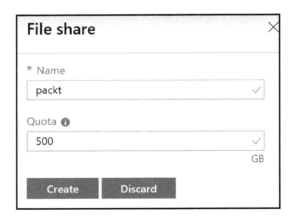

4. After the file share has been created, you will see the new share in your list of file shares:

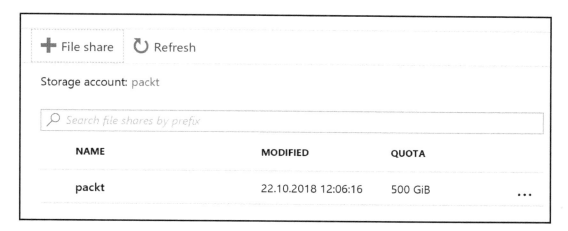

Summary

Now, you should have learned about the different types of storage that are available in Azure as well as which replication and availability options they have. Also, we have created a storage account and a few storage services in it. You should also be familiar with some basic tools and PowerShell cmdlets to interact with Azure Storage.

6
Implementing Azure-Managed Kubernetes and Azure Container Service

The next level of virtualization is **containers** as they provide a better solution than virtual machines within Hyper-V, as containers optimize resources by sharing as much as possible of the existing container platform.

This chapter will describe the basics of containers, how to design and implement them, and how to choose the proper solution for orchestrating containers. You will get an overview of how Azure can help you to implement services based on containers and get rid of traditional virtualization stuff with redundant OS resources that need to be managed, updated, backed-up, and optimized.

Containers started with Docker in Linux and came to Windows Server version 2003, without any official feature statement or public announcement because it has been driven by Microsoft Azure, and was a feature that had been used and proofed there for years before Windows Server 2016 Container Services in Windows was officially announced and used.

One of the best things is that a container could be run on Linux and on Windows as a **container host**, without modifications if the service is built up properly, and without breaking the barriers and modifying the general concept of containers.

The following topics will be covered in this chapter:

- Technical design of containers
- Designing microservices
- Container registries
- Container instances
- Container orchestration
- **Azure Container Service** (ACS)

Technical requirements

To run containers in a cloud environment, no specific installations are required, as you only need the following:

- A computer with an internet browser
- An Azure subscription (if not available, a trial could work too: https://azure.microsoft.com/en-us/free/)
- The code in this chapter can be found at https://github.com/PacktPublishing/Implementing-Azure-Putting-Modern-DevOps-to-Use

Containers – the concept and basics

Containers are a mechanism to run software reliably even when moving them from one computer environment to another. The open sources project Docker in Linux has provided such a service for some years now. It containerizes the application and its dependencies (OS and underlying infrastructure) and abstracts the interaction between each; they isolate applications from each other but use a shared OS. This idea works based on the microservice design of services, because it performs as a service that is independent, flexible, and scalable by default, using predefined APIs for communications:

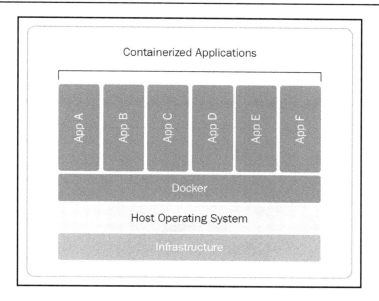

The basic features of containers are as follows:

- They are *run-everywhere apps*
- They are developed on a microservice-style architecture
- They enable a higher density of resources

The generic platform for running these containerized applications is Docker, which is available for the following:

- Windows containers
- Docker for Linux
- Docker for Mac
- Boot2Docker
- VirtualBox

In this chapter, we will focus on Linux and Windows containers. With the launch of Window Server 2016, we had two different version of containers in Windows—Hyper-V and generic containers. As the concept of Hyper-V containers has since been deprecated, we will not waste time on this concept any further.

The following image describes the design on container services on a high level:

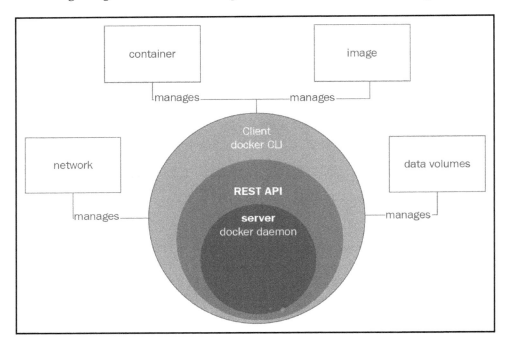

Microservices – the concept

To design a solution using containers, you will need to design a solution based on the microservices concept. This new architectural style is an approach to developing a single application as a suite of small services, each running in its own process and communicating with lightweight mechanisms, often an HTTP resource API. This provides an easy mechanism that can even replace technologies, for example, moving from PostgreSQL to MS SQL as you will not have to modify the microservices; just by replacing one microservice, the others will run properly.

The following images describes the concept of container services:

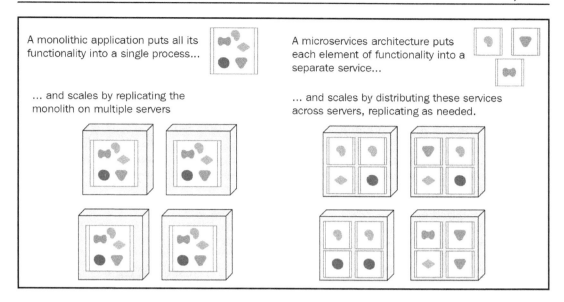

Now, let's combine microservices and containers. The result is a flexible and scalable environment that gives the possibility to spin up additional containers to provide better performance and latency in the app, without any specific configuration changes.

Workloads to run in containers

Docker containers are not the one and only solution for every single workload. There are services that do not fit into this concept, too. The major services that do not fit are as follows:

- Containers are not as fast as *bare-metal* installations. Even though a Docker container has less overhead than VMs, it does not have zero overhead. If your solution needs bare-metal speed, especially from the app point of view, you will have no choice but to run it directly from a bare-metal server, without using containers or virtual machines.

- Containers provide cross-platform compatibility, which means that a container designed to run in a Docker container may run in a Windows container, and vice versa. If you design your container to be flexible with the underlying operating system, you may lose features that often lead software architects to not provide this OS compatibility within containers at all.

- Containers are not designed to run applications with graphical interfaces. Although some tricks may provide this feature, the result is more than clunky. Docker is not a good solution for applications that require rich interfaces.
- Using Docker may provide a way to improve security, as its concept involves isolating applications from the host system and breaking an application into small microservices. This means that if one microservice is compromised, the others are not necessarily compromised, too. On the other hand, containerization brings additional requirements for security as it is a highly scalable environment, and this means that you will need to monitor the complete solution somehow.

Deploying container hosts in Azure

Deploying a container host in Azure is quite easy, as it is just a VM extension. You just have to choose the appropriate Azure Marketplace item and deploy it as follows.

Docker on Linux

As you can see in the following screenshot, there is quite a huge amount of Docker/container stuff that is available in the Azure Marketplace:

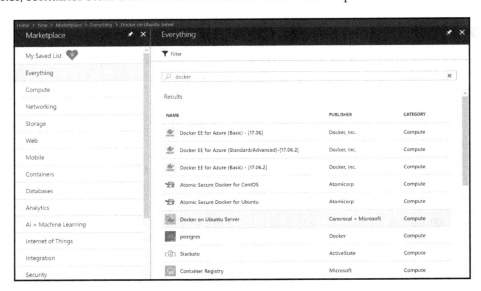

Windows Server Container VM

In addition to the huge number of containers, you could even upload your own
Azure custom IaaS image with Docker/container services enabled:

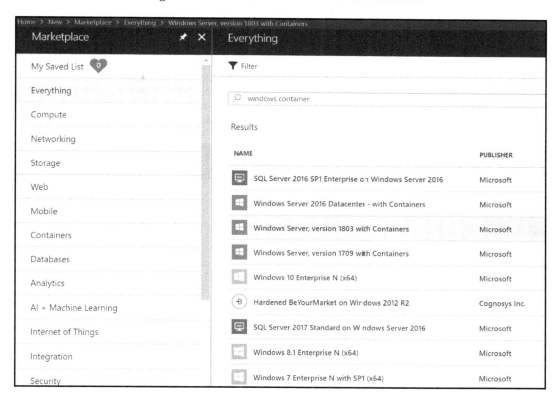

The way described previously is in general not the way you should provide
containers in a cloud environment. With Azure we have easier ways of doing so, but
if you need it, you could do it that way. As with Azure, you will have the option to
order a container directly in Azure as an **Azure Container Instance (ACI)** or a
managed Azure solution using Kubernetes as orchestrator, which we will talk about
later in this chapter.

> To administer a Docker container from the command line, Azure
> CLI provides a great implementation: `https://hub.docker.com/r/`
> `microsoft/azure-cli/`.

Azure Container Registry (ACR)

If you need to set up a container environment to be used by the developers in your Azure tenant, you will have to think about where to store your container images. In general, the way to do this is to provide a container registry. This registry could reside on a VM itself, but using PaaS services with cloud technologies always provides an easier and more flexible design.

This is where **Azure Container Service** (**ACS**) comes in, as it is a PaaS solution that provides high flexibility and even features such as replication between geographies.

This means you will need to fill in the following details:

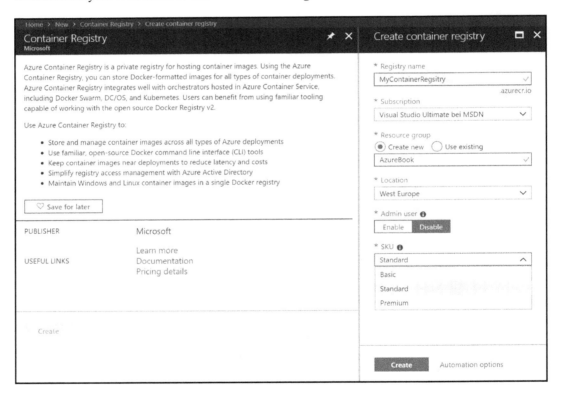

When you create your container registry, you will need to define the following:

- The registry name (ending with `azurecr.io`)
- The resource group the registry sits in

- The Azure location
- The admin user (if you will need to log in to the registry using an account)
- The SKU:
    - Basic
    - Standard
    - Premium

The following table details the features and limits of the basic, standard, and premium service tiers:

Resource	Basic	Standard	Premium
Storage	10 GiB	100 GiB	500 GiB
Max image layer size	20 GiB	20 GiB	50 GiB
ReadOps per minute	1,000	3,000	10,000
WriteOps per minute	100	500	2,000
Download bandwidth MBps	30	60	100
Upload bandwidth MBps	10	20	50
Webhooks	2	10	100
Geo-replication	N/A	N/A	Supported (https://docs.microsoft.com/en-us/azure/container-registry/container-registry-geo-replication)

Switching between the different SKUs is supported and can be done using the portal, PowerShell, or CLI.

If you still are on a classic ACR, the first step would be to upgrade to a managed registry using the following steps at https://docs.microsoft.com/en-us/azure/container-registry/container-registry-upgrade.

From the best-practice point of view, you should design your ACR that way, to provide it near to the region where you are planning to deploy the containers themselves.

ACI

As mentioned already, running just container instances in Azure is quite easy. By running your workloads in ACI, you don't have to set up a management infrastructure for your containers, you just can put your focus on design and building the applications.

Creating a first container in Azure

Let's create a first simple container in Azure using the portal:

1. Go to **Container Instances** under **New** | **Marketplace** | **Everything**, as shown in the following screenshot:

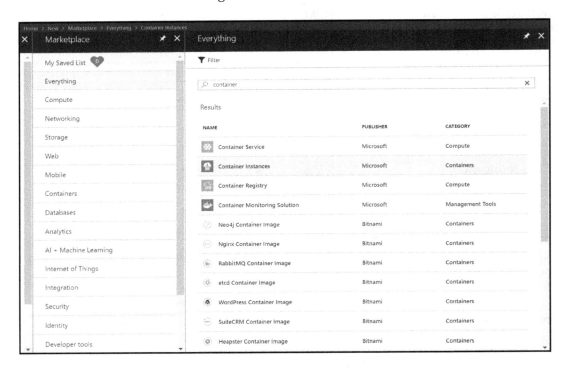

2. After having chosen the **Container Instances** entry in the resources list, you will have to define some properties, which are described as follows:

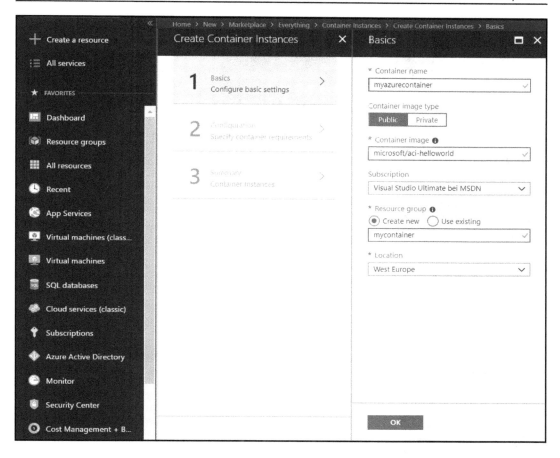

At first, we will need to define the Azure container name. Of course, this needs to be unique in your environment. Then, we will need to define the source of the image and to which resource group and region it should be deployed within Azure.

3. As already mentioned, containers can reside on Windows and Linux, because this needs to be defined at first. Afterwards, we will need to define the resources per container:
   - Cores
   - Memory
   - Ports
   - Port protocol

- Restart policy (if the container went offline)

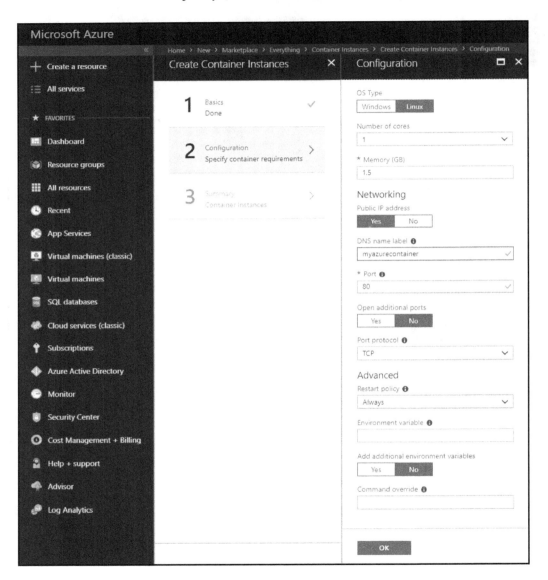

4. After having deployed the corresponding container registry, we can start working with the container instance:

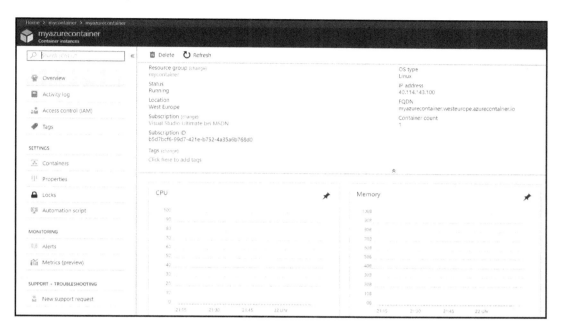

5. When hitting the URL posted in the left part, under FQDN, you should see the following screenshot:

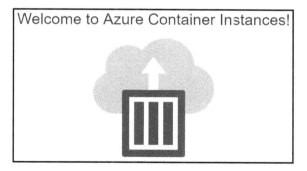

After we have finalized the preceding steps, we have an ACI up and running, which means that you are able to provide container images, load them up to Azure, and run them.

Azure Marketplace containers

In the public Azure Marketplace, you can find existing container images that just can be deployed to your subscription. These are pre-packaged images that give you the option to start with your first container in Azure. As cloud services provide reusability and standardization, this entry point is always good to look at first.

1. Before starting with this, we will need to check if the required resource providers are enabled on the subscription you are working with. Otherwise, we will need to register them by hitting the **Register** entry and waiting a few minutes for completion, as shown in the following screenshot:

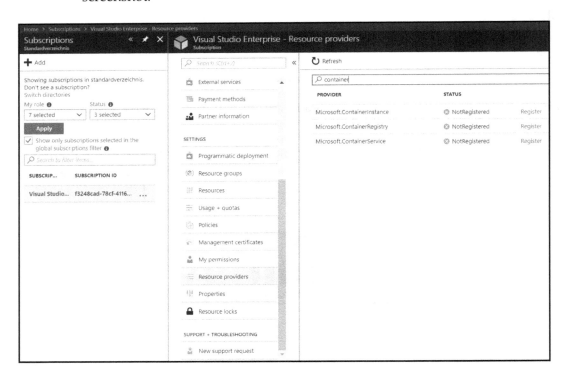

2. Now, we can start deploying marketplace containers such as the container image for WordPress, which is used as a sample, as shown in the following screenshot:

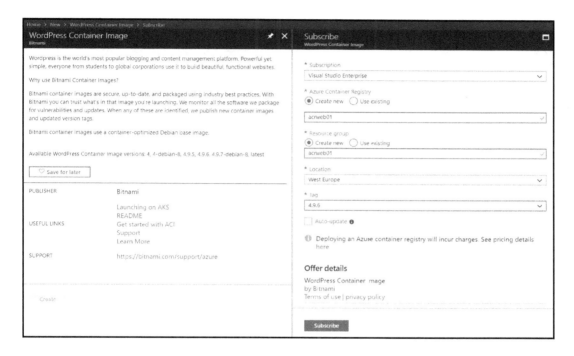

At first, we will need to decide for the corresponding image and choose to create a new ACR, or use an existing one. Furthermore, the Azure region, the resource group, and the tag (for example, version) need to be defined in the following dialog:

3. Now that the registry is being created, we will need to update the permission settings, also called enable admin registry. This can be done with the **Admin user Enable** button as shown in the following screenshot:

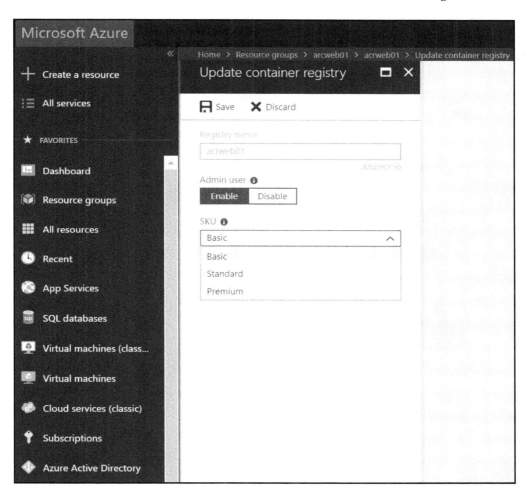

4. Regarding the SKU, this is just another point where we can set the priority and define performance. This may take some minutes to be enabled. Now, we can start deploying container images from the container registry, as you can see in the following screenshot with the WordPress image that is already available in the registry:

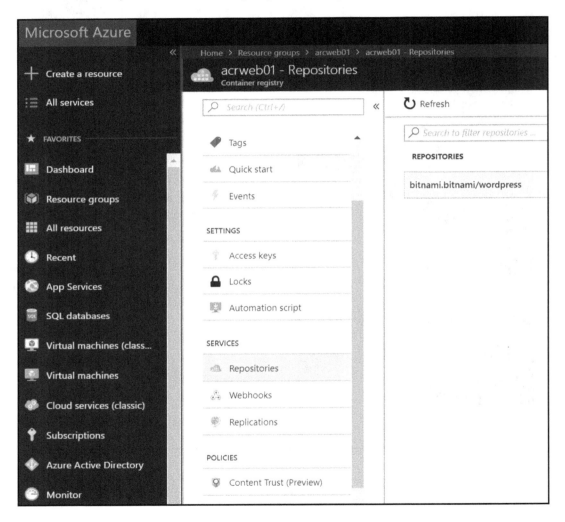

5. At first, we will need to choose the corresponding container from the registry; right-click the tag version from the **Tags** section:

6. Having done that, we will need to hit the **Deploy to web app** menu entry to deploy the web app to Azure:

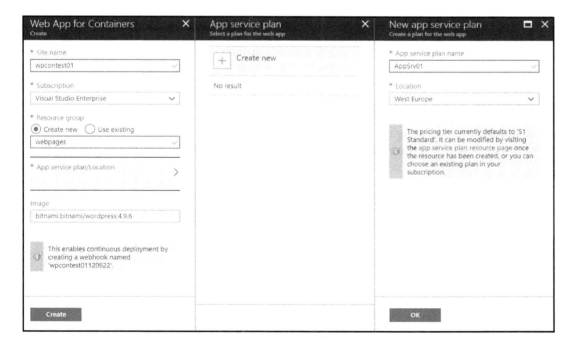

7. As the properties that need to be filled are some defaults for **Web Apps**, it is quite easy to set them:

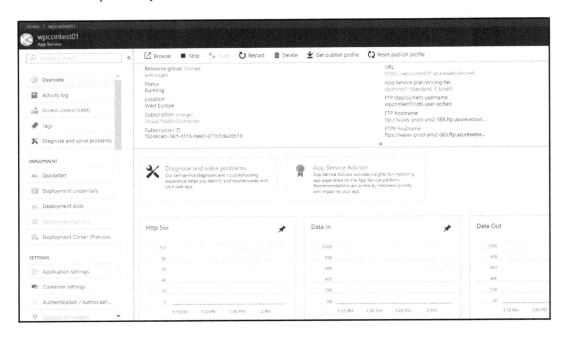

Finally, the first containerized image for a web app has been deployed to Azure.

Creating custom containers

Having now learned how containers in general work, and how to create the required infrastructure around them (for example, **registries**), let's have a look how to create a customer container from a custom app.

Before creating a container from a custom app, it is quite important to think about the design of containers we talked about earlier in this chapter (for example, no GUI and already microservice).

A good tutorial on creating a custom container from your app can be found at `https://docs.microsoft.com/en-us/azure/container-instances/container-instances-tutorial-prepare-app`.

Container orchestration

In the first part of this chapter, we understood the concept of containers, how they are designed, how you can prepare a service to create your own container, and how to deploy them in an Azure environment.

One of the most interesting topics with regard to containers is that they provide a technology for scaling. For example, if we need more performance on a website that is running containerized, we would just spin off an additional container to load-balance the traffic. This could even be done if we needed to scale down.

The concept of container orchestration

Regarding this technology, we need an orchestration tool to provide this feature set. There are some well-known container orchestration tools available on the market, such as the following:

- Docker swarm
- DC/OS
- Kubernetes

Kubernetes is the most-used one, and therefore could be deployed as a service in most public cloud services, such as in Azure. In general, it provides the following features:

- **Automated container placement:** On the container hosts, to best spread the load between them
- **Self-healing**: For failed containers, restarting them in a proper way
- **Horizontal scaling:** Automated horizontal scaling (up and down) based on the existing load

- **Service discovery and load balancing**: By providing IP-addresses to containers and managing DNS registrations
- **Rollout and rollback**: Automated rollout and rollback for containers, which provides another self-healing feature as updated containers that are newly rolled-out are just rolled back if something goes wrong
- **Configuration management**: By updating secrets and configurations without the need to fully rebuild the container itself

Azure Kubernetes Service (AKS)

Installing, maintaining, and administering a Kubernetes cluster manually could mean a huge investment of time for a company. In general, these tasks are one-off costs and therefore it would be best to not waste these resources. In Azure today, there is a feature called **AKS**, where **K** emphasizes that it is a managed Kubernetes service.

Right after containers became interesting for cloud services, Microsoft launched a first service called which was in general the same, but if you ordered it, Azure created a custom ACS environment (dedicated to your tenant) for templated deployments. With ACS, the choice was just available to the most popular orchestrators—**Mesos**, **Swarm**, and **Kubernetes**. With ACS, you have to pay for the master servers of the orchestrator.

For AKS, there is no charge for Kubernetes masters, you just have to pay for the nodes that are running the containers.

Before you start, you will have to fulfill the following prerequisites:

- An Azure account with an active subscription
- Azure CLI installed and configured
- Kubernetes command-line tool, `kubectl`, installed

- Make sure that the Azure subscription you use has these required resources—storage, compute, networking, and a container service:

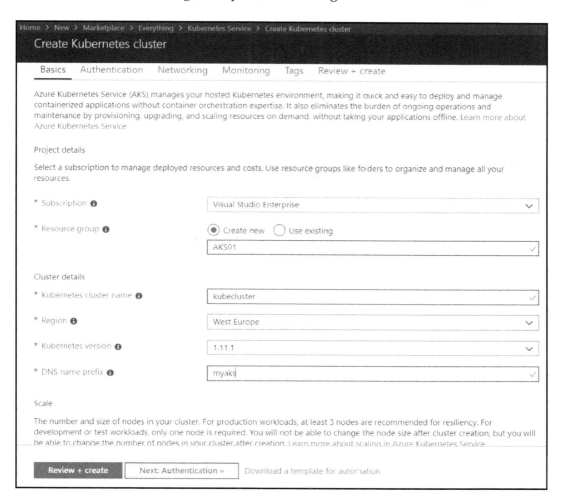

1. For the first step, you need to choose **Kubernetes service** and choose to create your AKS deployment for your tenant. The following parameters need to be defined:
   - Resource group for the deployment
   - Kubernetes cluster name
   - Azure region
   - Kubernetes version
   - DNS prefix

2. Then, hit the **Authentication** tab, as shown in the following screenshot:

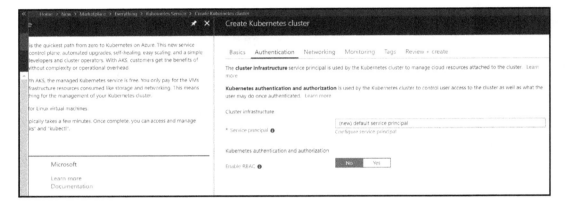

3. On the **Authentication** tab, you will need to define a service principal or choose and existing one, as AKS needs a service principal to run the deployment. In addition, you could enable the RBAC feature, which gives you the chance to define fine-grained permissions based on Azure AD accounts and groups.

 For more information on RBAC with AKS, visit the following URL at https://docs.microsoft.com/en-us/azure/aks/aad-integration.

4. On the **Networking** tab, you can choose either to add the Kubernetes cluster into an existing VNET, or create a new one. In addition, the HTTP routing feature can be enabled or disabled:

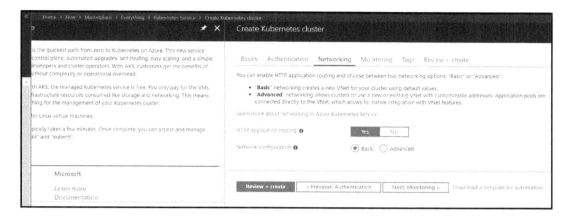

5. On the **Monitoring** tab, you have the option to enable container monitoring and link it to an existing Log Analytics workspace, or create a new one:

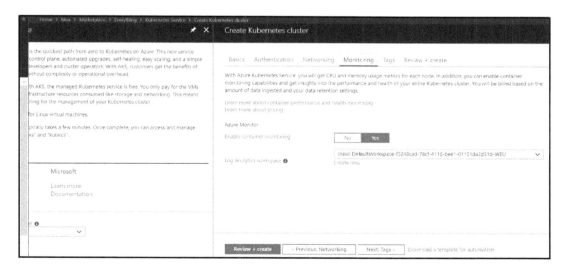

6. As Azure tags are a major feature and requirement for Azure Governance, the following is the source from which to set your required tags:

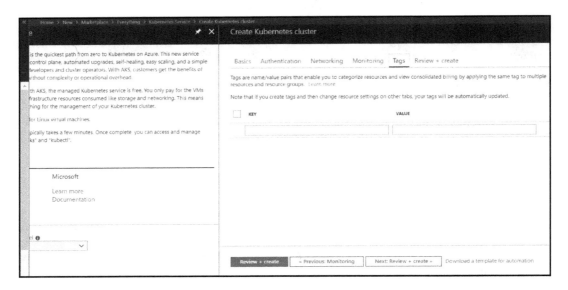

7. Finally, the validation will check for any misconfigurations and create the Azure ARM template for the deployment. Clicking the **Create** button will start the deployment phase, which could run for several minutes or even longer depending on the chosen feature, and scale:

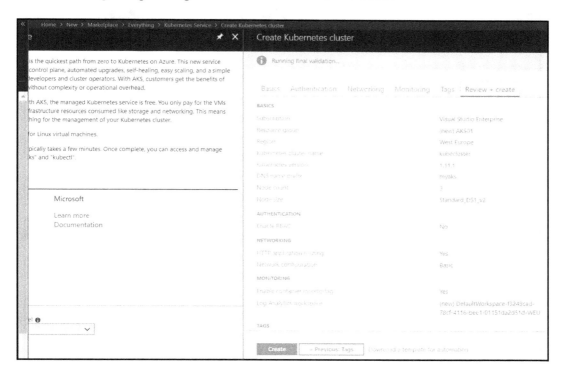

8. After the deployment has finished, the Kubernetes dashboard is available. You can view the Kubernetes dashboard by clicking on the **View Kubernetes dashboard** link, as shown in the following screenshot:

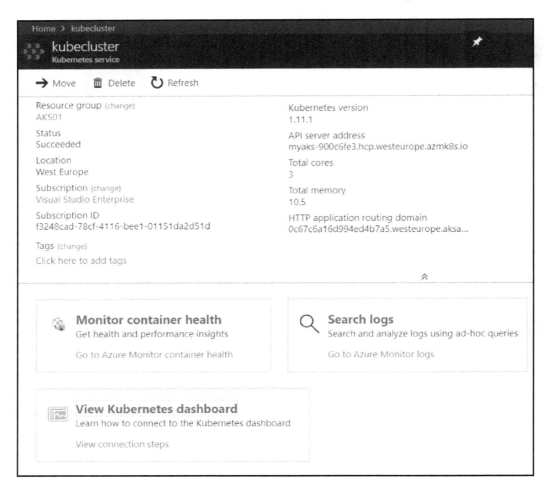

The dashboard looks something like the one shown in the following screenshot:

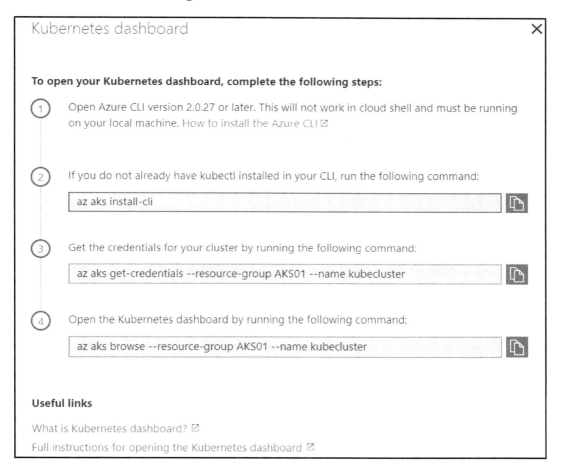

9. As you can see in the preceding screenshot, there are four steps to open the dashboard. At first, we will need to install the Azure CLI in its most current version using the statement that is mentioned in the following screenshot:

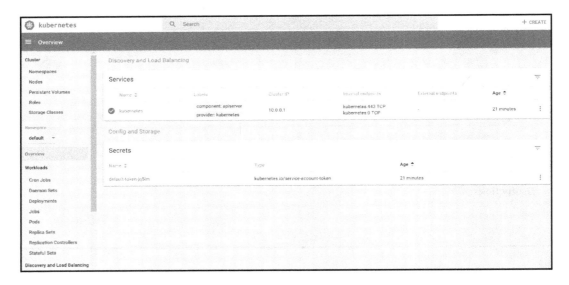

Afterward, the AKS CLI needs to be enabled. It is called `kubectl.exe`.

10. Finally, after setting all the parameters (and when you have performed steps 3 and 4 from the preceding task list), the following dashboard should open in a new browser window:

The preceding dashboard provides a way to monitor and administer your Azure Kubernetes environment, in general, from a GUI.

11. If a new Kubernetes version becomes available, you can easily update it from the Azure portal yourself with one click, as shown in the following screenshot:

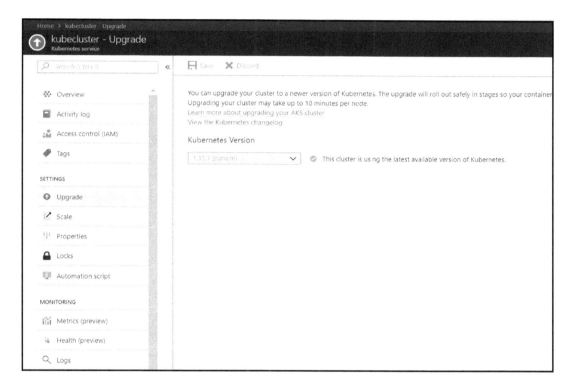

12. If you need to scale your AKS hosts, this is quite easy too, as you can do it through the Azure portal. A maximum of 100 hosts with 3 vCPUs and 10.5 GB RAM per host is currently possible:

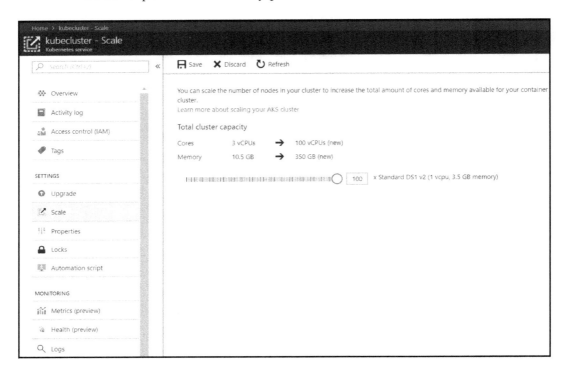

- To enable autoscaler with AKS, the following URL will provide detailed information: `https://docs.microsoft.com/en-us/azure/aks/autoscaler`.

- If you would like to implement AKS using the Azure CLI, the following link is a great source of information: `https://docs.microsoft.com/en-us/azure/aks/kubernetes-walkthrough`.

With all the steps done, you can now upload your containers to your AKS-enabled Docker, and have a huge scalable infrastructure with a minimum of administrative tasks and time for the implementation itself.

 If you are working with Terraforms to centrally manage your ARM templates, a valuable description is available at `https://docs.microsoft.com/en-us/azure/terraform/terraform-create-k8s-cluster-with-tf-and-aks?toc=%2Fen-us%2Fazure%2Faks%2FTOC.jsonbc=%2Fen-us%2Fazure%2Fbread%2Ftoc.json.`

13. If you need to monitor AKS, the integration with Azure monitoring is integrated completely. By clicking the **Monitor container health** link, you will be directed to the following overview:

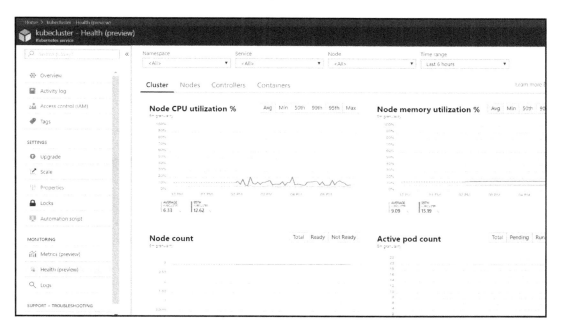

The **Nodes** tab provides the following information per node:

This not only gives a brief overview of the health status, but also the number of containers and the load on the node itself.

14. The **Controllers** view provides detailed information on the AKS controller, its services, status, and uptime:

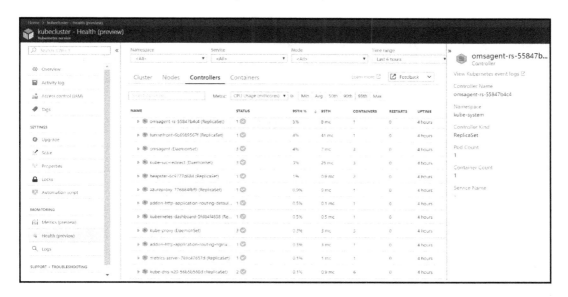

15. And finally, the **Containers** tab gives a deep overview of the health state of each container running in the infrastructure (system containers included):

16. By hitting the **Search logs** section, you can define your own custom Azure monitoring searches and integrate them in your custom portal:

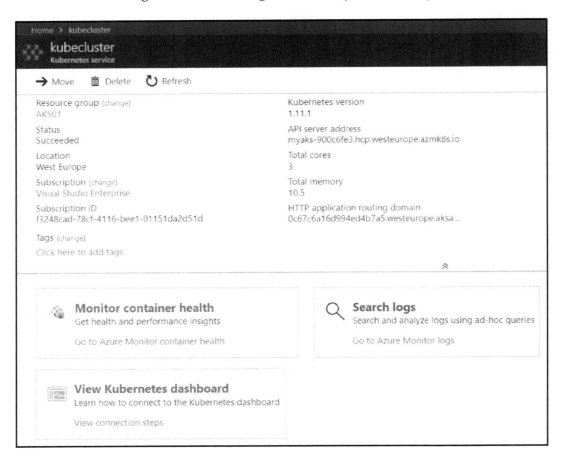

To finally get everything up-and-running, the following to-do list gives a brief overview of all the tasks needed to provide an app within AKS:

1. **Prepare the AKS App**: https://docs.microsoft.com/en-us/azure/aks/tutorial-kubernetes-prepare-app

2. **Create the container registry**: https://docs.microsoft.com/en-us/azure/aks/tutorial-kubernetes-prepare-acr

3. **Create the Kubernetes cluster:** https://docs.microsoft.com/en-us/azure/aks/tutorial-kubernetes-deploy-cluster

4. **Run the application in AKS**: https://docs.microsoft.com/en-us/azure/aks/tutorial-kubernetes-deploy-application

5. **Scale the application in AKS**: https://docs.microsoft.com/en-us/azure/aks/tutorial-kubernetes-scale

6. **Update the application in AKS**: https://docs.microsoft.com/en-us/azure/aks/tutorial-kubernetes-app-update

AKS has the following service quotas and limits:

Resource	Default limit
Max nodes per cluster	100
Max pods per node (basic networking with KubeNet)	110
Max pods per node (advanced networking with Azure CNI)	301
Max clusters per subscription	100

If you already have ACS in place and need to migrate to AKS, the following URL should help: https://docs.microsoft.com/en-us/azure/aks/acs-aks-migration.

As you have seen, AKS in Azure provides great features with a minimum of administrative tasks.

Summary

In this chapter, we have talked about all the basics that are required to understand, deploy, and manage container services in a public cloud environment, including the following:

- The concept of containers
- Container registries
- Container environments
- Container orchestrators (including AKS)

Basically, the concept of containers is a great idea and surely the next step in virtualization that applications need to go to. Setting up the environment manually is quite complex, but by using the PaaS approach, the setup procedure is quite simple (because of automation) and allows you to just start using it.

Azure Hybrid Data Center Services

7

Azure public cloud services provide cloud services all around the world, through a technology based on the following high-level design on the left-hand side. If there are scenarios where Azure does not fit the requirements of a customer and services need to be put on-premise, Microsoft has released a product called Azure Stack that has nearly the same technical design as Azure, but runs a smaller footprint. The high-level design for Azure Stack is as follows on the right-hand side of the following diagram:

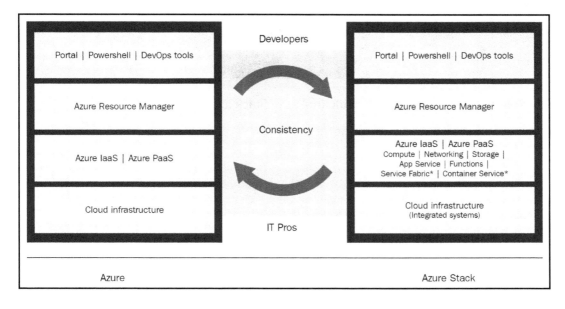

As you can see, the only difference is the infrastructure design on the bottom; in Azure this is something special, based on Windows server technology and in Azure Stack it is Windows Server 2016.

The following diagram provides a way to place Azure (and Azure Stack) all around the world:

The following features are available in Azure Stack as of today:

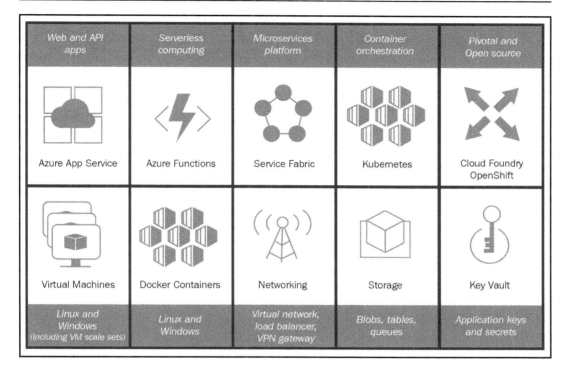

Web and API apps	Serverless computing	Microservices platform	Container orchestration	Pivotal and Open source
Azure App Service	Azure Functions	Service Fabric	Kubernetes	Cloud Foundry OpenShift
Virtual Machines	Docker Containers	Networking	Storage	Key Vault
Linux and Windows (including VM scale sets)	*Linux and Windows*	*Virtual network, load balancer, VPN gateway*	*Blobs, tables, queues*	*Application keys and secrets*

In this chapter, we will discuss this hybrid technology a little bit more in depth.

 If you want a more detailed reading on this, we would advise that you have a look at this specific book discussing only Azure Stack itself at `https://www.packtpub.com/virtualization-and-cloud/building-hybrid-clouds-azure-stack`.

The chapter will cover the following topics:

- The **Azure Stack Development Toolkit** (**ASDK**) versus multi-host deployments
- Setting up an ASDK
- Working with Azure Stack
- Monitoring Azure Stack
- Use cases for Azure Stack

Technical requirements

For working with Microsoft Azure Stack, no specific installations are required, as you only need:

- A computer with an internet browser
- An Azure subscription (if not available, a trial could work, too: `https://azure.microsoft.com/en-us/free/`)

Code in this chapter can be found here at `https://github.com/PacktPublishing/Implementing-Azure-Putting-Modern-DevOps-to-Use`

ASDK

Microsoft Azure Stack can only be ordered with the corresponding hardware, which has been tested and certified. The following are the hardware vendors:

- HPE
- DELL EMC
- Lenovo
- Cisco
- Huawei
- Wortmann
- Fujitsu

The typical scenarios which Azure Stack could fit in are:

- Disconnected/Edge scenarios (for example, running services of Azure on a ship or a plane)
- Data privacy reasons (data could, should, or must not leave the company location)
- Modern cloud app development on-premise

As Azure Stack can only be bought as an integrated system, there is no software available that could be downloaded and place it on dedicated hardware. But for testing **proof of concept (PoC)** purposes, Microsoft offers a trial version of Azure Stack, called **ASDK**. As it is running on one physical host, no performance or availability tests are suitable, but in general all features are available with ASDK, too.

The required hardware for an ASDK is documented here at `https://docs.microsoft.com/en-us/azure/azure-stack/asdk/asdk-deploy-considerations`. To finally double check if all hardware requirements are met, you can run the prerequisite script from here at `https://go.microsoft.com/fwlink/?LinkId=828735 clcid=0x409`.

Preparing the ASDK host

The most recent download of the ASDK can be found here at `https://azure.microsoft.com/en-us/overview/azure-stack/development-kit/?v=try`. This is how to download the ASDK:

1. The Azure Stack Downloader will help you with a nice UI to make it work:

2. Now we will need to extract the files to a folder of your choice on the local hard disk:

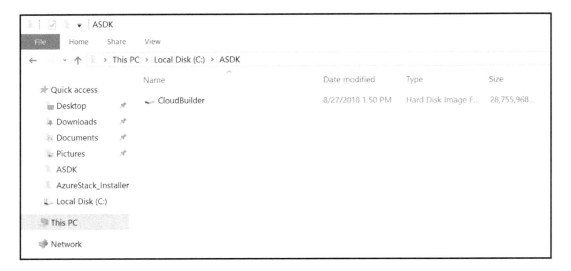

3. The `CloudBuilder.vhdx` is the source that all Azure Stack services boot from. You should place this `.vhdx` file in a destination folder of your choice and start the ASDK installer script, which is available here at `https://docs.microsoft.com/en-us/azure/azure-stack/asdk/asdk-install`.

4. Now let's start with choosing the option on the left and prepare the environment:

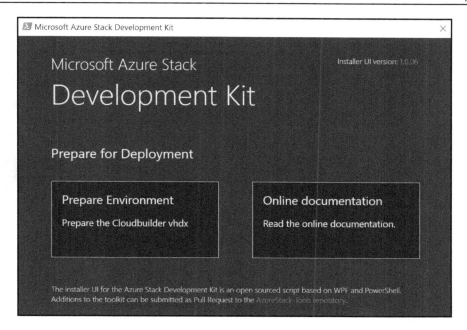

5. We will need to choose the correct virtual disk of Azure Stack and load corresponding drivers for the hardware, if needed:

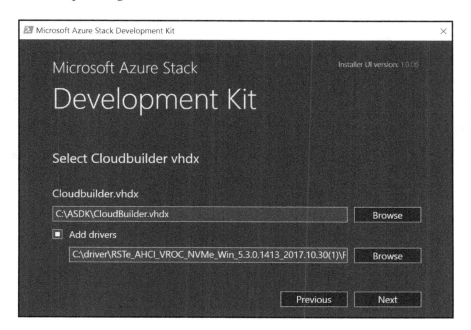

6. The installer now mounts the .vhdx file and boots from it. The next required parameters are the local administrator account and password, which will be set identically for all accounts in Azure Stack. If you are running your ASDK host in a non-DHCP networking environment, you would need to define the networking properties and even the time zone and computer name:

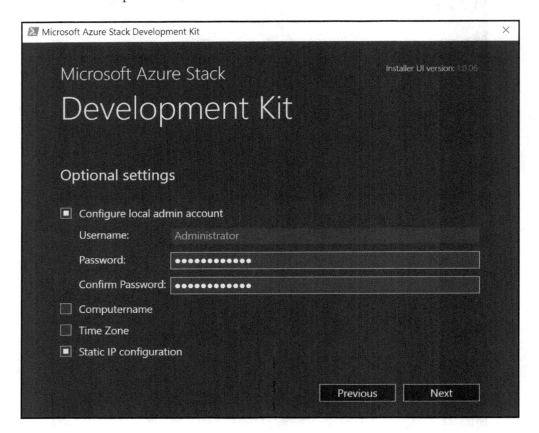

7. Because ASDK only supports one network card, we will need to choose it. All others will be disabled by default, if they are not already:

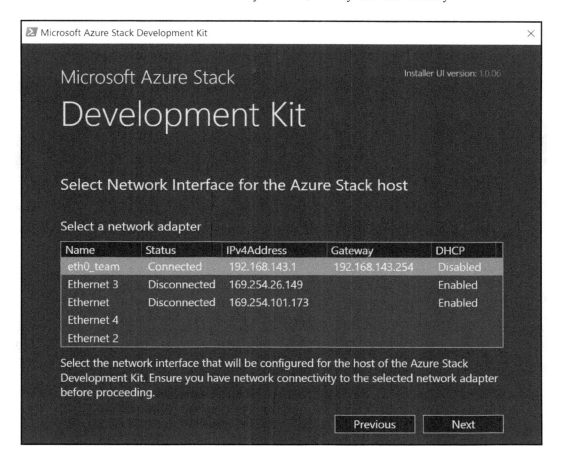

8. If you are deploying ASDK with a fixed IP, it is a must to set a proper time server, as about 80% of all broken ASDK installations are caused by time server issues. If you have no other one available, `time.windows.com` could help you:

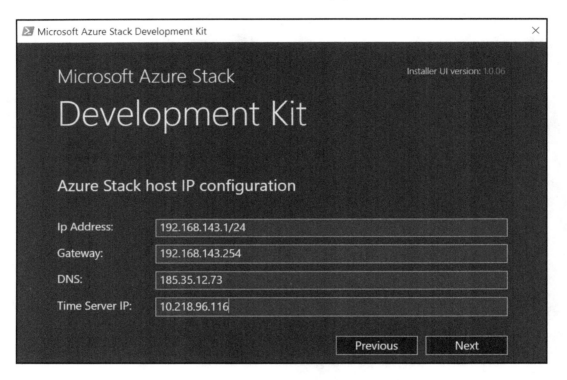

9. Now, the `CloudBuilder.vhdx` is being mounted and a final reboot will bring the system online in the VHDX itself:

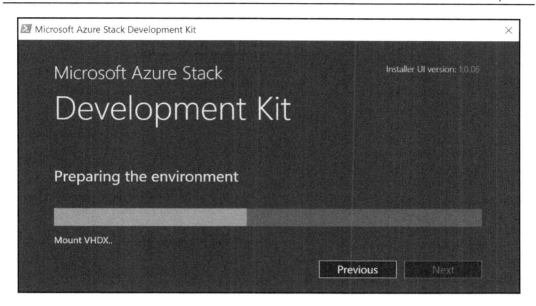

10. After the reboot is successfully done, we will need to run the installer again to get to the second phase of the installation:

11. Therefore, we will need to hit the **Install** box on the left-side of the
following screenshot:

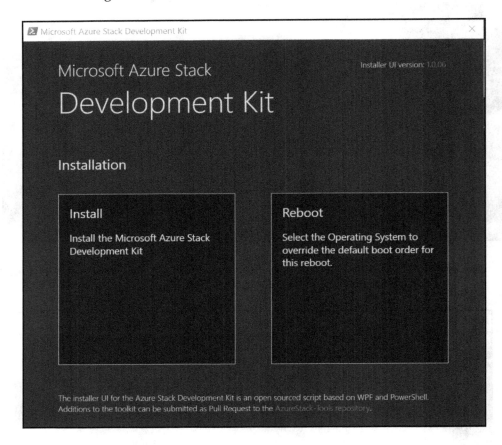

Identity management configuration

During the installation, the appropriate identity management solution (also called
connected mode or **disconnected mode**) needs to be selected:

As you can see in the preceding screenshot, Azure Stack is supported to run in:

- **Azure China Cloud**
- **Azure Cloud**
- **ADFS** (although called disconnected mode)

This means that if you run it in connected mode (using Azure Cloud or Azure China Cloud), the identity management is moved to Azure AD. To enable this, you will need to have proper permission (global administrator) in Azure AD. This is because the registration of applications needs to be done during the setup. The following table gives an overview of the tasks in detail:

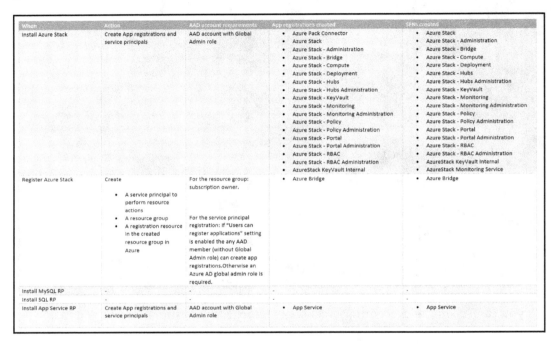

When	Action	AAD account requirements	App registrations created	SPNs created
Install Azure Stack	Create App registrations and service principals	AAD account with Global Admin role	• Azure Pack Connector • Azure Stack • Azure Stack - Administration • Azure Stack - Bridge • Azure Stack - Compute • Azure Stack - Deployment • Azure Stack - Hubs • Azure Stack - Hubs Administration • Azure Stack - KeyVault • Azure Stack - Monitoring • Azure Stack - Monitoring Administration • Azure Stack - Policy • Azure Stack - Policy Administration • Azure Stack - Portal • Azure Stack - Portal Administration • Azure Stack - RBAC • Azure Stack - RBAC Administration • AzureStack KeyVault Internal	• Azure Stack • Azure Stack - Administration • Azure Stack - Bridge • Azure Stack - Compute • Azure Stack - Deployment • Azure Stack - Hubs • Azure Stack - Hubs Administration • Azure Stack - KeyVault • Azure Stack - Monitoring • Azure Stack - Monitoring Administration • Azure Stack - Policy • Azure Stack - Policy Administration • Azure Stack - Portal • Azure Stack - Portal Administration • Azure Stack - RBAC • Azure Stack - RBAC Administration • AzureStack KeyVault Internal • AzureStack Monitoring Service
Register Azure Stack	Create • A service principal to perform resource actions • A resource group • A registration resource in the created resource group in Azure	For the resource group: subscription owner. For the service principal registration: If "Users can register applications" setting is enabled the any AAD member (without Global Admin role) can create app registrations.Otherwise an Azure AD global admin role is required.	• Azure Bridge	• Azure Bridge
Install MySQL RP	-	-	-	-
Install SQL RP	-	-	-	-
Install App Service RP	Create App registrations and service principals	AAD account with Global Admin role	• App Service	• App Service

After the specific registrations have been done, there is no need to have the global administrator permissions anymore. If Azure Stack is using disconnected mode, it relies on ADFS and creates the federation trust during the deployment. This means that ADFS has to be already in place before starting the setup:

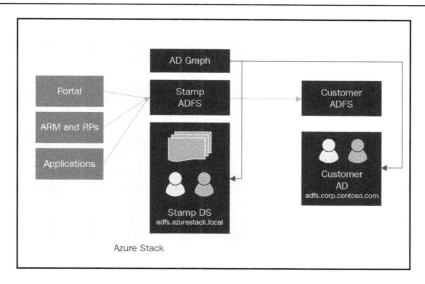

For the Microsoft Graph configuration, a service account with read permission in the existing AD needs to be available. The requirements for AD and ADFS are Windows Server 2012, Active Directory 2012, and above.

The technical differences between both modes regarding available services are described in the following table:

	Disconnected from the internet	Connected to the internet
Billing	Must be Capacity Enterprise Agreement (EA) only	Capacity or Pay-as-you-use EA or Cloud Solution Provider (CSP)
Identity	Must be AD FS	Azure AD or AD FS
Marketplace	Supported BYOL licensing	Supported BYOL licensing
Registration	Recommended, requires removable media and a separate connected device.	Automated
Patch and update	Required, requires removable media and a separate connected device.	Update package can be downloaded directly from the Internet to Azure Stack.

For more details regarding identity configuration, the following URL could help at `https://docs.microsoft.com/en-us/azure/azure-stack/azure-stack-integrate-identity`.

Networking configuration

The next important step during the setup is the networking configuration. With the ASDK, all networking relies on a VM called BGPNAT, which simulates the networking switch in the multi-node deployments. As all outgoing or incoming traffic passes this VM, it also represents the bottleneck of ASDK. As only one network interface card is supported, all other available ones need to be disabled, which will be done during the setup itself. This is how to set up:

1. In a multi-node environment, the BGPNAT VM is replaced with a physical top of the rack switch:

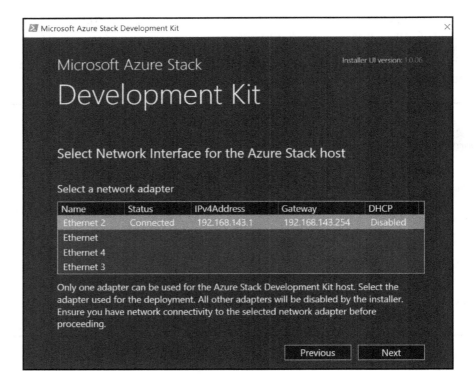

2. For the ASDK, we will need to set up the BGPNAT IP and all other required TCP/IP parameters as shown in the following screenshot:

3. With these parameters filled in, all required information is available and the setup is ready to start:

4. After having hit the **Deploy** button, the setup continues. If you have chosen the connected mode, within the next few minutes an authentication request for AAD will be displayed. If no AAD is in place, no further input is needed:

5. Depending on the performance of the physical host, the setup may run for four to five hours or more:

6. During the first steps of the deployment phase, a Windows cluster will be set up while the ASDK host is rebooting. After this step, it is important to log on as `Azurestack\AzureStackAdmin` to double check the installation progress:

```
================================= ValidateUpdate =================================
MpSigStub successfully updated Microsoft Windows Defender (RS1+) using the Platform update
package.

          Original:        Updated to:
 Platform: 4.10.14393.2273  4.18.1807.18075

End time: 2018-09-09 21:05:53Z
---------------------------------------------------------------------------------

 - 9/9/2018 2:05:53 PM
VERBOSE: [Cloud:UpdateCloudSecurity] Done applying Windows Defender Platform update to individual
nodes - 9/9/2018 2:05:53 PM
VERBOSE: [Cloud:UpdateCloudSecurity] Done applying Windows Defender Platform update - 9/9/2018
2:05:55 PM
VERBOSE: [Cloud:UpdateCloudSecurity] Done updating Common Antimalware Platform (Windows Defender).
 - 9/9/2018 2:05:55 PM
VERBOSE: Interface: Interface UpdateCloudSecurity completed. - 9/9/2018 2:05:55 PM
COMPLETE: Task Cloud - UpdateCloudSecurity
VERBOSE: Task: Task completed. - 9/9/2018 2:05:55 PM
COMPLETE: Step 305 - (SEC) Finalize cloud security
VERBOSE: Step: Status of step '305 - (SEC) Finalize cloud security' is 'Success'. - 9/9/2018
2:05:55 PM
VERBOSE: Checking if any of the in progress steps are complete. The following steps are currently
in progress: '305'. - 9/9/2018 2:05:55 PM
VERBOSE: Action: Step 305 completed successfully. - 9/9/2018 2:05:55 PM
VERBOSE: The following steps have completed and will be removed from the collection of in-progress
 steps: '305'. - 9/9/2018 2:05:55 PM
VERBOSE: Action plan execution completed for action plan 'Deployment'. - 9/9/2018 2:05:55 PM
VERBOSE: Action: Action plan 'Deployment' completed. - 9/9/2018 2:05:55 PM
COMPLETE: Action 'Deployment'
PS C:\Windows\system32> _
```

7. If no errors occur, the setup will be finished with the preceding screen. If there are any issues, the installation log files (saved to `..\CloudDeployment\Logs`) are the single point of truth. You can collect them using the following PowerShell command:

```
Get-AzureStackLog -OutputPath C:\AzureStackLogs (or any
other folder)
```

The first and easiest troubleshooting step is to run the setup again using the `/rerun` parameter.

VM design of Azure Stack (ASDK)

After Azure Stack ASDK has been set up properly, the following virtual machines are available on the host:

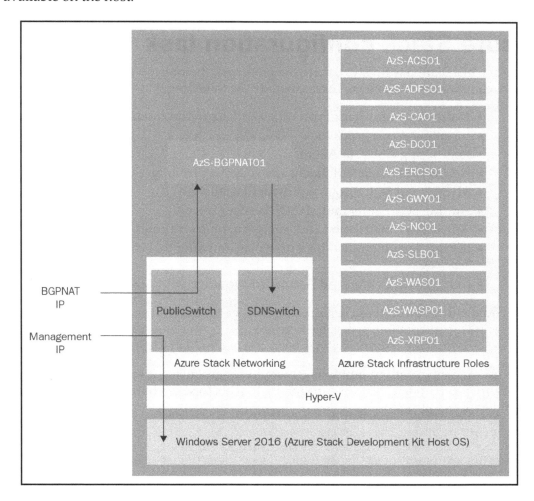

For the multi-node environments, these VMs are available at minimum redundantly with load balancers in front, but as these are secured by default, you would never see the VMs from the operational perspective.

Azure Stack configuration task

After the installation is finished, there are more tasks before you could call Azure Stack ready for the customers. Theses include the following:

- Installing Azure Stack PowerShell and AzureRM modules
- Installing Azure Stack tools
- Registering ASDK to Azure
- Adding Microsoft VM Extensions to gallery from marketplace
- MySQL and SQL resource provider installation
- Adding SQL Server and MySQL hosting servers
- App service installation and configuration (certificates generation)
- Setting default quotas and a base plan and offer that contain all deployed services
- Configuring Python and Azure CLI for usage with ASDK

You could either run all these tasks manually (per the description available within the Microsoft Documentation, accessible here at `https://github.com/mattmcspirit/azurestack`) or using a script that has been created by Matt McSpirit.

As it makes configurations quite easy, I would suggest using it every time following the Azure Stack update cycle. It runs for another six to seven hours and a sample should look as follows:

```
.\ConfigASDK.ps1 -azureDirectoryTenantName "contoso.onmicrosoft.com" -
authenticationType AzureAD -downloadPath "D:\ASDKfiles" -ISOPath
"D:\WS2016EVALISO.iso" -azureStackAdminPwd 'YourPassword' -VMpwd
'YourPassword' -azureAdUsername "admin@contoso.onmicrosoft.com" -
azureAdPwd 'YourAADPassword' -registerASDK -
useAzureCredsForRegistration -azureRegSubId "YourAzureSubscriptionID"
```

If you run into issues while the script is running, you should correct the setup and simply rerun it.

This should be the last step to finally start with Azure Stack testing.

Operating Azure Stack

In this chapter so far, we have discussed what Azure Stack is and how to install the ASDK. Now it is time to have a look at Azure Stack and see how it works.

Basically, there are three ways to connect to Azure Stack endpoints and work with them from the operations side:

- Admin portal and tenant portal
- PowerShell
- The Azure (Stack) CLI

Working with the portals

With Azure Stack, you will get an administrative portal, which is lacking with Microsoft Public Azure, as there Microsoft is running Azure. Azure Stack will be operated by your operations team. Therefore, Azure Stack provides an administrative portal that is accessible through the following URL (using ASDK, as with the multi-node environment, is something you have to decide during the setup): `https://adminportal.local.azurestack.external`.

Depending on which scenario Azure Stack has been set up with (connected or disconnected mode), you either have to authenticate against **Azure AD** or as **Cloudadmin**:

This portal is used to fulfil the following tasks:

- Manage the infrastructure (including system health, updates, capacity, and so on)
- Populate the marketplace
- Create user subscriptions
- Create plans and offers

In Azure Stack, a plan is a way to group one or more services into a basic service plan; for example, you could create a plan that includes the compute, network, and storage resource providers. It gives a subscriber the ability to provision virtual machines by then. Resources can be budgeted using **quotas**. A quota can exist per resource.

An **offer** is a group of one or more plans to be presented to a customer.

After having created plans and offers, a user would have to **subscribe** to them. This could be done in two different ways:

- The cloud operator can create the subscription for a user in the administrative portal
- A tenant can subscribe to a public offer using the tenant portal

Now, let's have a look at the tenant portal, which is accessible using the following URL `https://portal.local.azurestack.external/` (in ASDK; in multi-node environments it could be different). This is a screenshot of the tenant portal:

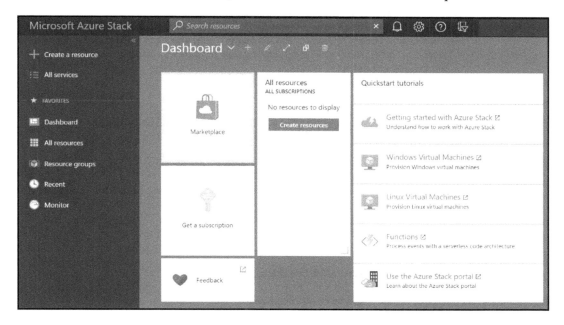

The tenant portal will be used to create resources (virtual machines or PaaS solutions) as a self-service portal.

Working with PowerShell

If your work is not GUI-based, PowerShell could be your friend. You can set up your computer by installing Azure Stack PowerShell upon Azure PowerShell by running the following commands:

1. Install Azure PowerShell (in PowerShell evaluated admin mode):

```
install-module AzureRM
```

2. Install Azure Stack PowerShell (in PowerShell evaluated admin mode):

```
Import-Module -Name PowerShellGet -ErrorAction Stop
Import-Module -Name PackageManagement -ErrorAction Stop
Get-PSRepository -Name "PSGallery"
Register-PsRepository -Default
Set-PSRepository -Name "PSGallery" -InstallationPolicy Trusted
# Install the AzureRM.Bootstrapper module. Select Yes when
prompted to install NuGet
Install-Module -Name AzureRm.BootStrapper
# Install and import the API Version Profile required by Azure
Stack into the current PowerShell session.
Use-AzureRmProfile -Profile 2018-03-01-hybrid -Force
Install-Module -Name AzureStack -RequiredVersion 1.5.0
```

As an example, let's have a look at how to create a storage resource using PowerShell:

```
# Create variables to store the storage account name and the storage
account SKU information
$StorageAccountName = "mystorageaccount"
$SkuName = "Standard_LRS"

# Create a new storage account
$StorageAccount = New-AzureRMStorageAccount `
  -Location $location `
  -ResourceGroupName $ResourceGroupName `
  -Type $SkuName `
  -Name $StorageAccountName
Set-AzureRmCurrentStorageAccount `
  -StorageAccountName $storageAccountName `
  -ResourceGroupName $resourceGroupName

# Create a storage container to store a virtual machine image
$containerName = 'osdisks'
$container = New-AzureStorageContainer `
  -Name $containerName `
  -Permission Blob
```

Everything is possible through PowerShell, so the following link may help to dive deeper into Azure Stack PowerShell: https://docs.microsoft.com/en-us/azure/azure-stack/user/azure-stack-quick-create-vm-windows-powershell.

Working with the CLI

A third option to operate Azure Stack is the **Command Line Interface** (**CLI**), which is available for:

- Windows
- Linux
- Mac

 You can install them using the URL at `https://docs.microsoft.com/en-us/cli/azure/install-azure-cli?view=azure-cli-latest`.

Now, let's have a look at how to create a virtual machine using the CLI. At first, we would need to register the corresponding environment:

- As administrative environment, you would need to run the following script:

```
az cloud register \
  -n AzureStackAdmin \
  --endpoint-resource-manager
  "https://adminmanagement.local.azurestack.external" \
  --suffix-storage-endpoint "local.azurestack.external" \
  --suffix-keyvault-dns
".adminvault.local.azurestack.external" \
  --endpoint-vm-image-alias-doc <URI of the document which
  contains virtual machine image aliases>
az cloud set \
  -n AzureStackAdmin
```

- As user environment, the following script could help:

```
az cloud register \
  -n AzureStackUser \
  --endpoint-resource-manager
  "https://management.local.azurestack.external" \
  --suffix-storage-endpoint "local.azurestack.external" \
  --suffix-keyvault-dns ".vault.local.azurestack.external"
\
  --endpoint-vm-image-alias-doc <URI of the document which
  contains virtual machine image aliases>
az cloud set \
  -n AzureStackUser
```

- Now, let's log on to the Azure Stack environment with the following command:

```
az login \
  -u <Active directory global administrator or user
account. For example:
username@<aadtenant>.onmicrosoft.com> \
  --tenant <Azure Active Directory Tenant name. For
example: myazurestack.onmicrosoft.com>
```

- And finally, let's create a virtual machine:

```
az group create --name myResourceGroup --location local
az vm create \
  --resource-group "myResourceGroup" \
  --name "myVM" \
  --image "Win2016Datacenter" \
  --admin-username "Demouser" \
  --admin-password "Demouser@123" \
  --use-unmanaged-disk \
  --location local
```

Hybrid cloud patterns

Now that we have an overview of what Azure Stack is, how it works, and how we could work with it, let's go on and discuss some scenarios where Azure Stack could fit. Here are some examples:

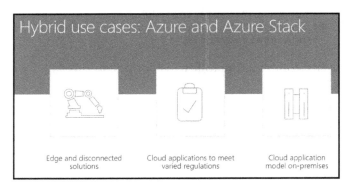

Basically, you should in general think about public Azure and how to move your IT services to it. If there is a reason why a service does not fit public Azure, Azure Stack might work.

The general scenarios for Azure Stack are as follows:

- **Edge and disconnected solutions**: Edge and disconnected solutions are everything when not much internet connectivity is available or not intended. Therefore, the disconnected mode is suitable, because with Azure AD an internet connection is really needed.
- **Data sovereignty**: Data sovereignty is the most important reason, as if a customer is not able to, not willing to, or does not have to move specific data to the public cloud, Azure Stack fits completely, as stack lives on the premise, where the data needs to reside.
- **Cloud applications**: Developing cloud applications is often something that needs to be done on the premises, therefore Azure Stack is the one and only option. After a major release or update is available, the application could then be moved from development stage to public Azure.

To make the corresponding use cases for Azure Stack a little bit easier to understand, Microsoft has published some use cases that might fit and has described them in a little bit more detail. These are the following:

- Configure hybrid cloud connectivity
- Machine learning solution with Azure Stack
- Azure Stack staged data analysis
- Azure Stack cloud burst scenario
- Azure Stack geo-distributed applications

While working through these scenarios, you will figure out that there is a step-by-step guide available to easily understand and set up these scenarios.

Let's have a little bit of a deeper look into each of them.

Configure hybrid cloud connectivity

Azure Stack often needs to be integrated into public Azure or other on-premise infrastructure setups. This is where a site-to-site VPN connection needs to be in place to connect the different infrastructure services. As Azure Stack nowadays is working with a shared VPN device for all customers on it, you will need to set up the site-to-site connection between some devices on premise, in Azure, or even using a network virtual appliance from a third party vendor to set up the connectivity needed.

For more information, please refer to: `https://docs.microsoft.com/en-us/azure/azure-stack/user/azure-stack-solution-hybrid-identity`.

Machine learning solution with Azure Stack

This solution is suitable if your company is using a DevOps approach and set up a CI/CD pipeline across stack and public Azure.

 For more information, please refer to: `https://docs.microsoft.com/en-us/azure/azure-stack/user/azure-stack-solution-machine-learning`.

Azure stack staged data analysis

This solution could be useful to learn how to set up cross-cloud environments to meet the demand of multi-facility enterprises, as the solution describes a way to easily collect data as a basis for quick decisions with no internet access.

Learn how to use both on-premises and public cloud environments to meet the demands.

 For more information, please refer to: `https://docs.microsoft.com/en-us/azure/azure-stack/user/azure-stack-solution-staged-data-analytics`.

Azure Stack cloud burst scenario

This scenario describes an environment where the customer is running its application (for example, a web application) on Azure Stack on-premise and, based on an automatic or manually triggered process (for example, excessive load on the solution), the system auto scales to public Azure through traffic manager to ensure flexibility and scalability.

For more information, please refer to: `https://docs.microsoft.`
`com/en-us/azure/azure-stack/user/azure-stack-solution-`
`cloud-burst.`

Azure Stack geo-distributed Application

As you will see in this scenario, an application is being deployed on public Azure and on one or more Azure Stack environments. In combination with using DNS services and Azure Traffic manager, your environment automatically decides the proper cloud to answer an application request. If one is unavailable, it even automatically fails over to another one.

 For more information, please refer to: `https://docs.microsoft.`
`com/en-us/azure/azure-stack/user/azure-stack-solution-geo-`
`distributed.`

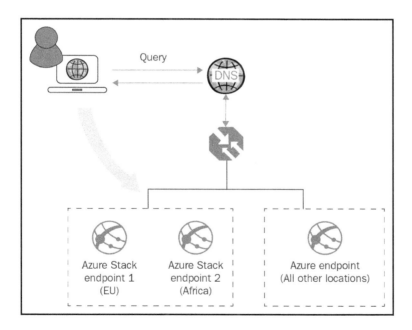

Monitoring Azure Stack

As Azure Stack is an integrated system, the monitoring solution for Azure Stack itself (and not the tenant workloads) has two pillars:

- Hardware monitoring
- Azure Stack monitoring

Hardware monitoring: As the Azure Stack hardware is vendor based, the monitoring of the components works with the hardware vendor-based monitoring solutions that already exist and have been proofed in the based without Azure Stack itself:

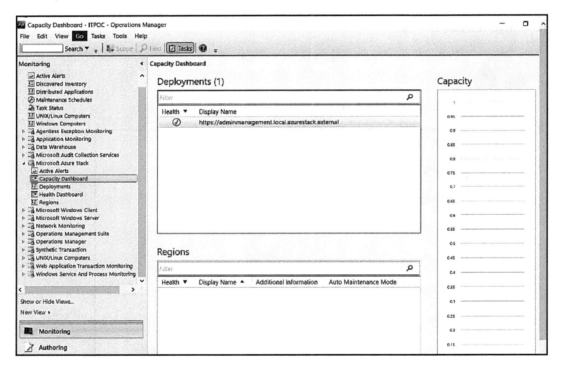

Azure Stack monitoring: The Azure Stack software monitoring is based on the corresponding health APIs. If you are running **System Center Operations Manager** (**SCOM**) on-premise, a SCOM solution is available to monitor multiple Azure Stacks with one SCOM:

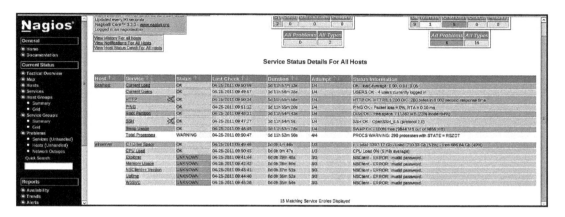

If your primary monitoring solution is Nagios based, there is an integration available, too.

Summary

As you have seen in this chapter, a true hybrid cloud environment using Azure Stack and Azure as consistent solutions is possible and quite easy to implement. Azure Stack is a complex service and in general needs to be integrated in the data center if all required teams are part of the project.

8
Azure Web Apps Basics

In this chapter, we will be introducing Azure App Service, App Service Environment and its types. We will then cover App Service plans and the different pricing plans on offer in order to understand which plan will fulfill your needs. Lastly, you will learn how to create these service in the Azure portal.

The following topics will be covered in this chapter:

- Introduction to Azure App Service
- App Service plans
- App Service Environment
- Creating an App Service plan
- Creating an App Service

Introduction to Azure App Service

Azure App Service is one of Microsoft Azure's **Platform as a service** (**PaaS**) offerings. It is used to run your applications on Azure in a fully managed service environment.

This offering provides the following services:

- **Web Apps**: Used to host your web apps that need to scale with your business
- **API Apps**: Used to easily build and consume APIs on the cloud
- **Mobile Apps**: Used to build mobile apps for any device
- **Logic apps**: Used to automate business processes across **Software as a service** (**SaaS**) and on-premises systems
- **Function apps**: Used to integrate systems, work with IoT, process data, and even build simple APIs and microservices.

In this chapter, we will be focusing on Azure Web Apps specifically.

Azure Web Apps

As mentioned earlier, Azure Web Apps is one of the Azure App Service. Azure Web Apps runs on top of **virtual machines** (**VMs**), where a lot of IIS clusters are deployed in Microsoft data centers. Therefore, when you want to deploy your own web app, you do not have to be responsible for deploying and managing the VMs—just build your app and deploy it on Azure Web Apps.

You can deploy web apps built using one of the following languages: .NET, .NET Core, PHP, Ruby, Python, Java, and Node.js. These apps can be hosted on Windows, Linux, or even in containers such as Docker, although this mode is still in preview at the time of writing.

App Service plans

When you create an App Service, such as a Web App for example, you will be asked to specify the App Service plan.

An App Service plan is like the hardware host on which you run your VMs. It contains the resources that are shared among the App Service. As a result, we can look at App Service as VMs running on the host, which is the App Service plan.

The App Service plan also defines many settings for the App Service that will be built on it, such as the region, number of instances, whether it will be able to scale out/in or not, and much more, which will be covered later on.

Azure offers different plans to fulfill different customers' needs, such as the following:

- **Shared infrastructure plans**:
    - **Free plan**: This is the entry level plan, and as its name implies, it's available for free. It's meant for dev/test scenarios, or if you wish to deploy a website for temporary purposes, where your app would be running with other apps on the same VM with a limited CPU quota per day and no SLA guarantee. This option is suitable, as long as you don't care about your domain name.
    - **Shared plan**: This plan is also meant for dev/test scenarios, but offers a higher CPU quota than the free plan, and the ability to add a custom domain name to the app. This is the lowest cost plan.

- **Dedicated infrastructure plans**:
    - **Basic plan**: Although this plan is meant for dev/test scenarios, it can also be considered as the entry level for a small business. Also, it provides a dedicated VM with an OS (Windows/Linux) of your choice on which the apps will be run, greater hardware resources for your apps, the ability to add SSL certificates to secure your apps, and manual scaling up to three instances. Unlike the shared plans, it offers a 99.95% SLA.
    - **Standard plan**: This plan offers more resources than the previous plans. It also offers autoscaling, deployment slots, distribution of traffic using Traffic Manager, and daily backups.
    - **Premium plan**: This plan offers even more advanced hardware resources, more deployment slots than the standard plans, and more instances when it comes to scalability. There's the Premium plan and Premium V2 plan. The advantage of the Premium V2 plan is that it runs on a Dv2 series VM.
    - **Isolated infrastructure plan**: This plan offers an isolated hosting environment that is located in its own virtual networks and virtual machines. Like the Premium V2 plan, it is based on the Dv2 virtual machine series. It offers the other features available with similar level plans, but with higher specifications.

Deployment slots provide the ability to develop and test your app without affecting the production environment. Whenever you want to swap the dev/test environment with the production one, you can do it with one click, without causing any downtime. Also, if you find something wrong with the new release of your application, you can roll back by swapping to the slot that used to run the production before.

Azure App Service Environments

Generally speaking, when you deploy an App Service on an App Service plan, these apps will be deployed in a multi-tenant environment. In other words, the VMs that will host the apps will be in a shared pool, hosting other customers' apps as well.

Azure's App Service Environment will not do this. Instead, it will provide you with an isolated environment, such as that available on the isolated service plan, which needs an App Service Environment to function in a way that takes advantage of the benefits it offers.

App Service Environment provides the following benefits:

- Isolation—you will run your own app on a single tenant, so you can make it compliant with your policy standards
- Bring your own virtual network—you can use specific virtual networks for the VMs running your App Service, giving you more control over the traffic flow
- Support for scaling app instances can reach up to 100 instances at the time of writing

App Service Environment types

App Service Environment is available in a number of different types and versions.

Azure's App Service Environment has the following versions:

- **App Service Environment v1**: This version has the common benefits of App Service Environments, discussed previously
- **App Service Environment v2**: This version comes with fewer complications, as you will not have to configure frontends and workers to auto-scale your App Service plan.

Azure App Service Environment offerings are also divided along the lines of accessibility:

- **External**: This type exposes the apps on App Service Environment to allow for access via the internet by either the public IP address assigned to it, or the external domain name provided by Azure, such as `*.p.azurewebsites.net` or a custom domain name.

- **Internal**: This type exposes the apps internally on the virtual network it is built on, via an internal load balancer. If you want to expose it to the internet, you will have to add a custom domain name that will resolve to the internal load balancer, as it does not provide any external domain names, nor a public IP address.

Creating an App Service Environment

Creating an App Service Environment is not a hard process. To do it, perform the following steps:

1. Navigate to Azure portal, and search for `app service environments`, as shown in the following screenshot:

2. Click on it, and a new blade will be opened where you can view or add new App Service Environments, as shown in the following screenshot:

3. To add a new App Service Environment, click on **Add** and a new blade will be opened, where you have to specify the following:
   - **Name**: Specify the name for the app service environment
   - **Subscription**: Select the subscription that will be charged for using this service
   - **Resource group**: Specify the resource group within which the app service environment will exist as a resource.
   - **Virtual Network/Location**: When you click on it, a new blade will be opened where you have to specify the following:
     - **Virtual Network**: Either create a new one or select an existing one
     - **VIP type**: This is the accessibility type that we covered earlier; choose external or internal:

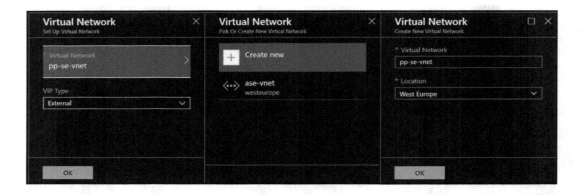

- Once you specify the previous settings, you will be asked to specify the subnet in the virtual network where the App Service Environment will exist:

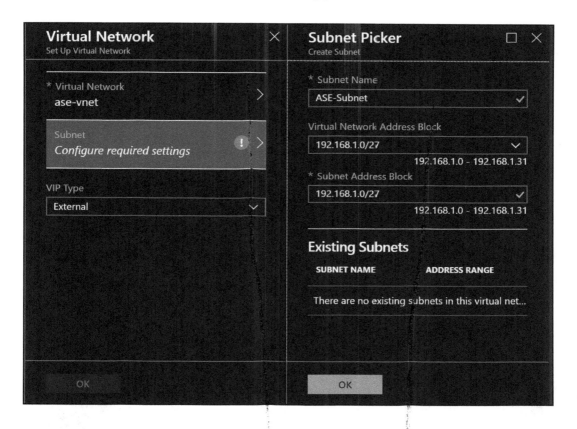

- **App Service Environment pricing details**: If you want more information about the pricing, you can click on the pricing details option, which will open a new blade displaying the App Service Environment pricing details:

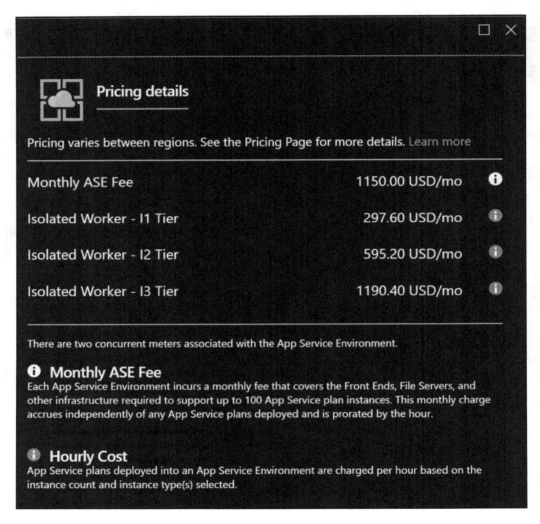

4. Once you are done with specifying the settings of the App Service Environment, you can click on **Create** to start creating App Service Environment.

- It will take a while for your App Service Environment to be created.
- The location of the virtual network you assign to the App Service Environment is the region within which the App Service Environment will operate.
- If you are going to use an existing virtual network for your App Service Environment, make sure that it has spare IPs to create a dedicated subnet for the App Service Environment. Providing an external App Service Environment with no service plans will use 12 IP addresses of the subnet, and the internal one with the same specifications will use 13 IP addresses.
- You can only have one App Service Environment per subscription.
- App Service Environment can only be used with Isolated App Service plan.
- We will be using App Service Environment for demo purposes. Delete App Service Environment once you are done with the demo, because it is a very expensive service.

Creating an App Service plan

With the information we have seen so far, you should be excited to get started and create an App Service plan. Therefore, without further ado, let's get started:

1. Navigate to the Azure portal and search for `app service plans`, as shown in the following screenshot:

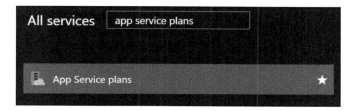

2. A new blade will be opened, where you can view/add new App Service plans, as shown in the following screenshot:

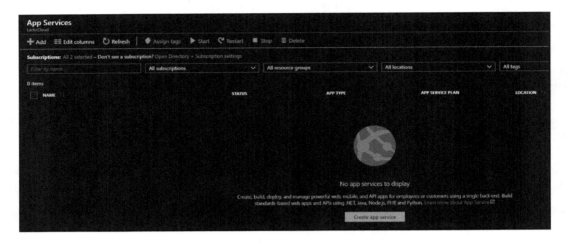

3. When you click on **Add**, a new blade will be opened where you have to specify the following:

- **App Service plan**: Specify a descriptive name for the plan
- **Subscription**: Specify the subscription that will be charged for using this service
- **Resource group**: Specify the resource group in which the app service plan will exist as a resource.
- **Operating system**: Specify whether the plan is Windows-based or Linux-based
- **Location**: Select the region where you want to deploy your app service plan

- **Pricing tier**: Specify the App Service plan that suits your needs, as shown in the following screenshot:

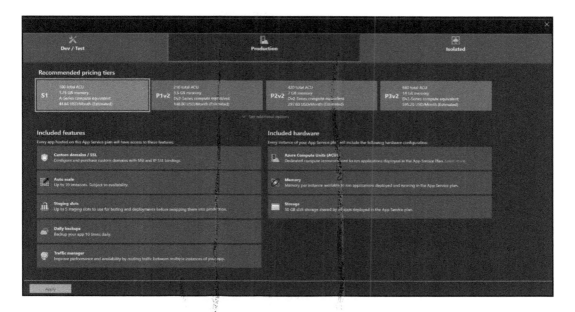

4. Once you are done with specifying the required settings, you can start the creation of the App Service plan by clicking on **Create**:

If you want to build the App Service plan within the App Service Environment, you need to select the App Service Environment as the location for the App Service plan.

Creating an App Service

Creating an App Service is a very straightforward process too. To do it, perform the following steps:

1. Navigate to the Azure portal and search for `App Services`:

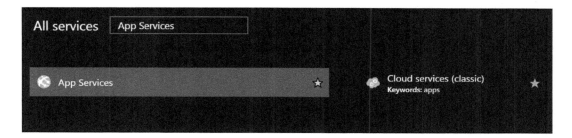

2. When you click on it, a new blade will be opened, where you can view/add App Service:

3. When you click on **Add**, a new blade will be opened, where you can select from different App Service and even some templates for HTML5, WordPress, Joomla, and much more:

4. In our case, we will select **Web App**. Once selected, you will be navigated to a new blade, which will give you an overview of Azure Web Apps:

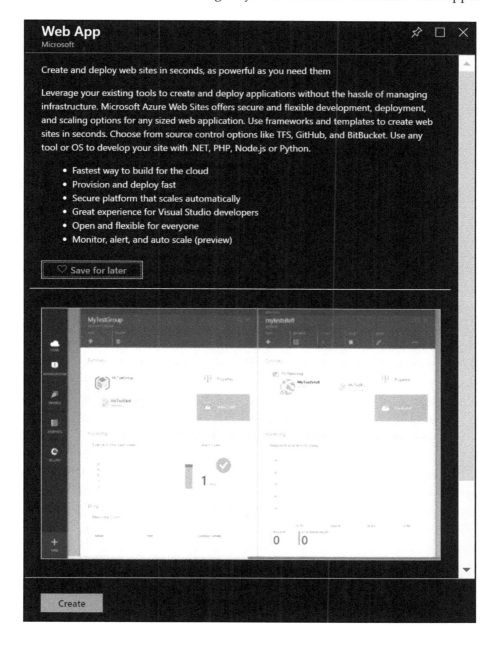

5. Next, click on **Create**, which will open a new blade where you have to specify the following:

- **App name**: Specify a name for your app
- **Subscription**: Select the subscription that will be charged for using this service
- **Resource Group**: Specify the resource group in which the app will exist as a resource
- **OS**: Linux or Windows
- **Publish**: Specify whether you want to publish code directly to the App Service, or to a container within which a Docker image will be running. If you select a container, you will be asked to configure it.
- **App Service plan/Location**: Select an existing App Service plan or create a new one.
- **Application Insights**: This solution will help you to detect and diagnose quality issues in your web apps and web services, and help you understand what your users are actually doing with them. At the time of writing, you can turn it on for Windows-based web apps that are not published via Docker images

6. Once you are done, click on **Create**.

7. Once the app is created, you can navigate to it, and in the **Overview** blade, you will note that you can **Browse, Stop, Restart**, and much more:

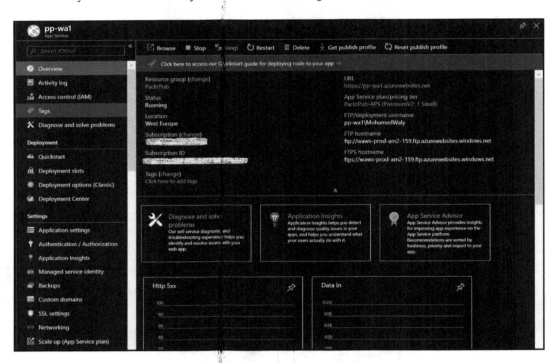

 You cannot select an OS for a web app different than the App Service plan. The App Service must operate in the same region as that of the App Service plan.

Summary

In this chapter on Azure App Service, we were introduced to some highlights of App Service plans and App Service Environments, so you can now specify the differences between them, and how and when to use each one.

Managing Azure Web Apps

In this chapter, we will continue discussing Azure Web Apps and how to work with them. The chapter will be kicked off by looking at deployment slots, which help you to have multiple environments for testing and development, while not affecting the production environment. Then, the application settings of the App Service in Azure will be covered. This is followed by a discussion of the scalability solutions offered for App Service. Finally, we will go through the backup process of the App Service.

The following topics will be covered in this chapter:

- Deployment slots
- App Service application settings
- Azure App Service scalability
- Azure App Service backup

Deployment slots

Deployment slots is one of Azure App Service greatest features. With deployment slots in place, you shouldn't be worried if your new release doesn't work appropriately when it is released to production. This is because you can have different slots for dev/test purposes and a different slot for production.

Using deployment slots, you can verify that the application is functioning properly before publishing it. Then, you can swap it with the production slot, which will cause almost no downtime. If the application does not behave as expected, you can swap it with the application that was working in production right before you swapped the slots. When you create an App Service, it's running on the default production slot.

To add an additional deployment slot, follow these steps:

1. Navigate to the App Service that you want to add another deployment slot to.

2. Under **Deployment**, click on **Deployment slots**, as shown in the following screenshot:

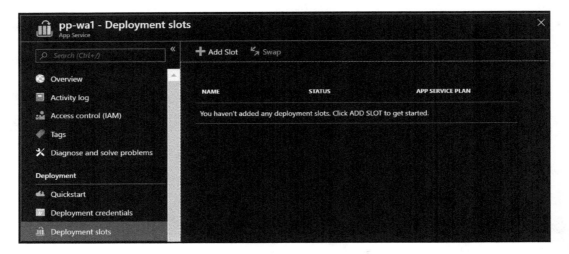

3. Click on **Add Slot**, and a new blade will pop up where you have to specify the following:
   - **Name**: Specify a descriptive name for the slot.
   - **Configuration Source**: Specify whether you want to clone the configuration from another slot or not:

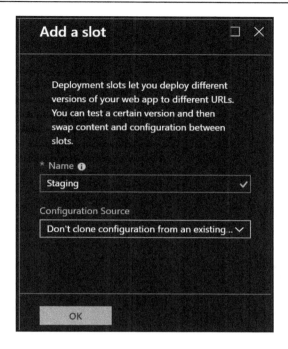

Deployment slots key points

The following key points will give you more information about deployment slots:

- If you have cloned the configuration of one of the deployment slots, you can edit these configurations later.
- When you swap a deployment slot with another, you will note that some of the settings will be swapped, while others won't:
    - The following are the settings that will be swapped:
        - Handler mappings
        - WebJobs content
        - App settings (unless they are stuck to a slot)
        - General settings, such as web sockets, framework version, and 32/64 bit
        - Connection strings (unless they are stuck to a slot)
        - Monitoring and diagnostic settings

- The following are settings that won't be swapped:
  - Custom domain names
  - Scale settings
  - SSL certificates and bindings
  - Publishing endpoints
  - WebJobs scheduler
- Before swapping, make sure that the settings that haven't been swapped are properly configured in the staging slot to avoid any failures after swapping.
- When you swap slots, the traffic will be redirected to the swapped slot and no requests will be dropped. Therefore, you will notice no downtime.

App Service application settings

Each App Service you will create in Azure will have some app settings to configure. These app settings are some configurable items that you would like to configure for the app without changing any piece of the code. The application settings of the App Service can be accessed by navigating to App Service and select the App Service you wish and click on **Application settings**.

The application settings are classified into the following categories:

- **General settings**: Here, you can specify the following:
  - **Framework**: Framework versions that the app is using, such as .NET, PHP, Java, and Python.
  - **Platform**: Specify the platform architecture that you want to run your web app on, whether it is 32 bit or 64 bit.
  - **Web sockets**: You can enable web sockets for your applications in case your web app is using socket.io or ASP.NET SignalR. In addition to that, web sockets allow for more flexible connectivity between web apps and modern browsers. Your web app would need to be built to leverage these capabilities.

- **Always On**: This setting would load your web app all the time, because by default, web apps are unloaded after they have been idle for a while. It's recommended to enable this setting if you have continuous WebJobs running on the web app.
- **Managed pipeline version**: This setting identifies the IIS application pool mode. It's recommended to use the integrated mode unless you have a legacy application that depends on IIS versions older than IIS 7; then you can select **Classic**.
- **HTTP version**: Select the HTTP version that suits your needs.
- **ARR affinity**: If you turn on this setting, it will ensure that the client is routed to the same VM when you have multiple VMs hosting your web app during the life of the session.
- **Auto swap**: This setting can be configured for any deployment slot, other than the production one. In order to configure it for a deployment slot, you have to navigate to App Service then select **Deployment slots** and then select the deployment slot you want to configure this setting for. A new blade will be opened for the deployment slots with the same configurations in the blade of the original App Service, from there you can click on **Application settings** to be able to view the app settings of the slot and configure it accordingly. Therefore, if this setting is enabled, it will automatically swap this slot with the slot that you will specify in the next step whenever an update is pushed to that slot.
- **Auto swap slot**: If the previous setting is enabled, you have to specify which slot you should swap.

- **FTP access**: Specify the way in which FTP accesses the App Service, whether by enabling it for FTP and FTPS, or FTPS only, or just disable it if you do not want to use it:

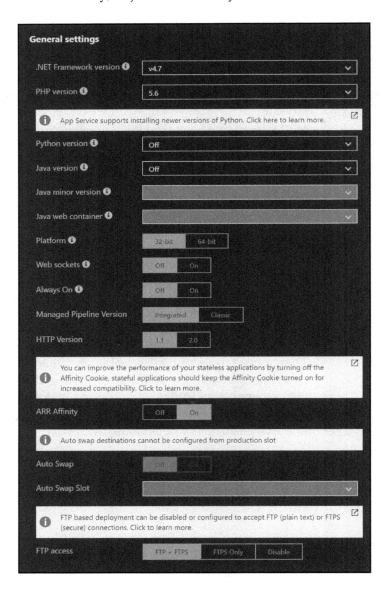

- **Debugging**: In this category, you can specify the following:
  - **Remote debugging**: You can specify whether you want to enable or disable remote debugging for this App Service. If it is enabled, the remote debugger of Visual Studio can be connected directly to the web app.
  - **Remote Visual Studio version**: Specify the version of Visual Studio you have. Only the **2015** and **2017** versions are supported at the time of writing:

- **Application settings:** In this category, you can provide some settings that you want to force your web application to load on every startup in the form of name/value pairs. For example, if you want to configure the application to be monitored by Application Insights, you can set the application setting's name and value, as shown in the following screenshot:

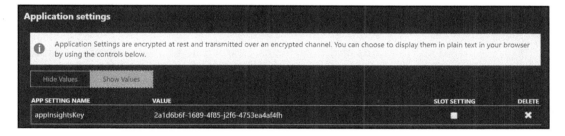

If you want to stick this setting to this slot only, you have to tick on **SLOT SETTING**.

- **Connection strings**: You can specify the connection strings between the application and the databases.
- **Default documents**: In this category, you can specify the documents that would be displayed at the home page of the web app.

- **Handler mappings**: In this category, you can add custom script processors so you can handle requests based on a specific file extension by specifying the following:
  - **Extension**: The extension of the file you want to be handled.
  - **Script processor path**: This is an absolute path to the script processor that will operate to process requests for files that corresponds to the pattern specified in the extension.
  - **Optional arguments**: This can be used to add another path to a script for the script processor. Therefore, any arguments you would like to specify when the script processor is enabled can be proceeded with.

The script processor is responsible for executing the scripts that would be stored in the **SCRIPT PROCESSOR** path.

- **Virtual applications and directories**: In this category, you can add virtual applications and directories, where you can specify the virtual directory and its physical path according to the root of the website.

For more information about the application settings, check the following article: `https://docs.microsoft.com/en-us/azure/app-service/web-sites-configure`.

Application settings key points

The following key points will give you more information about application settings:

- If you want to specify a 64-bit environment for the web app, you need to make sure that the plan is in the basic tier at the least, because it does not support the free or shared hosting plans.

- If you want to improve the performance of stateless applications, ensure that the **ARR affinity** setting is disabled, because stateless applications don't save the client data generated in a session to be used in the next one, and that might lead to some instances serving more requests than other servers. However, if it is disabled, the load balancer will be able to distribute the traffic evenly.
- If you have Traffic Manager in place to load balance the traffic, it is recommended to disable **ARR affinity**, because Traffic Manager does not support sticky sessions.
- The key/value pairs you will be providing as application settings will be encrypted when stored.
- The connection strings are encrypted when stored.

Azure App Service scalability

In this section, I'll be discussing the scalability options for Azure App Service. Using these scalability solutions will help you to have a highly available application.

There are two types of supported scalability:

- **Scaleup**: Here, you increase the size of the resources on which the web app operates. For example, memory, CPU, and disk space.
- **Scaleout**: Here, you increase the number of instances on which the apps operate. For example, if you are facing a high load over the instance on which the web app operates, another one will be created to load balance with it.

Scaling up

When you notice that your application is consuming too many of the App Service plan's resources, you can scale the App Service plan up. This gives it more resources so that it can fulfill the application's needs.

When you scale up an App Service plan, you get more hardware resources, such as CPU, memory, and storage.

You will also get more supportability for features, such as the following:

- Custom domain/SSL
- The number of instances you can auto scale to
- The number of staging slots you can have
- The number of daily backups of your applications that you can make
- Traffic Manager

To scale up the App Service plan that your application is a part of, follow these steps:

1. Navigate to the Azure portal and then to App Service. Choose the App Service you want to scale up and then select **Scale up (App Service plan)**, as shown in the following screenshot:

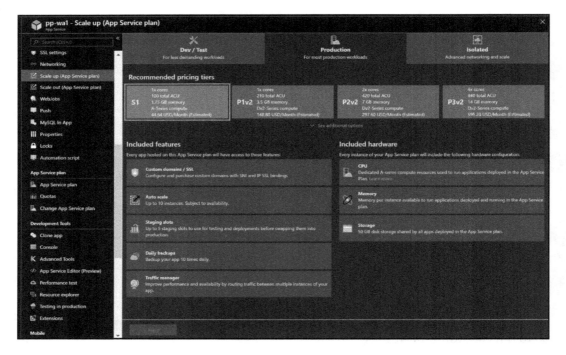

2. Then, select a plan that fits your criteria and click on **Apply**.
3. You can also scale up the App Service plan if you know which plan your application is a part of by navigating to **App Service plans**. From here, select the App Service plan you want to scale up and click **Scale up (App service Plan)**, as shown in the following screenshot:

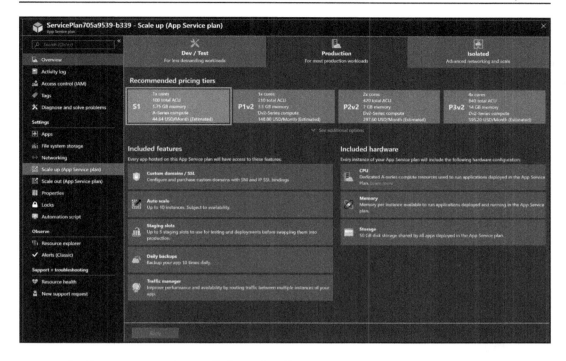

4. Once you are done, click on **Apply**.

App Service plan scaleup key points

The following key points will give you more information about the App Service plan:

- When you scale up an App Service plan, it affects all of the applications within this plan in a matter of seconds, provided that you do not have to either change anything in the code or redeploy the application.
- When you notice that the use of your apps is decreasing, you can scale it down. Otherwise, you will be still charged for the pricing tier you have scaled up to because it has reserved a VM that's running in the background.

Scaling out

Scaling out is a credible solution for applications that have usage peaks from time to time. By scaling out, you can increase the number of instances (VMs) in which the App Service are running instead of increasing the hardware resources of it. You can also enable auto scale. By doing this, when a specific threshold is triggered, the App Service plan will be scaled out to handle the load.

There are two ways to scale out your App Service plan, and we will discuss these options in the upcoming sections.

Scaling out the App Service plan manually

To scale out the App Service plan manually, you need to follow these steps:

1. Navigate to App Service. Choose the App Service you want to scale up and then click **Scale out (App Service plan)**, as shown in the following screenshot:

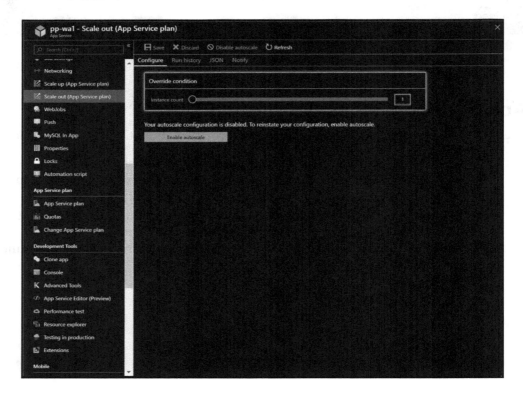

2. Then, you can increase the number of instances up to the number you want to scale out to.

3. Once you are done, click on **Save**.

 You can also do the same by navigating to **App Service plans**, selecting the App Service plan you want to scale out, and then choosing **Scale out (App Service plan)**.

Scaling out the App Service plan automatically

To scale out the App Service plan automatically, you need to follow these steps:

1. Navigate to App Service and choose the App Service you want to scale out.

2. Click on **Enable autoscale**.

3. Then, you will need to configure the autoscale settings by specifying the following:

- **Autoscale setting name**: Specify a descriptive name for the purpose of the autoscale
- **Resource group**: Specify a resource group for the autoscale setting
- **Scale conditions**: You can add scale conditions according to your needs by specifying the following:
    - **Scale mode**:
        - **Scale based on a metric**: Specify a metric based on which a scale out will be performed. For example, when CPU usage exceeds 70%, it will add one more instance.
        - **Scale to a specific instance count**: Specify the number of instances you want to scale to. If you have selected this option, you do not have to proceed with the upcoming settings.

- **Rules**: Click on **Add a rule** to create a rule that will determine how the App Service plan will scale out/in. A new blade will open where you have to specify the following:
    - **Metric source**: Specify the source for which you will specify metrics that will determine the scale out/in.
    - **Resource type**: If you have selected **Other resource** in the metric source, you will have to specify the resource type.
    - **Resource**: If you have selected a metric source other than the current resource, you will need to specify that source. For example, if you selected **Storage queue** as a metric source, you will have to specify which storage account to use as a resource.
    - **Time aggregation**: This is the aggregation method that's used to aggregate sampled metrics. For example, *time aggregation = average* will aggregate the sampled metrics by taking the average of them.
    - **Metric name**: Specify which metric you want to measure so that the rule can determine whether to scale out/in.
    - **Time grain statistic**: This is the aggregation method within the *timeGrain* period. For example, *statistic = average* and *timeGrain = PT1M* means that the metrics will be aggregated every 1 minute by taking the average.

- **Operator**: Specify the measure operator that will specify when the value of the metric has exceeded the threshold. For example, this operator will specify when the actual value of the resource is greater, lesser, equal to, and so on, compared to the threshold.
- **Threshold**: This is the threshold on which the action will be performed to specify whether the plan scales out/in.
- **Duration**: This is the duration of time required to look back for metrics. For example, 10 minutes means that every time autoscale runs, it will query metrics for the past 10 minutes. This allows the metrics to stabilize and avoids reacting to transient spikes.
- **Operation**: Specify whether to decrease or increase instances count/percentage when a threshold is exceeded.
- **Instance count**: The instance count will be increased/decreased according to the operation you specified in the previous step.

- **Cool down**: The amount of time to wait after a scale operation before scaling again. For example, if the cool-down time is 10 minutes and a scale operation has just occurred, autoscale will not attempt to scale again until after 10 minutes. This is to allow the metrics to stabilize first. The following screenshot shows the scale rule:

- **Instance limits**: There are three instance limits that need to be specified
    - **Minimum**: Specifies the minimum instance count.
    - **Maximum**: Specifies the maximum instance count.
    - **Default**: If there's a problem reading the resource metrics and the current capacity is below the default capacity, then to ensure the availability of the resource, autoscale will scale out to the default. If the current capacity is already higher than the default capacity, autoscale will not scale in.
- **Schedule**: By default, the first added rule is executed when none of the other scale conditions match. If you are adding other conditions, you can specify the start/end date or specific days for the rule:

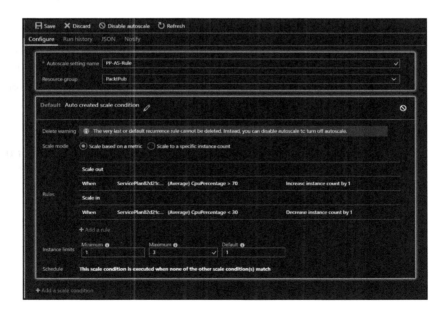

4. Once you are done, click on **Save**.

Key points for autoscaling your App Service plan

The following key points will give you more information about App Service plan autoscaling:

- You cannot assign more than one autoscale setting to one resource.
- When you have more than one instance, the threshold will be calculated according to the average of the metric across all of the instances. This is done to decide whether to scale out/in.
- If you want to investigate an autoscale operation failure, you can use the activity log.
- Make sure that you have different values for the minimum and maximum number of instances with a reasonable margin.
- If you have manually scaled out/in at the same time that you have autoscale rules, the autoscale rules will overwrite the manual scaling you have done.
- Ensure that you have scale out and scale in rules so that you can get benefits from the usage savings. For example, when the App Service plan scales out after hitting a threshold, it can be scaled in again after going below another threshold that indicates that the resource usage is quite acceptable to be scaled in.
- It is not recommended to set the scale out/in rules threshold when it goes above or below the same value. For example, do not make the threshold for the scale out when it is above 70% and scale in when it is below 70%.
- If you have added multiple rules to the same autoscale setting, it will scale out when any scaleout rule is met, but it will not scale in until all of the scale-in rules are met to maintain the performance and the availability of the apps. For example, if we have different scale in rules, such as a scale-in rule for the CPU and another one for the memory, and then one of these rules is met but the other is not. In this case, the scale in will not be triggered to maintain the performance because we have another rule that would affect the performance that not been met yet.
- When the metrics are not available, it will use the default number of instances. Therefore, make sure that you have set a reasonable number of instances so that you can get your apps up and running with no negative impact on performance.

Azure App Service backup

To avoid any unexpected scenarios regarding your apps, it is recommended that you back up your apps regularly. Therefore, in the worst-case scenario, you can retrieve your application with minimal data loss.

To configure backup for your app, follow these steps:

1. Navigate to the App Service you want to back up.
2. Under **Settings**, click on **Backup**, as shown in the following screenshot:

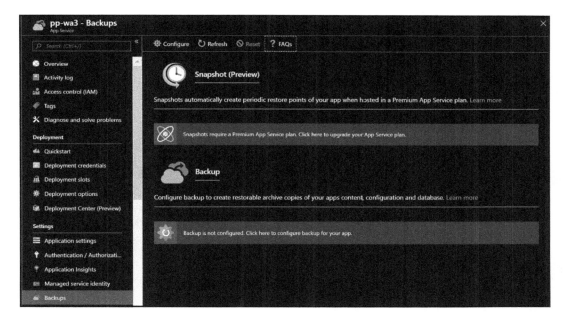

3. When you click on **Configure**, a new blade will open where you have to specify the following:
   - **Storage settings**: Specify a container in a storage account where the backup will be stored. If you do not have a storage account, you will have to create one.
   - **Backup schedule**: Specify whether you want to run the backup based on a schedule or not. If you enabled scheduling, you will have to specify the following:
     - **Backup every**: Specify the frequency of the backup either in days or hours.

- **Specify backup schedule from**: Specify when to trigger the backup schedule for the first time.
- **Retention**: Specify for how long you want to retain the backup files. You can set it to **0** to keep the backup files indefinitely.
- **Keep at least one backup**: Specify whether you want to keep at least one backup or not.

4. If you want to back up the database of the app, tick **INCLUDE IN BACKUP** to back it up too. If you have other backup policies for your databases, you do not have to include it:

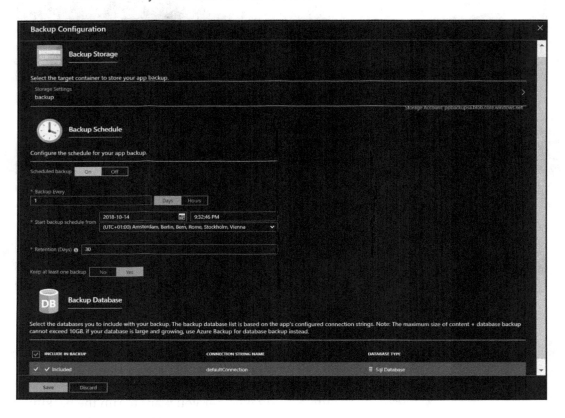

App Service backup key points

The following key points will give you more information about App Service backup:

- Ensure that the storage account in which you are going to store your backup is in the same subscription as the App Service. At the time of writing, it only supports the general-purpose storage account v1 as a storage account type.
- The backup size should not exceed 10 GB of the application and its database (if the database is backed up too). Otherwise, an error will occur.
- You cannot back up an SSL-enabled Azure MySQL database.
- Do not use firewall-enabled storage accounts to store the backup of your apps.
- If you want to back up the database of an application, but you cannot find it displayed under the **Backup Database**, ensure that its connection string has been added in the application settings.

Summary

So far, we have covered the most important parts of Azure Web apps. In this chapter, we continued the journey by covering some of the interesting solutions, such as the deployment slots, the App Service settings, scalability, and how to back up your App Service.

10
Basics of Azure SQL Database

In this chapter, we will go through one of the trendiest topics for IT professionals, developers, and DBAs: Azure SQL Database. This chapter will be kicked off by an introduction to Azure SQL Database. We'll look at why you should use this service and the difference between SQL Database in the IaaS and PaaS models. Then, we'll look at the different SQL database types available on Azure, followed by service tiers and performance levels. Finally, we will demonstrate how to create Azure SQL Database and how to connect to it.

The following topics will be covered in this chapter:

- Introduction to Azure SQL Database
- SQL Database (IaaS/PaaS)
- Azure SQL Database types
- Service tier types
- Creating Azure SQL Database
- Connecting to Azure SQL Database

Introduction to Azure SQL Database

A database is the most important component of many modern applications. Therefore, it is no surprise that we have two chapters where I will cover most of the important key points and best practices for using Azure SQL Database.

Azure SQL Database is a relational database as a service, which means it follows the **Platform as a Service (PaaS)** cloud service model, where you do not have to manage the underlying infrastructure, including networks, storage, servers, the virtualization layer, the operating system, middleware, or runtime. You only have to manage your databases and do not even have to think about patching and updating your servers.

Why Azure SQL Database?

There are lots of other reasons for using Azure SQL Database. These include the following:

- **Scalability**: Azure SQL Database can be scaled according to your needs and usage. More information about this topic will be covered later in the chapter.
- **Online scaling**: No downtime is needed to scale your database size. For example, you can start your application with a size that fits it in the beginning, and Azure SQL Database can respond to the database's requirements by scaling whenever necessary without causing any downtime.
- **Hardcore monitoring**: Azure SQL Database provides built-in monitoring and alerting tools that can be used to identify potential problems and even recommend actions to be taken in order to fix an issue. Alerts can also be generated based on the monitoring metrics, so you can receive an alert that something has gone wrong according to the monitoring baseline that the user can define according to his needs.
- **Built-in intelligence**: One of the coolest features of Azure SQL Database is built-in intelligence. It helps to reduce the costs involved in running databases and increases the performance of the application that uses Azure SQL Database as a backend.

- **Intelligent threat detection**: This feature utilizes SQL Database auditing in order to detect any harmful attempts to access data. It simply provides alerts for any abnormal behaviors.
- **High availability**: Microsoft provides many ways to ensure that Azure SQL Database is highly available:
    - **Automatic backup**: To avoid any issues that might cause data loss, automatic backups are performed on SQL Databases (these include full, differential, and transaction log backups).
    - **Point in time restores**: Azure SQL Database can be recovered to any point-in-time within the automatic backup retention period.
    - **Active geo-replication**: If you have an application that needs to be accessed from across the globe, you can use active geo-replication to avoid facing a high load on the original SQL Database. Azure geo-replication will create four secondary databases for the original database, with read access.
    - **Failover groups**: This feature is designed to help customers to recover from databases in secondary regions if a disaster occurs in the region that the original database is stored in.

This is a sneak peek of Azure SQL Database's most common features.

SQL Database (IaaS/PaaS)

An SQL Database can be implemented in Azure in two ways:

- **Using Azure SQL Database**: This follows the PaaS model, and will be covered in this chapter and the next one
- **Using Azure VMs and building SQL on them**: This follows the IaaS model, and will be covered in more detail shortly

Azure SQL Database (PaaS)

Azure SQL Database is a relational database as a service, built and hosted on Azure. It minimizes the cost of managing and provisioning databases. Using this model will reduce the responsibility for managing the virtual machines that host SQL Server, the operating system, and even the SQL Server software.

This model eliminates concerns regarding upgrades, backups, and even the high availability of databases, because they are not your responsibility anymore. Moreover, you can add databases as you wish, whenever you want. Taking this into account, you will pay less in credits because in this scenario you will not pay for a VM with SQL installed on it, plus the license credits; you will only pay for the database you are using.

Scenarios that would fit Azure SQL Database

Azure SQL Database would be a best fit for the following scenarios:

- Cloud applications that need to be developed quickly
- Building a highly-available and auto-upgradable database that is recoverable in the event of disasters
- A database with less management needed for its OS and configuration
- Building a **Software as a Service** (**SaaS**) application
- If you want complete management of your SQL installation, but no worries about hardware

SQL on Azure VMs (IaaS)

This type of deployment of SQL Server is much more complicated than using Azure SQL Database, as a VM built on Azure and SQL Server built upon it requires more administration. Also, you can use whichever versions you want to use (2008 R2, 2012, 2014, 2016, 2017, and 2019), and whichever edition you need (Developer, Express, Web, Standard, or Enterprise).

Scenarios that would suit SQL on Azure VMs

The following scenarios would be the best fit for building SQL on Azure VMs:

- Migrating existing on-premises apps to Azure with minimal changes
- Having a SQL environment that you have full access to
- Needing databases of up to 64 TB storage, since Azure SQL Database can support only up to 4 TB
- Building hybrid applications with SQL Database as a backend

Azure SQL Database types

Azure SQL Database is available in three flavors:

- Elastic database pools
- Single databases
- Managed instances

Elastic database pools

Elastic database pools are a great solution for managing multiple databases and scaling their performance according to the databases' needs, which means it is a good fit for databases with unpredictable usage demands, and this leads to a saving on credits. Elastic database pools share performance across many databases, since all of these databases are built on a single Azure SQL Database server.

Single databases

Single databases are a good fit for a set of databases with predictable performance, where the required resources for the databases are predetermined.

SQL database managed instance

This type allows you to run SQL Server with all the features of Microsoft SQL Server Enterprise in the cloud without needing to manage Windows VMs. It offers all the functionalities of Azure SQL Enterprise on Azure with the PaaS solution.

Service tier types

At the time of writing, there are two types of service tiers:

- DTU service tiers
- vCore service tiers

DTU service tiers

At the time of writing, there are three DTU service tiers for Azure SQL Database: Basic, Standard, and Premium. All of these offer support for elastic database pools and single databases only, but not the SQL database managed instance. The performance of these tiers is expressed in **Database Transaction Units** (**DTUs**) for single databases, and **elastic Database Transaction Units** (**eDTUs**) for elastic database pools.

DTUs specify the performance for single databases, as they provide a specific amount of resources to that database.

On the other hand, eDTUs do not provide a dedicated set of resources for a database, as they share resources within a specific Azure SQL Server with all the databases which run that server.

For more information about DTUs and eDTUs, you can check out the following article: https://docs.microsoft.com/en-us/azure/sql-database/sql-database-what-is-a-dtu.

To calculate your required DTUs, especially when you are migrating an on-premises SQL Server database, you can use the Azure SQL DTU calculator, which can be accessed at the following link: http://dtucalculator.azurewebsites.net/.

The following is a table from Microsoft that illustrates the different tiers' performance levels for elastic database pools:

	Basic	Standard	Premium
Maximum storage size per database	2 GB	1 TB	1 TB
Maximum storage size per pool	156 GB	4 TB	4 TB
Maximum eDTUs per database	5	3,000	4,000
Maximum eDTUs per pool	1,600	3,000	4,000
Maximum number of databases per pool	500	500	100

The following illustrates the different tiers' performance levels for single databases:

	Basic	Standard	Premium
Maximum storage size	2 GB	1 TB	4 TB
Maximum DTUs	5	3,000	4,000

 For a detailed comparison of performance levels for single and elastic database pools, you can check out the following link: `https:/ /docs.microsoft.com/en-us/azure/sql-database/sql-database- resource-limits-logical-server#single-database-storage- sizes-and-performance-levels`.

vCore service tiers

At the time of writing, there are three vCore service tiers for Azure SQL Database:

- **General purpose**: This tier provides scalable compute and storage options with IOPs up to 7,000 and 5-10 ms latency.
- **Hyperscale**: At the time of writing, this service tier is in preview, and it provides on-demand scalable storage with 200,000 IOPS and 1.2 ms latency for data and 7,000 IOPS, 5-10 ms latency for logs.

- **Business critical**: This tier is designed for high transaction rates and high resiliency with 200,000 IOPS and 1-2 ms latency. Moreover, it provides the option to have enhanced availability by spreading replicas across availability zones within one region.

For all the vCore service tiers, you can specify one of the two compute generations that are supported by Azure at present, according to your scenario:

- **Gen4**: Provides up to 24 cores and memory up to 168 GB
- **Gen5**: Provides up to 80 cores and memory up to 408 GB

Creating an Azure SQL Database

In order to create an Azure SQL Database, you need to create an Azure SQL Server first:

1. Navigate to the Azure portal, then to **All services**, and search for `SQL servers`.
2. When you open **SQL servers**, a new blade pops up, and if there are any SQL Servers that you created earlier, they will be displayed here. But since no SQL Servers have been created so far, it will be blank, as shown in the following screenshot:

3. To create a new Azure SQL Database, click on **Add**.
4. Once you have clicked on **Add,** a new blade will be opened where you have to specify the following:

- **Server name**: Specify a descriptive server name for the server, although the name you might provide will not be valid because it has been used before for another SQL Server in the `database.windows.net` domain.
- **Server admin login**: Specify the SQL Server admin username.
- **Password**: Specify a strong password for the SQL Server.
- **Subscription**: Specify the subscription that will be charged for using this service.
- **Resource group**: Specify the resource group in which this resource will exist.
- **Location**: Select the nearest location to the service for which you are creating Azure SQL Server. For example, if you are going to use it for a web app, make sure they are in the same region, or if you are going to use it as a backend of an application hosted on-premises or somewhere else, it's recommended to use the nearest region.
- **Allow Azure services to access server**: If you enable this option, you are allowing other Azure services to access this server.
- **Advanced Threat Protection**: This is a unified security package for discovering and classifying sensitive data, surfacing, mitigating potential database vulnerabilities, and detecting anomalous activities that could indicate a threat to your database. If you want to use it, you can have a trial for 60 days, and then it is 15 USD/server/month:

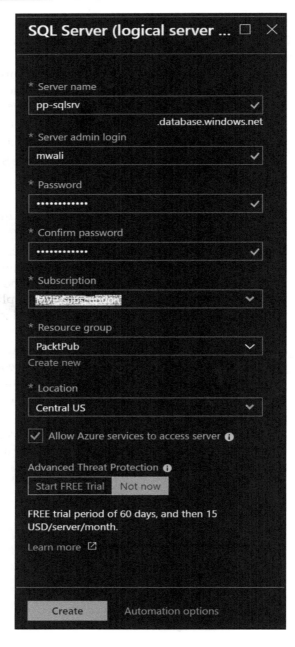

5. Once you are done, click on **Create** and the server will be created after few moments.

With SQL Server in place, you can now start to create the database by performing the following steps:

1. Navigate to the Azure portal, then to **All services**, and search for SQL database.
2. When you open **SQL databases**, a new blade pops up, and if there are any SQL Databases that you created earlier, they will be displayed here. But since no SQL Servers have been created so far, it will be blank, as shown in the following screenshot:

3. To create a new Azure SQL Database, click on **Add**.
4. A new blade will be opened where you have to specify the following:
   - **Database name**: A descriptive name for the database.
   - **Subscription**: Specify the subscription the SQL Server you have created earlier is using.
   - **Resource group**: Specify the resource group in which this database exists.

- **Select source**: You can select one of the following as a source for the database:
  - **Blank database**: An empty database where you can create your own tables.
  - **Sample (AdventureWorksLT)**: You can use this option to have a sample database provided by Azure. If selected, it loads the **AdventureWorks** schema and data into your new database.
  - **Backup**: If you want to restore a previously backed-up Azure SQL Database to be used in this case.
- **Server**: Specify the SQL Server you want to build the database into. You can either select an existing one, such as the one we have just created, or create a new one, as shown in the following screenshot:

- **Want to use SQL elastic pools**: If you select **Not now**, it means this database will be a single database.

- **Pricing tier**: Choose a SQL service tier and performance level that best fits your application needs. There are two purchasing models:

  - **DTU-base model**: This consists of the DTU service tiers we discussed earlier (Basic, Standard, and Premium), where you can specify the DTUs and the size that can be used by the database:

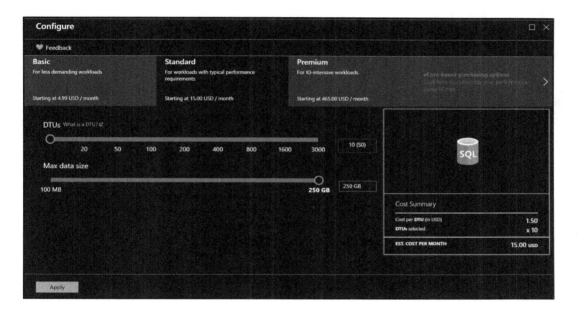

- **vCore-based model**: This is a more customizable model, where you can select compute and storage resources. Moreover, you can make use of Azure Hybrid Benefit for SQL Server to save costs:

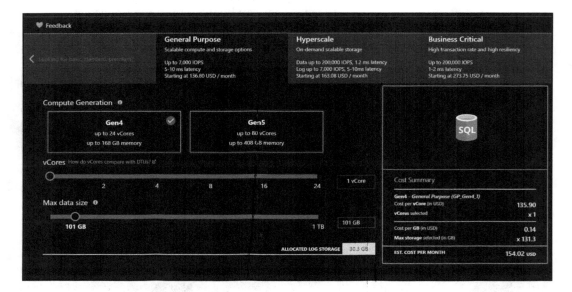

- **Collation**: Database collation defines the rules that sort and compare data, and cannot be changed after database creation. The default database collation is SQL_Latin1_General_CP1_CI_AS

5. Once you are ready, click on **Create**:

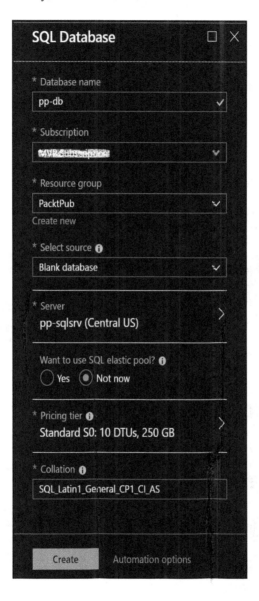

Connecting to Azure SQL Database

As mentioned earlier, when you create an Azure Database via the Azure portal, all Azure services will be allowed to access this database with no further configuration.

However, when you want to connect to the database from anywhere else, there is some configuration that needs to be done.

Server-level firewall

To allow access to Azure SQL Database from somewhere else, you will have to set a server-level firewall rule, as described in the following steps:

1. Navigate to the SQL Server and select **Firewalls and virtual networks**, as shown in the following screenshot:

2. Then, you can specify the range of IP addresses you would like to allow access for, but if you want to specify a single IP address, you can add it as **START IP** and **END IP**. In this scenario, we will click on **Add client IP,** which will detect your own public IP address and add it, as shown in the following screenshot:

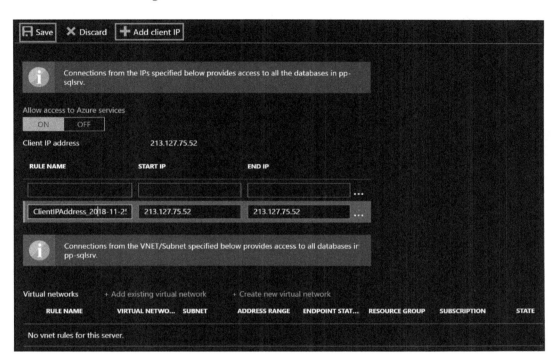

3. Once you are done, click on **Save**.
4. You can do the same thing on the level of the database by navigating to the database and clicking on **Set server firewall**, as shown in the following screenshot:

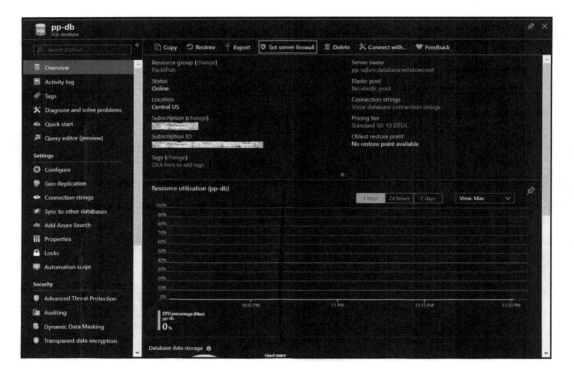

 Make sure that port 1433 is open in your environment, which is used for communication between the SQL Server and the client (**SQL Server Management Studio (SSMS)**).

Connecting to Azure SQL Database using SQL SSMS

To connect to the created database via SSMS, you can follow these steps:

1. Navigate to the database blade and copy **Server name** from the overview page.

2. Open SSMS, paste the name of the server, change the **Authentication** to **SQL Server Authentication**, and enter the SQL Server credentials that you entered during SQL Server creation, as shown in the following screenshot:

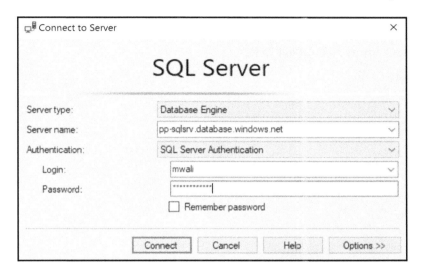

3. Once you click on **Connect**, you will be connected to your database on Azure, as shown in the following screenshot:

Summary

So far, we have gone through the basics of Azure SQL Database by understanding what it is, its types, and why we would use it.

Then, a creation for Azure SQL Database has been demonstrated with a guide about how to do it and how to connect to it.

11
Managing Azure SQL Database

In this chapter, you will continue to learn about Azure SQL Database. We will cover how to work with Azure SQL elastic database pools, how to set Active Directory authentication in Azure SQL Database, the business continuity for Azure SQL Database, and how to work with an Azure SQL Managed Instance.

The following topics will be covered in this chapter:

- Azure SQL elastic database pools
- Azure AD authentication
- Azure SQL Database business continuity
- Azure SQL Managed Instances

Azure SQL elastic database pools

In the previous chapter, we gave you a sneak peek at elastic database pools. In this section, you will learn more about them, and you will work on creating and managing them.

Benefits of using elastic database pools

An elastic database pool can help you to achieve the following:

- Simplify performance management for multiple databases, especially when usage patterns are unpredictable
- Reduce the cost of multiple databases and provide a convenient way to control the budget

- Perfect choice for **Software as a service** (**SaaS**) apps that provision a single database per tenant, to get isolation benefits

 It's not recommended to use elastic database pools for mission critical applications that require specific consumption and can be degraded by other databases running in the same pool.

Creating an elastic database pool

To get your elastic database pool up and running, follow these steps:

1. Navigate to the **SQL servers** blade and click on **New pool**, as shown in the following screenshot:

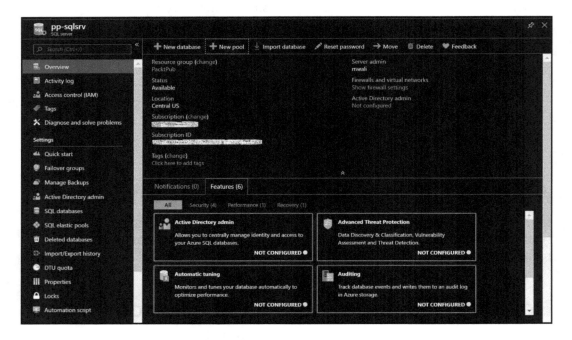

2. A new blade will open, and you will have to specify the following:
   - **Name**: Specify a descriptive name for the pool.
   - **Configure pool**: Specify a service tier:

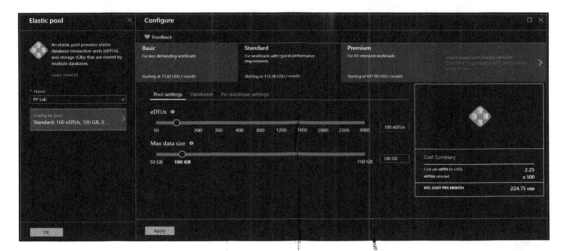

3. When you have finished, click on **OK**.

4. To view and manage the pool after its creation, navigate to **SQL elastic pools**, in the same blade of the SQL Server that you are creating the pool in:

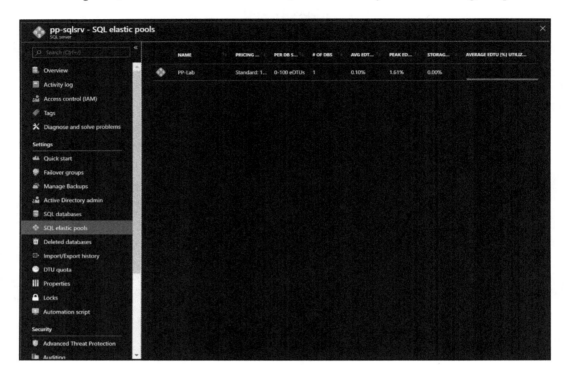

Adding a database to an elastic pool

Once your elastic database pool is up and running, you can add databases to it; to do so, follow these steps:

1. Navigate to the SQL Server in which you created the pool.
2. Then, go to **SQL elastic pools** and click on the pool that you want to add databases to.

3. A new blade will open. In the **Overview** blade, click on **Create database**, as shown in the following screenshot:

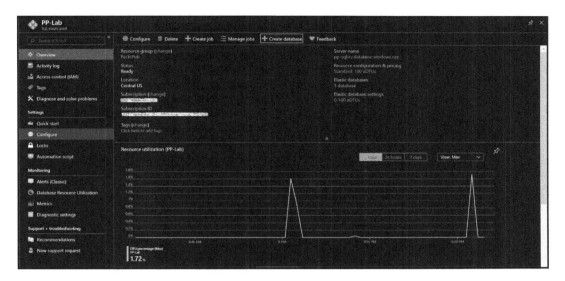

4. A new blade will open, where you will have to specify the following:
   - **Database name**: Provide a name for the database.
   - **Select source**: The source for the database.

- **Collation**: Database collation defines the rules that sort and compare data, and cannot be changed after database creation. The default database collation is `SQL_Latin1_General_CP1_CI_AS`:

5. When you are done, click on **OK**, and a new database will be created and added to the pool.

Setting Azure Active Directory authentication

So far, we have been using SQL authentication to connect to Azure SQL Database, as we did in the previous chapter, via SQL Server Management Studio. Using Azure **Active Directory** (**AD**) will provide centralized administration for database users' identities, providing the following benefits:

- Another method of SQL Server authentication
- Controlling the password change for a centralized location
- Assigning user permissions on the database level
- Support of token-based authentication for the applications that connect to the database
- Protection of user profiles across the database servers
- Avoidance of the need to store passwords, as you will be able to use different methods of authentication, which we will cover shortly

In the next chapter, Azure Active Directory will be covered in more detail.

To enable Azure AD authentication for Azure SQL Database, follow these steps:

1. Navigate to the Azure SQL Server that you want to enable this feature for.

2. Under **Settings**, click on **Active Directory admin**, as shown in the following screenshot:

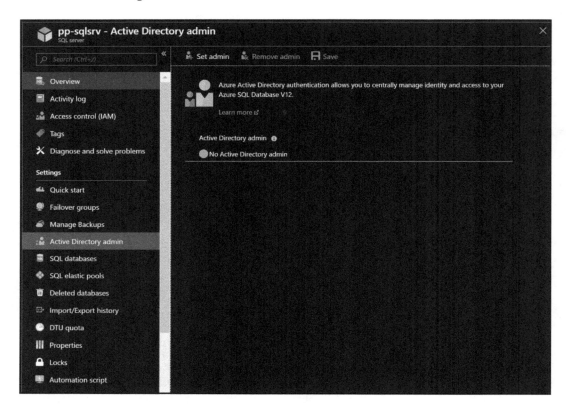

3. Click on **Set admin**, and a new blade will open, in which you can choose
   the AD user that you want to grant access to that SQL Server, as shown in
   the following screenshot:

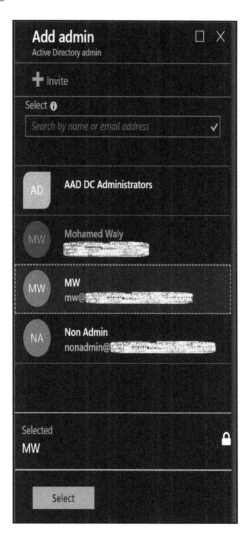

4. Once you are done, click on **Save**:

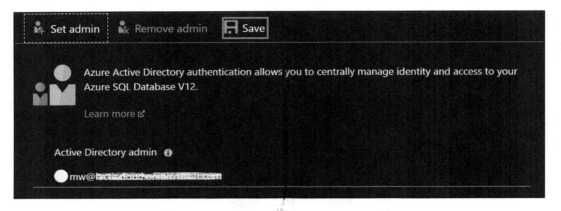

5. If you want to connect to Azure SQL Database using your Azure AD user, you can select one of the following authentication methods:

- **Active Directory - Universal with MFA support**: You can use this option if MFA is enabled for the AD user that you will be logging in with.
- **Active Directory - Password**: With this option, you can set the AD user and password manually, in the SSMS.
- **Active Directory - Integrated**: This option should be used if you are logged into the machine using your Azure AD user, and you will not have to enter the username and password to log in, as the credentials that you used to log into the machine will be considered.

The following screenshot depicts the **Active Directory – Password** option:

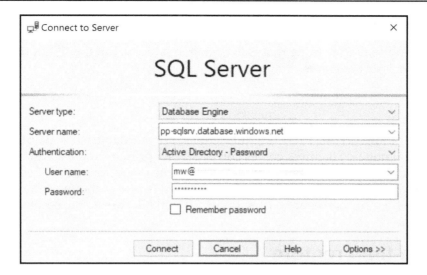

 If you have an SQL Server running on an Azure VM, you cannot do it using an Azure AD account, but the domain AD account is supported.

Azure SQL Database business continuity

You now have your database up and running in the cloud, and you can even connect to it, and create, delete, and update the tables as you wish.

In this section, you will learn how to build a highly available and business continuity database.

How business continuity works in Azure SQL Database

Microsoft does its best to address any issues that may occur in Azure SQL Database, and it provides solutions to the following issues.

Hardware failure

Hardware failure is something that is expected to happen, but it will not be the reason that you lose your databases.

Just as replication is provided for storage, there is a similar safeguard for Azure SQL Databases.

If hardware failure occurs, there are three copies of your database, separated across three physical nodes. The three copies consist of one primary replica and two secondary replicas, and, to avoid any data loss, write operations are not committed in the primary replica until they have been committed to one of the secondary replicas. Therefore, whenever hardware failure occurs, it will fail over to the secondary replica.

Point-in-time restore

To avoid any issues that might cause data loss, automatic backups are performed on SQL databases (these include full, differential, and transaction log backups).

Azure SQL Database can be recovered to any point in time, within the automatic backup retention period.

The retention period varies from one tier to another: seven days for the Basic tier, 35 days for the Standard tier, and 35 days for the Premium tier. This solution would suit a scenario in which your database has been corrupted and you want to restore it to the last healthy point.

To restore your database to the last healthy point, you have to follow these steps:

1. Navigate to the database that you want to restore to the last healthy point, and click on **Restore**, as shown in the following screenshot:

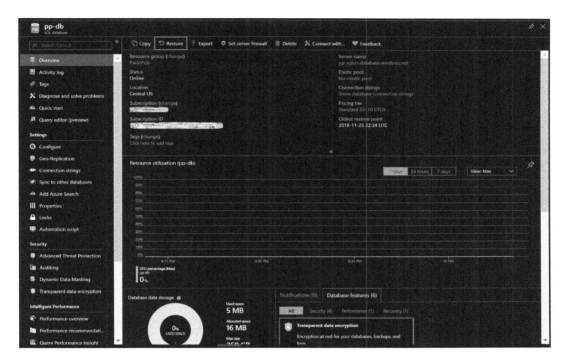

2. Once you have clicked on **Restore**, a new blade will pop up, where you can provide the restored database with a new database name, determine the time that you want to restore to, and change the pricing tier for the restored database, as shown in the following screenshot:

3. When you click on **OK**, the database will start to be restored.

Point-in-time restoration key points

The following key points provide more information about point-in-time restoration:

- When you restore a database, a new database is created, which means that you will have to pay for the new database, too.
- You cannot provide the new database with the same name as the original database, because the original still exists; to do so, you would have to remove the original one.
- You can choose a restoration point between the earliest point and the latest backup time, which is six minutes before the current time.
- The database recovery time varies from one database to another, according to many factors; some of them are as follows:
  - The database's size
  - The number of transaction logs involved in the operations
  - The database's performance level
  - If you are restoring the database from a different region, the network bandwidth might cause a delay

Restoring a deleted database

You can accidentally remove a database, or you might remove a database and figure out that you still need it later on. This can be a tough situation. However, Microsoft Azure supports database recovery, even in the case of deletion. (The SQL Server on which the database was built cannot have been deleted; at the time of writing this book, there was no support for the recovery of deleted SQL Servers.)

To restore a deleted database, follow these steps:

1. Navigate to SQL Servers and select the server in which the deleted database was built.
2. Scroll down to **Deleted databases** in the **SQL server** blade, as shown in the following screenshot:

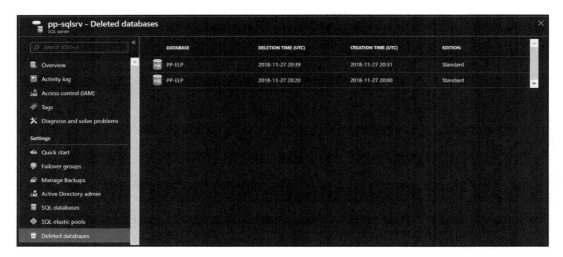

3. Select the database that you want to restore, and name it as you wish, considering that you cannot provide the name of an existing database that is already running on the same SQL Server (but you can give it its old name), as shown in the following screenshot:

4. Once you are done, click on **OK**, and it will start the restoration process.

Active geo-replication

Active geo-replication is one of the most important business continuity methodologies.

When using active geo-replication, you can configure up to four secondary databases within the same region, or in different regions with reading access. This will help to reduce latency for users or applications that need to query the database from different regions.

If a catastrophic disaster occurs, you can fail over to the other region by using a failover group. Failover groups are mainly designed to manage every aspect of geo-replication automatically, such as connectivity, relationships, and failover. Provided it is available for all databases in respective service tiers in all the regions.

To implement active geo-replication, follow these steps:

1. Navigate to the desired database in the Azure portal and click on **Geo-Replication**, under **Settings**, as shown in the following screenshot:

2. Click on the region that you want to replicate to, as shown in the following screenshot:

3. Once the region has been selected, a new blade will pop up, asking you to configure the secondary server for which the database will be replicated; you will have to specify the following:

- **Target server**: If you have not created another Azure SQL Server in that region to act as a secondary server, you can click on **Target server** and go through the wizard for creating a new SQL Server (or select an existing one, if you have already created it).
- **Pricing tier**: Select a pricing tier that is not lower that the original one.

4. Once you are done, click on **OK**.

Auto-failover groups

Auto-failover groups make good use of active geo-replication by providing group-level replication and automatic failover. Moreover, you will not have to change the SQL connection string if a failover occurs. To create an auto-failover group, follow these steps:

1. Navigate to the SQL Server in which the databases exist.
2. Under **Settings**, click on **Failover groups**, as shown in the following screenshot:

3. Click on **Add group** to add an auto-failover group.
4. A new blade will pop up, where you will have to specify the following:
   - **Failover group name**: Specify a descriptive name for the failover group.
   - **Secondary server**: Specify the secondary server that will host the replicated database.

- **Read/Write failover policy**: You can let this process be done automatically, which is the default, and is recommended. Otherwise, you will have to do it manually.
- **Read/Write grace period (hours)**: Specify the time between every automatic failover.
- **Database within the group**: Select the databases in that Azure SQL Server that you would like to add to the auto-failover group:

5. Once you are done, click on **Create**.

Azure SQL Managed Instances

In the previous chapter, Azure SQL Managed Instances were introduced as one of the Azure SQL Database types. In this section, we will provide more information on them.

Azure SQL Managed Instances offer the full functionalities of SQL Server Enterprise. If you need some features that were not available in the previous types that we discussed (such as SQL Agent or linked servers), this type will fulfill your needs.

Azure SQL Managed Instances can be better than the other Azure SQL Database types, for the following reasons:

- **SQL Server Enterprise edition features support**: All of the features that you used to work with an SQL Server on-premises can be used with this type.
- **Dedicated instance**: Unlike with the other types of Azure SQL Databases, you will not be sharing the server on which you run your database with others.
- **Backward compatibility**: If you have legacy versions of SQL Servers on-premises, you can migrate the databases to Azure SQL Managed Instances with no problems. Notice that you cannot migrate versions earlier than SQL Server 2005.

Azure SQL Managed Instance types

The following are the two types of Azure SQL Managed Instance:

- **General purpose**: This type is meant for applications with no high tech requirements for performance and I/O latency
- **Business critical**: This type is meant for applications that need high Input/Output Operations Per Second and high stability during the maintenance of the instance

Creating an Azure SQL Managed Instance

Creating an Azure SQL Managed Instance is a straightforward process; all you need to do is follow these steps:

1. Navigate to **All services** and search for `SQL managed instance`; fill in the following fields:

2. Click on it, and a new blade will open; click on **Add**, and a new blade will open, where you have to specify the following:

   - **Subscription**: Specify the subscription that will be charged for using this service
   - **Managed instance name**: Specify a descriptive name for the managed instance
   - **Managed instance admin login**: Specify the admin of the managed instance
   - **Password**: Specify a strong password for the managed instance
   - **Location**: Select the nearest region to the service/application that will work with the managed instance.
   - **Virtual network**: You have two options, as follows:
     - **Create a new virtual network**: This option will create a new virtual network, compliant with the rules required for the SQL Managed Instance.
     - Select one of the virtual networks/subnets that you already have.
   - **Resource group**: Select the resource group in which it will exist as a resource.
   - **Pricing tier**: Select one of the types that were covered in the previous section, in order to fulfill the needs of your applications. You also need to set the number of vCores and the storage size that you need. It supports two compute generations, as follows:
     - **Gen 4**: Based on Intel E5-2673 v3 (Haswell) 2.4 GHz processors, this generation supports 8/16/24 vCores and storage ranging from 32 GB to 8 TB.
     - **Gen 5**: Based on Intel E5-2673 v4 (Broadwell) 2.3 GHz processors, this generation supports 8/16/24/32/40/64/80 vCores and storage ranging from 32 GB to 4 TB.

3. Once you are done, click on **Create**:

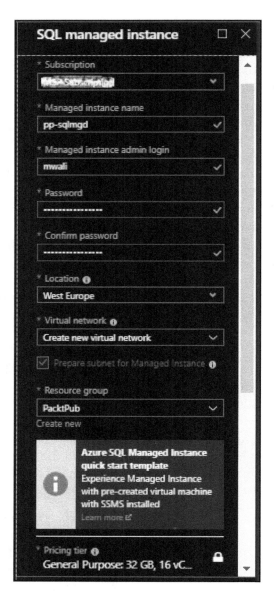

Connecting to an Azure SQL Managed Instance

Connecting to the SQL Managed Instance can be done by using SQL Server Management Studio, but only under the following conditions:

- You are trying to connect to the server from an Azure VM that exists in the same VNet as the SQL Managed Instance.
- You are connecting from an Azure VM that does not share the same VNet as the Managed Instance; you need to make sure that it has network connectivity to the VNet where the Managed Instance exists (via a VNet peering, for example).
- You can connect from on-premises, but with a network connection in place between your on-premises and Azure, via one of the following options:
  - Point-to-site VPN connection
  - Site-to-site VPN connection
  - Express route

When you have achieved one of the preceding conditions, you can run SSMS and connect to the Managed Instance in the same way that you did in the previous chapter.

Azure SQL Managed Instance key points

The following key points will provide more insight into Azure SQL Managed Instances:

- If you are planning to use a precreated subnet for the SQL Managed Instance when you create it, ensure that the following conditions are met:
  - It is not a gateway subnet
  - There are not any service endpoints enabled for it
  - The subnet is not used by any other service
  - At least 16 IP addresses are available in the subnet

- **Prepare subnet for managed instance** is an option during the SQL Managed Instance creation, and it will handle the following:
    - It will create a user-defined table for the subnet `0.0.0.0/0` next-hop internet
    - A network security group will be created with some security rules, to be compliant with the Managed Instance deployment requirements
- When you increase the storage size in the **Pricing tier** blade, the custom amount to the nearest value divided by 32 would be rounded.
- You can make use of the hybrid use benefit and reuse an SQL Server license, saving up to 55% off the Managed Instance costs.

 You can configure a VNet for Azure SQL Database Managed Instance at `https://docs.microsoft.com/en-us/azure/sql-database/sql-database-managed-instance-vnet-configuration`.

Summary

By now, most of the important topics about Azure SQL Database have been covered. In this chapter, we covered more information about Azure SQL elastic database pools and Azure SQL Managed Instance. In addition, we discussed enabling AD authentication, which will help you to have well-managed, secure authentication to databases. We also discussed some solutions that will allow for business continuity.

Microservices 2013; Getting to Know the Buzzword

12

The world of information technology today is witnessing a revolution influenced by cloud computing. Agile, inexpensive, scalable infrastructure which is completely self-serviced and pay-per-use has a critical part to play in optimizing the operational efficiency and time-to-market for software applications enabling all major industries. With the changing nature of underlying hardware and operational strategies, many companies find it challenging to meet competitive business requirements of delivering applications or application features which are highly scalable, highly available, and continuously evolving by nature.

The agility of this change has also compelled solution architects and software developers to constantly rethink their approach of architecting a software solution. Often, a new architecture model is inspired by learnings from the past. Microservices-driven architecture is one such example which is inspired by **Service-Oriented Architecture (SOA)**. The idea behind Microservices-based architecture is heavily based on componentization, abstraction, and object-oriented design, which is not new to a software engineer.

In a traditional application, this factorization is achieved by using classes and interfaces defined in shared libraries accessed across multiple tiers of the application. The cloud revolution encourages developers to distribute their application logic across services to better cater to changing business demands such as faster delivery of capabilities, increased reach to customers across geographies, and improved resource utilization.

What are Microservices?

In simple words, a Microservice can be defined as an autonomous software service which is built to perform a single, specific, and granular task.

The word *autonomous* in the preceding definition stands for the ability of the Microservice to execute within isolated process boundaries. Every Microservice is a separate entity which can be developed, deployed, instantiated, scaled, and managed discretely.

The language, framework, or platform used for developing a Microservice should not impact its invocation. This is achieved by defining communication contracts which adhere to industry standards. Commonly, Microservices are invoked using network calls over popular internet protocols such as REST.

On cloud platforms, Microservices are usually deployed on a **Platform as a Service** (**PaaS**) or **Infrastructure as a Service** (**IaaS**) stack. It is recommended to employ a management software to regulate the lifecycle of Microservices on a cloud stack. This is especially desirable in solutions which require high density deployment, automatic failover, predictive healing, and rolling updates. Microsoft Azure Service Fabric is a good example of a distributed cluster management software which can be used for this purpose. More about this is covered in later sections of this book.

Microservices are also highly decoupled by nature and follow the principle of minimum knowledge. The details about the implementation of the service and the business logic used to achieve the task are abstracted from the consuming application. This property of the service enables it to be independently updated without impacting dependent applications or services. Decoupling also empowers distributed development as separate teams can focus on delivering separate Microservices simultaneously with minimal interdependency.

It is critical for a Microservice to focus on the task it is responsible for. This property is popularly known as the **Single Responsibility Principle** (**SRP**) in software engineering. This task ideally should be elementary by nature. Defining the term *elementary* is a key challenge involved in designing a Microservice. There is more than one way of doing this:

- Restricting the cyclomatic complexity of the code module defining the Microservice is one way of achieving this. Cyclomatic complexity indicates the complexity of a code block by measuring the linear independent paths of execution within it.
- Logical isolation of functionality based on the bounded context that the Microservice is a part of.

- Another simpler way is to estimate the duration of delivering a Microservice.

Irrespective of the approach, it is also important to set both minimum and maximum complexity for Microservices before designing them. Services which are too small, also known as **Nanoservices**, can also introduce crucial performance and maintenance hurdles.

Microservices can be developed using any programming language or framework driven by the skills of the development team and the capability of the tools. Developers can choose a performance-driven programming language such as C or C++ or pick a modern managed programming language such as C# or Java. Cloud hosting providers such as Azure and Amazon offer native support for most of the popular tools and frameworks for developing Microservices.

A Microservice typically has three building blocks – **code**, **state**, and **configuration**. The ability to independently deploy, scale, and upgrade them is critical for the scalability and maintainability of the system. This can be a challenging problem to solve. The choice of technology used to host each of these blocks will play an important role in addressing this complexity. For instance, if the code is developed using .NET Web API and the state is externalized on an Azure SQL Database, the scripts used for upgrading or scaling will have to handle compute, storage, and network capabilities on both these platforms simultaneously. Modern Microservice platforms such as Azure Service Fabric offer solutions by co-locating state and code for the ease of management, which simplifies this problem to a great extent.

Co-location, or having code and state exist together, for a Microservice has many advantages. Support for versioning is one of them. In a typical enterprise environment, it's a common requirement to have side-by-side deployments of services serving in parallel. Every upgrade to a service is usually treated as a different version which can be deployed and managed separately. Co-locating code and state helps build a clear logical and physical separation across multiple versions of Microservices. This will simplify the tasks around managing and troubleshooting services.

A Microservice is always associated with a unique address. In the case of a web-hosted Microservice, this address is usually a URL. This unique address is required for discovering and invoking a Microservice. The discoverability of a Microservice must be independent of the infrastructure hosting it. This calls for a requirement of a service registry which keeps track of where each service is hosted and how it can be reached. Modern registry services also capture health information of Microservices, acting like a circuit breaker for the consuming applications.

Microservices natively demands hyperscale deployments. In simpler words, Microservices should scale to handle increasing demands. This involves seamless provisioning of compute, storage, and network infrastructure. It also involves challenges around lifecycle management and cluster management. A Microservices hosting platform typically has the features to address these challenges.

Microservices hosting platform

The primary objective of a Microservices hosting platform is to simplify the tasks around developing, deploying, and maintaining Microservices while optimizing the infrastructure resource consumption. Together, these tasks can be called *Microservice lifecycle management tasks*.

The journey starts with the hosting platform supporting development of the Microservices by providing means for integrating with platform features and application framework. This is critical to enable the hosting platform to manage the lifecycle of a service hosted on it. Integration is usually achieved by the hosting platform exposing APIs (application programming interfaces) which can be consumed by the development team. These APIs are generally compatible with popular programming languages.

Co-locating code and state is desirable for improving the efficiency of a Microservice. While this is true, storing state locally introduces challenges around maintaining the integrity of data across multiple instances of a service. Hosting platforms such as Service Fabric come with rich features for maintaining consistency of state across multiple instances of a Microservice there by abstracting the complexity of synchronizing state from the developer.

The hosting platform is also responsible for abstracting the complexity around physical deployment of Microservices from the development team. One way this is achieved is by containerizing the deployment. Containers are operating system-level virtualized environments. This means that the kernel of the operating system is shared across multiple isolated virtual environments. Container-based deployment makes possible an order-of-magnitude increase in density of the Microservice deployed. This is aligned with the recommended cloud design pattern called **compute resource consolidation**. A good example to discuss in this context, as mentioned by Mark Fussell from Microsoft, is the deployment model for Azure SQL Databases hosted on Azure Service Fabric. A SQL Azure Database cluster comprises hundreds of machines running tens of thousands of containers hosting a total of hundreds of thousands of databases.

Each of these containers hosts code and state associated with multiple Microservices. This is an inspiring example of how a good hosting platform can handle hyperscale deployment of Microservices.

A good hosting platform will also support deployment of services across heterogeneous hardware configurations and operating systems. This is significant for meeting demands of services which have specific requirements around high-performance hardware. An example would be a service which performs **GPU** (**graphics processing unit**) intensive tasks.

Once the Microservices are deployed, management overhead should be delegated to the hosting platform. This includes reliability management, health monitoring, managing updates, and so on. The hosting platform is responsible for the placement of a Microservice on a cluster of virtual machines. The placement is driven by a highly optimized algorithm which considers multiple constraints at runtime to efficiently pick the right host virtual machine for a Microservice.

The following diagram illustrates a sample placement strategy of Microservices in a cluster:

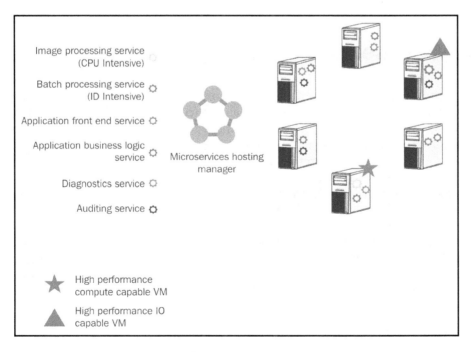

Microservice placement strategy

As the number of Microservices grows, so does the demand for automating monitoring, and diagnostics systems which takes care of the health of these services. The hosting platform is responsible for capturing the monitoring information from every Microservice and then aggregating it and storing it in a centralized health store. The health information is then exposed to the consumers and also ingested by the hosting platform itself, to take corrective measures. Modern hosting platforms support features such as preventive healing, which uses machine learning to predict future failures of a virtual machine and take preventive actions to avoid service outages. This information is also used by the failover manager subsystem of the hosting platform to identify failure of a virtual machine and to automatically reconfigure the service replicas to maintain availability. The failover manager also ensures that when nodes are added or removed from the cluster, the load is automatically redistributed across the available nodes. This is a critical feature of a hosting platform considering the nature of the cloud resources to fail, as they are running on commodity hardware.

Considering the fact that migrating to a Microservices architecture can be a significant change in terms of the programming paradigm, deployment model, and operational strategy, a question which usually rises is *why adopt a Microservice architecture?*

The Microservice advantage

Every application has a shelf life, after which it is either upgraded or replaced with another application with evolved capabilities or which is a better fit for changing business needs. The agility in businesses has reduced this shelf life further by a significant factor. For instance, if you are building an application for distributing news feeds among employees within a company, you would want to build quicker prototypes and get feedback on the application sooner than executing an elaborate design and plan phase. This, of course, will be with the cognizance that the application can be further optimized and revised iteratively. This technique also comes in handy when you are building a consumer application where you are unsure of the scale of growth in the user base. An application such as Facebook, which grew its user base from a couple of million to 1,500 million in a few years would have been impossible to plan for, if the architecture was not well architected to accommodate future needs. In short, modern-day applications demand architectural patterns which can adapt, scale and gracefully handle changes in workload.

To understand the benefits of Microservices architecture for such systems, we will require a brief peek at its predecessor, monolithic architecture. The term monolith stands for a single large structure. A typical client-server application for the previous era would use a tiered architecture. Tiers would be decoupled from one another and would use contracts to communicate with each other. Within a tier, components or services would be packed with high cohesion, making them interdependent on each other.

The following diagram illustrates a typical monolithic application architecture:

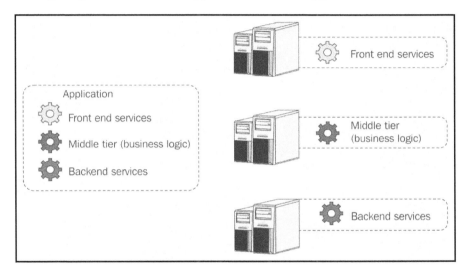

Monolithic application deployment topology

This works fine in simpler systems which are aimed to solve a static problem catering to a constant user base. The downside is that the components within a tier cannot scale independently, neither can they be upgraded or deployed separately. The tight coupling also prevents the components from being reused across tiers. These limitations introduce major roadblocks when a solution is expected to be agile by nature.

Microservices architecture addresses these problems by decomposing tightly coupled monolithic ties to smaller services. Every Microservice can be developed, tested, deployed, reused, scaled, and managed independently. Each of these services will align to a single business functionality. The development team authoring a service can work independently with the customer to elicit business requirements and build the service with the technology best suited to the implementation of that particular business scenario. This means that there are no overarching constraints around the choice of technology to be used or implementation patterns to be followed. This is perfect for an agile environment where the focus is more on delivering the business value over long-term architectural benefits. A typical set of enterprise applications may also share Microservices between them. The following diagram illustrates the architecture of such a Microservices-driven solution:

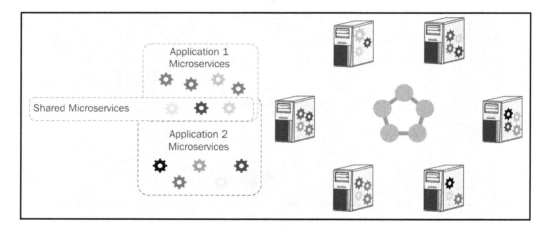

Microservice application deployment topology

The following are a few key advantages of a Microservice architecture:

Fault tolerance

As the system is decomposed to granular services, failure of a service will not impact other parts of the system. This is important for a large, business-critical application. For instance, if a service logging events of the system fails, it will not impact the functioning of the whole system.

The decomposed nature of the services also helps fault isolation and troubleshooting. With proper health monitoring systems in place, a failure of a Microservice can be easily identified and rectified without causing downtime to the rest of the application. This also applies to application upgrades. If a newer version of a service is not stable, it can be rolled back to an older version with minimal impact to the overall system. Advanced Microservice hosting platforms such as Service Fabric also come with features such as predictive healing, which uses machine learning to foresee failures and takes preventive measures to avoid service downtime.

Technology-agnostic

In today's world, when the technology is changing fast, eliminating long-term commitment to a single technology stack is a significant advantage. Every Microservice can be built on a separate technology stack and can be redesigned, replaced, or upgraded independently as they execute in isolation. This means that every Microservice can be built using a different programming language and use a different type of data store which best suits the solution. This decreases the dependency concerns compared to the monolithic designs, and makes replacing services much easier.

A good example where this ability of a Microservice maximizes its effect is a scenario where different data stores can be used by different services in alignment with the business scenario they address. A logging service can use a slower and cheaper data store, whereas a real-time service can use a faster and more performant data store. As the consuming services are abstracted from the implementation of the service, they are not concerned about the compatibility with the technology used to access the data.

Development agility

Microservices being handled by separate logical development streams makes it easier for a new developer to understand the functionality of a service and ramp up to speed. This is particularly useful in an agile environment where the team can constantly change and there is minimal dependency on an individual developer. It also makes code maintenance related tasks simpler as smaller services are much more readable and easily testable.

Often, large-scale systems have specific requirements which require specialized services. An example of this is a service which processes graphical data which requires specialized skills to build and test the service. If a development team does not have the domain knowledge to deliver this service, it can be easily outsourced or offloaded to a different team which has the required skill sets. This would be very hard in a monolithic system because of the interdependency of services.

Heterogeneous deployment

The ability of Microservices to be executed as an isolated process decouples it from the constraints around a specific hosting environment. For instance, services can be deployed across multiple cloud stacks such as IaaS and PaaS and across different operating systems such as Windows and Linux hosted on private data centers or on cloud. This decouples the technology limitations from the business requirements.

Most of the mid and large sized companies are now going through a cloud transformation. These companies have already invested significant resources on their on-premises data centers. This forces cloud vendors to support hybrid computing models where the IT infrastructure can coexist across cloud and on-premises data centers. In this case, the infrastructure configuration available on-premises may not match the one provisioned on cloud. The magnitude of application tiers in a monolithic architecture may prevent it from being deployed on less capable server machines, making efficient resource utilization a challenge. Microservices, on the other hand, being smaller, decoupled deployment units, can easily be deployed on heterogeneous environments.

Manageability

Each Microservice can be separately versioned, upgraded, and scaled without impacting the rest of the system. This enables running multiple development streams in parallel with independent delivery cycles aligned with the business demands. If we take a system which distributes news to the employees of a company as an example, and the notification service needs an upgrade to support push notifications to mobile phones, it can be upgraded without any downtime in the system and without impacting the rest of the application. The team delivering the notification service can function at its own pace without having a dependency on a big bang release or a product release cycle.

The ability to scale each service independently is also a key advantage in distributed systems. This lets the operations team increase or decrease the number of instances of a service dynamically to handle varying loads. A good example is systems which require batch processing. Batch jobs which run periodically, say once in a day, only require the batch processing service to be running for a few hours. This service can be turned on and scaled up for the duration of batch processing and then turned off to better utilize the computing resources among other services.

Reusability

Granularity is the key for reuse. Microservices, being small and focused on a specific business scenario, improve the opportunity for them to be reused across multiple subsystems within an organization. This in turn reflects as momentous cost savings.

The factor of reuse is proportional to the size of the organization and its IT applications. Bigger companies have more number of applications developed by multiple development teams, each of which may run their own delivery cycles. Often, the lack of ability to share code across these teams forces software components to be duplicated, causing a considerable impact on development and maintenance cost. Although service duplication across applications may not always be bad, with proper service cataloging and communication, Microservices can easily solve this problem by enabling service reuse across business units.

The SOA principle

SOA has multiple definitions that vary with the vendors that provide platforms to host SOA services. One of the commonly accepted SOA definitions was coined by Don Box of Microsoft. His definition is essentially a set of design guidelines which a service-oriented system should adhere to.

> *Boundaries are Explicit*
> *Services are Autonomous*
> *Services share Schema and Contract, not Class*
> *Compatibility is based upon Policy*
> *   – Don Box, Microsoft*

Although this definition was originally explained in relation to Microsoft Indigo (now WCF), the tenets still hold true for other SOA platforms as well. An understanding of this principle is that all the services should be available in the network. This tenet dictates that no modules, routines, or procedures can be considered as participants in SOA. Let's take a look at the original tenets in a little detail. The first tenet says that a service should implement a domain functionality and should be discoverable by the other services making up the system. The discovery of service is generally done by registering each service in a directory. The clients of the services can discover each service at runtime. The second tenet explains that the services should be independent of the other services that make up the system. Since the services are independent of each other, they may also enjoy independence of platform and programming language. The third tenet advices that each service should expose an interface through which the rest of the services can communicate with it. The knowledge of this contract should be sufficient to operate with the service. The fourth tenet dictates that the services define the boundaries in which they would work. An example of such a boundary can be a range of integers within which a service that performs arithmetic operations would operate. Such policies should be mentioned in the form of policy expressions and should be machine readable. In WCF, the policies are implemented by the **Web Services Policy (WS-Policy)** framework.

Although none of the original tenets dictate the size of individual services built using SOA architecture, to obtain independence from other services in the system, an individual service in SOA needs to be coarse-grained. To minimize interaction between services, each service should implement functionalities that work together.

In essence, both the Microservices architecture and the SOA architecture try to solve the problems of monolithic design by modularizing the components. In fact, a system already designed using the SOA architecture is a step in the right direction to realize Microservices architecture.

Issues with SOA

An inherent problem in the SOA architecture is that it tries to mimic the communication levels in an enterprise. SOA principles take a holistic look at the various communication channels in an enterprise and try to normalize them. To understand this problem in a better manner, let us take a look at a real-world SOA implementation done for an organization.

The following is the architecture of a real-life SOA-based application of a car rental company. The architecture diagram presented below has intentionally been simplified to ease understanding:

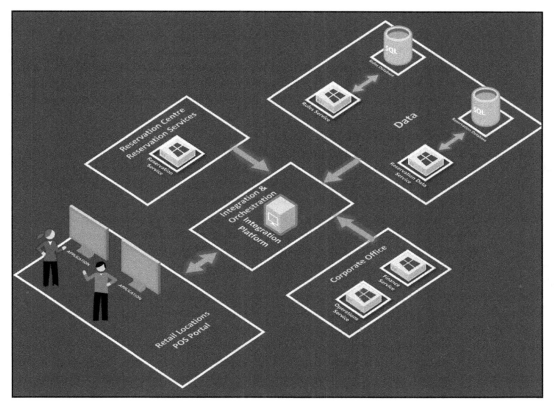

SOA architecture

This model is a classic example of an SOA-based system. The various participants in this SOA landscape are as follows:

- **The corporate office services**: These services provides data pertaining to fleet management, finances, data warehouse, and so on.
- **The reservation services**: These services help manage bookings and cancellations.
- **Backend services**: These services interface the systems that supply rules to the system and that supply reservation data to the system. There might be additional systems involved in the application, but we will consider only two of them at the moment.
- **Integration platform**: The various services of the system need to interact with each other. The integration platform is responsible for orchestrating the communication between the various services. This system understands the data that it receives from the various systems and responds to the various commands that it receives from the portal.
- **The Point of Sale portal**: The portal is responsible for providing an interface for the users to interact with the services. The technology to realize the frontend of the application is not important. The frontend might be a web portal, a rich client, or a mobile application.

The various systems involved in the application may be developed by different teams. In the preceding example, there can be a team responsible for the backend systems, one for the reservation center, one for the corporate office, one for the portal, and one for the integration services. Any change in the hierarchy of communication may lead to a change in the architecture of the system and thus drive up the costs. For instance, if the organization decides to externalize its finance systems and offload some of the information to another system, then the existing orchestrations would need to be modified. This would lead to increased testing efforts and also redeployment of the entire application.

Another aspect worth noting here is that the integration system forms the backbone of SOA. This concept is generally wrongly interpreted and **Enterprise Service Bus (ESB)** is used to hook up multiple monoliths which may communicate over complicated, inefficient, and inflexible protocols. This not only adds the overhead of complex transformations to the system but also makes the system resilient to change. Any change in contract would lead to composing of new transformations.

Typical SOA implementations also impede agility. Implementing a change in application is slow because multiple teams need to coordinate with each other. For example, in the preceding scenario, if the application needs to accept a new means of payment, then the portal team would need to make changes in the user interface, the payment team would need to make changes in their service, the backend team would need to add new fields in the database to capture the payment details, and the orchestration team would need to make changes to tie the communication together.

The participant services in SOA also face versioning issues. If any of the services modify their contract, then the orchestrator systems would need to undergo changes as well. In case the changes are too expensive to make, the new version of service would need to maintain backward compatibility with the old contract, which may not always be possible. The deployment of modified services requires more coordination as the modified service needs to be deployed before the affected services get deployed, leading to the formation of deployment monoliths.

The orchestration and integration system runs the risk of becoming a monolith itself. As most of the business logic is concentrated in the orchestration system, the services might just be administering data whereas the orchestration system contains all the business logics of the entire application. Even in a domain-driven design setting, any change in an entity that leads to a change in the user interface would require redeployment of many services. This makes SOA lose its flexibility.

The Microservices solution

Unlike SOA, which promotes cohesion of services, Microservices promote the principle of isolation of services. Each Microservice should have minimal interaction with other Microservices that are part of the system. This gives the advantage of independent scale and deployment to the Microservices.

Let's redraw the architecture of the car rental company using the Microservices architecture principle:

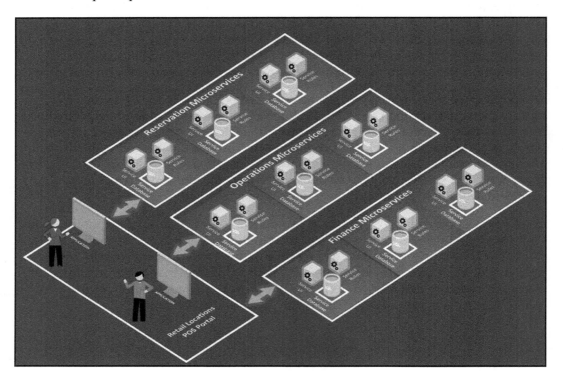

Microservices architecture

In the revised architecture, we have created a Microservice corresponding to each domain of the original system. This architecture does away with the integration and orchestration component. Unlike SOA, which requires all services to be connected to an ESB, Microservices can communicate with each other through simple message passing. We will soon look at how Microservices can communicate.

Also, note that we have used the principles of **Domain-Driven Design** (**DDD**), which is the principle that should be used for designing a Microservices-based system. A Microservice should never spawn across domains. However, each domain can have multiple Microservices. Microservices avoid communicating with each other and for the most part use the user interface for communication.

In the revised setup, each team can develop and manage a Microservice. Rather than distributing teams around technologies and creating multiple channels of communication, this distribution can increase agility. For instance, adding a new form of payment requires making a change in the payment Microservice and therefore requires communication with only a single team.

Isolation between services makes adoption of Continuous Delivery much simpler. This allows you to safely deploy applications and roll out changes and revert deployments in case of failures.

Since services can be individually versioned and deployed, significant savings are attained in the deployment and testing of Microservices.

Inter-Microservice communication

Microservices can rarely be designed in a manner that they do not need to communicate with each other. However, if you base your Microservices system on the DDD principle, there should be minimal communication required between the participant Microservices.

Cross-domain interactions of Microservices help reduce the complexity of individual services and duplication of code. We will take a look at some of the communication patterns in `Chapter 18`, *Microservices Architectural Patterns*. However, let us look at the various types of communication.

Communication through user interface

In most cases, the usability of a system is determined through the frontend. A system designed using Microservices should avoid using a monolithic user interface. There are several proponents of the idea that Microservices should contain a user interface and we agree with that.

Tying a service with a user interface gives high flexibility to the system to incorporate changes and add new features. This also ensures that distribution of teams is not by the communication hierarchy of the organization but by domains that Microservices are a part of. This practice also has the benefit of ensuring that the user interface will not become a deployment monolith at any point in time.

Although there are several challenges associated with integrating the user interface of Microservices, there are several ways to enable this integration. Let's take a look at a few.

Sharing common code

To ensure a consistent look and feel of the end user portal, code that ensures consistency can be shared with the other frontends. However, care should be taken to ensure that no business logic, binding logic, or any other logic creeps into the shared code.

Your shared code should always be in a state of being released publicly. This will ensure that no breaking changes or business logic gets added to the shared library.

Composite user interface for the web

Several high-scale websites such as Facebook and MSN combine data from multiple services on their page. Such websites compose their frontend out of multiple components. Each of these components could be the user interface provided by individual Microservices. A great example of this approach is Facebook's **BigPipe** technology, which composes its web page from small reusable chunks called *pagelets* and *pipes* them through several executing stages inside web servers and browsers:

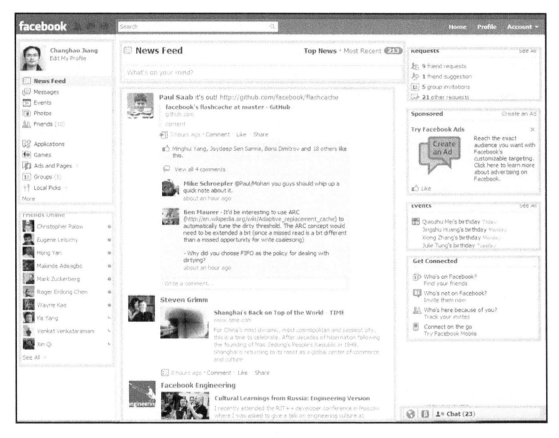

Facebook BigPipe (source: https://www.facebook.com/notes/facebook-engineering/bigpipe-pipelining-web-pages-for-high-performance/389414033919/)

The composition of a user interface can take place at multiple levels, ranging from development to execution. The flexibility of such integrations varies with the level they are carried out at.

The most primitive form of composition can be the sharing of code, which can be done at the time of development. However, using this integration, you have to rely on deployment monoliths as the various versions of user interface can't be deployed in parallel.

A much more flexible integration can also take place at runtime. For instance, Asynchronous JavaScript and XML (AJAX), HTML, and other dependencies can be loaded in the browser. Several JavaScript frameworks, such as Angular.js, Ember.js, and Ext.js, can help realize composition in single-page applications.

In cases where integration through JavaScript is not feasible, middleware may be used which fetches the HTML component of each Microservice and composes them to return a single HTML document to the client. Some typical examples of such compositions are the edge side includes of varnish or squid, which are proxies and caches. Server-side includes such as those available on Apache and NGINX can also be used to carry out transformations on servers rather than on caches.

Thin backend for rich clients

Unlike web applications, rich clients need to be deployed as monoliths. Any change in the Microservices would require a fresh deployment of the client application. Unlike web applications where each Microservice consists of a user interface, it is not the case for mobile or desktop applications. Moreover, structuring the teams in a manner that each team has a frontend developer for each rich client that the application can be deployed to is not feasible.

A way in which this dependency can be minimized is by having a backend for the rich client applications which is deployed with the application:

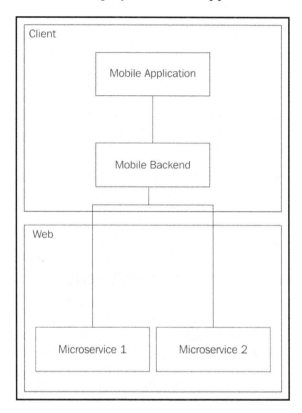

Microservices for rich clients

Although this approach is not perfect, it does ensure that part of the system conforms to Microservices architecture. Care should be taken to not alter any Microservice to encapsulate the business logic of the rich client. The mobile and desktop clients should optimize content delivery as per their needs.

Synchronous communication

A simple solution for synchronous communication between services is to use REST and transfer JSON data over HTTP. REST can also help in service discovery by using **Hypermedia as the Engine of Application State** (**HATEOAS**). HATEOAS is a component of REST which models relationships between resources by using links. Once the client queries the entry point of the service, it can use the links it receives to navigate to other Microservices.

If text-based transfers are not desired, protocol buffers (Google's data interchange format) may be used to transmit data. This protocol has been implemented in several languages to increase its adoption, for example, Ruby protobuf.

A protocol that can be used to transmit structured data across a network is **Simple Object Access Protocol** (**SOAP**). It can be used to make calls to different Microservices using various transport mechanisms such as JMS, TCP, or UDP. SOAP is language-neutral and highly extensible.

Asynchronous communication

Asynchronous message passing has the benefit of truly decoupling Microservices from each other. Since the communication is carried out by a broker, individual services need not be aware of the location of the receiver of the request. This also gives individual services the ability to scale independently and recover and respond to messages in case of failure. However, this communication pattern lacks the feature of immediate feedback and is slower than the synchronous communication format.

There are several tools available for such communication, such as MSMQ and Rabbit MQ. Microsoft Azure offers Service Bus Queues and Microsoft Azure Storage Queue for asynchronous messaging on cloud. Amazon SQS provides similar functionality in Amazon Web Services.

Orchestrated communication

This process is similar to the asynchronous communication process that we discussed earlier. Orchestrated communication still uses message stores to transmit data; however, the Microservice sending the data would insert different messages in different queues in order to complete the action. For example, an **Order Microservice** would insert the message in the queue consumed by the **Inventory Microservice** and another message in the queue consumed by the **Shipment Microservice**:

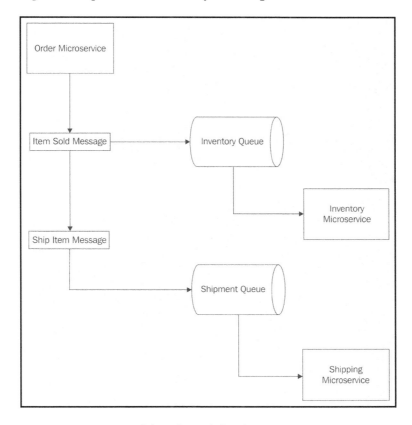

Orchestrated communications using queues

The orchestration may be carried out by a separate component, which is known as Saga, which we will read more about in `Chapter 18`, *Microservices Architectural Patterns*.

Shared data

Microservices should not share the same data store. Sharing data representation can make altering the database very difficult, and even if done, such a change always runs the risk of causing failure to services that are still using the old data representation. Such challenges ultimately lead to a bloated and complex database and accumulation of lots of dead data over time.

Data replication is a possible solution to sharing data across Microservices. However, data should not be blindly replicated across Microservices as the same problems that are present with shared databases would still remain. A custom transformation process should convert data available from the database to the schema used by the data store of the Microservice. The replication process can be triggered in batches or on certain events in the system.

Architecture of Microservices-based systems

Many of us have been curious about the representation of a Microservice by a hexagon. The reason for this is the inspiration behind the architectural pattern that drives *Microservices – the hexagonal architecture*. This pattern is also popularly known as **ports** and **adapters** in some parts of the globe. In a hexagonal architecture pattern, the code application logic is insulated with an isolation perimeter. This insulation helps a Microservice be unaware of the outside world. The insulation opens specific ports for establishing communication channels to and from the application code. Consuming applications can write adapters against these ports to communicate with the Microservice. The following diagram illustrates a hexagonal pattern for a Microservice:

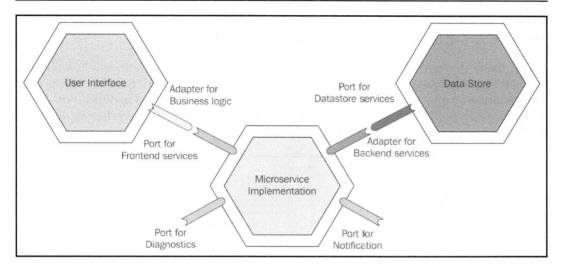

Hexagonal architecture

Protocols in the case of a Microservice architecture are usually APIs. These APIs are exposed using popular protocols for ease of consumption. Hexagonal architecture lets the Microservice treat all of its consumers alike, whether it is a user interface, test suit, monitoring service, or an automation script.

Conway's law

Melvin Edward Conway, an American computer scientist, coined a law that generally guides the design of the applications built by an organization.

> *Any organization that designs a system (defined broadly) will produce a design*
> *whose structure is a copy of the organization's communication structure.*
> *— Melvyn Conway 1967*

An important aspect of the law that should be noted is that the communication structure mentioned in the law is not the same as organizational hierarchy but rather how the various teams in the organization communicate with each other. For instance, an e-commerce company might have a product team and an invoicing team. Any application designed by this organization will have a product module and an invoicing module that will communicate with each other through a common interface.

For a large enterprise with many communication channels, the application architecture will be very complex and nearly impossible to maintain.

Using the law in conjunction with principles of domain driven design can actually help an organization enhance agility and design scalable and maintainable solutions. For instance, in an e-commerce company, teams may be structured around the domain components rather than the application layers that they specialize in, for instance, user interface, business logic, and database:

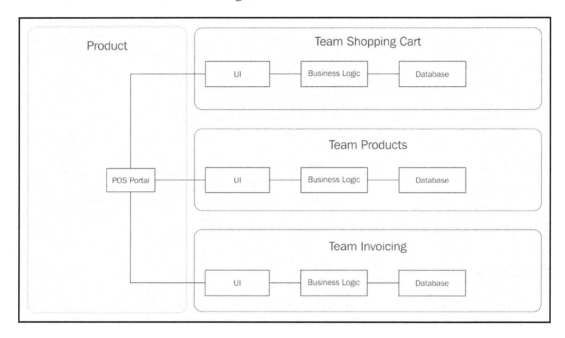

Team structure for Microservices development

Since the domains are clearly defined, the teams across domains will not need to interact too frequently. Also, the interfaces between teams would not be too complex and rigid. Such team layouts are commonly employed by large organizations such as Amazon, where each team is responsible for creating and maintaining a part of a domain.

Amazon practices the *two-pizza* rule to limit the size of teams. According to the rule, no team can be larger in size than what two pizzas can feed. Amazon also does not practice heavy communication between teams and all teams are required to communicate with each other through APIs. For instance, if the marketing team needs statistical data from a product team, they can't ask them for it. They need to hit the product team's API to get the data.

Microservices work better when coupled with the principles of domain driven design rather than communication channels. In the application architecture that we designed earlier, we could have ignored the domains of the application and classified teams by communication structure; for instance, two Microservices may be created, each of which handles product listing and product inventory. Such a distribution might lead to each of the teams to develop components independently of each other and will make moving functionalities between them very difficult if the communication hierarchy changes, such as when the two services need to be merged.

Summary

In this chapter, we learned about the concept of Microservices and its evolution. We also compared it with its predecessors, SOA and monolithic architecture. We then explored the requirement for a Microservices hosting platform and its properties.

We then discussed the various means of communications between Microservices and their advantages and disadvantages, after which we explored the architecture of a Microservices-based system.

To conclude, we also explored the philosophy behind hexagonal architecture and Conway's law.

Understanding Azure Service Fabric

13

Microservices architecture portrays efficient mechanisms of solving modern enterprise problems. However, this simplification comes at a cost. Manually managing hyperscale deployments of Microservices is nearly impossible. Automating Microservices lifecycle management becomes an inevitable requirement to achieve enterprise-grade environment stability. This is where the role of Azure Service Fabric becomes significant. To start with, let's try to understand what Service Fabric is.

Mark Fussell, a senior program manager in the Microsoft Azure Service Fabric team, defines Service Fabric as the following:

> *Service Fabric is a distributed systems platform that makes it easy to package, deploy, and manage scalable and reliable Microservices.*

Let's dig deeper into this definition. The definition categorizes Service Fabric as a platform. A platform, in theory, is a software component capable of hosting other software applications which are built to align with the constraints imposed by the platform and can use the features exposed by the platform for its execution. This is exactly what Service Fabric is for the Microservices services it hosts. Service Fabric is a platform which can host services and offers runtime features to support their execution.

The term distributed in the preceding definition highlights the capability of Service Fabric to host decoupled services. As a hosting platform, Service Fabric provides features to catalog, address, and access these services from other services hosted within the platform as well as from external applications.

The process involved in end-to-end delivery of a service can be categorized into different phases according to the activities performed during each phase. These phases are design, development, testing, deployment, upgrading, maintenance, and removal. The task of managing all these phases involved in the delivery of a service is commonly known as application lifecycle management. Service Fabric provides first-class support for end-to-end application lifecycle management of applications deployed on cloud as well as for the ones running on-premises data centers.

The last and most important part of the definition emphasizes the capability of Service Fabric to host Microservices. Service Fabric offers capabilities for building and managing scalable and reliable applications composed of distributed, stateless (which do not maintain a session between requests) and stateful (which maintain a session between requests), Microservices running at very high density on a shared pool of machines. Service Fabric hosts Microservices inside containers deployed and activated across the Service Fabric cluster. By using a containerized execution environment for Microservices, Service Fabric is able to provide an increase in the density of deployment and improved portability across heterogeneous environments.

The Service Fabric advantage

Now that we understand what Service Fabric is, let's look at the advantages of using it as a platform to host Microservices.

As discussed in the earlier section in this chapter, Service Fabric is a distributed systems platform used to build hyperscalable, reliable, and easily managed applications for the cloud. The following figure mentioned in MSDN, provides a good overview of capabilities of Service Fabric as a hosting platform for Microservices:

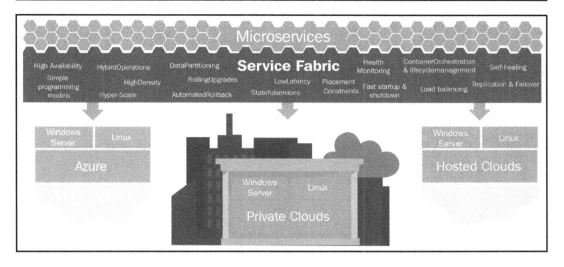

Service Fabric features

Apart from the capabilities of Service Fabric to manage the application lifecycle for Microservices, the preceding diagram provides an important aspect of its ability to be deployed across heterogeneous environments. We will talk about this in detail in later sections of this chapter. Let's now dive deeper in to few of the key features of Service Fabric which make it an ideal platform to build a Microservice-based applications.

Highly scalable

Every Microservice hosted on Service Fabric can be scaled without affecting other Microservices. Service Fabric will support scaling-based on Virtual Machine Scale Sets which means that these services will have the ability to be auto-scaled based on CPU consumption, memory usage, and so on.

Service Fabric enables scaling while maximizing resource utilization with features such as like load balancing, partitions, and replication across all the nodes in the cluster. A Microservice hosted on Service Fabric can be scaled either at partition level or at name level.

Support for partitioning

Service Fabric supports partitioning of Microservices. Partitioning is the concept of dividing data and compute into smaller units to improve the scalability and performance of a service.

A stateless Microservice can be of two types – one which stores the state externally and two which does not store a state. These Microservices are rarely partitioned as the scalability and the performance of the service can be enhanced by increasing the number of instances running the service. The only reason to partition a stateless service would be to achieve specialized routing requirements.

Service Fabric natively supports partitioning of state for a stateful service, thereby reducing the overheads on the developers around maintaining and replicating state across partition replicas. A partition of a stateful service can be thought of as a scale unit that is highly reliable through replicas distributed and load balanced across the nodes in a Service Fabric cluster. Service Fabric controls the optimal distribution of the partitions across multiple nodes, allowing them to grow dynamically. The partitions are rebalanced regularly to ensure resource availability to each service deployed on the cluster.

For instance, if an application with ten partitions each with three replicas is deployed on a five node cluster, Service Fabric will distribute the instances across the nodes with two primary replicas on each node:

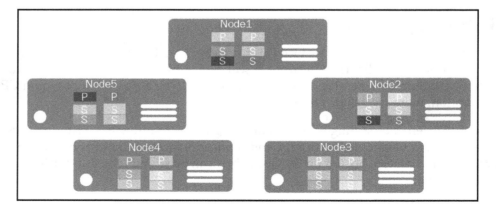

Partitioning on a five node cluster

Later, if you scale up the cluster to ten nodes, Service Fabric will rebalance the primary replicas across all the 10 nodes:

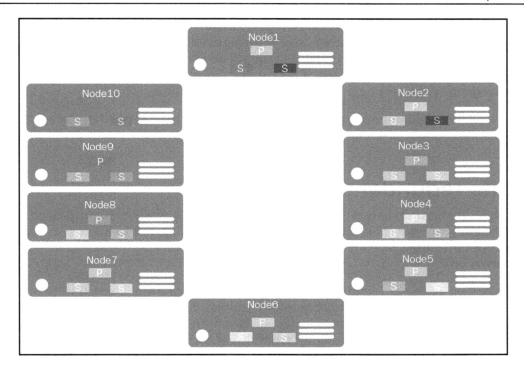

Partitioning on 10 node cluster

The same logic will apply when the cluster is scaled down.

Rolling updates

A Service Fabric application is a collection of services. Every service, the ones which are part of the Service Fabric framework or the ones which are hosted on it, will require an upgrade at some point in time. To achieve high availability and low downtime of services during upgrades, Service Fabric supports rolling updates. This means that the upgrade is performed in stages. The concept of update domains is used to divide the nodes in a cluster into logical groups which are updated one at a time.

First, the application manifests of the new and existing deployments are compared to identify services which need an upgrade and only the ones requiring an update is refreshed. During the process of an upgrade, the cluster may contain a version of new and old services running in parallel.

This forces the upgrades to be backward-compatible. A multi-phased upgrade can be used as a solution to achieve upgrade of non-compatible versions of services. In a multi-phased upgrade, the service is first upgraded to an intermediate version which is compatible with the old version of the service. Once this is successful, the intermediate version is upgraded to the final version of the service.

Service Fabric also supports non-rolling updates of services deployed in a cluster, a process also known as unmonitored upgrade.

State redundancy

For stateful Microservices, it is efficient to store state near compute for improved performance. Service Fabric natively integrates with a Microsoft technology called **Reliable Collections** to achieve collocation of compute and state for services deployed on it.

Reliable Collections can be thought of as a collection of state stores specifically designed for multi-computer applications. It enables developers to store state locally on a node within a Service Fabric cluster while assuring high availability, scalability, and low latency. For services running multiple instances, the state is replicated across nodes hosting different instances. Replication is the responsibility of the Reliable Services framework. This saves developers a significant amount of time and effort.

Reliable Services is also transactional by nature and supports asynchronous, non-blocking APIs. Presently, this technology supports two types of state stores – **Reliable Dictionary**, for storing key-value pairs, and **Reliable Queues**, a first-in-first-out data structure usually used for message passing.

High-density deployment

The recent revolution of containers has accelerated the ability to improve the density of deployment on a virtual machine. Microservices can be deployed within containers and the containers will provide the logical isolation for the services it hosts. Service Fabric enhances this ability to the next level by offering native support for Microservices. Every Microservice hosted on Service Fabric will be logically isolated and can be managed without impacting other services. This level of granularization in turn makes possible achieving a much higher density of deployment.

Another notable advantage of using Service Fabric is the fact that it is tried and tested. Microsoft runs services such as Azure DocumentDB, Cortana, and many core Azure services on Service Fabric.

Automatic fault tolerance

The cluster manager of Service Fabric ensures failover and resource balancing in case of a hardware failure. This ensures high availability of the services while minimizing manual management and operational overhead.

For a stateless service, Service Fabric lets you define an instance count, which is the number of instances of the stateless service that should be running in the cluster at a given time. The service can be scaled up by increasing the number of instances.

When Service Fabric detects a fault on an instance, it creates a new instance of the service on a healthy node within the cluster to ensure availability. This process is completely automated.

The story becomes a bit more complex for a stateful service. Service Fabric replicates a stateful service on different nodes to achieve high availability. Each replica will contain code used by the service and the state. All write operations are performed on one replica called the **primary replica**. All other replicas are called secondary replicas. Changes to state on the primary replica are automatically replicated to the secondary replicas by the framework. Service Fabric supports the configuration of a number of active secondary replicas. The higher the number of replicas, the better the fault tolerance of a service.

If the primary replica fails, Service Fabric makes one of the secondary replicas the primary replica and spins up a new instance of a service as a secondary replica.

Heterogeneous hosting platforms

It is common for enterprise environments to have heterogeneous hosting environments spread across multiple data centers managed and operated by different vendors. A key advantage of Service Fabric is its ability to manage clusters in and across heterogeneous environments. Service Fabric clusters can run on Azure, AWS, Google Cloud Platform, an on-premises data center, or any other third-party data center. Service Fabric can also manage clusters spread across multiple data centers. This feature is critical for services requiring high availability.

Service Fabric can manage virtual machines or computers running Windows Server or Linux operating systems. It can also operate on a diverse set of hardware configurations. While working with heterogeneous environments, usually there are scenarios where we want to host certain workloads on certain types of nodes. For instance, there may be services which execute GPU-intensive tasks which ideally should be placed on a node with a powerful GPU. In order to support such requirements, Service Fabric offers an option to configure placement constraints. Placement constraints can be used to indicate where certain services should run. These constraints are widely extensible. Nodes can be tagged with custom properties and constraints can be set for every service to be executed on certain types of nodes. Service Fabric also allows imposing constraints around the minimum resource capacity required to host a service on a node in a cluster. These constraints can be based on memory, disk space, and so on.

Technology agnostic

Service Fabric can be considered as a universal deployment environment. Services or applications based on any programming language or even database runtimes such as MongoDB can be deployed on Service Fabric.

Service Fabric supports four types of programming models – Reliable Services, Reliable Actors, Guest Executable, and Guest Containers. These topics are covered in detail in later parts of the book. Services can be written in any programming language and deployed as executables or hosted within containers.

Microsoft ships a rich **Software Development Kit (SDK)** for developing, packaging, and deploying services on Service Fabric managed clusters. Apart from .NET, Service Fabric also supports a native Java SDK for Java developers working on Linux. The Java SDK is supported by the Eclipse **integrated development environment (IDE)**.

Centralized management

Monitoring, diagnosing, and troubleshooting are three key responsibilities of the operations team. Services hosted on Service Fabric can be centrally managed, monitored, and diagnosed outside application boundaries. While monitoring and diagnostics are most important in a production environment, adopting similar tools and processes in development and test environments makes the system more deterministic. The Service Fabric SDK natively supports capabilities around diagnostics which works seamlessly on both local development setups and production cluster setups.

Service Fabric has native support for **Event Tracing for Windows** (**ETW**). Service Fabric code itself uses ETW for internal tracing. This allows developers to centrally access application traces interleaved with Service Fabric system traces, which significantly helps in debugging. ETW is fast and works exactly the same way on development and production environments. However, ETW traces are local to the machine. While running a multi-node cluster, it helps to have a centralized vision on logs produced by all the services running in the cluster. The Azure Diagnostics extension can be used for this purpose. The extension can collect the logs from configured sources and aggregate it in Azure Storage to enable centralized access. External processes can be used to read the events from storage and place them into a product such as Log Analytics or Elastic Search, or another log-parsing solution for better visualization.

Service Fabric as an orchestrator

From a service management point of view, Service Fabric can be thought of as an orchestrator. An orchestrator in general terms is an automated piece of software used to manage service deployments. This piece of software is supposed to abstract the complexities around provisioning, deploying, fault handling, scaling, and optimizing the applications it is managing, from the end user. For instance, an orchestration should be able to consume a configuration which specifies the number of instances of service to run and perform the task of deploying the services-based on multiple complex factors such as resource availability on nodes in a cluster, placement constraints, and so on

Orchestrators are also responsible for fault handling and recovery of services. If a node in a cluster fails, the orchestrator needs to gracefully handle this while ensuring service availability. Updating a service deployment or applying a patch to the underlying framework is also managed by orchestrators. Apart from Service Fabric, there are other orchestration services available in the market, such as Mesosphere, Core OS, Docker Swarm, and Kubernetes. Azure container services open opportunities for some of these powerful orchestration services to be hosted on Azure. More about this is discussed later in this book.

Orchestration as a Service

In Service Fabric, the responsibilities of orchestration are primarily handled by the resource manager subsystem. This service is automatically initiates when a cluster is spun up and it stays awake for the lifetime of the cluster. The key responsibilities of this subsystem include optimization of environment, enforcing constraints, and assisting with other cluster management operations.

Let's dig a little deeper to understand the architecture of the resource manager service.

Is a cluster resource manager similar to an Azure load balancer?

While load balancing is a key part of managing a cluster, this is not what a cluster resource manager does. A traditional load balancer can be of two types, a **network load balancer** (**NLB**) or an **application load balancer** (**ALB**). The primary job of a load balancer is to make sure that all of the services hosted receive a similar amount of work. Some load balancers are also capable of ensuring session stickiness and some are even capable or optimizing the request routing-based on the turnaround time or current machine load.

While some of these strategies are efficient and best suited for a monolithic or tiered architecture, they lack the agility to handle faults and upgrades. A more responsive, integrated solution is required to handle hyperscale deployments of Microservices. The Service Fabric cluster resource manager is not a network load balancer. While a traditional load balancer distributes the traffic to where services are hosted, the Service Fabric cluster resource manager moves services to where there is room for them, or to where they make sense based on other conditions. These conditions can be influenced by the resource utilization on a node, a fault, an upgrade request, or so on.

For instance, the cluster resource manager can move services from a node which is busy to a node which is underutilized based on the CPU and memory use. It can also move a service away from a node which is in the queue for an upgrade.

Architecture of cluster resource manager

The process of resource management is complex. It is based on multiple parameters which are highly dynamic in nature. To perform resource balancing, the resource manager has to know about all the active services and the resources consumed by each of the services at this point of time. It should also be aware of the actual capacity of every node in the cluster in terms of memory, CPU, and disk space, and the aggregate amount of resources available in the cluster. The resources consumed by a service can change over time, depending on the load it is handling. This also needs to be accounted for before making a decision to move a service from one node to another. To add to the complexity, the cluster resources are not static. The number of nodes in the cluster can increase or decrease at any point of time, which can lead to a change in load distribution. Scheduled or unscheduled upgrades can also roll through the cluster, causing temporal outages of nodes and services. Also, the very fact of cloud resources running on commodity hardware forces the resource manager to be highly fault tolerant.

To achieve these tasks, the Service Fabric cluster resource manager uses two components. The first component is an *agent* which is installed on every node of a cluster. The agent is responsible for collecting information from the hosting node and relaying it to a centralized service. This information will include CPU utilization, memory utilization, remaining disk space, and so on. The agent is also responsible for heartbeat checks for the node.

The second component is a service. Service Fabric is a collection of services. The cluster resource manager service is responsible for aggregating all of the information supplied by the agent and other management services and reacting to changes based on the desired state configuration of the cluster and service. The fault tolerance of the service manager is achieved via replication, similar to how it is done for the services hosted on Service Fabric. The resource manager service runs seven replicas to ensure high availability.

To understand the process of aggregation, let's take an example.

The following figure illustrates a Service Fabric cluster with six nodes. There are seven services deployed on this cluster with the names **A**, **B**, **C**, **D**, **E**, and **F**. The diagram illustrates the initial distribution of the services on the cluster based on placement rules configured for the services. Services **A**, **B**, and **C** are placed on node 5 (**N5**), service **D** on node 6 (**N6**), service **G** on node 2 (**N2**), service **F** on node 3 (**N3**) and service **E** on node 4 (**N4**). The resource manager service itself is hosted on node 1 (**N1**). Every node has a Service Fabric agent running which communicates with the resource manager service hosted on **N1**:

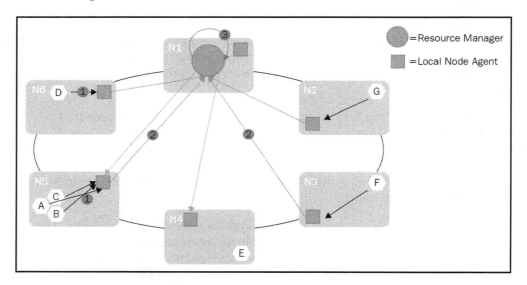

General resource manager functions

During runtime, if the amount of resources consumed by services changes, or if a service fails, or if a new node joins or leaves the cluster, all the changes on a specific node are aggregated and periodically sent to the central resource manager service. This is indicated by lines **1** and **2**. Once aggregated, the results are analyzed before they are persisted by the resource manager service. Periodically, a process within the cluster resource manager service, looks at all of the changes, and determines whether there are any corrective actions required. This process is indicated by the step **3** in the preceding figure.

To understand step **3** in detail, let's consider a scenario where the cluster resource manager determines that **N5** is overloaded. The following diagram illustrates a rebalancing process governed by the resource manager. This case is reported by the agent installed on **N5**. The resource manager service then checks available resources in other nodes of the cluster. Let's assume that **N4** is underutilized as reported by the agent installed on **N4**. The resource manager coordinates with other subsystems to move a service, which is service **B** in this instance, to **N4**. This is indicated by step **5** in the following diagram:

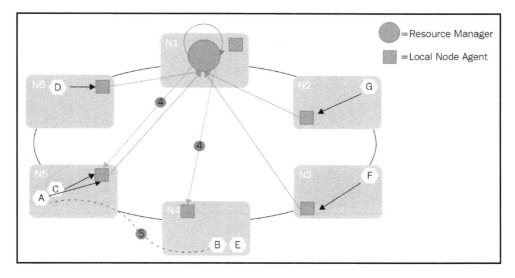

The Resource Manager reconfigures the clusters

This whole process is automated and its complexity is abstracted from the end user. This level of automation is what makes hyperscale deployments possible on Service Fabric.

Architecture of Service Fabric

Service Fabric is a collection of services grouped into different subsystems. These subsystems have specific responsibilities. The following diagram illustrates the major subsystems which form the Service Fabric architecture:

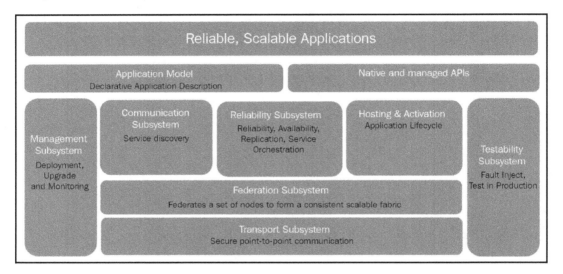

Subsystems of Service Fabric

The first layer from the bottom, the **Transport Subsystem** is responsible for providing secure communication channels between nodes in a Service Fabric cluster. The **Federation Subsystem** above it helps logically group physical or virtual nodes into a cluster so that it can be managed as a unit. This helps Service Fabric with tasks such as failure detection, leader election, and routing. Reliability of the workload hosted on Service Fabric is managed by the **Reliability Subsystem**. It owns the responsibility of replication, resource management, and failover. The **Hosting & Activation** Subsystem manages the lifecycle of the workload on every node and the **Management Subsystem** is responsible for managing the lifecycle of applications. The **Testability Subsystem** helps developers test their workload before and after deployment. Service location of services hosted on Service Fabric is managed by **Communication Subsystem**. The top three boxes capture the application programming models and the application model available for the developers to consume. More about application models is discussed in later parts of this book.

Transport Subsystem

The Transport Subsystem provides a communication channel for intra and inter cluster communication. The channels used for communication are secured by X509 certificate or Windows security. The subsystem supports both one-way and request-response communication patterns. These channels are in turn used by the Federation Subsystem for broadcast and multicast messaging. This subsystem is internal to Service Fabric and cannot be directly used by the developers for application programming.

Federation Subsystem

Federation Subsystem is responsible for logically grouping virtual or physical machines together to form a Service Fabric cluster. This subsystem uses the communication infrastructure provided by the Transport Subsystem to achieve this grouping. Grouping of nodes helps Service Fabric better manage the resources. The key responsibilities of this subsystem includes failure detection, leader election, and routing. The subsystem forms a ring topology over the nodes allocated for the cluster. A token-leasing mechanism along with a heartbeat check is implemented within the system to detect failures, perform leader election, and to achieve consistent routing.

Reliability Subsystem

Reliability of the service hosted on the platform is ensured by the Reliability Subsystem. It achieves these tasks by managing failover, replicating, and balancing resources across nodes in a cluster.

The replicator logic within this subsystem is responsible for replicating the state across multiple instances of a service. Maintaining consistency between the primary and the secondary replicas in a service deployment is its main task. It interacts with the failover unit and the reconfiguration agent to understand what needs to be replicated.

Any changes in the number of nodes in the cluster trigger the failover manager service. This in turn triggers automatic redistribution of services across the active nodes.

The resource manager plays the part of placing service replicas across different failure domains. It is also responsible for balancing the resources across the available nodes in the cluster while optimizing the load distribution and resource consumption.

Management Subsystem

The application lifecycle management of workloads deployed on a Service Fabric cluster is owned by the Management Subsystem. Application developers can access the Management Subsystem functionalities through administrative APIs or PowerShell cmdlets to provision, deploy, upgrade, or de-provision applications. All these operations can be performed without any downtime. The Management Subsystem has three key components – cluster manager, health manager, and image store.

The cluster manager interacts with the failover manager and the resource manager in the Reliability Subsystem for deploying the applications of available nodes considering the placement constraints. It is responsible for the lifecycle of the application, starting from provisioning to de-provisioning. It also integrates with the health manager to perform health checks during service upgrades.

Health manager, as the name suggests, is responsible for monitoring the health of applications, services, nodes, partitions, and replicas. It is also responsible for aggregating the health status and storing it in a centralized health store. APIs are exposed out of this system to query health events to perform corrective actions. The APIs can either return raw events or aggregated health data for a specific cluster resource.

The image store is responsible for persisting and distributing application binaries deployed on a Service Fabric cluster.

Hosting subsystem

The Hosting Subsystem takes care of managing application deployments within the scope of a node. The cluster manager signals the Hosting Subsystem, informing it about the application deployments to be managed on a particular node. The Hosting Subsystem then manages the lifecycle of the application on that node. It interacts with the Reliability Subsystem and Management Subsystem to ensure the health of each deployment.

Communication subsystem

The communication subsystem provides features for service discovery and intra-cluster messaging features using a naming service. The naming service is used to locate a service within a cluster. It also lets users securely communicate with any node on a cluster, retrieve service metadata, and manage service properties. The naming service also exposes APIs, which enables users to resolve network location or each service despite of them being dynamically placed.

Testability Subsystem

The Testability Subsystem provides a list of tools for developers, deployment engineers, and testers to introduce controlled faults and run test scenarios to validate state transitions and behaviors of services deployed on Service Fabric. The fault analysis service is automatically started when a cluster is provisioned. When a fault action or test scenario is initiated, a command is sent to the fault analysis service to run the fault action or test scenario.

Deconstructing Service Fabric

A Service Fabric application can be logically decomposed into multiple components. As a pro developer, you write your application using one of the programming models and supply the necessary configurations and data to make your code work, Service Fabric takes care of the rest of the stack and ensures that your code executes in a reliable and highly available environment. Let us take a look at the various components of a Service Fabric application and go through the individual components, starting from the infrastructure model:

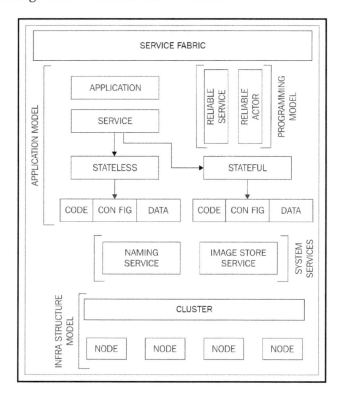

Components of Service Fabric application

Infrastructure model

In a distributed computing platform such as Service Fabric, the computing load is distributed over all the available compute units, which are actually a number of virtual machines that work together. Because Service Fabric clusters can be deployed on any platform and on physical or virtual machines, your Service Fabric applications can run on a variety of platforms without any modifications. Let us take a look at the components that make up the infrastructure of Service Fabric.

Cluster

In Service Fabric, a cluster is a network-connected set of virtual or physical machines into which your Microservices are deployed and managed. Clusters can scale to thousands of machines. In traditional data centers, the most deployed clusters are the failover cluster and the load balancing cluster. However, quite unique to the Service Fabric cluster is the Service Fabric cluster resource manager. The Service Fabric cluster resource manager is responsible for deploying the Microservices across the nodes, taking care of the node capacity, fault tolerance, and sufficient replication. Since multiple Microservices can be deployed on a node, the Service Fabric cluster resource manager ensures that there is proper utilization of the compute resources.

Node

A machine or VM that is part of a cluster is called a **node**. A node might be a a physical or virtual machine. A node in Service Fabric is identified by its string name. A cluster may have heterogeneous nodes and more nodes can be added to the existing capacity to scale out the cluster.

Each node on the cluster has Service Fabric runtime binaries installed in it. When the node starts, an auto-start Service Fabric runtime service named `FabricHost.exe` spins up two executables on the node which make up the node:

- `Fabric.exe`: This executable is responsible for managing the lifetime of the Microservices hosted on the node
- `FabricGateway.exe`: This executable is responsible for managing communication between the nodes

System services

A set of system services gets provisioned on every Service Fabric cluster that provides the underlying support for Service Fabric applications.

Naming service

A Service Fabric application is composed of multiple Microservices. The Service Fabric cluster manager may deploy your service instances to any nodes in the cluster, which can make it difficult to discover the service by the client application.

Every Microservice in a Service Fabric application is identified by a string name. A Service Fabric cluster has multiple instances of the naming service, which resolves service names to a location in the cluster. A client can securely communicate with any node in the cluster using the naming service to resolve a service name and its location. When a client requests the location of a Microservice, the naming service responds with the actual machine IP address and port where it is currently running. This makes the Microservice independent of the hardware on which it is hosted.

Image store service

Once your application is ready to be deployed, the application package files are versioned and copied to Service Fabric cluster's image store. The image store is made available to the cluster and other services through a hosted service called the image store service. Once your application package has been uploaded, you need to register the application package to make the application type and version known to the cluster. After the application type is provisioned, you can create named applications from it.

Upgrade service

Azure cloud-based Service Fabric clusters are managed and upgraded by the **Service Fabric Resource Provider (SFRP)**. The SFRP calls into a cluster through the HTTP gateway port on the management endpoint to get information about nodes and applications in the cluster. SFRP also serves the cluster information that is available to you in the **Azure Management Portal**. The HTTP Gateway ports is also used by the **Service Fabric Explorer** to browse and manage your cluster. The SFRP is an Azure-only service and is not available in the local development environment or any other infrastructure, such as Windows Server.

The upgrade service coordinates upgrading the Service Fabric itself with the SFRP.

Failover manager service

Each Service Fabric cluster node runs an agent that collects and sends load reports to a centralized resource balancer service. The resource balancer service is responsible for generating placement recommendations based on the load on the nodes and the placement requirements. The agent also sends failure reports and other events to a failover manager service. In a event of a change to the available node count, such as when a node fails or when a node is added to the cluster, the failover manager communicates with the resource balancer to get a placement recommendation. Once the failover manager receives a recommendation from the resource balancer service, it places a new service replica on the recommended node.

Cluster manager service

The cluster manager service is available over the HTTP Port `19080` and the TCP port `19000` of the cluster. It allows the Fabric client (available in the `System.Fabric` namespace), REST, and PowerShell clients to perform management operations, such as restarting a node, on the Service Fabric cluster.

Service placement

The System Services are deployed in a redundant manner across multiple nodes so that they are highly available. The following diagram shows a possible distribution of the **System Services** in a six node cluster:

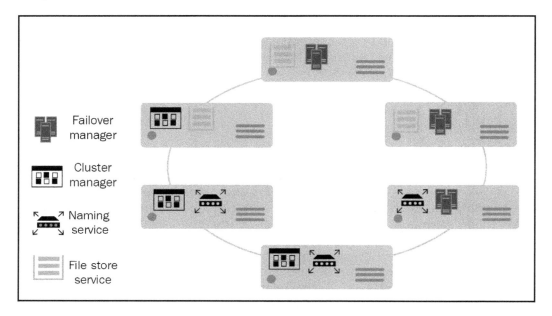

System Services

Application model

A Service Fabric application is made up of one or more Microservices. Each Microservice consists of the executable binaries or code of the Microservice, the configuration or setting that is used by the Microservice at runtime and static data used by the Microservice. All the individual components of the Microservices can be versioned and upgraded independently:

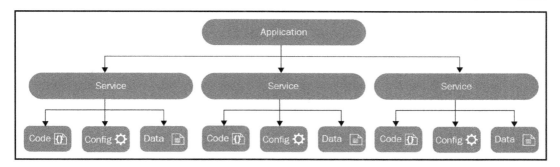

Application model

Applications and Microservices in Service Fabric are denoted by their type names. An application type can have a number of service types. You can create instances of application types (for example, by using the PowerShell command New-ServiceFabricApplication) and also service type (for example by using PowerShell command New-ServiceFabricService) which can have different settings and configurations, but the same core functionality.

The application types and service types are described through the application manifests (ApplicationManifest.xml) and service manifests (ServiceManifest.xml) respectively, which are XML files. These manifests serve as the templates against which applications can be instantiated from the cluster's image store.

Once you have installed the Service Fabric SDK, you can find the schema definition for the ServiceManifest.xml and ApplicationManifest.xml files saved in your developer machine at: C:\Program Files\Microsoft SDKs\Service Fabric\schemas\ServiceFabricServiceModel.xsd.

A Service Fabric node can host multiple application instances, some of which might belong to the same application; however, the code for different application instances will run as separate processes. Each application instance can be upgraded and managed independently. The following diagram shows how application types are composed of service types, which in turn are composed of code, configuration, and packages. Each of the service types would include some or all of the code, configuration and data packages:

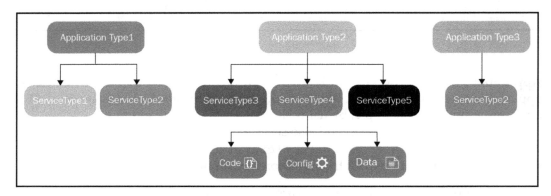

Service Types

A stateful Microservice can split its state and save its state across several partitions. A partitioned service can be deployed across nodes in a cluster. A partition is made highly available through replication. A partition has a primary replica and may have multiple secondary replicas. The state data of a stateful Microservice is synchronized automatically across replicas. Whenever a primary replica goes down, a secondary replica is promoted to primary to ensure availability. Later, the number of secondary replicas is brought back up to ensure there is enough redundancy available. There can be one or more instances of a service type active in the cluster.

The following diagram represents the relationship between applications and service instances, partitions, and replicas:

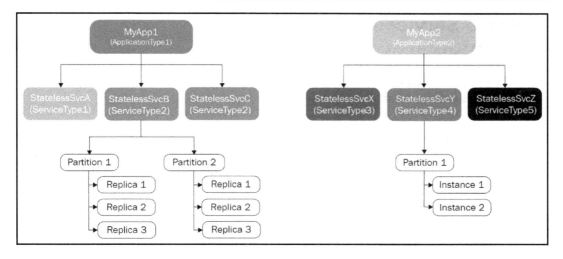

Instances, Partitions, and Replicas

Programming model

Service Fabric provides two .NET framework programming models for you to build your Microservices. Both the frameworks provide a minimal set of APIs that allow Service Fabric to manage your Microservices. Additionally, Service Fabric allows you to package your application binaries as a compiled executable program written in any language and host it on a Service Fabric cluster. Let's take a look at the programming models.

Guest Executables

You can package an arbitrary executable, written in any language, such as Node.js, Java, or native applications in Azure Service Fabric, and host it on a Service Fabric cluster. These type of applications are called **Guest Executables**. Guest Executables are treated by Service Fabric like stateless services. Service Fabric handles orchestration and simple execution management of the executable, ensuring it stays up and running according to the service description. However, since the executables do not interact with the Service Fabric platform through Service Fabric APIs, they do not have access to the full set of features the platform offers, such as custom health and load reporting, service endpoint registration, and stateful compute.

Reliable Services

The Reliable Services framework is used for writing Microservices using traditional .NET constructs. The framework helps Service Fabric provide reliability, availability, consistency and scalability to your service. Using the Reliable Services model, you can create both stateless and stateful Microservices.

- **Stateless Reliable Service**: A stateless Microservice in Service Fabric does not contain any state data that needs to be stored reliably or made highly available. There is no affinity of requests to the services, therefore stateless services store any state data in external store such as Azure SQL database or Redis cache.
- **Stateful Reliable Service**: A stateful Microservice in Service Fabric can reliably maintain state that is co-located with the executing code of the Microservice. The Service Fabric platform ensures that the state data is replicated, consistent and highly available. The Service Fabric application programming framework provides a few collection types that can be used to store state data with reliability guarantees. These collection classes are part of `Microsoft.ServiceFabric.Data.Collections` namespace and are called **Reliable Collections**. High availability and strong consistency of state data in these collections is guaranteed by writing transactional state data to a majority quorum of replicas, including the primary replica.

At the time of writing, the namespace `Microsoft.ServiceFabric.Data.Collections` contains three collections:

- `ReliableDictionary`: `ReliableDictionary` is similar to the `ConcurrentDictionary` collection in the `System.Collections.Concurrent` namespace. However, unlike the `ConcurrentDictionary` collection, it represents a replicated, transactional, and asynchronous collection of key-value pairs. Similar to `ConcurrentDictionary`, both the key and the value can be of any type.
- `ReliableQueue`: `ReliableQueue` is similar to the `ConcurrentQueue` collection in the `System.Collections.Concurrent` namespace. Just like the `ReliableDictionary` collection, it represents a replicated, transactional, and asynchronous collection of values. However, it is a strict **first-in, first-out** (**FIFO**) queue. The value stored in a `ReliableQueue` can be of any type.

- ReliableConcurrentQueue: ReliableConcurrentQueue is a new Reliable Collection of persisted, replicated values that allows concurrent reads and writes with best-effort. FIFO ordering. ReliableConcurrentQueue supports higher throughput and therefore does not guarantee FIFO behavior like the ReliableQueue does. Also, while ReliableQueue restricts concurrent consumers and producers to a maximum of one each, ReliableConcurrentQueue imposes no such restriction, allowing multiple concurrent consumers and producers.

We will learn more about Reliable Services in the next chapter.

Reliable Actors

You must be familiar with the object-oriented programming paradigm which models problems as a number of interacting objects that contain some data which forms the state of the object. The Actor model of computation breaks down problems into a number of Actors which can function independently and interact with each other by messaging.

The Service Fabric Reliable Actors API provides a high-level abstraction for modelling your Microservices as a number of interacting Actors. This framework is based on the Virtual Actor pattern, which was invented by the Microsoft research team and was released with the codename **Orleans**.

The Actor pattern has been implemented in multiple languages through various frameworks such as Akka.NET, ActorKit, and Quasar. However, unlike Actors implemented on other platforms, the Actors in Orleans are virtual. The Orleans runtime manages the location and activation of Actors similarly to the way that the virtual memory manager of an operating system manages memory pages. It activates an Actor by creating an in-memory copy (an activation) on a server, and later it may deactivate that activation if it hasn't been used for some time. If a message is sent to the Actor and there is no activation on any server, then the runtime will pick a location and create a new activation there.

You can read more about the *Orleans* project from the Microsoft Research website at: https://www.microsoft.com/en-us/research/project/orleans-virtual-actors/.

As a general guidance, you should consider using the Actor pattern in the following scenarios:

- Your system can be described by a number of independent and interactive units (or Actors), each of which can have its own state and logic
- You do not have significant interaction with external data sources and your queries do not span across the Actors
- Your Actors can execute as single-threaded components and do not execute blocking I/O operations

The Service Fabric Reliable Actors API is built on top of the Service Fabric Reliable Services programming model and each Reliable Actor service you write is actually a partitioned, stateful Reliable Service. The Actor state can be stored in memory, on disk, or in external storage.

Since the Service Fabric Actors are virtual, they have a perpetual lifetime. When a client needs to talk to an Actor, the Service Fabric will activate the Actor if it has not been activated or if it has been deactivated. After an Actor has been lying unused for some time, the Service Fabric will deactivate it to save resources. We will read more about Reliable Actors later in this book.

Creating a cluster on Azure

We have discussed quite a few concepts by now. Let's create a Service Fabric cluster in Azure and map the concepts that we learnt with the components. These steps to create a Service Fabric cluster on Azure are also documented on the Microsoft Azure documentation site at: `https://azure.microsoft.com/en-us/documentation/articles/service-fabric-cluster-creation-via-portal/`.

 Although you can work with almost all the samples in this book on your system, you would need a Microsoft Azure subscription to deploy your production workload. We recommend that you get a Microsoft Azure subscription now. You can get started with a free one month trial at: `https://azure.microsoft.com/en-us/free/`.

Perform the following steps to create a **Service Fabric Cluster**:

1. Sign in to the Azure Management Portal at: `https://portal.azure.com`.
2. Click **New** to add a new resource template. Search for the **Service Fabric Cluster** template in **Marketplace** under **Everything**:

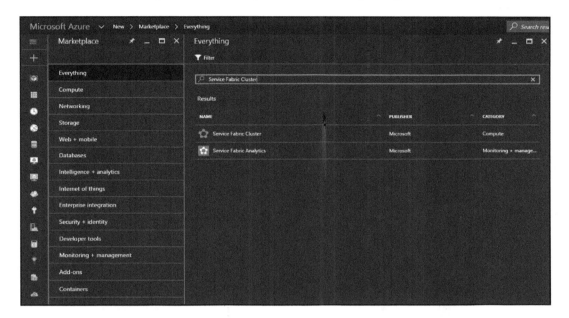

Service Fabric cluster template

3. Select **Service Fabric Cluster** from the list.
4. Navigate to the **Service Fabric Cluster** blade and click **Create**.

The **Create Service Fabric cluster** blade has the following four steps:

Basics

In the **Basics** blade you need to provide the basic details for your cluster:

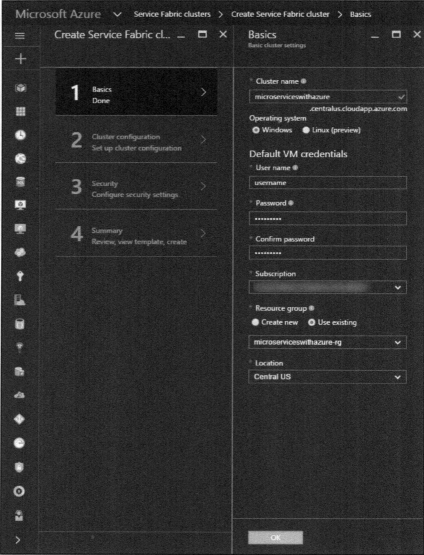

Service Fabric cluster configuration: Basic Blade

You need to provide the following details:

1. Enter the name of your cluster.
2. Enter a **User name** and **Password** for remote desktop for the VMs.
3. Make sure to select the **Subscription** that you want your cluster to be deployed to, especially if you have multiple subscriptions.
4. Create a new **Resource group**. It is best to give it the same name as the cluster, since it helps in finding them later, especially when you are trying to make changes to your deployment or delete your cluster.
5. Select the region in which you want to create the cluster. You must use the same region that your key vault is in.

Cluster configuration

Configure your cluster nodes. Node types define the VM sizes, the number of VMs, and their properties. Your cluster can have more than one node type, but the primary node type (the first one that you define on the portal) must have at least five VMs, as this is the node type where Service Fabric system services are placed. Do not configure **PlacementProperties** because a default placement property of **NodeTypeName** is added automatically:

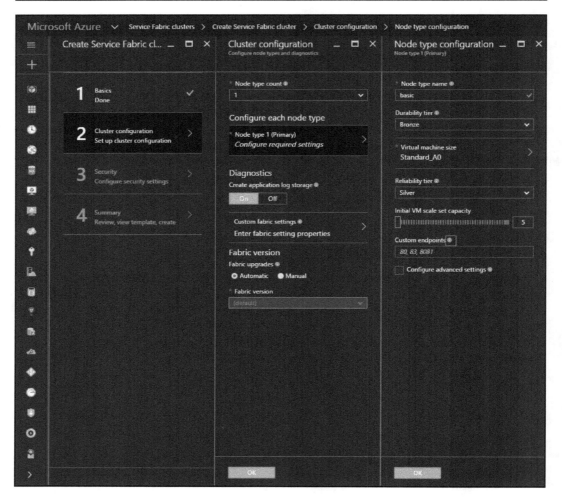

Service Fabric cluster configuration: Node Configuration Blade

For configuring your cluster, you need to perform the following steps:

1. Choose a name for your node type (1 to 12 characters containing only letters and numbers).

2. The minimum size of VMs for the primary node type is driven by the durability tier you choose for the cluster. The default for the durability tier is **Bronze**.

3. Select the VM size and pricing tier. D-series VMs have SSD drives and are highly recommended for stateful applications. Do not use any VM SKU that has partial cores or has less than 7 GB of available disk capacity.

4. The minimum number of VMs for the primary node type is driven by the reliability tier you choose. The default for the reliability tier is **Silver**.

5. Choose the number of VMs for the node type. You can scale up or down the number of VMs in a node type later on, but on the primary node type, the minimum is driven by the reliability level that you have chosen. Other node types can have a minimum of one VM.

6. Configure custom endpoints. This field allows you to enter a comma separated list of ports that you want to expose through the Azure load balancer to the public Internet for your applications. For example, if you plan to deploy a web application to your cluster, enter 80 here to allow traffic on port 80 into your cluster.

7. Configure cluster diagnostics. By default, diagnostics are enabled on your cluster to assist with troubleshooting issues. If you want to disable **Diagnostics**, change the status toggle to **Off**. Turning off diagnostics is not recommended.

8. Select the **Fabric upgrades** mode you want set your cluster to. Select **Automatic**, if you want the system to automatically pick up the latest available version and try to upgrade your cluster to it. Set the mode to **Manual**, if you want to choose a supported version.

Security

The final step is to provide certificate information to secure the cluster. You can secure communication between the clients and the cluster and the communication between the nodes of the cluster using X509 certificates. The communication security can be implemented by adding X509 certificates to a key vault store and configuring the cluster to apply the certificates in this step. To keep this walk-through simple, we will not secure our cluster this time:

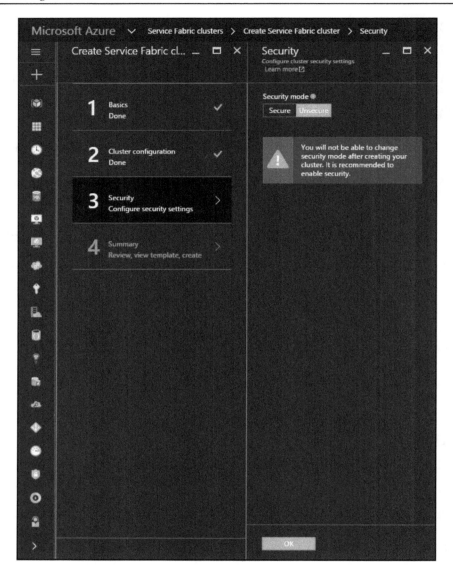

Service Fabric cluster configuration: Security Blade

It is highly recommended that you always use a secured cluster for your production workloads. You have to plan for security at initial stages of development as an unsecure cluster cannot be secured later and a new cluster would need to be created if you decide to secure your cluster later. You can read more about securing your cluster in `Chapter 19`, *Securing and Managing Your Microservices*.

Summary

To complete the cluster creation, click **Summary** to see the configurations that you have provided, or download the Azure Resource Manager template that can be used to deploy your cluster. After you have provided the mandatory settings, the **OK** button becomes green and you can start the cluster creation process by clicking it:

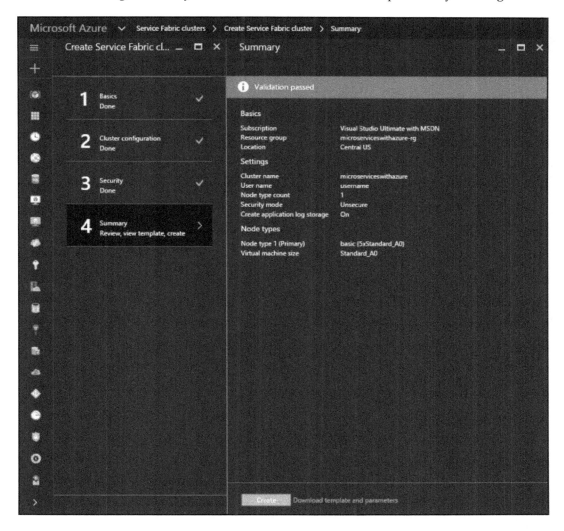

Service Fabric cluster configuration: Summary

You can see the creation progress in the notifications. (Click the *bell* icon near the status bar at the upper-right of your screen.) If you clicked **Pin to Startboard** while creating the cluster, you will see **Deploying Service Fabric cluster** pinned to the **Start** board.

Viewing your cluster status

Once your cluster is created, you can inspect your cluster in the portal:

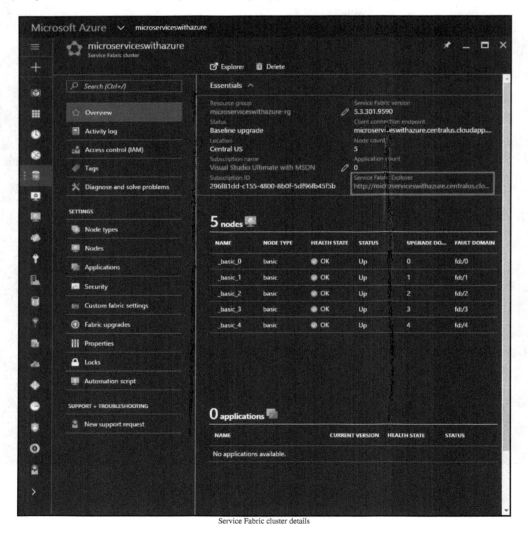

Service Fabric cluster details

To view your cluster status, perform the following steps:

1. Go to browse and click **Service Fabric Clusters**.
2. Locate your cluster and click it.
3. You can now see the details of your cluster in the dashboard, including the cluster's public endpoint and a link to **Service Fabric Explorer**.

The **nodes** monitor section on the cluster's dashboard blade indicates the number of VMs that are healthy and not healthy. Click on the **Service Fabric Explorer** link now to explore the various components of your cluster.

 You can create Service Fabric cluster using Azure Resource Manager. In fact, using ARM is the recommended strategy for deploying workloads. Using Resource Manager, you can repeatedly deploy your solution throughout the development lifecycle and have confidence that your resources are deployed in a consistent state The step-by-step guide to provision a Service Fabric cluster on Azure is available here: `https://azure.microsoft.com/en-us/documentation/articles/service-fabric-cluster-creation-via-arm/`.

Service Fabric Explorer

Service Fabric Explorer is a web-based tool that is built using HTML and AngularJS and is included in every cluster, including the local cluster, at port `19080`. You can access the explorer at `http(s)://clusteraddress:19080/Explorer`.

You can use the Service Fabric Explorer tool for inspecting and managing applications and nodes in an Azure Service Fabric cluster. The left-side section of **Service Fabric Explorer** provides a tree view of your cluster and to the right is a pane showing details of the selected item and an **ACTIONS** button with possible actions you can perform on the item:

Service Fabric Explorer

Let's take a look at the layout of Service Fabric Explorer.

Summary view

The cluster dashboard provides an overview of your cluster, including a summary of application and node health:

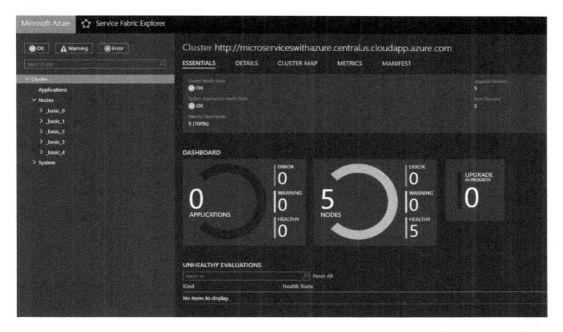

Service Fabric Explorer Cluster Summary

Cluster Map

You can also view the placement of nodes in your cluster by clicking on the **Cluster Map** button. To ensure high availability of your services, your cluster nodes are placed in a table of fault domains and upgrade domains:

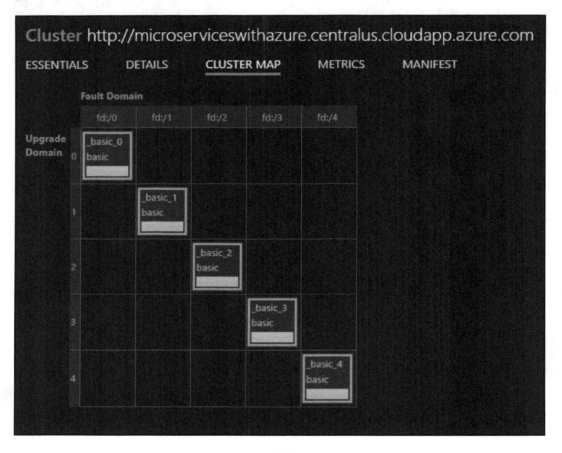

Cluster Map

At this point, you might be interested in knowing what fault domains and upgrade domains are.

Fault domains

A **fault domain** (FD) is an area of coordinated failure. FDs are not restricted to a rack of servers. Several other factors are considered while composing a fault domain such as connection to the same ethernet switch and connection to the same power supply. When you provision a Service Fabric cluster on Azure, your nodes are distributed across several Fault Domains. At runtime, the Service Fabric cluster resource manager spreads replicas of each service across nodes in different fault domains so that failure of a node does not bring down the application.

Service Fabric's cluster resource manager prefers to allocate replicas of your service in a balanced tree of fault domains so that failure of a particular domain does not cause failure of the application. The following is a representation of an imbalanced and a balanced domain configuration:

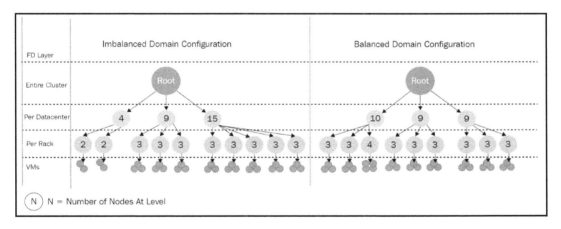

Fault domains

Note that in the imbalanced domain configuration, the extreme right domain may bring down the application if it contains all the replicas of a service. This is something that you don't need to be worry about if you are deploying your cluster in Azure, but something that you need to be aware of when you are deploying your cluster on premises.

Upgrade domains

The **upgrade domains** (**UDs**) are sets of nodes to which an upgrade package (application package, Service Fabric runtime update, or OS update) is applied simultaneously. During an upgrade, all the nodes that are part of the same UDs will go down simultaneously. Unlike fault domains, you can decide the number of upgrade domains that you want and the nodes that should be part of the each upgrade domain.

The following figure shows a setup where we have three upgrade domains spread across three fault domains. The replicas of a stateful service (one primary and two secondary) may be placed across these nodes. Note that they are all in different fault and upgrade domains. This means that we could lose a fault domain while in the middle of a service upgrade and there would still be one running copy of the code and data in the cluster:

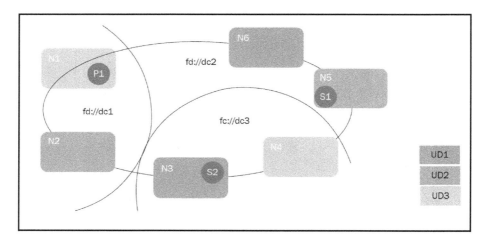

Upgrade domains

You need to be careful when deciding upon the number of upgrade domains that you require. Too few upgrade domains may affect the capacity of your service, as during an upgrade, the remaining nodes may not be able to cater to the load on application. On the other hand, too many upgrade domains may make the upgrade propagation a slow process.

Viewing applications and services

The cluster node contains two more subtrees, one for applications and one for nodes. Since, we haven't yet deployed an application to the cluster, this node contains no items. We will revisit this part of the explorer once we are done developing our first Service Fabric application.

Cluster nodes

Expanding the nodes tree will list the nodes present in the cluster. The details view will show you, which FD and UD each node is a part of. You can also view which application is currently executing on the node and, more importantly, which replica is running on it:

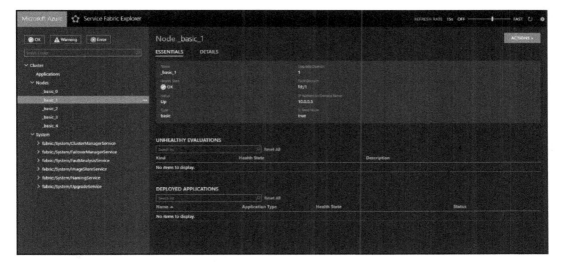

Cluster Nodes

Actions

The **ACTIONS** button is available on the nodes, applications, and services view in the explorer. You can invoke actions on the particular element through this button. For instance, in the **Nodes** view, you can restart a node by selecting **Restart** from the **ACTIONS** menu:

Actions Button

The following table lists the actions available for each entity:

Entity	Action	Description
Application type	Unprovision type	Remove the application package from the cluster's image store. Requires all applications of that type to be removed first.
Application	Delete application	Delete the application, including all its services and their state (if any).
Service	Delete service	Delete the service and its state (if any).
Node	Activate	Activate the node.
Node	Deactivate (pause)	Pause the node in its current state. Services continue to run but Service Fabric does not proactively move anything onto or off it unless it is required to prevent an outage or data inconsistency. This action is typically used to enable debugging services on a specific node to ensure that they do not move during inspection.
Node	Deactivate (restart)	Safely move all in-memory services off a node and close persistent services. Typically used when the host processes or machine need to be restarted.

Entity	Action	Description
Node	Deactivate (remove data)	Safely close all services running on the node after building sufficient spare replicas. Typically used when a node (or at least its storage) is being permanently taken out of commission.
Node	Remove node state	Remove knowledge of a node's replicas from the cluster. Typically used when an already failed node is deemed unrecoverable.

Since many actions are destructive, you may be asked to confirm your intent before the action is completed.

System

The various system services that we previously discussed are listed in this node:

System Services

If you expand the individual service nodes, you will be able to see the placement of the services. Notice that all the services have been deployed to multiple nodes; however, the primary and secondary replicas of each service have been spread across multiple fault and upgrade domains for instance, in the preceding figure, you can see that the primary replica of the **ClusterManagerService** is deployed on the node named (**_basic_2**) while that of the **FailoverManagerService** is deployed on the node named (**_basic_4**).

Preparing your system

To get started with developing applications on Service Fabric, you will need to the following:

1. Install the runtime, SDK, and tools.
2. A Service Fabric cluster to deploy your applications.
3. Configure PowerShell to enable SDK script execution.

We are going to use C#, Visual Studio 2015, and Windows 10 to develop all samples in this book.

 You can find the steps to to prepare your development environment on various operating systems at this link: `https://azure.microsoft.com/en-us/documentation/articles/service-fabric-get-started/`.

To install the SDK, tools, and Service Fabric runtime, use the Web Platform Installer (Visual Studio 2015) or enable Service Fabric workload (Visual Studio 2017). You can read more about these options at:

`https://docs.microsoft.com/en-us/azure/service-fabric/service-fabric-get-started`.

Service Fabric uses Windows PowerShell scripts for creating a local development cluster and for deploying applications from Visual Studio. By default, Windows blocks these scripts from running. To enable them, you must modify your PowerShell execution policy. Open PowerShell as an administrator and enter the following command:

```
Set-ExecutionPolicy -ExecutionPolicy Unrestricted -Force -Scope
CurrentUser
```

After you have completed the installation steps, you should be able to find the Service Fabric local cluster manager installed in your system, along with new Service Fabric project templates in your Visual Studio. Let's get started with building our first application on Service Fabric in the next chapter.

Summary

In this chapter, we covered the features of Service Fabric which make it an ideal platform to host Microservices. We discussed how Service Fabric acts as an orchestrator for managing Microservices.

In the second section of the chapter, we covered the architecture of Service Fabric in detail and studied the cluster services. Next, we discussed the infrastructure model, system services, and programming models available to build and host applications on Service Fabric.

Finally, we walked through the steps for creating a Service Fabric cluster on Azure and preparing our system to get started with developing applications on Service Fabric.

14
Hands-on with Service Fabric – Guest Executables

Service Fabric as a platform supports multiple programming models, each of which is best suited for specific scenarios. Each programming model offers different levels of integration with the underlying management framework. Better integration leads to more automation and fewer overheads. Picking the right programming model for your application or service is the key to efficiently utilizing the capabilities of Service Fabric as a hosting platform. Let's take a deeper look into these programming models.

To start with, let's look at the least integrated hosting option – **Guest Executables**. Native Windows applications or application code using Node.js or Java can be hosted on Service Fabric as a Guest Executable. These executables can be packaged and pushed to a Service Fabric cluster like any other services. As the cluster manager has minimal knowledge about the executable, features such as custom health monitoring, load reporting, state store, and endpoint registration cannot be leveraged by the hosted application. However, from a deployment standpoint, a guest executable is treated like any other service. This means that for a guest executable, Service Fabric cluster manager takes care of high availability, application lifecycle management, rolling updates, automatic failover, high-density deployment, and load balancing.

As an orchestration service, Service Fabric is responsible for deploying and activating an application or application service within a cluster. It is also capable of deploying services within a container image. This programming model is addressed as Guest Containers. The concept of containers is best explained as an implementation of operating system level virtualization. They are encapsulated deployable components running on isolated process boundaries sharing the same kernel. Deployed applications and their runtime dependencies are bundles within the container with an isolated view of all operating system constructs. This makes containers highly portable and secure. The Guest Container programming model is usually chosen when this level of isolation is required for the application. As containers don't have to boot an operating system, they have fast boot up time and are comparatively small in size.

A prime benefit of using Service Fabric as a platform is the fact that it supports heterogeneous operating environments. Service Fabric supports two types of containers to be deployed as Guest Containers:

- Docker Containers on Linux
- Windows Server Containers

Container images for Docker Containers are stored in Docker Hub and Docker APIs are used to create and manage the containers deployed on a Linux kernel.

Service Fabric supports two different types of containers in Windows Server 2016 with different levels of isolation:

- Windows Server Containers
- Windows Hyper-V Containers

Windows Server Containers are similar to Docker Containers in terms of the isolation they provide. Windows Hyper-V Containers offer a higher degree of isolation and security by not sharing the operating system kernel across instances. These are ideally used when a higher level of security isolation is required, such as systems requiring hostile multitenant hosts.

The following figure illustrates the different isolation levels achieved by using these containers:

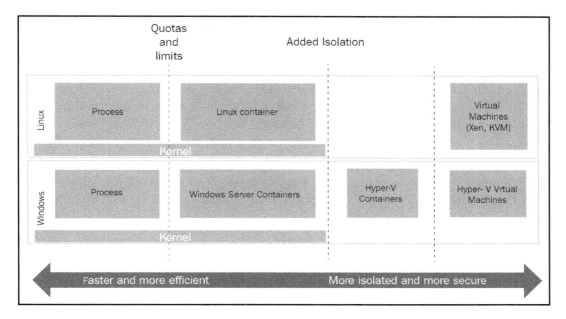

Container isolation levels

The Service Fabric application model treats containers as an application host which can in turn host service replicas. There are three ways of utilizing containers within a Service Fabric application mode. Existing applications such as Node.js and JavaScript applications, or other executables can be hosted within a container and deployed on Service Fabric as a Guest Container. A Guest Container is treated similar to a Guest Executable by the Service Fabric runtime. The second scenario supports deploying stateless services inside a container hosted on Service Fabric. Stateless services using Reliable Services and Reliable Actors can be deployed within a container. The third option is to deploy stateful services in containers hosted on Service Fabric. This model also supports Reliable Services and Reliable Actors.

Service Fabric offers several features to manage containerized Microservices. These include container deployment and activation, resource governance, repository authentication, port mapping, container discovery and communication, and the ability to set environment variables. Later in this chapter, we will explore ways of deploying containers on Service Fabric.

While containers offer a good level of isolation, it is still heavy in terms of deployment footprint. Service Fabric offers a simpler, powerful programming model to develop your services, which they call Reliable Services. Reliable Services let you develop stateful and stateless services which can be directly deployed on Service Fabric clusters. For stateful services, the state can be stored close to the compute by using Reliable Collections. High availability of the state store and replication of the state is taken care by the Service Fabric cluster management services. This contributes substantially to the performance of the system by improving the latency of data access. Reliable Services come with a built-in pluggable communication model which supports HTTP with Web API, WebSockets, and custom TCP protocols out-of-the-box.

A Reliable Service is addressed as stateless if it does not maintain any state within it or if the scope of the state stored is limited to a service call and is entirely disposable. This means that a stateless service does not need to persist, synchronize, or replicate state. A good example for this service is a weather service such as MSN weather service. A weather service can be queried to retrieve weather conditions associated with a specific geographical location. The response is totally based on the parameters supplied to the service. This service does not store any state. Although stateless services are simpler to implement, most of the services in real life are not stateless. They either store state in an external state store or an internal one. Web frontend hosting APIs or web applications are good use cases to be hosted as stateless services.

A stateful service typically will utilize various mechanisms to persist its state. The outcome of a service call made to a stateful service is usually influenced by the state persisted by the service. A service exposed by a bank to return the balance on an account is a good example for a stateful service. The state may be stored in an external data store such as Azure SQL Database, Azure Blobs, or Azure Table store. Most services prefer to store the state externally, considering the challenges around reliability, availability, scalability, and consistency of the data store. With Service Fabric, state can be stored close to the compute by using Reliable Collections.

To make things more lightweight, Service Fabric also offers a programming model based on the Virtual Actor pattern. This programming model is called Reliable Actors. The Reliable Actors programming model is built on top of Reliable Services. This guarantees the scalability and reliability of the services. An Actor can be defined as an isolated, independent unit of compute and state with single-threaded execution. Actors can be created, managed, and disposed independent of each other.

A large number of Actors can coexist and execute at a time. Service Fabric Reliable Actors are a good fit for systems which are highly distributed and dynamic by nature. Every Actor is defined as an instance of an Actor type, the same way an object is an instance of a class. Each Actor is uniquely identified by an Actor ID. The lifetime of Service Fabric Actors is not tied to their in-memory state. As a result, Actors are automatically created the first time a request for them is made. Reliable Actor's garbage collector takes care of disposing unused Actors in memory.

Now that we understand the programming models, let's take a look at how the services deployed on Service Fabric are discovered and how the communication between services takes place.

Service Fabric discovery and communication

An application built on top of Microservices is usually composed of multiple services, each of which runs multiple replicas. Each service is specialized in a specific task. To achieve an end-to-end business use case, multiple services will need to be stitched together. This requires services to communicate to each other. A simple example would be a web frontend service communicating with the middle-tier services, which in turn connects to the backend services to handle a single user request. Some of these middle-tier services can also be invoked by external applications.

Services deployed on Service Fabric are distributed across multiple nodes in a cluster of virtual machines. The services can move across dynamically. This distribution of services can either be triggered by a manual action or be result of Service Fabric cluster manager rebalancing services to achieve optimal resource utilization. This makes communication a challenge as services are not tied to a particular machine. Let's understand how Service Fabric solves this challenge for its consumers.

Service protocols

Service Fabric, as a hosting platform for Microservices, does not interfere in the implementation of the service. On top of this, it also lets services decide on the communication channels they want to open. These channels are addressed as service endpoints. During service initiation, Service Fabric provides the opportunity for the services to set up the endpoints for incoming requests on any protocol or communication stack. The endpoints are defined according to common industry standards, that is *IP:Port*. It is possible that multiple service instances share a single host process. In which case, they either have to use different ports or a port sharing mechanism. This will ensure that every service instance is uniquely addressable:

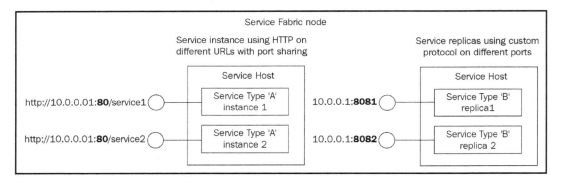

Service endpoints

Service discovery

Service Fabric can rebalance services deployed on a cluster as a part of orchestration activities. This can be caused by resource balancing activities, failovers, upgrades, scale-outs, or scale-ins. This will result in changes in service endpoint addresses as the services move across different virtual machines.

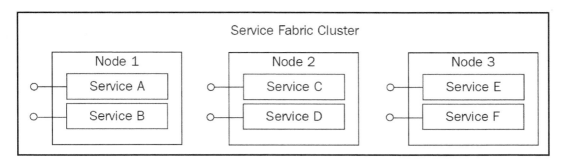

Service distribution

The Service Fabric Naming Service is responsible for abstracting this complexity from the consuming service or application. The Naming Service takes care of service discovery and resolution. All service instances in Service Fabric are identified by a unique URL such as `fabric:/MyMicroServiceApp/AppService1`. This name stays constant across the lifetime of the service, although the endpoint addresses which physically host the service may change. Internally, Service Fabric manages a map between the service names and the physical location where the service is hosted. This is similar to the DNS service which is used to resolve website URLs to IP addresses.

The following figure illustrates the name resolution process for a service hosted on Service Fabric:

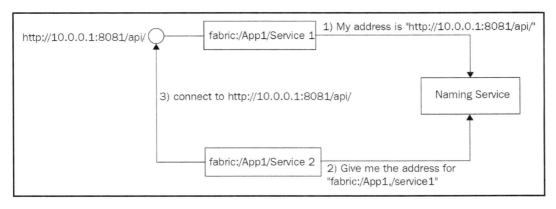

Name resolution

Connections from applications external to Service Fabric

Service communications between services hosted in Service Fabric can be categorized as internal or external. Internal communication between services hosted on Service Fabric is easily achieved using the Naming Service. External communication, originated from an application or a user outside the boundaries of Service Fabric, will need some extra work. To understand how this works, let's dive deeper into the logical network layout of a typical Service Fabric cluster.

A Service Fabric cluster is usually placed behind an Azure load balancer. The load balancer acts like a gateway to all traffic which needs to pass to the Service Fabric cluster. The load balancer is aware of every post open on every node of a cluster. When a request hits the load balancer, it identifies the port the request is looking for and randomly routes the request to one of the nodes which has the requested port open. The load balancer is not aware of the services running on the nodes or the ports associated with the services.

The following figure illustrates request routing in action:

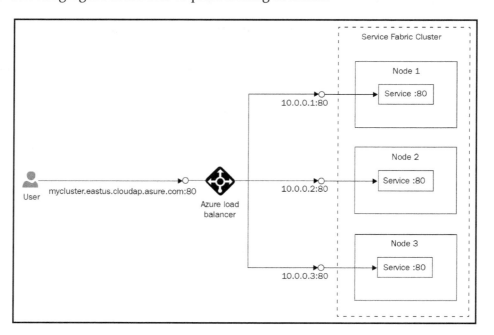

Request routing

Configuring ports and protocols

The protocol and the ports to be opened by a Service Fabric cluster can be easily configured through the portal. Let's take an example to understand the configuration in detail.

If we need a web application to be hosted on a Service Fabric cluster which should have port 80 opened on HTTP to accept incoming traffic, the following steps should be performed.

Configuring the service manifest

Once a service listening to port 80 is authored, we need to configure port 80 in the service manifest to open a listener in the service. This can be done by editing Service Manifest.xml:

```
<Resources>
    <Endpoints>
        <Endpoint Name="WebEndpoint" Protocol="http" Port="80" />
    </Endpoints>
</Resources>
```

Configuring the custom endpoint

On the Service Fabric cluster, configure port 80 as a **Custom endpoint**. This can be easily done through the Azure Management Portal:

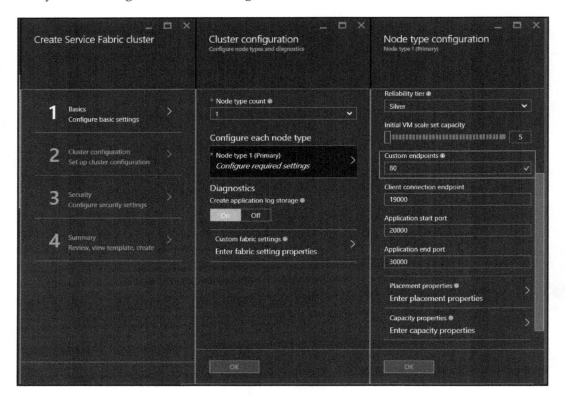

Configuring custom port

Configuring the Azure load balancer

Once the cluster is configured and created, the Azure load balancer can be instructed to forward the traffic to port `80`. If the Service Fabric cluster is created through the portal, this step is automatically taken care for every port which is configured on the cluster configuration:

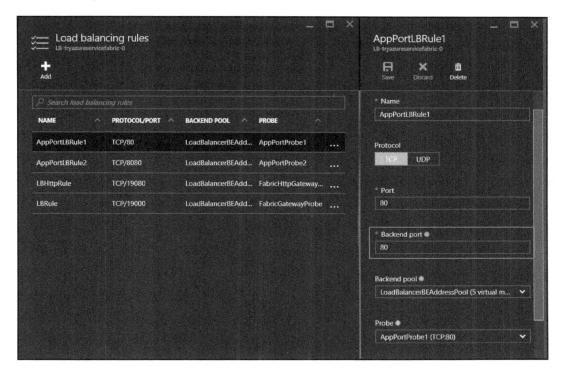

Configuring Azure Load Balancer

Configuring the health check

Azure load balancer probes the ports on the nodes for their availability to ensure reliability of the service. The probes can be configured on the Azure Portal. This is an optional step as a default probe configuration is applied for each endpoint when a cluster is created:

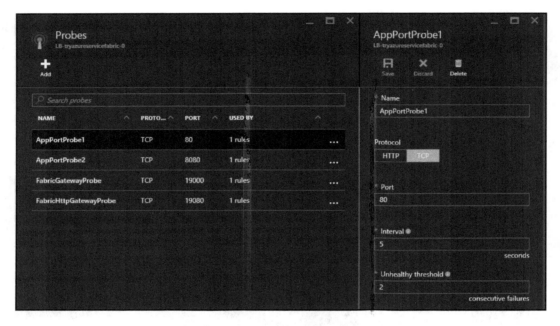

Configuring the probe

Built-in communication API

Service Fabric offers many built-in communication options to support inter-service communications. Service remoting is one of them. This option allows strong typed remote procedure calls between Reliable Services and Reliable Actors. This option is very easy to set up and operate with as service remoting handles resolution of service addresses, connection, retry, and error handling. Service Fabric also supports HTTP for language-agnostic communication.

Service Fabric SDK exposes `ICommunicationClient` and `ServicePartitionClient` classes for service resolution, HTTP connections, and retry loops. WCF is also supported by Service Fabric as a communication channel to enable legacy workload to be hosted on it. The SDK exposed `WcfCommunicationListener` for the server side and `WcfCommunicationClient` and `ServicePartitionClient` classes for the client to ease programming hurdles.

Deploying a Guest Executable

Service Fabric supports hosting packaged executables developed using .NET, Node.js, Java, or any similar programming languages. These executables are addressed as Guest Executables in the Service Fabric world. Although they are not developed using Service Fabric SDK, Service Fabric still ensures high availability and high-density deployment of Guest Executables on a cluster. Service Fabric is also capable of performing basic health monitoring for these executables and managing their application lifecycle.

Let's explore the details around the steps to be followed to deploy a Guest Executable on a Service Fabric cluster.

Understanding the manifests

Service Fabric uses two XML files - the *Application Manifest* and the *Service Manifest* for the purpose of packaging and deploying the applications. An application in Service Fabric is a unit of deployment. An application can be deployed, upgraded, or even rolled back as a unit. The rollback usually occurs in case of a failure on upgrade and is automatically handled by the Service Fabric orchestrator to ensure system stability.

Application manifest, as the name suggests, is used to describe the application. It defines the list of services and the parameters required to deploy these services. Number of service instances being one of them.

Service manifest defines the components of a service. This includes data, code, and configuration. We will look deeper in these manifests in later sections of this book.

Package structure

Service Fabric expects the application to be packages in a specific directory structure. Let's take an example to understand this further:

```
|-- ApplicationPackageRoot
    |-- GuestService1Pkg
        |-- Code
            |-- existingapp.exe
        |-- Config
            |-- Settings.xml
        |-- Data

        |-- ServiceManifest.xml
    |-- ApplicationManifest.xml
```

`ApplicationPackageRoot`, is the root folder containing the application manifest file - `ApplicationManifest.xml`. Each sub directory under this folder specifies a service which is part of this application. In the preceding example, `GuestService1Pkg` is one such service. Every service folder in turn holds the service components. This includes three sub folders holding the code, configuration, and data. The `Service` folder also holds the service manifest file - `ServiceManifest.xml`. The `Code` directory contains the source code for the service. The `Config` directory contains a settings file - `Settings.xml` which store the service configuration. The `Data` folder stores transient data which is used by the service locally. This data is not replicated across service instances. The `Config` and `Code` folders are optional.

There are two ways to package a Service Fabric Guest Executable. The easiest way is to use Visual Studio template for Guest Executables. The other way is to package it manually. Let's take a look at both these options.

Packaging Guest Executables using Visual Studio

Installing the Service Fabric SDK is a pre-requisite for performing this exercise. The following steps can be followed to create a Guest Executable package using Visual Studio:

1. Open Visual Studio and choose **New Project**.
2. Select **Service Fabric Application**.
3. Choose the **Guest Executable** service template.
4. Click **Browse** and select the folder holding the executable to be packaged.

5. Fill in other parameters:
   - **Code Package Behavior**: This is ideally set to copy all the content of the folder to the Visual Studio project. There is also an option to link a folder if you require the project to dynamically pick up the executables every time it executes.
   - **Program**: Choose the executable that should run to start the service.
   - **Arguments**: Input parameters to be passed in as arguments to the executable should be specified here.
   - **Working Folder**: The working folder can be set to one of these three values:
     - **CodeBase**: If you want to set the working folder to the code directory.
     - **CodePackage**: If you want to set the working folder to the root directory.
     - **Work**: If you want to place the files in a sub directory called **Work**

6. Name your service.
7. Click **OK**.
8. If the service requires an endpoint communication, you need to edit `ServiceManifest.xml` to open an endpoint. We will see how this can be done in the next section.
9. You can now debug the solution and use package and publish action to deploy the Guest Executable on your local cluster.
10. When ready, you can publish the application to a remote cluster using Visual Studio.

Manually packaging a Guest Executable

The process of manually packaging a Guest Executable can be divided into four steps.

Creating the directory structure

To start with, the directory structure for the deployment package needs to be created as per the hierarchy mentioned earlier in this chapter. This package structure will host the code, configuration, and data required for the deployment.

Adding code and configuration

Once the directory structure is ready, the code and the configuration files can be placed under the respective directories. It is allowed to have multiple levels of subdirectories within these folders. It is important to ensure that all the dependencies required for the application to run are included in the folders. Service Fabric replicates the content of these folders across nodes in a cluster.

Updating service manifest

Service manifest file stores the configuration for service deployment. This file needs to be updated to provide a name to the service, to specify the command used to launch the application, and to specify and setup or configure scripts which need to be executed. Following is an example of a service manifest file:

```xml
<?xml version="1.0" encoding="utf-8"?>
<ServiceManifest xmlns:xsd="http://www.w3.org/2001/XMLSchema"
xmlns:xsi="http://www.w3.org/2001/XMLSchema-instance" Name="NodeApp"
Version="1.0.0.0" xmlns="http://schemas.microsoft.com/2011/01/fabric">
    <ServiceTypes>
      <StatelessServiceType ServiceTypeName="NodeApp"
UseImplicitHost="true"/>
    </ServiceTypes>
    <CodePackage Name="code" Version="1.0.0.0">
      <SetupEntryPoint>
        <ExeHost>
            <Program>scripts\launchConfig.cmd</Program>
        </ExeHost>
      </SetupEntryPoint>
      <EntryPoint>
        <ExeHost>
          <Program>node.exe</Program>
          <Arguments>bin/www</Arguments>
          <WorkingFolder>CodePackage</WorkingFolder>
        </ExeHost>
      </EntryPoint>
    </CodePackage>
    <Resources>
      <Endpoints>
        <Endpoint Name="NodeAppTypeEndpoint" Protocol="http"
Port="3000" Type="Input" />
      </Endpoints>
    </Resources>
</ServiceManifest>
```

To break this down further, let's go through every section in the service manifest:

```
<ServiceTypes>
    <StatelessServiceType ServiceTypeName="NodeApp"
UseImplicitHost="true" />
</ServiceTypes>
```

ServiceTypeName is a custom parameter which can be assigned to the deployed service. This value will be later used in the application manifest file. It is important to set the UseImplicitHost as true as this specifies the service as self-contained:

```
<CodePackage Name="Code" Version="1.0.0.0">
```

CodePackage element specifies the location of the folder holding the code and the version of the application packaged:

```
<SetupEntryPoint>
    <ExeHost>
        <Program>scripts\launchConfig.cmd</Program>
    </ExeHost>
</SetupEntryPoint>
```

SetupEntryPoint is an optional element used to specify the executable of batch files which should be executed before the service code is launched. This can be ignored as there are no startup scripts for the application. There can only be one SetupEntryPoint for a package:

```
<EntryPoint>
    <ExeHost>
        <Program>node.exe</Program>
        <Arguments>bin/www</Arguments>
        <WorkingFolder>CodeBase</WorkingFolder>
        <ConsoleRedirection FileRetentionCount="5"
FileMaxSizeInKb="2048"/>
    </ExeHost>
</EntryPoint>
```

The EntryPoint element specifies the details about application launch. The Program element specifies the name of the executable to be launched, Arguments element specifies the parameters to be passed in as arguments to the executable and the WorkingFolder specifies the working directory. ConsoleRedirection can be used to setup logging. This element helps redirect console output to a working directory:

```
<Endpoints>
    <Endpoint Name="NodeAppTypeEndpoint" Protocol="http" Port="3000"
Type="Input" />
</Endpoints>
```

The `Endpoints` element specifies the endpoint this application can listen on.

Updating the application manifest

Application manifest defines the list of services and the parameters required to deploy these services. Following is an example:

```xml
<?xml version="1.0" encoding="utf-8"?>
<ApplicationManifest xmlns:xsd="http://www.w3.org/2001/XMLSchema"
xmlns:xsi="http://www.w3.org/2001/XMLSchema-instance"
ApplicationTypeName="NodeAppType" ApplicationTypeVersion="1.0"
xmlns="http://schemas.microsoft.com/2011/01/fabric">
   <ServiceManifestImport>
      <ServiceManifestRef ServiceManifestName="NodeApp"
ServiceManifestVersion="1.0.0.0" />
   </ServiceManifestImport>
</ApplicationManifest>
```

The `ServiceManifestImport` element specifies the services that are included in the app.

Deployment

A PowerShell script can be used to manually deploy a package to a Service Fabric cluster:

```powershell
Connect-ServiceFabricCluster localhost:19000

Write-Host 'Copying application package...'
Copy-ServiceFabricApplicationPackage -ApplicationPackagePath
'C:\Dev\MultipleApplications' -ImageStoreConnectionString
'file:C:\SfDevCluster\Data\ImageStoreShare' -
ApplicationPackagePathInImageStore 'nodeapp'

Write-Host 'Registering application type...'
Register-ServiceFabricApplicationType -ApplicationPathInImageStore
'nodeapp'

New-ServiceFabricApplication -ApplicationName 'fabric:/nodeapp' -
ApplicationTypeName 'NodeAppType' -ApplicationTypeVersion 1.0

New-ServiceFabricService -ApplicationName 'fabric:/nodeapp' -
ServiceName 'fabric:/nodeapp/nodeappservice' -ServiceTypeName
'NodeApp' -Stateless -PartitionSchemeSingleton -InstanceCount 1
```

The `InstanceCount` parameter in the preceding script specifies the number of instances of the application to be deployed in the cluster. This value can be set to −1 if the application needs to be deployed on every node of the Service Fabric cluster.

Deploying a Guest Container

Service Fabric supports hosting containerized Microservices. It offers specialized features to manage containerized workloads. Some of these features are container image deployment and activation, resource governance, repository authentication, container port to host mapping, container-to-container discovery and communication, support for environment variables, and so on. Service Fabric supports two types of container workloads - Windows Containers and Docker Containers. Let's pick them one by one and understand the packaging and deployment process.

Deploying Windows Container

Similar to Guest Executables, Service Fabric will support packaging Guest Containers either through Visual Studio or manually. However, the Visual Studio wizard for Guest Containers is still under development. Let's dive deeper into the process of packaging and deploying a Guest Container manually.

The packaging process consists of four major steps - publishing the container to a repository, creating the package directory structure, updating the service manifest, and updating the application manifest.

Container image deployment and activation

Service Fabric treats a container as an application host capable of hosting multiple service replicas. To deploy and activate a container, the name of the container image must be put into the `ContainerHost` element of the service manifest. The following example deploys a container called `myimage:v1` from a repository `myrepo`:

```
<CodePackage Name="Code" Version="1.0">
    <EntryPoint>
      <ContainerHost>
        <ImageName>myrepo/myimagename:v1</ImageName>
        <Commands></Commands>
      </ContainerHost>
    </EntryPoint>
</CodePackage>
```

The `Commands` element can be used to pass commands to the container image. The element can take comma-separated values as commands.

Resource governance

The `ResourceGovernancePolicy` element is used to restrict the resources consumed by a container on a host. The limits can be set for `Memory`, `MemorySwap`, `CPUShares`, `MemoryReservationInMB`, or `BlkioWeight` (bulk I/O weight). The following sample shows the use of `ResourceGovernancePolicy` element:

```
<ServiceManifestImport>
    <ServiceManifestRef ServiceManifestName="FrontendServicePackage"
ServiceManifestVersion="1.0"/>
    <Policies>
        <ContainerHostPolicies CodePackageRef="FrontendService.Code">
            <RepositoryCredentials AccountName="TestUser"
Password="12345" PasswordEncrypted="false"/>
        </ContainerHostPolicies>
    </Policies>
</ServiceManifestImport>
```

The password specified in the `RepositoryCredentials` element should be encrypted using a certificate deployed on the machine.

Container port to host port mapping

`PortBinding` element in the application manifest can be used to configure the ports used for communication by the container. The binding maps the ports internal to the container to the ones open on the hosting machine. Following is an example:

```
<ServiceManifestImport>
    <ServiceManifestRef ServiceManifestName="FrontendServicePackage"
ServiceManifestVersion="1.0"/>
    <Policies>
        <ContainerHostPolicies CodePackageRef="FrontendService.Code">
            <PortBinding ContainerPort="8905"/>
        </ContainerHostPolicies>
    </Policies>
</ServiceManifestImport>
```

Container-to-container discovery and communication

The `PortBinding` element is also used to map a port to an endpoint. The `Endpoint` element in a `PortBinding` can be used to specify a fixed port or left blank to choose a random port available to the cluster port range. The `Endpoint` element in the `ServiceManifest` enables Service Fabric to automatically publish the element to the Naming Service to enable discovery of the container. Following is an example:

```
<ServiceManifestImport>
    <ServiceManifestRef ServiceManifestName="FrontendServicePackage"
ServiceManifestVersion="1.0"/>
    <Policies>
        <ContainerHostPolicies CodePackageRef="FrontendService.Code">
            <PortBinding ContainerPort="8905"
EndpointRef="Endpoint1"/>
        </ContainerHostPolicies>
    </Policies>
</ServiceManifestImport>
```

Configuring and setting environment variables

Environment variables for the service can be set within the service manifest. They can also be overridden in the application manifest or by application parameters supplied at runtime. Following is an example explaining how this can be done in a service manifest:

```
<ServiceManifest Name="FrontendServicePackage" Version="1.0"
xmlns="http://schemas.microsoft.com/2011/01/fabric"
xmlns:xsi="http://www.w3.org/2001/XMLSchema-instance">
    <Description>a guest executable service in a
container</Description>
    <ServiceTypes>
        <StatelessServiceType
ServiceTypeName="StatelessFrontendService"  UseImplicitHost="true"/>
    </ServiceTypes>
    <CodePackage Name="FrontendService.Code" Version="1.0">
        <EntryPoint>
        <ContainerHost>
            <ImageName>myrepo/myimage:v1</ImageName>
            <Commands></Commands>
        </ContainerHost>
        </EntryPoint>
        <EnvironmentVariables>
            <EnvironmentVariable Name="HttpGatewayPort" Value=""/>
```

```
            <EnvironmentVariable Name="BackendServiceName" Value=""/>
        </EnvironmentVariables>
    </CodePackage>
</ServiceManifest>
```

The following example shows how this can be overridden in an application manifest:

```
<ServiceManifestImport>
    <ServiceManifestRef ServiceManifestName="FrontendServicePackage"
ServiceManifestVersion="1.0"/>
    <EnvironmentOverrides CodePackageRef="FrontendService.Code">
        <EnvironmentVariable Name="BackendServiceName"
Value="[BackendSvc]"/>
        <EnvironmentVariable Name="HttpGatewayPort" Value="19080"/>
    </EnvironmentOverrides>
</ServiceManifestImport>
```

Deploying a Linux container

Containers in Linux can be packaged for Service Fabric either using a Yeoman template or manually. The Service Fabric SDK for Linux comes with a built-in Yeoman generator to ease things for application developers. Yeoman generator facilitates creating an application and adding it to a container image with minimal effort.

 Yeoman is a development stack that combines several development tools and runs as a command-line interface. Yeoman has a pluggable architecture and it only orchestrates the development tools plugged into it. The many available Yeoman plugins, called generators in Yeoman terms, create starter templates, manage dependencies, run unit tests, and optimize deployment code, among many other things. You can read more about Yeoman here: `http://yeoman.io/`.

Manifest files can be later updated to add or update services. Once the application is built, the Azure CLI can be used to deploy the local cluster.

Summary

We started this chapter by discussing service discovery and communication protocols used by Service Fabric. Next, we dived deeper into configuring the manifest for custom endpoints, load balancer, and health checks.

Towards the end of the chapter, we briefly discussed methods for deploying Guest executables and Guest Containers on Service Fabric.

15
Hands on with Service Fabric – Reliable Services

By now, we have set a strong foundation for us to explore the internals of Service Fabric. Let's get started by building our first Service Fabric application. We will build a simple application that will print the customary *Hello World* message.

The companion GitHub repository of this title contains code for all the samples that we have used in this book. You can visit `https://github.com/PacktPublishing/Microservices-with-Azure` to download the samples. Let's start building our application:

1. Launch Visual Studio as an administrator. This is necessary because we are going to test our application in Service Fabric local cluster that needs administrator privileges to work.
2. Click **File** | **New Project** | **Cloud** | **Service Fabric Application**.

3. Name the application `HelloWorldApplication` and click **OK**.

Create new Service Fabric application

4. On the next page, choose **Stateless Service** as the service type to include in your application. Name it `HelloWorldService` and click **OK**.

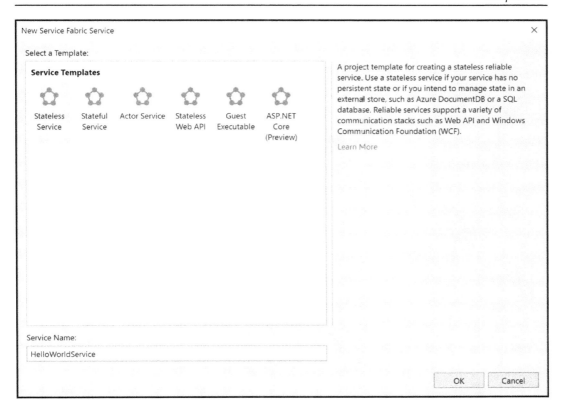

New Service Fabric Service   ×

Select a Template:

Service Templates

Stateless Service   Stateful Service   Actor Service   Stateless Web API   Guest Executable   ASP.NET Core (Preview)

A project template for creating a stateless reliable service. Use a stateless service if your service has no persistent state or if you intend to manage state in an external store, such as Azure DocumentDB or a SQL database. Reliable services support a variety of communication stacks such as Web API and Windows Communication Foundation (WCF).

Learn More

Service Name:

HelloWorldService

OK   Cancel

Create new stateless service dialog

Wait for the project template to unfold. In your solution, you will find two projects – the Service Fabric application project, named `HelloWorldApplication` and the stateless Microservice named `HelloWorldService`. Remember that in Service Fabric an application is a collection of Microservices. We will go through the various components of the project in a little while. For now, let us make our `HelloWorldService` generate some output. Navigate to the `HellcWorldService.cs` file and locate the `HelloWorldService` class.

```
namespace HelloWorldService
{
    /// <summary>
    /// An instance of this class is created for each
service
            instance by the Service Fabric runtime.
    /// </summary>
```

```
            internal sealed class HelloWorldService :
StatelessService
        {
            public HelloWorldService(StatelessServiceContext
                                            context)
                : base(context)
        { }

            /// <summary>
            /// Optional override to create listeners (for
example,
                TCP, HTTP) for this service replica to handle
client
                or user requests.
            /// </summary>
            /// <returns>A collection of listeners.</returns>
            protected override
IEnumerable<ServiceInstanceListener>
                CreateServiceInstanceListeners()
            {
                return new ServiceInstanceListener[0];
            }

            /// <summary>
            /// This is the main entry point for your
                service instance.
            /// </summary>
            /// <param name="cancellationToken">Canceled when
                                                Service
                Fabric needs to shut down this service
                instance.</param>
            protected override async Task
RunAsync(CancellationToken
                cancellationToken)
            {
                ...
            }
        }
    }
```

A Service Fabric stateless Microservice derives from the
StatelessService class. Service Fabric internally uses the functions
exposed by the StatelessService class to govern the lifecycle of your
stateless Microservice. The RunAsync method is a general-purpose entry
point for your service code.

Let's replace the definition of this method with the following one:

```
protected override async Task RunAsync(CancellationToken
    cancellationToken)
{
    long iterations = 0;
    while (true)
    {
        cancellationToken.ThrowIfCancellationRequested();
        ServiceEventSource.Current.ServiceMessage(this.Context,
            $"Hello World {++iterations}");
        await Task.Delay(TimeSpan.FromSeconds(1),
            cancellationToken);
    }
}
```

Service Fabric does not force your Microservices to communicate through
any specific communication stack. Since we haven't implemented any
communication stack for our service in this example, our service will
behave as a background service akin to Windows Service, Azure WebJob, or
Cloud Service Worker Role.

The Service Fabric solution template also adds an Event Source
implementation to create events for **Event Tracing for Windows (ETW)** for
you. ETW is an efficient kernel-level tracing facility that lets you log kernel
or application-defined events. Service Fabric runtime itself logs events using
ETW and using the same logging mechanism would help you understand
how your service communicates with the Service Fabric runtime. ETW can
work across cloud environments and even on your local system. Therefore,
using ETW can make your application platform independent.

5. Run the application by clicking on Run or by pressing F5. At this time, visual studio will spin up a local cluster for development. Once your application gets deployed on the cluster, you would be able to see the ETW trace events in **Diagnostic Events** Viewer window of Visual Studio:

Output of Hello World stateless service

6. You can expand any event to see more details. For instance, in the preceding event, you can view the node and partition on which your Microservice is running.

Exploring the Service Fabric Explorer

Service Fabric SDK installs a *Service Fabric Application management* tool in your system named Service Fabric Explorer (or SFX as Microsoft calls it). You can view the explorer UI by navigating to `http://localhost:19080/Explorer/`.

It is a two-panel web application in which the left panel displays an overview of your cluster in a tree format and the right panel displays detailed information about the currently selected item. Let's take a quick overview of the tree menu on the left:

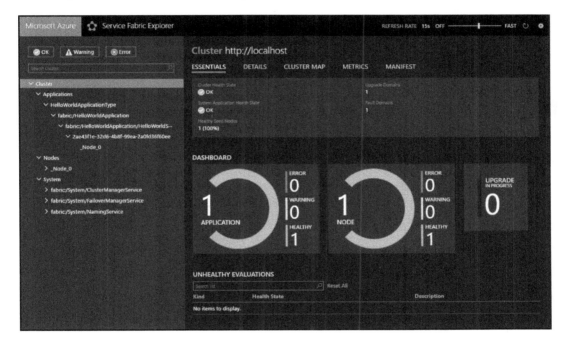

Service Fabric Explorer overview

Application Type

This node represents the type of your application, which in the case of our sample is `HelloWorldApplicationType`. Defining the application type grants the flexibility for an application administrator to tailor the application type to a specific application to be deployed to a Service Fabric cluster by specifying the appropriate parameters of the `ApplicationType` element in the application manifest.

Application instance

Below the application type node is the application instance node. The application type and application instance are analogous to the class and object concepts in object oriented programming. Your application instance is identified by a name, `fabric:/HelloWorldApplication`, in our case. This name is configurable and can be specified in the format of `fabric:/{name}` where `{name}` is any string.

Service type

An application type consists of a bundle of service types. Just as the application types are a template for application instances, the service types are templates for your service instances. In Service Fabric Explorer, you will find a service type corresponding to each Microservice that you have in your application. Since in our example, we have added only one service to our application, we can find the `HelloServiceType` representing the registered service type in our application. Each service in a Service Fabric application has a name in the format of `fabric:/{application name}/{service name}`. A Service Fabric cluster named the Naming Service, resolves this name to actual service instance address on every request.

Partition

Right below the Service Type node, you will find a GUID. This GUID represents the partition in which your Microservice instance is deployed. The Naming Service is responsible for routing requests to appropriate partitions and therefore your application should be oblivious to this identifier.

Replica

Each partition of a Microservice can have a configurable number of replicas. These replicas ensure that your service is highly available. The individual replicas that are executing the code of your Microservices are displayed at this level:

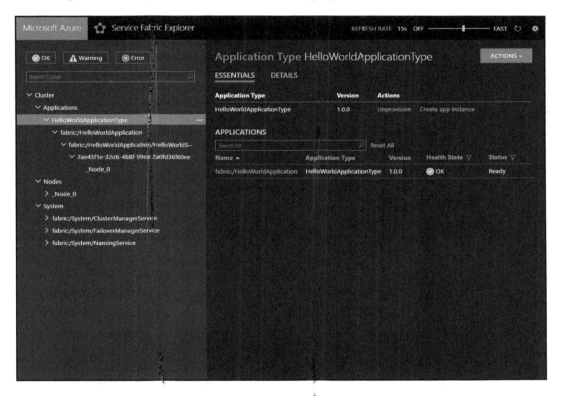

Service Fabric Explorer – application hierarchy

To explore the tool further, click on the application instance node, `fabric:/HelloWorldApplication`, in the left menu and in the **DETAILS** pane, click the **ACTIONS** button and then click the **Delete Application** menu. In the following dialog box, confirm that you want to delete your application instance:

Service Fabric Explorer – ACTIONS button

Prior to deleting the application, the explorer will prompt you to confirm whether you want to carry out the operation:

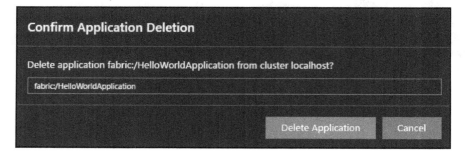

Confirmation to delete application

Once the UI of the application refreshes, your application instance will be removed from the list of available application instances:

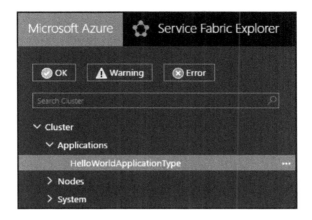

Updated list of applications after delete

Note that we have only deleted an application instance, so the application type is still preserved. Click on the **Create app instance** link to provision another instance of the application:

Create application instance

Stateless Reliable Services

A stateless service treats each request as a separate transaction that is independent of any previous request sent to the service. This service can not maintain an internal session store. A stateless service takes all the parameters that it needs to perform an operation at once.

However, you would rarely find applications that are truly stateless. In most of the scenarios, you would find that the state is externalized and stored separately. For instance, a service might use Azure Redis Cache to store state data and not maintain state internally.

Most of the stateless services built on Service Fabric are frontend services that expose the functionality of the underlying system. Users interact with the frontend services, which then forward the call to the correct partition of appropriate stateful services.

Stateless service architecture

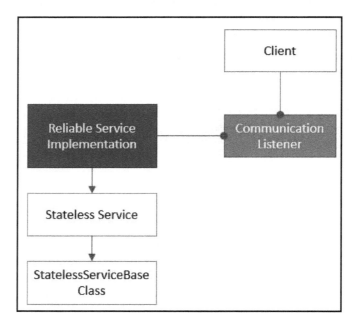

Reliable stateless service architecture

A stateless service implementation derives from the `StatelessService` class which manages the lifetime and role of a service.

The service implementation may override virtual methods of the base class if the service has work to do at those points in the service lifecycle or if it wants to create a communication listener object. Note that, although the service may implement its own communication listener object exposing `ICommunicationListener`, in the preceding diagram, the communication listener is implemented by Service Fabric as that service implementation uses a communication listener that is implemented by Service Fabric.

Stateless service lifecycle

Let's take a close look at the lifecycle of a stateless Service Fabric Reliable Service. The lifetime of a stateless Microservice starts as soon as you register a new instance of the service with the Service Fabric runtime. The following are the major lifetime events of a stateless Microservice:

- `CreateServiceInstanceListeners()`: This method is used to setup communication listeners for client requests. Although, Service Fabric provides a default communication listener based on RPC proxy, you can override this method to supply our communication stack of choice. The endpoints returned by the communication listeners are stored as a JSON string of listener name and endpoint string pairs like `{"Endpoints":{"Listener1":"Endpoint1","Listener2":"Endpoint2" ...}}`

- `OnOpenAsync(IStatelessServicePartition, CancellationToken)`: This method is called when the stateless service instance is about to be used. This method should generally be used in conjunction with its counterpart method `OnCloseAsync` to initialize resources that are used by the service such as open connections to external systems, start background processes and setup connections with databases, and so on.

- `RunAsync(CancellationToken)`: This method is a general-purpose entry point for the business logic of your Microservice. This method is invoked when a service instance is ready to begin execution. A cancellation token is provided as input to the method to signal your Microservice that processing should stop. You should only implement this method if your service is continuously processing some data, for example consuming messages from a queue and processing them.

- `OnCloseAsync(CancellationToken)`: In multiple scenarios, your Microservice may be requested to shut down, for example when the code of your service is being upgraded, when the service instance is being moved due to load balancing, or when a transient fault is detected. In such cases, the Service Fabric runtime will trigger the `OnCloseAsync` method to signal your Microservice to start performing the clean-up operations. This method should be used in conjunction with the `OnOpenAsync` method to clean up resources after they have been used by the service.
- `OnAbort()`: `OnAbort` is called when the stateless service instance is being forcefully shut down. This is generally called when a permanent fault is detected on the node, or when Service Fabric cannot reliably manage the service instance's lifecycle due to internal failures:

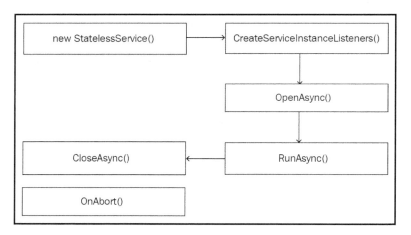

Stateless service lifetime

Scaling stateless services

There are two typical models that are used to build three tier applications using stateless Microservices.

Stateless frontend and stateless middle-tier

In this model, you build stateless web apps such as ASP.NET and Node.js and deploy your application's frontend as stateless Reliable Services. The **Front End** can communicate with **Stateless Middle-tier Compute** using **Queue** in case asynchronous processing is desired or using HTTP protocol in case synchronous communication is desired. The middle-tier is built using stateless web framework such as Web API or can execute as a continuously executing process. The model can be seen in the following image:

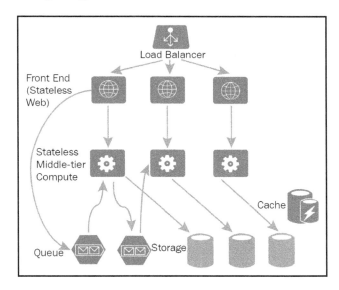

Stateless frontend and stateless middle-tier

Stateless frontend and stateful middle-tier

In this model, you build stateless web apps such as ASP.NET and Node.js and deploy your application's frontend as stateless Reliable Services. The model can be seen in the following image:

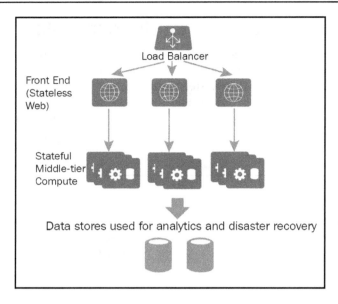

Stateless front-end and stateful middle-tier

The **Front End** can communicate with **Stateful Middle-tier Compute** using queues, in case asynchronous processing is desired, or using HTTP protocol, in case synchronous communication is desired. This model delivers better performance because the state lives near the compute, which avoids network hops. This model also helps ensure data consistency using transactions to commit data in data stores. In this model, the middle-tier can be built using stateless web framework such as Web API or it can execute as a continuously executing process.

You might have noticed that in both the models we have used a load balancer to route traffic to appropriate stateless service that hosts the frontend of our application. That is because web browsers don't have the ability to interact with the Naming Service to resolve the endpoint of a healthy instance of the service. When you provision your Service Fabric cluster on Azure, you get the ability to add a load balancer to proxy your instances. The load balancer uses a probe to determine the health of the frontend nodes and routes traffic only to the healthy nodes. Addition of a load balancer also makes the process of scaling of frontend invisible to the clients of your application. The load balancer automatically distributes the incoming traffic to the healthy nodes, thus ensuring that your resources get utilized optimally.

Reliable Services communication

Azure Service Fabric gives you the flexibility to implement custom communication stacks using protocols of your choice. To implement a custom communication stack, you need to implement the `ICommunicationListener` interface. The Reliable Services application framework provides a couple of inbuilt communication stacks that you can use, such as the default stack built on RPC proxy, WCF, REST (Web API), and HTTP (ASP.NET).

Let us build a custom stack using ASP.NET, Web API, and open web interface for .NET (OWIN) self-hosting in Service Fabric stateless Reliable Service.

This sample is inspired from the official *Service Fabric Web API services with OWIN self-hosting* sample from MSDN: `https://azure.microsoft.com/en-us/documentation/articles/service-fabric-reliable-services-communication-webapi/`.
If you are not familiar with Web API. This is a great link to start: `https://www.asp.net/web-api/overview/getting-started-with-aspnet-web-api/tutorial-your-first-web-api`.
You can find an overview of the Katana project here: `https://www.asp.net/aspnet/overview/owin-and-katana/an-overview-of-project-katana`.

Using Visual Studio, create a Service Fabric application with a single stateless service named `AgeCalculatorService`:

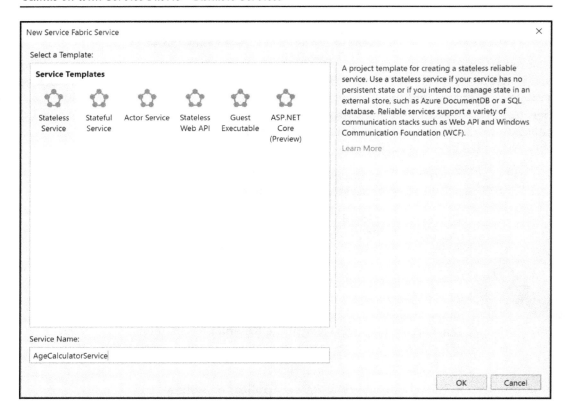

Create stateless service template

Once the project is ready, we will pull in the
`Microsoft.AspNet.WebApi.OwinSelfHost NuGet` package for Web API in the
service project. This package includes all the necessary Web API packages and the
host packages.

After installing the package, we will build a basic Web API project structure. Let us
add a `Controllers` directory and a simple controller named `AgeController`:

```
public class AgeController : ApiController
{
    public string Get(DateTime dateOfBirth)
    {
        return $"You are {DateTime.UtcNow.Year - dateOfBirth.Year}
        years old.";
    }
}
```

Next, to register routes and other configurations, add a `Startup` class in the project root directory:

```
namespace AgeCalculatorService
{
    using System.Web.Http;

    using Owin;

    public static class Startup
    {
        public static void ConfigureApp(IAppBuilder appBuilder)
        {
            var config = new HttpConfiguration();

            config.Routes.MapHttpRoute(
                "DefaultApi",
                "api/{controller}/{id}",
                new { id = RouteParameter.Optional });

            appBuilder.UseWebApi(config);
        }
    }
}
```

Our application is now ready. Service Fabric executes your service in service host process, which is an executable that runs your service code. You compile your service in the form of an executable file that registers your service type and executes your code. When you open the `Program.cs` file, you will find the `Main` method which is the entry point of the service host process. This method contains the code essential for mapping your service to the related service type. You will find that a parameter named context is passed to your service instance, which, depending on the service type, stateful or stateless, will either be a `StatefulServiceContext` or a `StatelessServiceContext`. Both the context classes are derived from `ServiceContext`. If you want to setup dependency injection in your service, you can utilize the `RegisterServiceAsync` method to do that:

```
internal static class Program
{
    private static void Main()
    {
        try
        {
            ServiceRuntime.RegisterServiceAsync(
                "AgeCalculatorServiceType",
                context => new
```

```
                AgeCalculatorService(context)).GetAwaiter().GetResult();

                ServiceEventSource.Current.ServiceTypeRegistered(
                    Process.GetCurrentProcess().Id,
                    typeof(AgeCalculatorService).Name);

                Thread.Sleep(Timeout.Infinite);
            }
            catch (Exception e)
            {
    ServiceEventSource.Current.ServiceHostInitializationFailed(e.ToString(
    ));
                throw;
            }
        }
    }
```

Your application runs in its own process and this code shows just that. Your application is nothing but a console application that is managed by the Service Fabric runtime. **OWIN** decouples ASP.NET from web servers. Therefore, you can start a self-hosted OWIN web server inside your application process. We will implement the `ICommunicationListener` interface to launch an OWIN server, which will use the `IAppBuilder` interface to initialize the ASP.NET Web API. The `ICommunicationListener` interface provides three methods to manage a communication listener for your service:

- `OpenAsync`: Start listening for requests
- `CloseAsync`: Stop listening for requests, finish any in-flight requests, and shut down gracefully
- `Abort`: Cancel everything and stop immediately

Before we implement the communication stack, we need to configure the endpoints for our service. Service Fabric ensures that the endpoints are available for our service to use. The Service Fabric host process runs under restricted credentials and therefore your application won't have sufficient permissions to setup ports that it needs to listen on. You can setup endpoints for your service in `PackageRoot\ServiceManifest.xml`:

```xml
<Resources>
  <Endpoints>
    <Endpoint Name="ServiceEndpoint" Type="Input" Protocol="http"
        Port="80" />
  </Endpoints>
</Resources>
```

By using the endpoint configuration, Service Fabric knows to set up the proper Access Control List (ACL) for the URL that the service will listen on. Service Fabric guarantees that only one instance of a stateless service will be deployed on a single node. Therefore, you don't need to worry about multiple applications listening on the same port in this case. In other cases, your service replicas might get deployed to the same host and therefore might be listening on the same port. Therefore, your communication listener must support port sharing. Microsoft recommends that your application communication listeners listen to traffic on an endpoint that is built using combination of partition ID and replica/instance ID, which is guaranteed to be unique.

Create a class named `OwinCommunicationListener` that implements the `ICommunicationListener` interface. We will add private class member variables for values and references that the listener will need to function. These private members will be initialized through the constructor and used later when you set up the listening URL.

```
internal class OwinCommunicationListener : ICommunicationListener
{
    private readonly string appRoot;

    private readonly string endpointName;

    private readonly ServiceEventSource eventSource;

    private readonly ServiceContext serviceContext;

    private readonly Action<IAppBuilder> startup;

    private string listeningAddress;

    private string publishAddress;

    private IDisposable webApp;

    public OwinCommunicationListener(
        Action<IAppBuilder> startup,
        ServiceContext serviceContext,
        ServiceEventSource eventSource,
        string endpointName)
        : this(startup, serviceContext, eventSource, endpointName,
                null)
    {
    }

    public OwinCommunicationListener(
```

```
            Action<IAppBuilder> startup,
            ServiceContext serviceContext,
            ServiceEventSource eventSource,
            string endpointName,
            string appRoot)
    {
        if (startup == null)
        {
            throw new ArgumentNullException(nameof(startup));
        }

        if (serviceContext == null)
        {
            throw new ArgumentNullException(nameof(serviceContext));
        }

        if (endpointName == null)
        {
            throw new ArgumentNullException(nameof(endpointName));
        }

        if (eventSource == null)
        {
            throw new ArgumentNullException(nameof(eventSource));
        }

        this.startup = startup;
        this.serviceContext = serviceContext;
        this.endpointName = endpointName;
        this.eventSource = eventSource;
        this.appRoot = appRoot;
    }
}
```

Now, let's implement the OpenAsync method. In this method, we will start the web server and assign it the URL it will listen on. Since this is a stateless service, we do not need to have the partition and replica identifiers suffixed to the URL to make it unique:

```
public Task<string> OpenAsync(CancellationToken cancellationToken)
{
    var serviceEndpoint =
        this.serviceContext.CodePackageActivationContext.
            GetEndpoint(this.endpointName);
    var protocol = serviceEndpoint.Protocol;
    var port = serviceEndpoint.Port;

    if (this.serviceContext is StatefulServiceContext)
```

```
{
    var statefulServiceContext = this.serviceContext as
      StatefulServiceContext;

    this.listeningAddress = string.Format(
        CultureInfo.InvariantCulture,
        "{0}://+:{1}/{2}{3}/{4}/{5}",
        protocol,
        port,
        string.IsNullOrWhiteSpace(this.appRoot) ?
          string.Empty : this.appRoot.TrimEnd('/') + '/',
        statefulServiceContext.PartitionId,
        statefulServiceContext.ReplicaId,
        Guid.NewGuid());
}
else if (this.serviceContext is StatelessServiceContext)
{
    this.listeningAddress = string.Format(
        CultureInfo.InvariantCulture,
        "{0}://+:{1}/{2}",
        protocol,
        port,
        string.IsNullOrWhiteSpace(this.appRoot) ?
          string.Empty : this.appRoot.TrimEnd('/') + '/');
}
else
{
    throw new InvalidOperationException();
}

this.publishAddress = this.listeningAddress.Replace("+",
  FabricRuntime.GetNodeContext().IPAddressOrFQDN);

try
{
    this.eventSource.Message("Starting web server on " +
      this.listeningAddress);

    this.webApp = WebApp.Start(this.listeningAddress,
      appBuilder => this.startup.Invoke(appBuilder));

    this.eventSource.Message("Listening on " +
      this.publishAddress);

    return Task.FromResult(this.publishAddress);
}
catch (Exception ex)
{
```

```
                        this.eventSource.Message(
                            "Web server failed to open endpoint {0}. {1}",
                            this.endpointName,
                            ex.ToString());

                        this.StopWebServer();

                        throw;
                }
        }
```

This method starts the web server and returns the address that the server is listening on. This address is registered with the Naming Service, which is a cluster service. A client can use the service name and get this address from the Naming Service of the cluster. Let's implement the `CloseAsync` and the Abort methods to complete the implementation:

```
public void Abort()
{
    this.eventSource.Message("Aborting web server on endpoint
      {0}", this.endpointName);

    this.StopWebServer();
}

public Task CloseAsync(CancellationToken cancellationToken)
{
    this.eventSource.Message("Closing web server on endpoint
      {0}", this.endpointName);

    this.StopWebServer();

    return Task.FromResult(true);
}
private void StopWebServer()
{
    if (this.webApp != null)
    {
        try
        {
            this.webApp.Dispose();
        }
        catch (ObjectDisposedException)
        {
            // no-op
        }
    }
```

}

Finally, we need to override the `CreateServiceInstanceListeners` method in our service implementation to create and return an instance of `OwinCommunicationListener` in the `AgeCalculatorService` class.

```
        protected override IEnumerable<ServiceInstanceListener>
CreateServiceInstanceListeners()
        {
            var endpoints =
                Context.CodePackageActivationContext.GetEndpoints()
                    .Where(endpoint => endpoint.Protocol ==
EndpointProtocol.Http || endpoint.Protocol == EndpointProtocol.Https)
                    .Select(endpoint => endpoint.Name);

            return endpoints.Select(endpoint => new
ServiceInstanceListener(
                serviceContext => new
OwinCommunicationListener(Startup.ConfigureApp, serviceContext,
ServiceEventSource.Current, endpoint), endpoint));
        }
```

Remove the default implementation of `RunAsync` in the `AgeCalculatorService` class as we don't need to perform any processing in the background. Build and deploy the application on your local cluster. You can find the address of the application in Service Fabric Explorer on which you can send a request to your API:

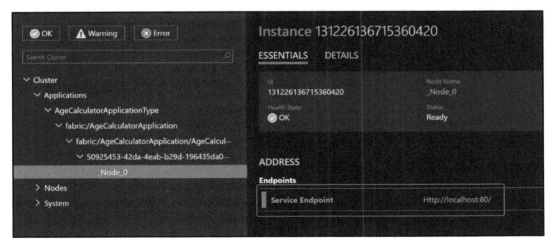

Service endpoint

In the browser, send a request to your application with your date of birth appended as a query string parameter to the request. For example: `http://localhost/api/Age?dateOfBirth=12-12-2001.`

After submitting the request, you should see a result as follows:

Output of age calculator

Exploring the application model

A service fabric application is made up of several Microservices. A Microservice is further made up of three parts:

- **Code**: These are the executable binaries of the Microservice. The binaries are packaged in code package.
- **Configuration**: These are the settings that can be used by your Microservices at run time. These are packaged into a configuration package.
- **Data**: Any static data that is used by the Microservice is packaged in data package.

A Service Fabric application is described by a set of versioned manifests, an application manifest, and several service manifests, one each for each of the Microservices that make up the application. Let's explore the components of a Service Fabric application by navigating through the Service Fabric application package.

To package your application, right click on your Service Fabric application project and click on the **Package** option:

Package application

Once the application has finished packaging, open the package folder by navigating to the package location that is shown in the output window. Your application package will have a layout like that shown in the following image:

```
D:\TEMP\MYAPPLICATIONTYPE
|    ApplicationManifest.xml
|
└───MyServiceManifest
     |    ServiceManifest.xml
     |
     ├───MyCode
     |        MyServiceHost.exe
     |
     ├───MyConfig
     |        Settings.xml
     |
     └───MyData
              init.dat
```

Let's discuss the various files available in your package in a bit more detail:

- **Application manifest**: The application manifest is used to describe the application. It lists the services that compose it, and other parameters that are used to define how one or more services should be deployed, such as the number of instances.

  In Service Fabric, an application is a unit of deployment and upgrade. An application can be upgraded as a single unit where potential failures and potential rollbacks are managed. Service Fabric guarantees that the upgrade process is either successful, or, if the upgrade fails, does not leave the application in an unknown or unstable state.

- **Service manifest**: There is one service manifest for each reliable service in the application. The service manifest describes the components of a Microservice. It includes data, such as the name and type of service, and its code and configuration. The service manifest also includes some additional parameters that can be used to configure the service once it is deployed.

- **Code package**: Each Microservice has a code package that contains the executable and the dependencies that are required by the executable to run.

- **Config Package**: You can package the configurations that are required by your Microservice in this folder. A config package is simply a directory in your project which can contain multiple configuration files. Except for Settings.xml file, which is added by default to your reliable service project, the rest of the configurations are not processed by Service Fabric and would need to be processed by the code of your Microservice.

  The Settings.xml file can store custom configuration sections and parameters that you can use in your application. For example, you can add a custom configuration section with parameters in your Settings.xml file.

```
<Section Name="CustomConfigSection">
        <Parameter Name="MyParameter" Value="Value1" />
</Section>
You can retrieve this configuration value from your service code.
        var configPkg =  context.CodePackageActivationContext.
          GetConfigurationPackageObject("Config");
        var customSection = configPkg.Settings.
          Sections["CustomConfigSection"];
        var value = customSection.
          Parameters["CustomConfigSection"].Value;
```

Service Fabric allows you to override the configurations based on the environment where the application is hosted as well.

- **Data package**: Any static data that is required by your application can be placed inside folders in the `PackageRoot` directory. Each folder represents one data package and can contain multiple data files. Service Fabric does not process any file that you place inside the folders and the code of your service is responsible for parsing and reading the data.

When you deploy your application from Visual Studio, it creates a package and uses the `Deploy-FabricApplication.ps1` script present in the `Script` folder to deploy your application package to Azure. To deploy your application to Azure, right click on the application project and select the `Publish` option in the context menu to bring up the publish dialog.

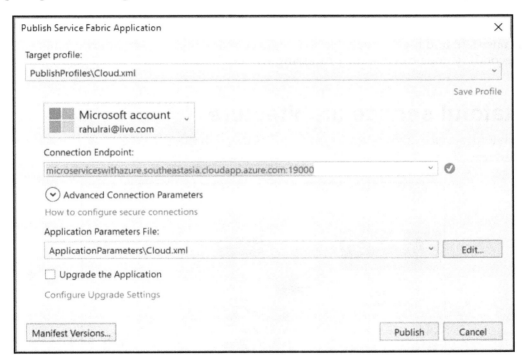

Publish application dialog

In the publish dialog, you can select the relevant application parameter file that you want to get deployed with your application. You can modify the parameters just before deployment by clicking the **Edit** button. In the dialog box that follows, you can enter or change the parameter's value in the **Parameters** grid. When you're done, choose the **Save** button.

You can deploy your application to the selected cluster by clicking on the **Publish** button.

Stateful service

A stateful Microservice stores state information stored in a consistent and highly available manner using reliable data structure. By default, the state data is saved on the disk of the compute node. However, you can write your own state providers to store state data externally and consume it. Service Fabric ensures that your state data is consistent and highly available so that, in case of failure of primary compute node, a secondary node can resume processing without loss of data.

Stateful service architecture

A stateful service takes requests from clients through the `ICommunicationListener` interface:

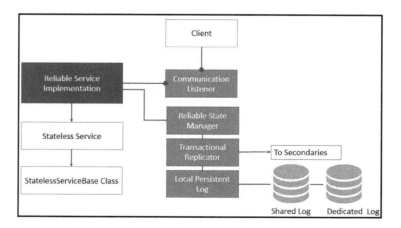

Stateful Reliable Service architecture

The implementation of a stateful reliable service derives from `StatefulService` class. Service Fabric runtime manages the lifetime of your stateful Microservice through the `StatefulService` class. The service can use Reliable Collections to persist state information, which are similar to collections in `System.Collections` namespace but with added features for *high availability* and *consistency*. The read and write operations of Reliable Collections go through **Reliable State Manager**. The state is replicated to secondary nodes by a **Transactional Replicator**. This replication ensures that state data is reliable, consistent, and highly available. After ensuring that state data has been copied to secondary replicas, the **Transactional Replicator** invokes the logger. The logger is responsible for persisting state data to disks by using append-only log files. In case of failure, state can be restored by replaying the logs.

There are two types of logs that store the state data. The shared logs are stored under node-level working directory. The logs in shared log are copied lazily to dedicated logs that are stored under service working directory.

Reliable Collections

The `Microsoft.ServiceFabric.Data.Collections` namespace contains various collections that act as reliable state providers and are known as Reliable Collections. You must have used standard data collections such as dictionary and queue present in the `System.Collections` namespace in your applications; the interfaces in Reliable Collections allow you to interact with the state provider in a similar manner. The Reliable Collections differ from the classes in `System.Collections`, in that they are:

- **Replicated**: The state data is replicated across nodes for high availability
- **Persisted**: The state data is persisted both in memory and in disk for durability against large-scale outages
- **Asynchronous**: The Service Fabric API supports asynchronous operations on the Reliable Collections to ensure that threads are not blocked when incurring I/O
- **Transactional**: Service Fabric APIs utilize the abstraction of transactions so you can manage multiple Reliable Collections within a service easily

The Service Fabric API implements the Reliable Collections in a pluggable manner, so you can expect to see new collections being added to the existing offering from time to time. Service Fabric currently provides three Reliable Collections:

- **Reliable Dictionary**: It represents a replicated, transactional, and asynchronous collection of key/value pairs. Similar to `ConcurrentDictionary`, both the key and the value can be of any type.
- **Reliable Queue**: It represents a replicated, transactional, and asynchronous strict **first-in, first-out (FIFO)** queue. Similar to `ConcurrentQueue`, the value can be of any type.
- **Reliable Concurrent Queue**: This queue is similar to Reliable Queue but offer a higher throughput in lieu of doing away with FIFO restrictions that Reliable Queue has.

The Reliable State Manager manages the lifetime of the state providers. Since the data structure needs to be replicated to several nodes, coordination among nodes is required to create instance of the data structure. Using the `IReliableStateManager` interface, your service can access the state manager to create new instances of Reliable Collections. The Reliable State Managers also support transactions. Using transactions, your service can operate with several collections in an atomic manner.

All state data that your site writes or modifies must go through the primary replica. Service Fabric ensures that there are is more than one primary replica of a service available at any point of time. However, data can be read from either the primary replica or secondary replicas.

Let's build a simple application which will help us understand how we can work with Reliable Collections.

Up and down counter application

Let's build a simple stateful application that would help us understand the various aspects of a reliable stateful application. We will build an up and down counter that will increment or decrement a counter value depending on the partition it belongs to. We will save the counter value in a `ReliableDictionary` instance and trace the current state of the dictionary so that we can visualize it in the **Diagnostics Event Viewer** console.

To begin, using Visual Studio create a new Service Fabric application named
`StatefulUpDownCounterApplication` and add a Stateful Reliable Service to it.
Name the service `UpDownCounterService`:

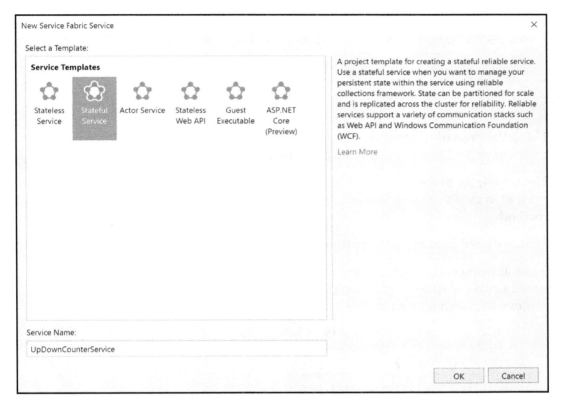

Create Stateful Service dialog

Let's first create two partitions of this service. For this sample, we will use the named
partitioning scheme. Applications that use named partitions usually work with
categorized data, for instance an election service that persists vote data by state.
Clients of applications that use the named partition scheme need to explicitly specify
which partition they want to access at runtime.

To create a named partition, navigate to the `ApplicationManifest.xml` file and update the contents of the `Service` node to the following:

```xml
<Service Name="UpDownCounterService">
  <StatefulService ServiceTypeName="UpDownCounterServiceType"
TargetReplicaSetSize="[UpDownCounterService_TargetReplicaSetSize]"
MinReplicaSetSize="[UpDownCounterService_MinReplicaSetSize]">
    <NamedPartition>
      <Partition Name="UpCounter" />
      <Partition Name="DownCounter" />
    </NamedPartition>
  </StatefulService>
```

Using the preceding configuration Service Fabric will create two partitions named `UpCounter` and `DownCounter` for your service.

Next, navigate to the `UpDownCounterService` class and clear the default code present in the `RunAsync` method. Let's start placing our counter code inside this method.

First, we need to identify the partition in which our process is getting executed.

The following code block, creates an instance of `ReliableDictionary` named `counter`. We use the `Partition` property of the base class `StatefulService` to retrieve the partition information.

```csharp
var myDictionary = await
this.StateManager.GetOrAddAsync<IReliableDictionary<string,
long>>("counter");
var myPartitionName = (this.Partition.PartitionInfo as
NamedPartitionInformation)?.Name;
```

The variable `myPartitionName` will contain the name of one of the partitions that we had created earlier. Let's consider the case when the value of the `myPartitionName` variable will be `"UpCounter"`. In this case, we will initialize the dictionary with 0 and keep updating the value by one every five seconds. The code is as follows:

```csharp
switch (myPartitionName)
{
    case "UpCounter":
        while (true)
        {
cancellationToken.ThrowIfCancellationRequested();
            using (var tx = this.StateManager.
                CreateTransaction())
            {
```

```
                    var result = await myDictionary.
                        TryGetValueAsync(tx, "Counter");
                    ServiceEventSource.Current.ServiceMessage(
                        this,
                        "Current Counter Value: {0}",
                        result.HasValue ? result.Value.
                        ToString() : "Value does not
                                                exist.");
                    await myDictionary.AddOrUpdateAsync(tx,
                        "Counter", 0, (key, value) =>
                                            ++value);
                    await tx.CommitAsync();
                }

                await Task.Delay(TimeSpan.FromSeconds(5),
                    cancellationToken);
            }
        case "DownCounter":
...
        }
```

All operations on Reliable Collections happen inside transaction scope. This is because the data in the collections need to be actively replicated to majority of secondary nodes to ensure high availability of state data. A failure to replicate data to majority of replicas would lead to failure of transaction.

Next, we need to implement the down counter. We will write a similar implementation as we did for up counter, except that the counter value will get initialized with 1000 and it will decrement every five seconds. The code for down counter is as follows:

```
        case "DownCounter":
            while (true)
            {
cancellationToken.ThrowIfCancellationRequested();
                using (var tx = this.StateManager.
                    CreateTransaction())
                {
                    var result = await myDictionary.
                        TryGetValueAsync(tx, "Counter");
                    ServiceEventSource.Current.ServiceMessage(
                        this.Context,
                        "Current Counter Value: {0}",
                        result.HasValue ? result.Value.
                        ToString() : "Value does not
                                        exist.");
                    await myDictionary.AddOrUpdateAsync(tx,
```

```
                                    "Counter", 1000, (key, value) => --
                                                                value);
                        await tx.CommitAsync();
            }
            await Task.Delay(TimeSpan.FromSeconds(5),
                cancellationToken);
      }
```

Let's also set the replica count of the service to 3 so that we have multiple secondary replicas of the service. Locate the parameter file `Local.5Node.xml` in the `ApplicationParameters` folder. This file is used to supply parameters when you are running your local cluster in five node mode. This mode spins five host processes on your machine to mimic deployment on five nodes. Validate that the minimum number of replicas and target number of replicas is set to three (at least):

```
<Parameters>
  <Parameter Name="UpDownCounterService_MinReplicaSetSize" Value="3"
/>
  <Parameter Name="UpDownCounterService_TargetReplicaSetSize"
Value="3"
     />
</Parameters>
```

Next, switch the cluster mode to **5 Node**, if not done already, by right clicking the Service Fabric Local Cluster Manager icon in the task bar and selecting the appropriate mode:

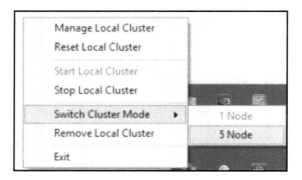

Switch cluster mode

Let's quickly deploy our application to the local cluster by pressing *F5*. Open the **Diagnostic Events** window and observe the output of the application:

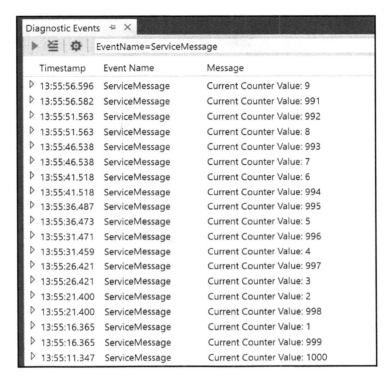

Output in Diagnostic Events

You would notice that even though both the counters referenced the same dictionary named `counter`, the two counters are progressing independently. That is because the Reliable Collections are not shared across partitions, but only across replicas.

Next, let's kill the primary replicas of both the partitions to see whether the state data is lost. To do so, open the Service Fabric Explorer and find out which node is hosting the primary replica of your service partitions:

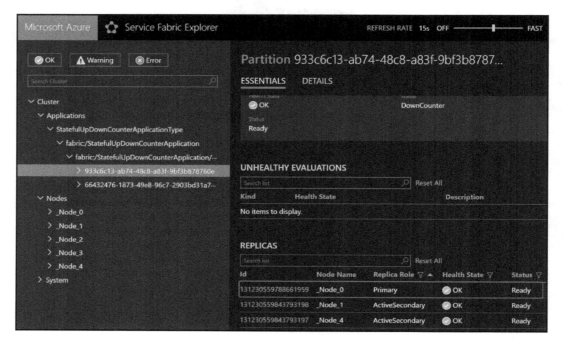

Primary replicas in Service Fabric Explorer

In my case **_Node_0** and **_Node_3** host the primary replicas of the two partitions of the service that we just built. Let's deactivate the nodes and observe the counter value. Click on the ellipsis next to the node to reveal the various node operations. Let's simulate a complete node crash by selecting the **Deactivate (remove data)** option:

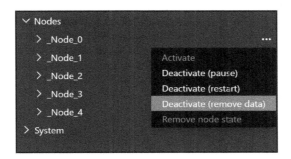

Deactivate node operation

You will notice that as soon as you deactivate the node, an active secondary replica on another node, **_Node_1** in my case, gets promoted to primary status and resumes processing without loss of state data which you can verify by looking at the logs accumulated in the **Diagnostic Events** window:

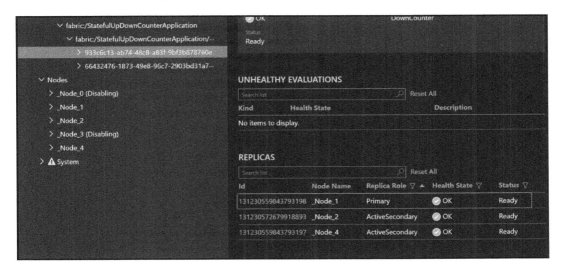

New primary replica

Stateful service lifecycle

Let's explore the lifecycle of a stateful service. The lifetime of a stateful Microservice replica starts as soon as you register a new instance of the service with the Service Fabric runtime. Most of the lifetime methods are same as that of stateless Microservice. Let's look at those that are different:

- `RunAsync (CancellationToken)`: In a stateful service, the platform performs additional work on your behalf before it executes `RunAsync ()`. This work can include ensuring that the Reliable State Manager and Reliable Collections are ready to use. This method executes only in the active primary replica.
- `OnChangeRoleAsync (ReplicaRole, CancellationToken)`: `OnChangeRoleAsync` is called when the stateful service replica is changing role, for example to primary or secondary. Primary replicas are given write status (are allowed to create and write to Reliable Collections). Secondary replicas are given read status (can only read from existing Reliable Collections). Most work in a stateful service is performed at the primary replica. Secondary replicas can perform read-only validation, report generation, data mining, or other read-only jobs. The stateful service lifetime can be seen in the following image:

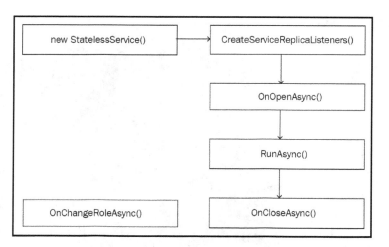

Service partitioning

To support scalability and reliability, Service Fabric supports setting up multiple instances of service and supports partitioning a service. Let's see what this concept means for stateless and stateful services.

Stateless services do not store any data locally. When you add a new stateless service in your Service Fabric application, you will find that a configuration is automatically created in `ApplicationManifest.xml` to configure the service to use `SingletonPartition`:

```
<Service Name="Stateless1">
  <StatelessService ServiceTypeName="Stateless1Type"
    InstanceCount="[Stateless1_InstanceCount]">
    <SingletonPartition />
  </StatelessService>
</Service>
```

`SingletonPartition` means that, number of partitions is one, which means that there is a single instance of state. If you set the value of `[Stateless1_InstanceCount]` parameter to 2, you will have two instances of the service running on different nodes. If you put a breakpoint in the `RunAsync()` method of `Stateless1` class, you would find that it will be invoked twice, once for each node on which it is deployed.

Due to absence of state data, other partitioning schemes do not make sense for stateless services. To explore the other partitioning schemes, let's add a stateful service to the project. After the template unfolds, you would find the following configuration in the application manifest file:

```
<Service Name="Stateful1">
  <StatefulService ServiceTypeName="Stateful1Type"
TargetReplicaSetSize="[Stateful1_TargetReplicaSetSize]"
MinReplicaSetSize="[Stateful1_MinReplicaSetSize]">
    <UniformInt64Partition
PartitionCount="[Stateful1_PartitionCount]"
LowKey="-9223372036854775808" HighKey="9223372036854775807" />
  </StatefulService>
</Service>
```

You will notice that instance count is no longer present in the configuration and is replaced with replica count. A replica is a copy of code and state data of a service. Let's simplify the preceding configuration to make it easier to understand:

```
<Service Name="Stateful1">
  <StatefulService ServiceTypeName="Stateful1Type"
    TargetReplicaSetSize="3" MinReplicaSetSize="2">
    <UniformInt64Partition PartitionCount="2" LowKey="1"
      HighKey="10" />
  </StatefulService>
</Service>
```

By default, your stateful services uses uniform partitioning scheme named `UniformInt64Partition`. This partitioning scheme uniformly distributes a continuous key range to the number of partitions that you specify. Using the preceding configuration, the state data will be partitioned in two parts, one partition will serve keys ranging from 1 to 5 and the other partition will serve keys ranging from 6 to 10. Each of these partitions will have a minimum of two replicas, which can expand up to three. If you deploy your application, you will find that six instances of your application will spin up, three replicas for each partition. However, if you put breakpoint in `RunAsync ()` method, it will be hit only twice, once for each primary replica of a partition because the rest of the replicas won't be in active state.

Next, let's change the partitioning scheme to `NamedPartition`. Named partition scheme is useful in cases where the number of partitions are known in advance and remain static over time, for example partitioning an application by states in a country:

```
<Service Name="Stateful1">
  <StatefulService ServiceTypeName="Stateful1Type"
    TargetReplicaSetSize="3" MinReplicaSetSize="2">
    <NamedPartition>
      <Partition Name="A" />
      <Partition Name="B" />
      <Partition Name="C" />
      <Partition Name="D" />
    </NamedPartition>
  </StatefulService>
</Service>
```

If you deploy the solution now, you will find that twelve instances of your application will get deployed, three for each partition. However, the breakpoint on the `RunAsync` method will only be hit four times, once for each primary replica of a partition.

Service replicas

As discussed previously, the replica is a copy of state data and code of your application. When you deploy a partitioned stateful service, replicas of each partition form a replica set. Each replica in a replica set takes one of the following roles:

1. **Primary**: This replica caters to all the write requests. A replica set can have only one primary replica. Whenever the state data is created or modified, the change is communicated to the secondary replicas that needs to be acknowledged by them. The primary replica waits for acknowledgements from a quorum of replicas to commit the change.

2. **Active secondary**: The replicas in active secondary participate in the write quorum. All participant active secondaries in the write quorum must acknowledge the change in state after committing the change to their own storage.

3. **Idle secondary**: The idle secondaries receive update from the primary but do not participate in the write quorum. In case an active secondary instance fails, an instance of idle secondary will be promoted to the status of active secondary.

4. **None**: A replica with this state does not hold any state. A replica that is being decommissioned holds this state.

You can view the replica states in Service Fabric Explorer by drilling down to the replica level.

Summary

We started this chapter by building our first Service Fabric stateless application. After which we took a thorough look at the Service Fabric Explorer. Next, we studied stateless and stateful service architecture and lifecycles using Service Fabric Reliable Services. Lastly, we looked at service partition and replicas in detail.

16
Reliable Actors

Actor model

Built on top of Reliable Services, the Reliable Actor framework is an application framework that implements the virtual Actor pattern based on the actor design pattern. The Reliable Actor framework uses independent units of compute and state with single-threaded execution called Actors. The Reliable Actor framework provides built-in communication for Actors and pre-set state persistence and scale-out configurations.

As Reliable Actors itself is an application framework built on Reliable Services, it is fully integrated with the Service Fabric platform and benefits from the full set of features offered by the platform.

What is an Actor?

An Actor is a specialized service that is much more granular in intent than the typical services that we build. The Actor programming model ensures that individual entities in your solution are highly cohesive and decoupled. An Actor is designed to work within a set of constraints:

- The various Actors of an application can only interact through asynchronous message passing. The messages that are exchanged between Actors should be immutable.
- An Actor can function within the boundary of domain that it is designed for. For instance, a shopping cart actor cannot implement or expose functionality of a product listing Actor.

- An Actor can only change its state when it receives and processes a message.
- An Actor should be single-threaded and it should process only one message at a time. Another message should be picked up by the Actor only when the Actor operation has completed.
- An Actor may spawn new Actors and send a finite number of messages to the other Actors in the application.

Actors in Service Fabric

Each Reliable Actor service you write is a partitioned and stateful Reliable Service. Service Fabric API provides a asynchronous and single-threaded programming model to implement Actors. You only need to work on the Actor implementation, the platform takes care of lifecycle, upgrades, scale, activation, and so on.

Actors closely resemble objects in object-oriented programming. Similar to the way a .NET object is an instance of a .NET type, every Actor is defined as an instance of an Actor type. For example, there may be an Actor type that implements the functionality of a sensor monitor and there could be many Actors of that type that are distributed on various nodes across a cluster. Each such Actor is uniquely identified by an Actor ID. Repeated calls to the same Actor ID are routed to the same Actor instance. For this reason, Actor services are always stateful services.

Actor lifetime

Unlike Actor implementation on other platforms, such as **Akka.net** (`https://petabridge.com/bootcamp/`), Service Fabric Actors are virtual. What this means is that the Service Fabric Reliable Actors runtime manages the location and activation of Actor instances. The Reliable Actors runtime automatically activates an Actor the first time it receives a request for that Actor ID. If an Actor instance remains unused for a period of time, the Reliable Actors runtime garbage-collects the in-memory object. The Reliable Actors runtime also maintains knowledge of the Actor's existence in the state manager for any future Actor reactivations. Actor instances are activated only when the runtime receives a message that is intended to be served by the Actor. If a message is sent to the Actor instance and there is no activation of that Actor on any cluster node, then the runtime will pick a node and create a new activation there.

Every Actor has a unique identifier and calling any Actor method for an Actor ID makes the runtime activates that Actor. For this reason, the Actor constructors are not called by the client but are called implicitly by the runtime. Therefore, an Actor type's constructor can not accept parameters from the client code, although parameters may be passed to the Actor's constructor by the service itself. There is no single entry point for the activation of an Actor from the client.

Even though the client of an Actor does not have the capability to activate the Actor's constructor, the client does have the ability to explicitly delete an Actor and its state. The following diagram shows the lifecycle of an actor:

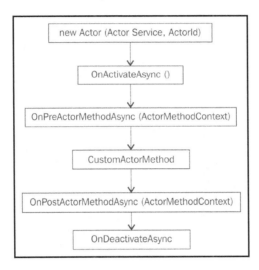

Reliable Actors lifetime

Every Actor derives from the *Actor* class. The runtime is responsible for invoking the Actor constructor. Every time an Actor instance is activated the OnActivateAsync method is invoked. You can override this method to initialize your Actor instance. Next, for every request sent to the Actor a pre-handle and a post-handle is available. If you want to log all operations that your Actor performs, then you can override these methods to add logging statements. Finally, the OnDeactivateAsyc method can be used to perform cleanup activities in Actor.

Saving state

Actors generally need to persist their internal state so that they can recover it in case an Actor is started or restarted, in case of node crashes, or migrated across nodes in cluster. State persistence is also necessary to build complex Actor workflows that transform and enrich input data and generate resultant data that helps make decisions to carry out further operations.

For example, for an automobile system, a fuel Actor may persist the fuel consumption in its state to later calculate the mileage of the vehicle, which may later help decide whether the vehicle requires a maintenance check.

The Actor base class contains the read only `StateManager` property that can be used to operate with state data. The following lines of code, can save and retrieve state data where the argument `cancellationToken` is an object of type `CancellationToken`:

```
// Save state data
this.StateManager.TryAddStateAsync("count", 0);
// Read state data
var result = await this.StateManager.GetStateAsync<int>("count",
cancellationToken);
```

If you want to initialize the state, then you should do so in the `OnActivateAsync` method. Finally, since Actors are single-threaded, we do not need to add concurrency checks while saving or reading state data. Also, since the state is local to the Actor instance, you don't need to add Actor identifier while preserving the state. What this means is that if an Actor named *A* preserves something in state then the information won't be visible to another instance of the same Actor named *B*. The state information can only be operated upon by the Actor named *A*.

Distribution and failover

The Reliable Actors runtime manages scalability and reliability of Actors by distributing Actors throughout the cluster and automatically migrating them from failed nodes to healthy ones when required.

Actors are distributed across the partitions of the Actor Service, and those partitions are distributed across the nodes in a Service Fabric cluster. Each service partition contains a set of Actors. Service Fabric manages distribution and failover of the service partitions.

For example, an Actor service with nine partitions deployed to three nodes using the default Actor partition placement would be distributed like this:

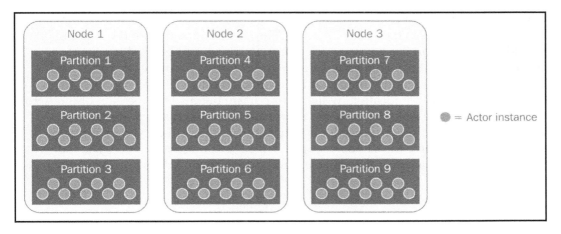

Actor instances distributed among partitions

The partition scheme and key range settings are taken care of by the runtime. Unlike Reliable Services, the Reliable Actors service is restricted to the range partitioning scheme (the uniform Int64 scheme) and requires you to use the full Int64 key range. By default, Actors are randomly placed into partitions resulting in uniform distribution. Communication between Actors happen over the network, which may introduce latency.

Actor communication

Actor interactions can only happen through contracts. Using the contracts, Actors can communicate with each other and also the clients can interact with Actors. Actors are responsible for implementing the interfaces which define these contracts. Using Service Fabric APIs, the client gets a proxy to an Actor via the same set of interfaces. Because this interface is used to invoke Actor methods asynchronously, every method on the interface must be task-returning.

Since any communication needs to take place over network, the communication interfaces should be serializable.

The Actor proxy

The Reliable Actors client API provides communication between an Actor instance and an Actor client. To communicate with an Actor, a client creates an Actor proxy object that implements the Actor interface. The client interacts with the Actor by invoking methods on the proxy object. The Actor proxy can be used for client-to-Actor and actor-to-Actor communication. An Actor proxy requires Actor ID and application name to identify the Actor it should connect to. The proxy does not expose the actual Actor location, which is important because the location of the Actor instance can change from time to time for reasons such as cluster node failure. Another important thing to consider is that Actors are required to be idempotent since they may receive the same message from a client more than once. The following line of code creates a proxy that can communicate with an Actor:

```
var proxy =
ActorProxy.Create<IHelloWorldActor>(ActorId.CreateRandom(),
"fabric:/APPLICATION NAME");
```

Here, `IHelloWorldActor` is the contract that the Actor implements. The proxy is generating a random Actor ID to which it wants to communicate with, which is in the Service Fabric application that contains the Actor service hosting the Actor object.

Concurrency

Since Actors are single-threaded, they can process only one request at a time. This means that requests to the same Actor instance need to wait for the previous request to get processed. Turn based concurrency ensures that no other Actor methods or timer/reminder callbacks will be in progress until this callback completes execution.

Actors can deadlock on each other if there is a circular request between two Actors while an external request is made to one of the Actors simultaneously. The Actor runtime will automatically time out on Actor calls and throw an exception to the caller to interrupt possible deadlock situations:

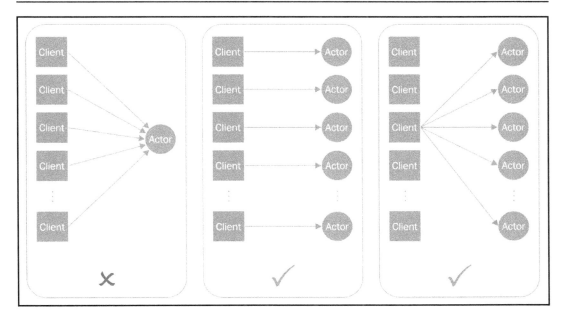

Actor Concurrency

Reentrancy

The Actors runtime allows reentrancy by default. This means that if an Actor method of Actor A calls a method on Actor B, which in turn calls another method on Actor A, that method is allowed to run. This is because it is part of the same logical call-chain context. All timer and reminder calls start with the new logical call context. However, reentrancy is a configurable property of Actors and you can disable this feature by decorating your Actor with the `Reentrant` attribute.

```
[Reentrant(ReentrancyMode.Disallowed)]
```

Asynchronous drivers

Most of the Actor actions are driven as reaction to an input received from the client. However, Actors can update their own state at regular intervals through **timers** and **reminders**. Actors can also post updates to the clients on the progress of operations using **events**. Let's take a brief look at each of these attributes.

Timers

Reliable Actor timers are modelled on timers available in the system.Timers namespace. The timers are usually used to carry out routine operations in the lifetime of an Actor, for example processing input data at a certain rate. You can declare and register a timer in your application using the following code, usually in the OnActivateAsync method:

```
private IActorTimer _updateTimer;
protected override Task OnActivateAsync()
   {
       ...

       _updateTimer = RegisterTimer(
          CallBackMethod,                       // Callback method
          ObjectParameter,                      // Parameter to pass to
                                                    the callback method
          TimeSpan.FromMilliseconds(15),   // Amount of time to delay
                                                before the callback is
                                                invoked
          TimeSpan.FromMilliseconds(15)); // Time interval between
                                                invocations of the
                                                callback method

       return base.OnActivateAsync();
   }
```

The CallBack method is simply a function that accepts the parameter that you passed while declaring the timer:

```
private Task CallBackMethod(object state)
{
    ...
    return Task.FromResult(true);
}
```

Finally, you can unregister a timer using the UnregisterTimer method:

```
protected override Task OnDeactivateAsync()
   {
       if (_updateTimer != null)
       {
           UnregisterTimer(_updateTimer);
       }
       return base.OnDeactivateAsync();
   }
```

Because of the turn wise concurrency feature of Reliable Actors, no two concurrent executions of the callback method will take place at any time. The time will be stopped while the callback is executing and will be restarted when it has completed.

It is important to note that if the Actor doesn't receive external invocations, it will be deactivated and garbage collected after a period of time. When this happens, the timers won't be activated any more. Therefore, it is important that you register the timer again in the `OnActivateAsync` method when the Actor is reactivated.

Actor reminders

Just like Actor timers, Actor reminders are a triggering mechanism to invoke callbacks at periodic intervals. However, unlike Actor timers, Actor reminder callbacks are always triggered until they are explicitly unregistered. If an Actor has been deactivated, an Actor reminder callback will reactivate the Actor and invoke the registered callback. Actor reminders are generally used to carry out asynchronous processing such as data aggregation by applications. The syntax for registering reminders is very similar to that of timers:

```
IActorReminder reminderRegistration = await
  this.RegisterReminderAsync(
    reminderName,                      // Name of reminder

    BitConverter.GetBytes(payload), // Parameter

    TimeSpan.FromDays(3),              // Amount of time to delay
                                    before the callback is invoked

    TimeSpan.FromDays(1)               // Recurrence period
  );
```

An Actor implementation that uses reminders needs to implement the `IRemindable` interface. This interface defines a single method named `ReceiveReminderAsync`. This method will be invoked for all the registered reminders, therefore, your application should be able to differentiate between reminders using either the name or the payload.

```
public Task ReceiveReminderAsync(string reminderName, byte[]
  context, TimeSpan dueTime, TimeSpan period)
{
    if (reminderName.Equals("Reminder Name"))
    {
        ...
}
```

```
    }
```

To unregister a reminder, if you have not persisted the reminder registration, then use the `GetReminder` method on the Actor base class to get a reference to the reminder registration, and then use the `UnregisterReminder` method to unregister the reminder:

```
IActorReminder reminder = GetReminder("Reminder Name");
Task reminderUnregistration = UnregisterReminderAsync(reminder);
```

Actor events

Actor events provide a mechanism for the application to send notifications to the clients using events. However, this Actor events do not guarantee reliable delivery and therefore if a guaranteed message delivery is desired then other notification mechanisms should be used. Due to its unreliable nature, this mechanism should only be used for Actor-client communication and never for Actor-Actor communication.

To use Actor events, you first need to define an event by extending it from the `IActorEvents` interface. This interface has no members and is only used by the runtime to identify events. All methods in the interface should return void and the parameters should be data contract serializable since they need to be sent to the client over the network:

```
public interface IReminderActivatedEvent : IActorEvents
{
    void ReminderActivated(string message);
}
```

The Actor who publishes this event would need to implement the `IActorEventPublisher<T>` interface. This interface has no members and is only used by the runtime to identify the event publisher:

```
internal class HelloWorldActor : Actor,
IActorEventPublisher<IReminderActivatedEvent>
    {
...
    }
```

On the client side, you need to declare an event handler, which is the component that will get invoked when an event is triggered. To define the handler, you simply need to implement the Actor event interface:

```
public class ReminderHandler : IReminderActivatedEvent
{
    public void ReminderActivated(string message)
    {
...
    }
}
```

Finally, using the Actor proxy, the client can register the handler with the event:

```
var actorClientProxy = ActorProxy.Create<IHelloWorldActor>(
                new ActorId(userName),
                "fabric:/HelloWorldActorsApplication");
await actorClientProxy.SubscribeAsync<IReminderActivatedEvent>(new
ReminderHandler());
```

The Actor proxy is a smart component and it abstracts fault handling and name resolution from the client. In case of failure of Actor host node, which leads to Actor migrations to new nodes, the proxy will automatically subscribe to the event again.

To unsubscribe an event, the client can use the `UnsubscribeAsync` method on the Actor proxy. To trigger an event, an Actor needs to use the `GetEvent<T >` method to get the event reference and then trigger events by calling methods on the event interface:

```
var evt = this.GetEvent<IReminderActivatedEvent>();
evt.ReminderActivated(reminderMessage.reminderMessage);
```

Your first Reliable Actors application

Now that we have understood all the carious concepts of a Reliable Actors Application in detail, let us cement our learning by building a sample that demonstrates all the key concepts that we have learned till now.

Create a new Service Fabric application named `HelloWorldActorsApplication` in Visual Studio and choose the Reliable Actors template.

You'd need to specify a name for the Actor service in the template dialog, let's name the service `HelloWorldActor`:

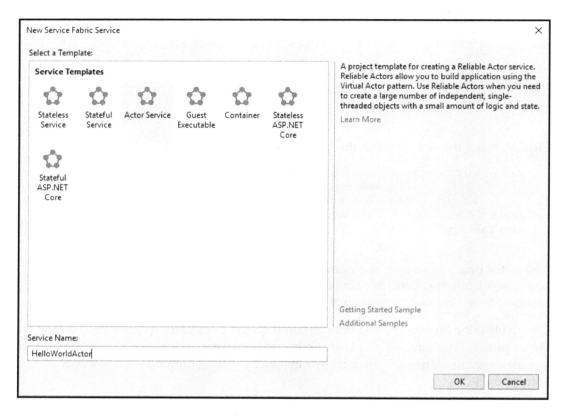

Creating HelloWorldActor service

After the template finishes unfolding, you would find three projects loaded in your solution as follows:

- `HelloWorldActorsApplication`: This is the application project that packages all the applications together for deployment. This project contains the deployment PowerShell script and the manifest file – `ApplicationManifest.xml`, that contains the name of packages that need to be deployed on Service Fabric cluster among other settings.

- `HelloWorldActor.Interfaces`: This project contains the communication contract for the Actor application and the clients. The clients of an Actor application uses these contracts to communicate with the application and the application implements those contracts. Although, it is not a requirement of Service Fabric to create a separate assembly to store the contracts, designing them in such a manner is useful since this project might be shared between the application and the clients.
- `HelloWorldActor`: This is the Actor service project which defines the Service Fabric service that is going to host our Actor. This project contains implementation of Actor interfaces defined in the Actor interfaces project. Let's take a deeper look into the primary class of this project – `HelloWorldActor` in `HelloWorldActor.cs` file.

This class derives from the Actor base class and implements the communication contract interfaces defined in the `HelloWorldActor.Interfaces` assembly. This class implements some of the Actor lifecycle events that we previously discussed. This class has a constructor that accepts an `ActorService` instance and an `ActorId` and passes them to the base Actor class.

```
[StatePersistence(StatePersistence.Persisted)]
internal class HelloWorldActor : Actor, IHelloWorldActor
{
    public HelloWorldActor(ActorService actorService, ActorId
      actorId)
        : base(actorService, actorId)
    {
}
...
}
```

When the Actor service gets activated, the `OnActivateAsync` is invoked. In the default template code, this method instantiates a state variable with count:

```
protected override Task OnActivateAsync()
{
    ActorEventSource.Current.ActorMessage(this, "Actor
      activated.");
    return this.StateManager.TryAddStateAsync("count", 0);
}
```

Let's now navigate to the `Main` method in `Program.cs` file which is responsible for hosting the Actor application. Every Actor service must be associated with a service type in the Service Fabric runtime. The `ActorRuntime.RegisterActorAsync` method registers your Actor type with the Actor service so that the Actor service can run your Actor instances. If you want to host more than one Actor types in an application, then you can add more registrations with the `ActorRuntime` with the following statement:

```
ActorRuntime.RegisterActorAsync<AnotherActor>();
```

Let's modify this application to allow users to save reminders with a message and later notify the user with the message at the scheduled time with an event.

To begin, add a new contract in the Actor interface, `IHelloWorldActor` to set a reminder and retrieve the collection of reminders that have been set:

```
public interface IHelloWorldActor : IActor
{
    Task<List<(string reminderMessage, DateTime
    scheduledReminderTimeUtc)>>
      GetRemindersAsync(CancellationToken
    cancellationToken);

     Task SetReminderAsync(string reminderMessage, DateTime
    scheduledReminderTimeUtc, CancellationToken
     cancellationToken);
}
```

The `SetReminderAsync` method accepts a message that should be displayed at the schceduled time. We will store the message in the Actor state in the form of a list. The `GetRemindersAsync` method will return a list of all the reminders that have been set by a user.

Let's navigate to the `HelloWorldActor` class to implement the members of this interface. First let's implement the `SetReminderAsync` method:

```
public async Task SetReminderAsync(
    string reminderMessage,
    DateTime scheduledReminderTimeUtc,
    CancellationToken cancellationToken)
{
    var existingReminders = await this.StateManager
        .GetStateAsync<List<(string reminderMessage, DateTime
         scheduledReminderTimeUtc)>>(
            "reminders",
            cancellationToken);
```

```
    // Add another reminder.
    existingReminders.Add((reminderMessage,
      scheduledReminderTimeUtc));
}
```

In this method, using the `StateManager`, we have first retrieved the reminders stored in the state. In the next statement, we added another reminder to the state.

The implementation of `GetReminderAsync` is very straightforward as well. In this method we simply retrive whatever is stored in the state and send it back as a response:

```
public async Task<List<(
    string reminderMessage,
    DateTime scheduledReminderTimeUtc)>> GetRemindersAsync(
    CancellationToken cancellationToken)
{
    return await
    this.StateManager.GetStateAsync<List<(string
    reminderMessage, DateTime scheduledReminderTimeUtc)>>
      ("reminders", cancellationToken);

}
```

The state is initialized in the `OnActivateAsync` method:

```
protected override Task OnActivateAsync()
{
    ActorEventSource.Current.ActorMessage(this, "Actor
      activated.");
    return this.StateManager.TryAddStateAsync("reminders", new
      List<(string reminderMessage, DateTime
        scheduledReminderTimeUtc)>());
}
```

The application side logic is covered. Let's create a client for our application now. Add a new console application named `HelloWorldActor.Client` to the solution. For this project, make sure that you choose the same .Net framework as your Service Fabric application and set the platform to x64. Since the clients and the application need to share the communication contract, therefore add reference to the `HelloWorldActor.Interfaces` assembly in this project.

Now, let us create a proxy to the Actor objects and invoke the Actor methods using the proxy:

```
private static async Task MainAsync(string[] args, CancellationToken
token)
        {
            Console.ForegroundColor = ConsoleColor.White;
            Console.WriteLine("Enter Your Name");
            var userName = Console.ReadLine();
            var actorClientProxy =
ActorProxy.Create<IHelloWorldActor>(
                new ActorId(userName),
                "fabric:/HelloWorldActorsApplication");
            await actorClientProxy.SetReminderAsync(
                "Wake me up in 2 minutes.",
                DateTime.UtcNow + TimeSpan.FromMinutes(2),
                token);
            await actorClientProxy.SetReminderAsync(
                "Another reminder to wake up after a minute.",
                DateTime.UtcNow + TimeSpan.FromMinutes(3),
                token);
            Console.WriteLine("Here are your reminders");
            var reminders = await
                        actorClientProxy.GetRemindersAsync(token);
            foreach (var reminder in reminders)
            {
                Console.ForegroundColor = ConsoleColor.Cyan;
                Console.WriteLine($"Reminder at:
                  {reminder.scheduledReminderTimeUtc} with message:
                    {reminder.reminderMessage}");
            }
        }
```

For this example, we will use the name of user to create and identify the Actor object that we want to work with. This will ensure that all our operations activate the same Actor instance and perform operations with it. After we have accepted the name of the user, we will use the `Create` method of `ActorProxy` class to create a proxy to the desired Actor instance. We can later use this proxy to invoke the methods exposed through the Actor interface. The `ActorProxy` abstracts the process to locate an Actor in the cluster and abstracts failure handling and retry mechanism in case of cluster node failures.

Next, we have used the proxy object that we have created to invoke the various methods on the Actor object.

You can run the application and the client now to test the functionalities that we have built till now. Till now the application only stores the reminders in state, however doesn't notify the user at the scheduled time. Now, let us add reminders to the application that will get invoked at the scheduled time.

Head back to the `HelloWorldActor` class and implement the `IRemindable` interface. This interface has a single method `ReceiveReminderAsync` which gets invoked every time a reminder gets triggered. To add a reminder, add the following statement to the `SetReminderAsync` method that we defined earlier:

```
await this.RegisterReminderAsync(
                       $"{this.Id}:{Guid.NewGuid()}",
    BitConverter.GetBytes(scheduledReminderTimeUtc.Ticks),
                       scheduledReminderTimeUtc - DateTime.UtcNow,
                       TimeSpan.FromMilliseconds(-1));
```

This statement will register a new reminder with the specified name, payload (which is the scheduled trigger time that we will use to identify the reminder), the scheduled occurrence time and the recurrence interval, which we have set to -1 to indicate that we don't want the reminder to recur.

Now that we have added a reminder, we need a mechanism to talk back to the client. Actor events give us the capability to do so. However, this mechanism doesn't guarantee message delivery and therefore should be used with caution in enterprise applications where guaranteed delivery might be a requirement. Also, this mechanism is designed for Actor-client communications only and is not supposed to be used for Actor-Actor communications.

To use Actor events, we need to define a class that implements the `IActorEvents` interface. Let's add a class named `IReminderActivatedEvent` in the `HelloWorldActor.Interfaces` which implements the `IActorEvents` interface. This interface doesn't contain any members and is only used by runtime to identify events:

```
public interface IReminderActivatedEvent : IActorEvents
{
    void ReminderActivated(string message);
}
```

Now that we have defined our event, we need to make sure that the runtime knows who is the publisher of the event. The runtime recognizes an event publisher using the `IActorEventPublisher` interface. This interface has no members that require implementation. Let's piggyback this interface on the `IHelloWorldActor` so that both the application and the client know that there are Actor events involved in the communication. The new `IHelloWorldActor` interface declaration should now look like the following:

```
public interface IHelloWorldActor : IActor,
IActorEventPublisher<IReminderActivatedEvent>
```

To complete the application side processing of events, let's implement the `ReceiveReminderAsync` method in the `HelloWorldActor` class which gets triggered every time a reminder is scheduled to trigger. In this function, we will try to extract the reminder from the state that got triggered, raise an Actor event, and finally unregister the reminder:

```
public async Task ReceiveReminderAsync(string reminderName,
  byte[] state, TimeSpan dueTime, TimeSpan period)
{
    var payloadTicks = BitConverter.ToInt64(state, 0);
    // Get the reminder from state.
    var cancellationToken = CancellationToken.None;
    var existingReminders = await this.StateManager
        .GetStateAsync<List<(string reminderMessage, DateTime
          scheduledReminderTimeUtc)>>(
            "reminders",
            cancellationToken);
    var reminderMessage =
        existingReminders.FirstOrDefault(
            reminder => reminder.scheduledReminderTimeUtc ==
            new DateTime(payloadTicks));
    if (reminderMessage.reminderMessage != string.Empty)
    {
        // Trigger an event for the client.
        var evt = this.GetEvent<IReminderActivatedEvent>();
  evt.ReminderActivated(reminderMessage.reminderMessage);
    }

    // Unregister the reminder.
    var thisReminder = this.GetReminder(reminderName);
    await this.UnregisterReminderAsync(thisReminder);
}
```

We do not need to construct an object of `IReminderActivatedEvent`, the base class Actor provides a `GetEvent` method that does it for us. By invoking the member function of `IReminderActivatedEvent`, we raise an event that gets published to the client.

Now let's tie things together on the client side. In the client we need to build an event handler and finally listen to the Actor event that gets raised by the application. It's time to head back to the `HelloWorldActor.Client` application and add a new class in the project named `ReminderHandler`. This class needs to implement the Actor event `IReminderActivatedEvent` which will get invoked when the application raises this event. For this sample, we will simply redirect the message to console when the event is raised:

```
public class ReminderHandler : IReminderActivatedEvent
{
    public void ReminderActivated(string message)
    {
        Console.ForegroundColor = ConsoleColor.Red;
        Console.WriteLine($"Reminder Activated: {message}");
        Console.ResetColor();
    }
}
```

To start listening to the event revisit the `Main` method which contains the implementation of the client. In this method, we are going to subscribe to the `IReminderActivatedEvent` and provide it with an object of the event handler that we just defined. The revised `Main` method should look something like the following:

```
private static async Task MainAsync(string[] args,
  CancellationToken token)
{
    ...
    Console.ResetColor();
    await
      actorClientProxy.SubscribeAsync<IReminderActivatedEvent>
        (new ReminderHandler());
    ...
}
```

Let's start the application and the client now to see it in action. Once you start the application, you should be able to see messages appearing in the **Diagnostics Events** viewer console:

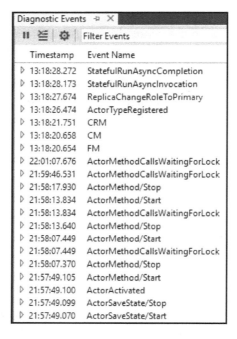

Diagnostic event messages from HelloWorldActor appliction

Finally, when you fire off the client application, you should be able to see new events being registered and reminders being triggered by the application and handled by the client:

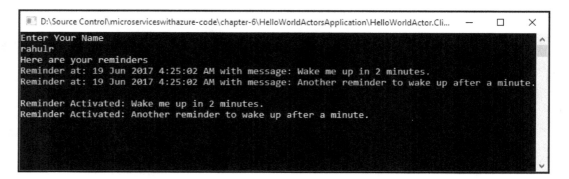

HelloWorldActor client

You might have noticed that we never used the Actor ID while persisting state or while operating with it. That is because the state is local to Actor, which means that no two instances of our application that supply different user names will write data to same store. Another noticeable fact is that we never used thread locking mechanisms in our code. That is because reliable Actors are by nature single-threaded. Which means that you can't invoke multiple methods in the same Actor simultaneously, which avoids thread locking problems.

Summary

We started this chapter with an introduction to the Actor framework and the virtual Actor model that Service Fabric Reliable Actors use. Next, we discussed the lifetime of a Service Fabric Actor and Service Fabric Reliable Actor model helps an Actor application persist state and maintain distribution and failover.

We discussed how Actors communicate among themselves and with the clients and how concurrency and reentrancy governs this behavior. We also discussed asynchronous communication drivers which are timers, reminders, and events.

Finally, to tie all the concepts together, we built a sample application and realized the various aspects of reliable Actors that we discussed.

17
Microservices Architecture Patterns Motivation

Use of patterns in architecting software solutions is not new to the industry. Design patterns and architectural patterns have been popular among application developers since 1990.

An architectural pattern can be defined as a verified and reusable solution to a commonly occurring problem in a software architecture. These patterns have numerous benefits; the most important of these is the ability to solve a recurring problem in a technology agnostic way. This level of abstraction increases the reusability of these patterns across different frameworks and programming paradigms.

Although the definition looks simple, learning the art of leveraging the patterns to define a software solution takes time and effort. Proper understanding of when and where to apply a pattern is the key to a good solution architecture. One way to gain this proficiency is to practice these patterns by designing and developing solutions with them. A good architecture for a solution is often a combination of multiple architectural patterns.

Creating an architecture

The task of creating an architecture for an enterprise-grade system can be organized into three steps:

1. Defining the solution boundaries.
2. Creating the solution structure.
3. Creating the component design.

Let's understand these steps in detail.

Defining the solution boundaries

The first step for a solution architect is to understand the boundaries of the proposed solution. This is an important task as, with boundaries, the solution can be a moving target which is difficult to contain. Defining clear solution boundaries helps the delivery team focus on the right scope for the solution to be designed and developed.

The main input for this process of defining the boundaries of a solution would be the business requirements driving the solution. External dependencies such as external systems or processes which needs to be integrated with the solution also influences this process. These inputs help the architect define the context and scope for the solution. It also enables normalization of the solution by abstracting external work flows from the internal ones.

Let's take a simple example to understand this further. Consider the requirement to build a system for booking a movie ticket. Let's assume that the system is driven by a two step process:

1. Verify the availability of a seat.
2. Book the ticket.

Let's also assume that there are two separate services made available for us to consume the preceding mentioned actions. The solution boundaries of such a system would look like the ones illustrated as follows:

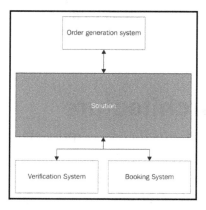

Solution boundaries

The box highlighted in green scopes the solution to be built and the other boxes are external systems which the solution is dependent on. This provides a clear understanding of the solution context to the application developers.

Creating the solution structure

After the solution boundaries are defined, the architect can now start working on the structure of the solution. A solution structure provides conceptual understanding of the solution space. The structure of the solution dictates the architectural framework to be used across the solution. The architectural framework is responsible for ensuring consistency throughout the solution there by making the solution more extensible and maintainable.

The key input for defining the structure of a solution is the system requirements. This will include both functional and non-functional requirements. The non-functional requirements will include requirements around security, performance, availability, reusability, and so on. The technologies used to develop the solution are largely influenced by their ability to deliver these requirements. Each non-functional requirement may force additional software components in the system. For instance, security requirements will require a security module for managing identity, authorization, and authentication of users accessing the system.

This step of the process is of most importance to us. During the definition of the solution structure, the solution architect can use architectural patterns to optimize and improve the solution architecture. We will discuss the common architectural problems surfaced for Microservice-based systems and the patterns which can be used to address these in detail in the next chapter, Microservices architectural patterns.

Let's use the previously described example and understand the solution structure for that system. Let's assume that there is a non-functional requirement to authenticate and authorize the users trying to book the ticket before performing the functionality. The following is a solution structure for this system:

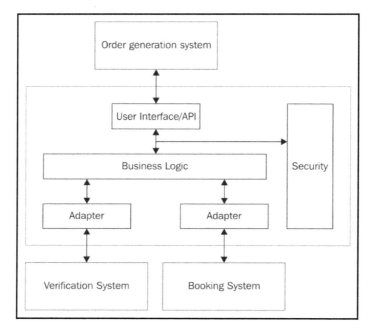

Solution structure

The solution structure defines the components within the solution, each of which specializes in a specific task. The adapters connecting to the external systems act like a bridge for communication to the externally hosted services.

 In terms of design patterns, an adapter is a component that allows two incompatible interfaces to work together. The adapter design pattern allows incompatible classes to work together by converting the interface of a class into another interface that the client expects. This eliminates friction between incompatible interfaces and allows them to work together. You can read more about adapters here: https://en.wikipedia.org/wiki/Adapter_pattern.

The user interface is used by the users to interact with the system and the core functionality is encapsulated within the component names as **Business Logic**. A separate component is introduced to handle the security requirements of the system. The user interfaces interact with the security module of authenticating and authorizing the user.

Component design

Once the solution structure is defined, every component can be designed in detail. The detailed design is mostly influenced by the functional requirements of the system and the relationship between the components which form the system. Tools such as UML can be used to identify the component relationships. This is where design patterns can be leveraged to improve the quality of the system. Design patterns are categorized into three types – structural, behavioral, and creational. Structural patterns are used to define the composition of objects and behavioral patterns are used to define the communications and algorithms within and across objects. Creational patterns are concerned with the instantiation of objects.

Classification of architectural patterns

Architectural patterns can be classified based on different properties. Componentization is a good example of one such property. Architectural patterns can be applied to monolithic systems or distributed systems. In this book, we will focus on the architectural patterns specific to Microservices-based distributed systems. Within this sub set we have classified the architectural patterns discussed in this book based on the problem type. This will ease the task for a solution architect to map a problem to an architectural pattern. The following are the architectural patterns we address through the patterns discussed in this book.

Optimization or non-functional patterns

Optimization or non-functional architectural patterns focus on enhancing the executional and evolutional quality of a system. The problems addressed by these patterns are oblivious of the system behavior or its functionality. Following are few problem categories addressed by these patterns:

- Resiliency
- Security
- Performance
- Scalability
- Availability

Operational patterns

Challenges in maintaining and managing the execution of a system needs to be thought through and accounted for while architecting a system. These common operational problems can be mapped to proven solutions with the help of architectural patterns. Following are the categories of major operational challenges:

- Orchestration
- Automation
- Centralization
- Deployment

Implementation or functional patterns

Implementation or functional patterns addresses common architectural problems related to a solution structure or framework used by an application. The solutions to these problems define standards for implementing all components in a system which makes these patterns very important. Following are a few challenges addressed by these patterns:

- Communication
- Abstraction
- Persistence

Picking up the right architecture pattern

You should follow a pragmatic approach for picking up the right patterns that address the problem that you are trying to solve. In the world of software development, each problem is unique and therefore building a universal pattern to address all scenarios is impossible. The process of selecting a pattern requires diligence from application architects and developers and should be done in a pragmatic manner. To select the right design pattern, you should first outline the following characteristics of the problem that you are trying to solve.

Context

A pattern documents a recurring problem-solution pairing within a given context. While selecting an architecture pattern for your application, you should be aware of the context of your application. A pattern that solves the messaging challenges of Facebook might not be a good fit for an application that caters to a small number of users. You need to resolve the applicability of a pattern by matching your problem with the associated scenario of the design pattern.

Forces

Forces describe what an effective solution for a problem must consider. An effective solution must balance the forces of a problem. A solution may not perfectly address all the forces. There might be consequences of implementing a solution that balances the forces, however, the benefits of implementation must outweigh the liabilities. For instance, for a system that makes multiple calls to another system on network, a force can be the need to improve application performance. You can solve this problem by batching the calls made by the system. This approach will introduce the liability of increased response time and storage space overhead but if configured precisely to balance response time, performance, and storage, it will adequately address the force without adding high liabilities.

You need to evaluate whether a pattern addresses the forces applicable to your problem, evaluate the benefits and liabilities of applying a pattern to your problem, and validate whether the liabilities arising out of application of a pattern are within acceptable limits of the requirements.

Complementing patterns

Most of the applications do not use a single pattern in isolation. For a pattern to make sense, it should list other patterns with which it competes or cooperates. We have listed related patterns for every pattern that you would be going through. We recommend that you consider the related patterns as well to compliment or compound the pattern under discussion.

Applying a pattern

Once you have selected a pattern to apply to your architecture, you should remodel it to fit your scenario. Due to unique nature of every application, you will need to apply diligence during the process of transforming a pattern to fit your scenario. Let's study the types of variations that you need to consider before applying a pattern to your scenario.

Structural variation

A pattern is not just an interconnection of components. The various components used in a pattern play a distinct role. These roles may be different from the requirements of your scenario. Let's consider the well-known observer design pattern, an observer may receive events from multiple sources or a single source. Also, the observer class may play the role of an observer in one relationship and the role of a subject in another. Therefore, you would need to remodel the observer pattern to fit in the scenario that you are trying to address.

The architecture patterns presented later in the book can be remodeled to fit the requirements of your scenario. You should consider how you can extend the pattern that you wish to apply to add value to your solution.

Behavioral variation

The desired behavior of your application may vary from the pattern. For example, your application may require messages to be processed in the order they are received, whereas the pattern may use concurrency optimization techniques to process messages without considering the message sequence. You should use the guidance of patterns to optimize the behavior of your application for time, space, and behavioral constraints within the application domains and runtime platforms.

Internal variation

The implementation of pattern and your application may vary. For example, a pattern uses *Service Fabric Concurrent Queues*, whereas your application may use *Azure Storage Queues*. Although, the objective of the pattern and your solution may concur, the implementation may vary. You should adapt the pattern to suit the needs of your application and not vice-versa.

Domain dependent variation

Depending on the desired functional, operational, and developmental requirements of your application, the implementation of a pattern may change. According to the principles of **domain-driven design** (**DDD**), within a bounded context a model can have a unique meaning. A pattern may exhibit such a behavior and there may be differences in the meaning of a term in the pattern and the context of the problem that you are trying to address. For instance, asynchrony may differ in meaning by context. For asynchronous communication using queues, your application may poll the queue at regular intervals or get triggered by a message-received event. You should remodel your chosen pattern to align the context of the pattern to the problem that you are addressing.

Summary

In this chapter, we walked through the steps of creating an architecture for a software solution. We then discussed the classification of architectural patterns and a few recommendations about picking the right architectural pattern for your application.

Towards the end of the chapter, we talked about methods of applying an architectural pattern on your application.

18 Microservices Architectural Patterns

The idea of componentizing software was first popularized in the world of computing in 1960s. Modern day enterprise distributed systems are build based on this principle of encapsulating functionalities as software components which are consumed by applications to assemble business work flows. These software components which provide functionality to other applications are popularly termed as services. The composite applications that use services can be anything ranging from a mobile application, a web application, or a desktop application.

In a traditional world, applications are monolithic by nature. A monolithic application is composed of many components grouped into multiple tiers bundled together into a single deployable unit. Each tier here can be developed using a specific technology and will have the ability to scale independently.

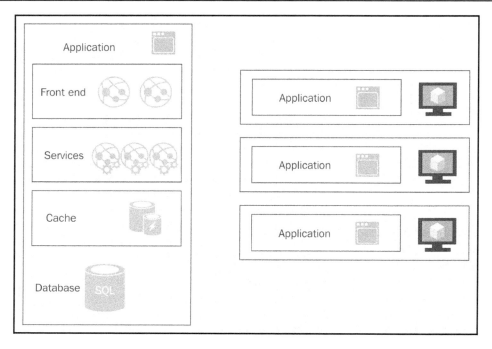

Monolithic application

Although a monolithic architecture logically simplifies the application, it introduces many challenges as the number of applications in your enterprise increases. Following are few issues with the monolithic design:

- **Scalability**: The unit of scale is scoped to a tier. It is not possible to scale components bundled within an application tier without scaling the whole tier. This introduces massive resource wastage resulting in increase in operational expense.
- **Reuse and maintenance**: The components within an application tier cannot be consumed outside the tier unless exposed as contracts. This forces development teams to replicate code which becomes very difficult to maintain.
- **Updates**: As the whole application is one unit of deployment, updating a component will require updating the whole application which may cause downtime thereby affecting the availability of the application.
- **Low deployment density**: The compute, storage and network requirements of an application, as a bundled deployable unit may not match the infrastructure capabilities of the hosting machine. This may lead to wastage of shortage of resources.

- **Decentralized management**: Due to the redundancy of components across applications, supporting, monitoring, and troubleshooting becomes expensive overheads.
- **Data store bottlenecks**: If there are multiple components accessing the data store, it becomes the single point of failure. This forces the data store to be highly available.
- **Cascading failure**: The hardware dependency of this architecture to ensure availability doesn't work well with cloud hosting platforms where designing for failure is a core principle.

A solution to this problem is to migrate to a distributed system architecture. A distributed system is highly maintainable and far less complex than a monolithic application. There is a clear separation between the various parts of the application in a distributed system. This gives third party service providers an opportunity to plug their applications to the services that the distributed system provides.

A distributed system is generally realized through a **Service-Oriented Architecture** (SOA). The idea behind using SOA is that instead of using modules within an application, use services to provide functionality to the client application. An advantage of SOA architecture is that there can be multiple independent clients of an application. For instance, same set of services may be used by a mobile client and a web client of an e-commerce application. The SOA architecture also supports the independence of client and functionalities. If the contracts of a service do not change, the service may be modified to provide the functionality without altering the clients.

Due to lack of standards and implementation consistency on what functionalities should be provided by each service realized through SOA architecture, traditional architectures resulted in large monolithic services. Because of size of the services, the services became hard to scale. SOA also lacks simplicity as it is generally realized through web services. Traditionally, web services use SOAP and XML, which today have been replaced with REST and JSON. Since services in SOA can encapsulate several functionalities, each of the individual SOA service becomes deployment monoliths. SOA tends to reduce delivery agility and does not gel well with recent DevOps practices such as continuous integration and continuous deployment.

The Microservices architecture is the evolution of SOA. The Microservice architecture is a software architecture pattern where applications are composed of small, independent services which can be aggregated using communication channels to achieve and end-to-end business use case. The services are decoupled from one another in terms of the execution space in which they operate.

Each of these services will have the capability to be scaled, tested and maintained separately:

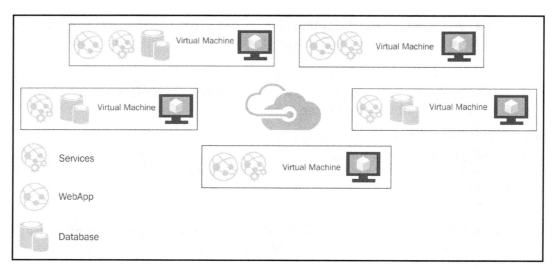

Microservices architecture

Microservices have all the features of SOA with additional service sizing constraints. Each Microservice has a single focus and it does just one thing and does it well. A distributed system composed of Microservices will have multiple Microservices that communicate with each other to provide a set of functionality for a specific part of the application.

Because the Microservices need to communicate with each other and with the clients, the communication mechanism needs to be quick and platform independent, for example, HTTP REST. A platform independent communication platform also ensures that Microservices and clients developed on different platform can communicate with each other for example a Java client communicating with .NET service.

Microservices are more agile than SOA. This helps development teams change part of systems quickly without affecting the rest of the system. Overall, added agility reduces the time to market of a product and allows the product to be adaptable to changing market conditions.

Microservices can also adapt to changing organizational systems. For instance, a change in account management product of a company would only alter the accounts service of the system without altering the other services such as the HR service or facility management service.

There are complex problems that need to be solved to host Microservices at scale. Such problems include preserving state, rolling upgrades, inter-service communication, and optimal use of machine resources. Such problems lead to slow adoption of Microservices architecture.

Azure Service Fabric is a distributed systems platform that makes it easy to package, deploy, and manage, scalable and reliable Microservices thereby addressing significant challenges in developing and managing Microservices. It does so by treating a collection of virtual machines as a worker pool on which Microservices can be deployed. Since, all that Service Fabric needs is a runtime, it can be executed on heterogeneous platforms on any data center.

Service Fabric is a reliable, tried and tested platform to build Microservices. It is already used to host some of the largest Microsoft services such as SQL Azure, Bing, Events hub, Cortana services, and so on.

Following are few advantages of a Service Fabric which makes it the ideal platform to build a Microservice based Application Platform:

- **Highly scalable**: Every service can be scaled without affecting other services. Service Fabric will support scaling based on VM scale sets which means that these services will have the ability to be auto-scale based on CPU consumption, memory usage, and so on.
- **Updates**: Services can be updated separately and different versions of a service can be co-deployed to support backward compatibility. Service Fabric also supports automatic rollback during updates to ensure consistency and stability of an application deployment.
- **State redundancy**: For stateful Microservices, the state can be stored alongside compute of a service. If there are multiple instances of a service running, the state will be replicated for every instance. Service Fabric takes care of replicating the state changes throughout the stores.
- **Centralized management**: The service can be centrally managed, monitored, and diagnosed outside application boundaries.

- **High density deployment**: Service Fabric supports high density deployment on a virtual machine cluster while ensuring even utilization of resources and even distribution of work load.
- **Automatic fault tolerance**: The cluster manager of Service Fabric ensures failover and resource balancing in case of a hardware failure. This ensures that your services are deigned for failure, a compulsory requirement of cloud ready applications.
- **Heterogeneous hosting platforms**: Service Fabric supports hosting your Microservices across public and private cloud environments. The Service Fabric cluster manager is capable of managing service deployments with instances spanning multiple data centers at a time. Apart from Windows operating system, Service Fabric also supports Linux as a host operating system for your Microservices.
- **Technology agnostic**: Services can be written in any programming language and deployed as executable or hosted within containers. Service Fabric also supports a native Java SDK for Java developers.

Architectural patterns

An application built with the Microservices architecture is composed of a set of small and independent services. Due to the granularity, diversity, high density, and scale of Microservices, a Microservices architecture is usually challenged by various problems related to optimization, operations, and implementation of these services. Most of these problems are best addressed with repeatable solutions or patterns which are tried and tested.

In the following sections, we will discuss few such architectural patterns which will help address challenges associated with a system build using Microservices. These patterns can speed up development process by providing tested, proven development paradigms. Each design pattern discussed here consists of the following sections:

- **Category**: The categories of challenges that the design pattern address
- **Problem**: The problem that the design pattern addresses
- **Solution**: How the design pattern solves the problem
- **Considerations**: Rationale that should be applied while applying the pattern in consideration
- **Related patterns**: Other patterns that are either used in conjunction with or are related to the pattern in consideration
- **Use Cases**: Typical scenarios where the pattern may be used

Let's start exploring these patterns one by one.

Each of the patterns discussed below belongs to a set of families, or categories, and is further classified by the problem areas it addresses, or the sub-categories. We have decorated each pattern with the following icons which will help you identify the appropriate categories and sub-categories to which the pattern belongs.

The following table summarizes the categories, which will be used across the chapter:

Category	Logo
Implementation	
Operational	
Optimization	

The following table summarizes the sub-category, which will be used across the chapter:

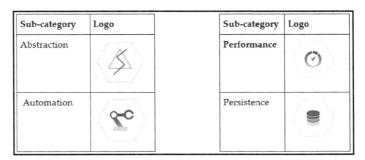

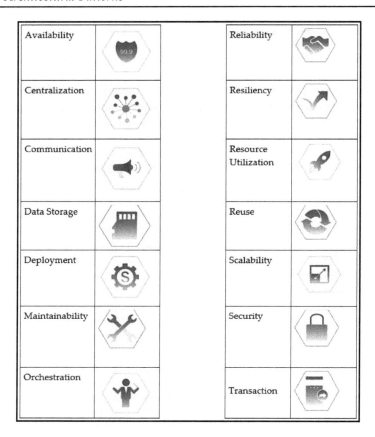

Availability		Reliability	
Centralization		Resiliency	
Communication		Resource Utilization	
Data Storage		Reuse	
Deployment		Scalability	
Maintainability		Security	
Orchestration		Transaction	

Service proxy

Problem

With Microservices hosted remotely, it is inefficient to instantiate a Microservice instance unless and until they are requested for by the client. During design/development time, this demands for a substitute object for the client to integrate with. Also, with cloud offering the ability to host multiple instances of Microservices across the globe, it is best that the deployment and implementation details are hidden from the client. Tightly coupled, deployment location aware communication can often result in service outages if the service deployment is relocated.

Following is an illustration of this scenario:

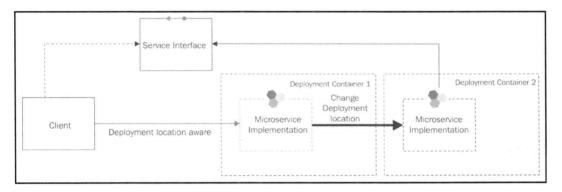

Service proxy (Problem)

Solution

Service proxy is an implementation pattern which solves a communication problem. Service proxy helps in abstracting the service implementation from the interface definitions. This lets you change the service implementation without affecting the contracts with the clients. To enable communication with an Actor or a Microservice, a client will create a proxy object of the Actor that implements the Actor or service interface. All interactions with the Actor or service is performed by invoking methods on the proxy object. The Actor or service proxy can be used for *client-to-Actor/service* and *Actor/service-to-Actor/service* communication. The proxy pattern does not change any interfaces. This defines substitute objects for other objects.

Following is an illustration of this pattern in action:

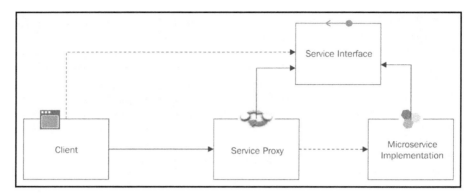

Service proxy (Solution)

Microsoft Azure Service Fabric exposes proxy classes for Reliable Actors and for Reliable Services. The proxy classes are also responsible for location resolution of Microservices.

Considerations

The following considerations should be taken into account while implementing this pattern:

- **Another layer of abstraction**: Adding layers to a system architecture results in some side effects such as increase in communication latency. The maintainability and testability of the code will also be impacted with introduction of additional classes.
- **Exception handling**: As the consuming application interacts with the proxy instead of the service directly, it must cater for scenarios where the backend Microservice is unavailable. The proxy will need to capture any service exceptions and relay it to the client.
- **Logging**: All exceptions and traces should be logged by the proxy to ensure better troubleshooting capabilities.
- **Abstraction**: Implementation or deployment details of the Microservice should be abstracted from the client.
- **Configurable**: The deployment location of the Microservice should be configurable and should have the ability to be updated without code re-compilation.

Related patterns

Following are the related design patterns which can be used in conjunction with this pattern:

- **Retry pattern**: Best used for transient fault handling which should be anticipated for cloud deployment of Microservices
- **Runtime reconfiguration pattern**: Making the configuration changes event-driven can help make the system more dynamic and ensure better availability
- **Gatekeeper pattern**: Best used to minimize the risk of clients gaining direct access to sensitive information and services
- **Circuit breaker pattern**: Handles transient faults to improve the stability and resiliency of an application

Use cases

Following are a few use cases where this pattern will be a right fit:

- **Controlling the object lifecycle**: The instantiation of server side objects can be controlled within the proxy pattern thereby supporting scenarios like lazy instantiation, singleton, object pooling, and so on.
- **Security**: Proxy can act like another layer of security as it prevents the client from directly interacting with the Microservice.
- **Transformation**: Proxy can perform certain degree of transformations to abstract these complexities from the client.

Service Façade \ API Gateway

Problem

Microservices architecture recommends services to be decomposed as simpler units which can be knit together to achieve an end-to-end business use case. This results in client being cognizant of services at a granular level thereby increasing the complexity of management overheads related to communication, transformation, and transaction. Any change in the API contracts of the Microservices will also impact the client impacting the stability of the system. Also, with an increase in the number of services in the system, the complexity of client applications increases to accommodate more communication channels and service discovery overheads. The following diagram illustrates such a scenario:

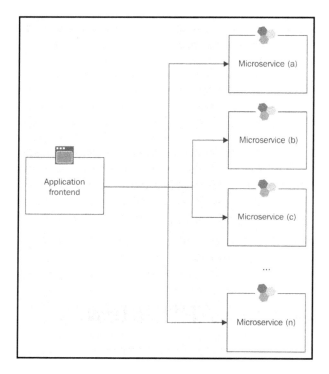

Service Façade (Problem)

Solution

Microservices, forced by the very idea behind the concept, recommend granularization of services to improve reuse and to enforce single responsibility principle. While this improves maintainability, it also introduces the requirement of having an abstraction layer which can aggregate multiple Microservices to expose a business functionality which can be easily consumed by an application. Services Façade will play this role of this abstract layer which a client can integrate with, without knowing the complexity of invoking one or more Microservices behind the scene.

As defined by Gang of Four, the role of the façade pattern is to provide different high-level views of subsystems whose details are abstracted from the client. The subsystems in our case would be specialized Microservices deployed over heterogeneous environments.

Design Patterns: Elements of Reusable Object-Oriented Software is a considered to be an authoritative book describing software design patterns. The book's authors are Erich Gamma, Richard Helm, Ralph Johnson and John Vlissides. The book discusses 23 classic software design patterns which are regarded as an important source for object-oriented design theory and practice. The authors of the book are often referred to as the **Gang of Four** (**GoF**).

Service Façade can be visualized as an orchestration layer responsible for integrating one or more Microservices to achieve a specific business use case. The Service Façade either routes the request to a service or fans out the request to multiple services. The business logic of the system is encapsulated in the Service Façade and is thus abstracted from the client. The Façade itself can be a Microservice participating in the application.

The following diagram illustrates this pattern in action:

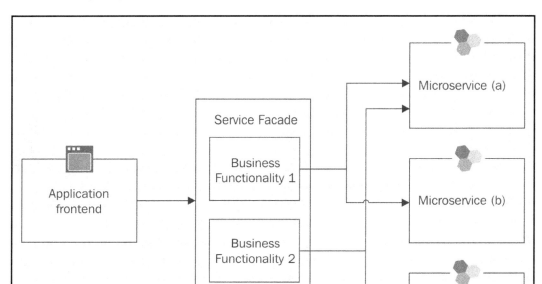

Service Façade (Solution)

Microsoft Azure API Management is a software as a service which enables orchestration, transformation and documentation of services. The service also provides other functionalities such as metering and analytics. API Management is a potential service to be considered to play the role of a Services Façade for Microservices based applications.

Considerations

The following considerations should be taken into account while implementing this pattern:

- **Cyclomatic complexity**: Cyclomatic complexity is a measure of complexity of a program. This metric measures independent paths through a program source code. An independent path is a path that has not been traversed before in a code execution flow. It is important to ensure that the cyclomatic complexity of the Service Façade is low. This will guarantee maintainability and readability of the code.

- **Transactions**: While integrating Microservices, it's important to ensure transactional integrity. If a business use case terminates before completion, compensatory transactions need to be executed by the Service Façade.

- **Another layer of abstraction**: Adding layers to a system architecture results in some side effects such as increase in latency. The maintainability and testability of the code will also be impacted with introduction of additional components.

- **Exception handling**: As the consuming application interacts with the façade instead of the service directly, it must cater for scenarios where the backend Microservice is unavailable. The Service Façade will need to capture any service exceptions and relay it to the client.

- **Logging**: All exceptions and traces should be logged in the same central location as the application by the Service Façade to ensure better trouble shooting capabilities.

- **Abstraction**: Implementation or deployment details of the Microservice should be abstracted from the client.

- **Configurable**: The deployment location of the Microservice should be configurable and should have the ability to be updated without code re-compilation.

Related patterns

Following are the related cloud design patterns which can be used in conjunction with this pattern:

- **Compensating Transaction pattern**: Used for maintaining transactional integrity of a system by handling workflow failures gracefully
- **Retry pattern**: Best used for transient fault handling which should be anticipated for cloud deployment of Microservices
- **Gatekeeper pattern**: Best used to minimize the risk of clients gaining direct access to sensitive information and services
- **Circuit Breaker pattern**: Handles transient faults to improve the stability and resiliency of an application

Use cases

Following are a few use cases where this pattern will be a right fit:

- **Service orchestration**: An ideal use case for this pattern would be to act like an orchestration layer to abstract out the complexity around integration of Microservices such as communication, transaction, deployment details, and so on
- **Security**: Service Façade can act like another layer of security as it prevents the client from directly interacting with Microservices
- **Fault tolerance**: Service Façade can be enriched by implementing a circuit breaker pattern within it to better tolerate transient faults

Reliable Data Store

Problem

Stateful Microservices are commonly associated with dependencies on external data stores. These dependencies often introduce bottle necks in terms of performance and availability as the data source can act like a single point of failure. This problem has enhanced impact where multiple instances of a service co-exists at a given point. Maintaining high availability of the data store becomes expensive as the data grows. The following diagram illustrates a system with a centrally externalized data store:

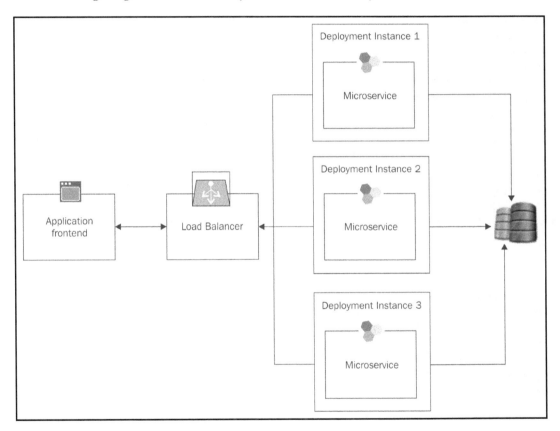

Reliable data store (Problem)

Solution

A solution to this problem is to co-locate Microservice state with compute. This will reduce application's dependency on external data stores (such as cache) for frequently accessed data. Having the data stored on the same deployment instance as the consuming application also contributes positively to the system performance and negates the risk introduced by the data store being a single point of failure.

However, this introduces challenges around maintaining data consistency and synchronization across multiple instances of the same service. A reliable data store with the following characteristics can be used to persist state to address these problems:

- **Replicated**: Data changes can be replicated across multiple instances
- **Persistence**: Data is persisted on a secondary storage to ensure durability
- **Asynchronous**: Supports asynchronous API model to ensure non-blocking calls
- **Transactional**: Should support transactions

The following diagram illustrates a system using Reliable Data Store instead of a centralized data store:

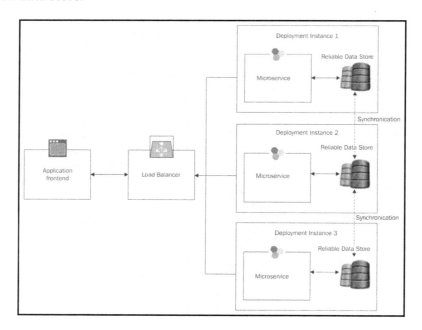

Reliable Data Store (Solution)

Microsoft Azure Service Fabric recommends the use of Reliable Collections for persisting data across instances of a Microservice. Reliable Collection is a natural evolution of the System.Collections library with the added ability to abstract out the complexities of replication, persistence, synchronization, and transaction management from the client. It also offers different isolation levels (repeatable read and snapshot) for accommodating diverse transactional systems.

Considerations

The following considerations should be taken into account while implementing this pattern:

- **Isolation levels**: While using this pattern, the isolation levels suited for the application need to be chosen based on characteristics of transactions. More about isolation levels supported by Reliable Collections can be found at: `https://docs.microsoft.com/en-us/azure/service-fabric/service-fabric-reliable-services-reliable-collections-transactions-locks`.
- **Persistence**: The persistence model required by the reliable data sore needs to be accounted for, before implementing this pattern. The frequency of write, replication, batching I/O operations, and so on are few things to consider while choosing a persistence model.
- **Timeouts**: It's important to introduce timeouts for every call associated with a reliable data store to avoid dead locks.
- **High availability**: To ensure high availability, consider running multiple instances of your Microservice at a time. Microsoft recommends at least three instances of a service to be active at any time.
- **Synchronization delay**: Where there are multiple instances of Microservices deployed, the data store on one of the instances will act as a primary and others would be considered as secondary. In case of an update, there will be a delay in reflecting changes across secondary instances of the data store. This may lead to chances of read operations retrieving stale data.

Related patterns

Following are the related cloud design patterns which can be used in conjunction with this pattern:

- **Retry pattern**: Can be used for handling transient faults on the Reliable Data Store.
- **Sharding pattern**: The data can be partitioned horizontally to improve scalability and performance. The pattern is advisable while handling large volumes of equally disperse data sets.
- **Leader Election pattern**: In case of multi-instance deployment, elect a leader to coordinate tasks to avoid conflicts around shared resources.

Use cases

Following are few use cases where this pattern will be a right fit:

- **Caching**: An ideal use case for this pattern would be application scenarios which require data to be cached. A Reliable Store will offer better performance compared to an external cache while ensuring a higher degree of availability.
- **Fault tolerance**: As the data stores are synchronized and persisted on every node, the system become more tolerant against hardware failures.

Cluster Orchestrator

Problem

Deploying a highly scalable and available set of Microservices on commodity hardware introduces the requirement having an efficient management system. Managing communication between services, monitoring health, maintaining a service catalog, managing application lifecycle, load balancing, scaling instances, data replication, handling failover, managing rolling updates, and so on are few challenges associated with operating enterprise scale Microservices.

It is nearly impossible to efficiently perform these tasks manually. The following diagram illustrates how complex manually managing such a system can become:

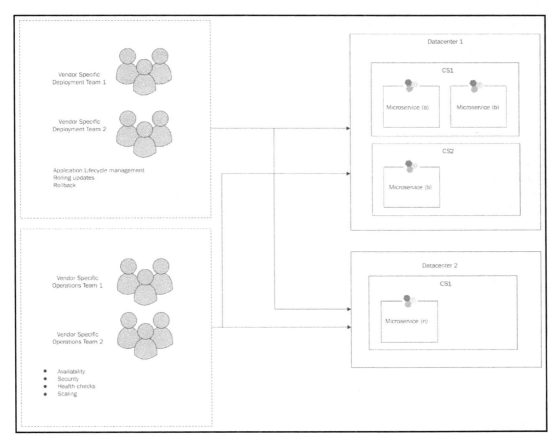

Cluster orchestrator (Problem)

Solution

A highly available, cluster orchestration system can be employed to manage Microservice deployments across heterogeneous environments. Cluster orchestrator will own the responsibility of ensuring the availability of Microservices with minimal human intervention. The system will consist of two components:

- **Cluster Orchestration Server(s)**: Centralized management server
- **Cluster Orchestration Agents**: A thin native software deployed on every instance (virtual machine) in a cluster dedicated for hosting the Microservices.

Cluster orchestrator deploys an agent on every hosting instance (virtual machine) in a cluster which is the used to control and communicate with the host operating system and the services deployed on the machine. Once a connection between the agent and the server is established, cluster orchestrator handles the following responsibilities associated with managing the Microservices:

- Availability
- Data replication
- Data partitioning
- Load balancing
- Rolling updates and rollbacks
- Resource placement (high density deployment)
- Failover and recovery
- Health monitoring and healing

The following diagram illustrates a cluster orchestrator in action:

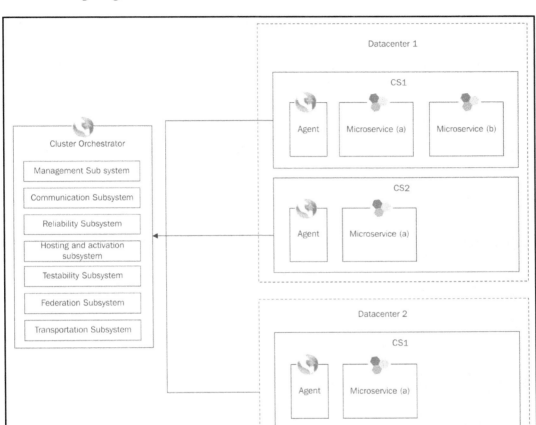

Cluster orchestrator (Solution)

Microsoft Azure Service Fabric has inbuilt orchestration capabilities capable of handling hyper scale Microservice deployments across heterogeneous environments. More about Service Fabric cluster orchestration capabilities can be found here: https://azure.microsoft.com/en-us/documentation/articles/service-fabric-architecture/.

Considerations

The following considerations should be taken into account while implementing this pattern:

- **High availability**: It is critical to ensure high availability of the cluster orchestrator as it can act like a single point of failure for your Microservices deployment. A three to five instance cluster is usually recommended for the orchestration software to handle availability.
- **Heterogeneity**: The ability of the orchestration tool to handle virtual machines of different configurations and operating environments is the key to support heterogeneity.
- **Resource allocation**: The orchestration tool should have an efficient resource allocation algorithm to manage high density deployments while optimizing the resource utilization.
- **Security**: The orchestration tool should be responsible to ensure isolation of services when performing high density deployments.
- **Configurable**: Thresholds for rollbacks, update domains, failover, and so on should be configurable to suit specific requirements of the ecosystem.

Related patterns

Following are the related cloud design patterns which can be used in conjunction with this pattern:

- **Compute Resource Consolidation Pattern**: This pattern is ideal to support high density deployments.
- **Health Endpoint Monitoring Pattern**: Employing agents (external processes) to verify that applications and services are performing correctly.
- **Leader Election Pattern**: In case of multi-instance deployment, elect a leader to coordinate tasks to avoid conflicts around shared resources. This is useful in managing a cluster of orchestration servers to ensure high availability.

Use cases

Following are few use cases where this pattern will be a right fit:

- **Hyper scale deployment of Microservices**: An ideal use case for this pattern would be environments which demand high density. Highly available, hyper scale deployments of Microservices.
- **Automated operations**: Cluster orchestrator minimizes the requirement of manual intervention for managing your Microservices by offering features like self-healing, rolling updates, rollback, and so on.
- **Cross platform deployments**: This pattern is best used to manage Microservice deployments across heterogeneous platforms (like different data centers, different operating systems, different hardware infrastructure, and so on).

Auto-scaling

Problem

The load on the services tier of enterprise system is typically nonlinear. Matching the infrastructure services to the workload is a key challenge faced by operation teams these days. The complexity starts with understanding the pattern around increase/decrease in the workload, mapping the workload with a scale-out / scale-up plan and then executing the plan manually. The challenges multiply if the workload keeps changing frequently altering the scalability requirements dynamically.

The following diagram illustrates a scenario where the operations team manually manages the scaling of services:

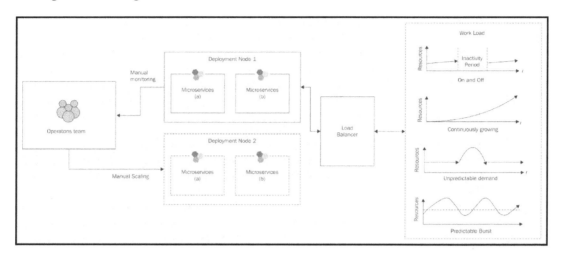

Auto-scaling (Problem)

Solution

The solution is to employ a software system to perform scaling automatically based on parameters such as number of requests, CPU utilization, memory utilization, and buffer size (queue size), and so on to improve the efficiency of the system and to optimize operational expense.

Auto-scaling is an elastic process which will provision resources based on the work load and a preconfigured collection of rules specifying the thresholds, scaling range, scaling factors, and so on. The system should be capable of scaling the resources vertically, by redeploying the service on a more capable hardware or, scaling horizontally, by provisioning additional instances of the services.

The following diagram illustrates an auto-scaling system in action:

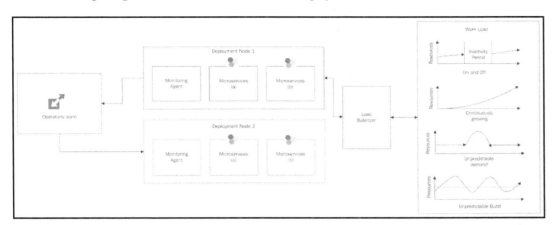

Auto-scaling (Solution)

Azure Service Fabric clusters are built on top of virtual machine scale sets and can be scaled either manually or with auto-scale rules. You can read more about building auto-scaling rules at: `https://docs.microsoft.com/en-us/azure/service-fabric/service-fabric-cluster-programmatic-scaling`.

Considerations

The following considerations should be taken into account while implementing this pattern:

- **System downtime**: Auto-scaling should be achieved without system downtime. This forces the requirement that existing instances hosting the service should not be impacted by the scaling operation.
- **Scale up or scale out**: Depending on the execution model of the application being hosted, the decision whether to scale up/down or scale out/in has to be made.
- **Start-up / shut-down threshold**: Starting up a new node or shutting down a node will take some time. This time needs to be accounted for before a decision on scaling is made. A good input for this decision is consistency of the load which can be evaluated against a threshold before scaling the system.

- **Max and min count for instances**: It is important to set bounds for auto-scaling to ensure that any erroneous/malicious activities are not impacting the availability or the operation expense of the system. Alerts should be configured to monitor any unusual scaling activities.
- **Logging and monitoring**: The scaling activity should be logged and the performance of the system should be monitored post scaling to ensure that the scaling operation was effective.

Related patterns

Following are the related cloud design patterns which can be used in conjunction with this pattern:

- **Throttling pattern**: This pattern can be used to handle graceful degradation of services when the load increases. Throttling can be used with auto-scaling pattern to ensure system availability while scaling out.
- **Health Endpoint Monitoring pattern**: Employing agents (external processes) to verify the load on the system to trigger the auto-scaling process.
- **Competing Consumers pattern**: This pattern helps scale out by enabling multiple concurrent consumers to process messages received on the same messaging channel.

Use cases

Following are few use cases where this pattern will be a right fit:

- **On and Off workload**: Scenarios where the service needs to be running only for a specific amount of time. Batch jobs and scheduled jobs are apt examples.
- **Growing fast**: When the demand for the service increases continuously. A new production release of a popular service would be an example for this scenario.
- **Unpredicted demand**: Unpredicted increase or decrease in workload demanding a scaling out/in. The load encountered on news site or stock exchanges can be classified in to this category.
- **Predictable burst**: Anticipated increase in load for an indefinite duration. Increase of load on movie ticking systems on a new release would be a perfect example.

Partitioning

Problem

Operational efficiency of a stateful Microservice is highly dependent on the way it stores and retrieves data as part of its operations. As the data store grows, time to access the data increases thereby causing significant impact on the performance, throughput, and scalability of a system. It is a commonly observed pattern that some sections of the data store are accessed more frequently compared to others. In a monolithic architecture, it is very difficult to scale the data store and the compute used to access the data separately for specific segments of the data store. The following figure illustrates such a scenario where the data store becomes a bottleneck:

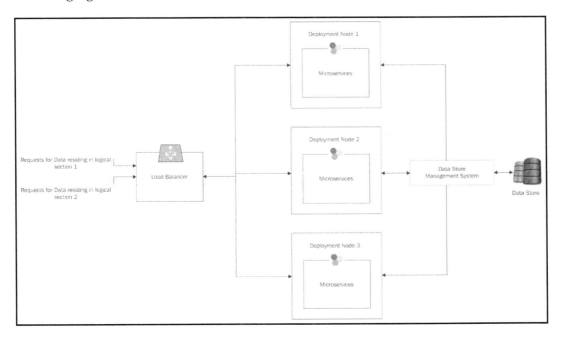

Partitioning (Problem)

Solution

A solution for this problem is to logically divide the state of the system in to partitions which can then be served separately with minimal dependency on one another.

Partitioning can be defined as the concept of dividing state and compute into smaller units to improve scalability and performance of a system. Partitioning is more suited for stateful Microservices than for stateless Microservices. Partitioning will define logical boundaries to ensure that a particular service partition is responsible for a portion of the complete state of the service. The services will be replicated on every partition.

Before implementing partitioning, it is important to device a partition strategy which supports scale out. Partition strategy should also ensure even distribution of the load across partitions.

The following figure illustrates a system which uses partitioned data store:

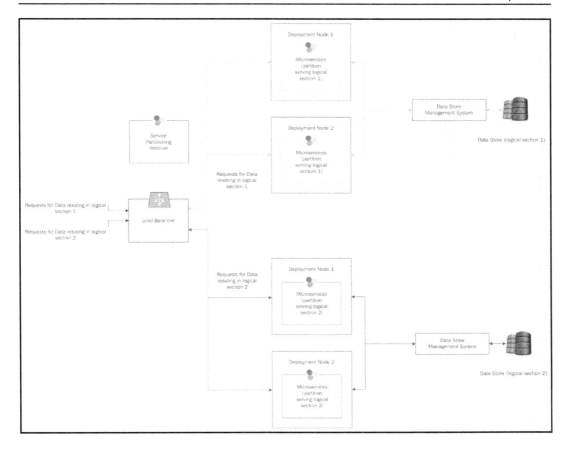

Partitioning (Solution)

Microsoft Azure Service Fabric natively supports partitioning for stateful Microservices. Service Fabric offers the following three choices for partitioning Microservices:

- Ranged partitioning
- Named partitioning
- Singleton partitioning

More of Service Fabric partitioning can be found at: `https://azure.microsoft.com/en-us/documentation/articles/service-fabric-concepts-partitioning/`.

Considerations

The following considerations should be taken into account while implementing this pattern:

- **Partitioning Strategy**: Choosing a partition strategy is the key to efficiently balance load across multiple partitions. Following are few of the partitioning strategies which can be considered:
    - Horizontal Partitioning (Sharding)
    - Vertical Partitioning
    - Functional Partitioning

    Data Partitioning guidelines published by Microsoft (`https://msdn.microsoft.com/en-us/library/dn589795.aspx`) is a good reference document to understand these strategies.

- **Data replication**: It is advisable to replicate static data and commonly used data across data partitions to avoid cross partition queries which can be resource consuming.
- **Rebalancing**: Always plan for rebalancing tasks for the partitions which may be required as the partitions age. Rebalancing may cause system downtime.
- **Referential integrity**: Consider moving the ownership of referential integrity to the application layer instead of the database layer to avoid cross partition queries
- **Transactions**: It is advisable to avoid transactions which access data across partitions as this may introduce performance bottlenecks
- **Consistency**: When data is replicated across partitions, it is important to decide on a consistency strategy. You will need to decide if your application requires strong consistency or if it can manage with eventual consistency

Related patterns

Following are the related cloud design patterns which can be used in conjunction with this pattern:

- **Throttling pattern**: Use this pattern if the load on a partition increases unexpectedly. Throttling is a leading indicator for the requirement of re-partitioning of data
- **Health Endpoint Monitoring pattern**: Continuous monitoring is advisable to regulate the load on each partition. Auto-scaling logic can be applied to alter the capability of a partition based on the load.
- **Sharding pattern**: This pattern can be used to horizontally partition your data to improve scalability when storing and accessing large volumes of data.
- **Command and Query Responsibility Segregation (CQRS) pattern**: Segregating operations that read data from operations that update data by using separate interfaces.

Use cases

Following are few use cases where this pattern will be a right fit:

- Near real-time systems: Systems which require near real time performance which cannot afford delays in data access from persistent stores.
- Priority workload: Not all operations in a system will hold equal priority. Operations which had to be executed on a higher priority can be separated as a different partition served with more capable hardware to optimize performance.
- Geo dispersed user base: Storing the data close to the users can be beneficial in case of a Geo-dispersed deployment. Partitioning data based on user local can be useful in this scenario.

Centralized Diagnostics Service

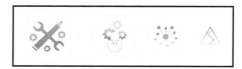

Problem

Diagnostics are a critical part of any system which provides insights about the state, health and transactions handled by the system. System logs and call-traces form the primary sources for diagnostics information. With every Microservice instance continuously generating logs and traces, maintaining, querying, and accessing these logs from different sources becomes an operational challenge. When logs are persisted in multiple stores, generating insights, and alerting also becomes complicated. Following is an illustration of an operations team receiving diagnostics information from distributed systems:

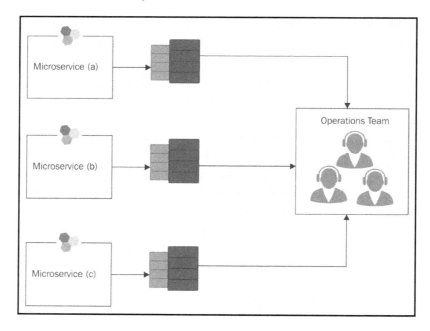

Centralized Diagnostics (Problem)

Solution

The solution to this problem is to delegate logging and tracing responsibilities to a separate service which can consolidate diagnostics information from multiple Microservices/Microservice-instances and persist it in a centralized store. This also helps in decoupling the diagnostics activities from business logic there by enabling the ability to scale services independently. The diagnostic service should also be capable of providing a live stream of trace information apart from persisting logs on secondary storage. Centralized logging also enables opportunities for drawing analytics around scenarios like patterns of faults, business trends, and threats. This service can be enhanced by coupling it with notification capabilities to send alerts to the operations team on a specific system state or event. Following is an illustration of a Centralized logging service in action:

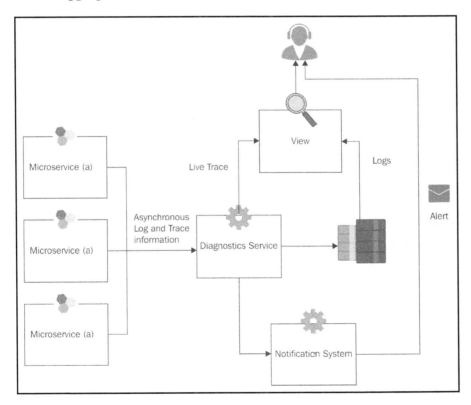

Centralized Diagnostics (Solution)

Microsoft Application Insights can be used to consolidate logs and tracing information from Microservices deployments. Application insights has the following inbuilt capabilities which simplify overheads around diagnostics for Microservice deployments:

- Centralized logging
- Proactive detection
- Continuous export (to blobs)
- Ability to search and filter logs
- Performance metrics
- Interactive data analytics
- Multilingual SDKs

More about application insights capabilities can be found at: `https://azure.microsoft.com/en-us/services/application-insights/`.

Considerations

The following considerations should be taken into account while implementing this pattern:

- **Logging agent**: The logging agent which is installed on every instance of a Microservice needs to be a lightweight in terms of resource consumption. Making the logging service asynchronous to ensure that the calls are unblocked is a key factor in implementing a diagnostics service.
- **Permissions**: With the logs stored in a centralized location, the rights to access the logs should be configurable, and Role Based Access Control (RBAC) method should be preferred.
- **Availability**: Diagnostics is an important part of a system. Especially if the system is transactional in nature. It is important to ensure high availability of the diagnostics service. Along with the service front end, the persistent log stores also need to be replicated to meet the availability requirements.
- **Querying**: Ability to search through the logs for an event or a state is an important capability of a diagnostics service. Enabling indexing around logs and traces can improve the efficiency around searching.

Related patterns

Following are the related cloud design patterns which can be used in conjunction with this pattern:

- **Retry pattern**: This pattern should be implemented on the logging agent to handle transient faults on the diagnostics service
- **Queue-Based Load Leveling pattern**: Queues can be introduced as buffers between logging agent and the diagnostics service to prevent data loss
- **Scheduler Agent Supervisor pattern**: A scheduler can be used to purge and archive logs to improve storage efficiency of the system
- **Index Table pattern**: This pattern can be used to index the log entries to improve the efficiency around searching.

Use cases

Following are few use cases where this pattern will be a right fit:

- **Hyper scale deployments**: This pattern is most effective in handling hyper scale deployment of Microservices as it helps in automating most of the diagnostics activity there by reducing operational overhead
- **High Availability systems**: For systems which require high availability, it's important to ensure that the turnaround time in case of a fault is minimal. This requires automation of diagnostics and capabilities around predictive detection and analytics.
- **Geo dispersed system**: Systems which are deployed across the globe usually has a centralized operations team. It is beneficial to equip the operations team with diagnostics capabilities like alerting and analytics to better offer round the clock support.

High Density Deployment

Problem

While architecting an enterprise system, separation of concerns is a commonly used design principle used to maintainability of the system. This leads to isolation of workloads as separate work packages (computational units) which are then deployed on hosting surrogates like web sites, virtual machines, containers, and so on, Often, this principle of isolation extends to the physical hosting infrastructure which may cause work packages to be deployed on separate virtual machines. Although this approach simplified the logical architecture it also causes underutilization of hardware resources there by increasing the operational and hosting cost.

The following diagram illustrates poorly utilized resources for a set of services:

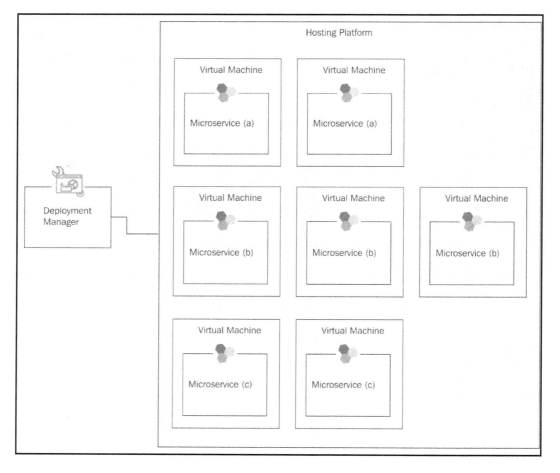

High Density Deployment (Problem)

Solution

Adopting high density deployment by enabling deployment of multiple Microservices on a single computation unit can be used to address this problem. Grouping the Microservice which can be co-deployed on a virtual machine can be based on features, communication patterns, scalability requirements, application lifecycle, resource requirement, and so on. The cluster manager managing the Microservice deployment should be able scale each of the Microservice separately. Cluster manager will also be responsible for the health of a virtual machine and failover to ensure high availability of a Microservice. Following is an illustration of how a cluster orchestrator can be used to achieve high density deployment:

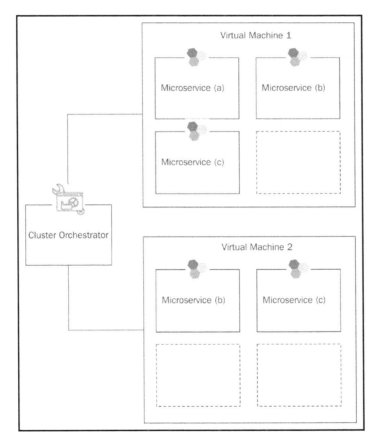

High Density Deployment (Solution)

Microsoft Azure Service Fabric offers natively supports high density deployment of Microservice on a cluster of virtual machines. The Service Fabric cluster manager also possesses rich cluster orchestration capabilities. This requires a detailed cluster design and capacity planning for both the stateful and stateless services. You can read more about capacity planning at:

`https://docs.microsoft.com/en-us/azure/service-fabric/service-fabric-cluster-capacity`.

More about Service Fabric cluster management can be found at: `https://azure.microsoft.com/en-us/documentation/articles/service-fabric-cluster-resource-manager-cluster-description/`.

Considerations

The following considerations should be taken into account while implementing this pattern:

- **Isolated namespaces**: Deploying multiple Microservices on a single virtual machine introduces challenges around securing resource boundaries around each service. Cluster manager should be responsible for managing the isolation.
- **Resource starvation**: Cluster manager that supports high density deployment should also support enforcing of limits around the resources each Microservice can consume to avoid resource starvation. Throttling logic should be implemented to gracefully handle resource requests after the thresholds are reached.
- **Release management**: Deploying, updating or de-allocating a Microservice should not impact the stability of other Microservices running on the same virtual machine.

Related patterns

Following are the related cloud design patterns which can be used in conjunction with this pattern:

- **Compute Resource Consolidation pattern**: A similar design pattern which supports high density deployment
- **Throttling pattern**: Helps control the consumption of resources used by a Microservice running on a shared hardware

- **Health Endpoint Monitoring pattern**: Continuous health monitoring pattern can be used to ensure requirements around high availability

Use cases

Following are few use cases where this pattern will be a right fit:

- **Enterprise scale Microservice deployment**: This pattern is applicable for any enterprise scale Microservice deployment considering requirements around optimizing operational and hosting expense.
- **Hybrid deployments**: Capability of the cluster manager to deploy Microservices on heterogeneous hardware environments comes handy in case of a hybrid data center where the hardware configurations can be different in different data centers.
- **High performance systems**: Optimizing the deployment based on the resource requirements of a Microservice and ensuring the availability of resources by setting thresholds ensures high performance of Microservices

API Gateway

Problem

Decomposing a monolithic architecture into a Microservice architecture exponentially increases the complexity in managing APIs. The challenges around API management can be categorized on to three divisions:

- **Abstraction**: Abstracting the API developers and the consumers from complexities around security, transformation, analytics, diagnostics, throttling and quota management, caching, and so on.
- **Publishing**: Publishing APIs, grouping APIs as bundles which can be associated with a business use case, deriving insights from consumption, and managing consumers.

- **Documentation**: Creating and maintaining a catalog of deployed APIs, documenting the ways they can be consumed, analytics, and so on.

Manually managing these responsibilities become extensively complex especially in hyper scale enterprise ready deployment of Microservices:

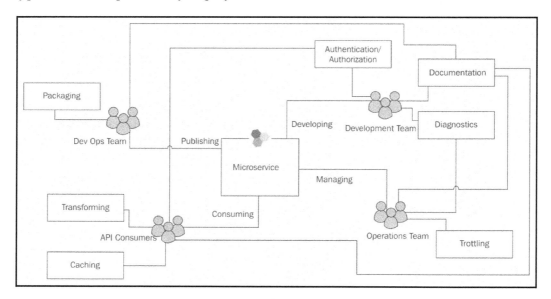

API Gateway (Problem)

Solution

Introducing an API gateway as a management service helps solve complexities around managing Microservices there by letting developers focus better on solving business problems. The API Gateway will be responsible to providing the supporting services for securing, managing, publishing, and consuming Microservices. This expedites consumer onboarding by automating most of the management processes.

API Gateway also have the capability of abstracting the deployment location of the actual APIs:

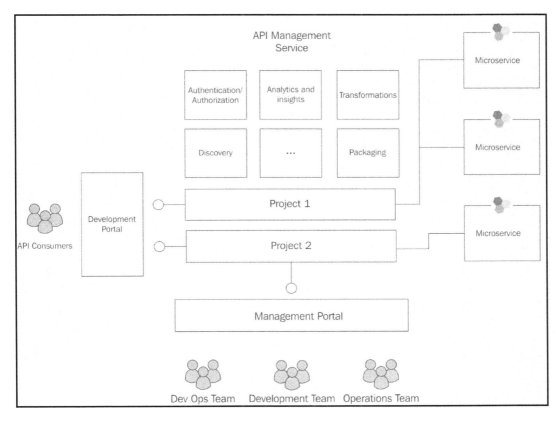

API Gateway (Solution)

Microsoft API Management is a feature rich service which can act like a gateway for Microservices. API management comes with built-in capabilities around discoverability, security, analytics, business insights, documentation, and transformations which can help enhance the experience around consumption of Microservices to a great extent. More about API management can be found at:
https://azure.microsoft.com/en-us/services/api-management/.

Considerations

The following considerations should be taken into account while implementing this pattern:

- **Another layer**: While introducing an API gateway, it is important to account for the increase in latency which may be caused in consuming the APIs. In most of the cases this is negligible and can be optimized by caching the API responses.
- **Centralizing diagnostics**: API gateway will have its own diagnostics components which logs information to a store which may be different from the one use by the hosted Microservices. It may be useful to consolidate these logs to improve operational efficiency.
- **Abstraction leads to information filtering**: Abstracting responsibilities will filter out information which may be relevant for the operation of a Microservice. A good example is user (consumer) context which may be of relevance to the Microservice will be filtered out by the API gateway as it is responsible for authentication/authorization.
- **Access control**: It is important that the API gateway supports role based access control as it needs to cater to different teams with different responsibilities.

Related patterns

Following are the related cloud design patterns which can be used in conjunction with this pattern:

- **Cache-Aside pattern**: Caching can be used to buffer API responses to optimize turnaround time
- **Circuit Breaker pattern**: Can be used to improve the stability and resiliency of an application by handling transient faults
- **Gatekeeper pattern**: This design pattern can be used to secure Microservices by preventing direct access
- **Throttling pattern**: Control the consumption of Microservice regulating the calls from a consuming application
- **Retry pattern**: A common pattern used to handle transient faults

Use cases

Following are few use cases where this pattern will be a right fit:

- **Multi datacenter deployment**: When your Microservices are deployed across multiple datacenters, API gateway acts as a façade for managing, packaging and consuming Microservices without being aware of the actual deployment location.
- **Developer focused**: With capabilities around packaging, maintaining catalogues and documenting Microservices, API gateway becomes single source of truth for developers to build applications using Microservices.
- **Analytics driven business**: A centralized channel for consuming APIs helps build better analytics which then can be used to build insights to identify trends which may impact the business.
- **Secure systems**: API gateway acts like a gatekeeper preventing consumers from directly accessing the Microservices. Responsibilities like authentication, authorization and throttling are owned by the API gateway there by providing a centralized control over all the Microservices running within an enterprise.

Latency Optimized Load Balancing

Problem

Microservice platforms today, supports geographically dispersed deployments. This means that multiple instances of a Microservice can be hosted in different continents on heterogeneous environments. While abstracting the service hosting location has advantages, it also introduces challenges around offering consistent performance for consumer requests from different parts of the globe.

Having a load balancer which uses a round robin or random routing algorithm cannot guarantee the most optimal response in most cases.

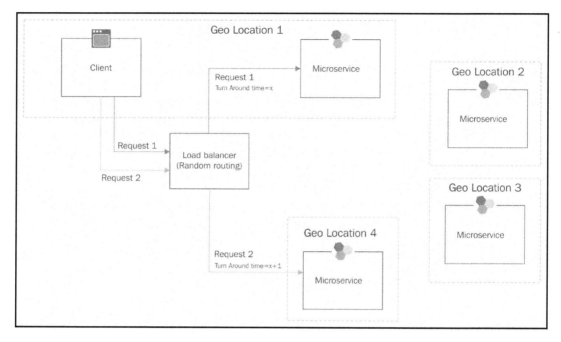

Latency optimized load balancing (Problem)

Solution

Load balancing plays an important role in optimal performance of any distributed system. This pattern optimizes the action of load balancing by considering the proximity of the Microservice deployment and the turnaround time from previous requests along with other parameters such as current load, health of the instance, and so on. This will enable the system to route a request from a consumer to the nearest performant Microservice instance.

Latency optimized load balancing is also effective in hybrid deployments of Microservices across public and private clouds:

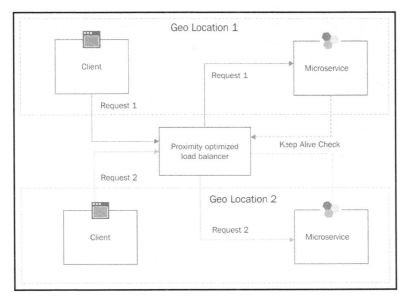

Latency optimized load balancing (Solution)

Microsoft Azure Traffic Manager allows you to control the distribution of traffic based on a rule set which can be configured to achieve high availability and performance. More and Traffic manager can be found at: `https://azure.microsoft.com/en-us/documentation/articles/traffic-manager-overview/`.

Apart from routing, traffic manager can also be used to enable automatic failover to improve the availability of your Microservice deployment.

Considerations

The following considerations should be taken into account while implementing this pattern:

- **Route optimization**: Optimizing a route is a complex process. Considering that load handled by an instance of a Microservice can change quickly, the records about previous response time may not lead to the most optimal route. Constant performance monitoring need to happen to analyze the load on virtual machines hosting Microservices.

- **Health checks**: Microservices can be hosted on commodity hardware which are susceptible to failure. Load balancer should be cognizant about the health of the virtual machines hosting Microservices.
- **Point of failure**: Load balancer can act like a single point of failure. It is critical to make load balancing service and its associated state highly available. Geo-replicating instances of the load balancer is advisable to achieve high availability.

Related patterns

Following are the related cloud design patterns which can be used in conjunction with this pattern:

- **Gatekeeper pattern**: The load balancer implicitly acts like a gatekeeper. Load balancing service can be enhanced with capabilities of this pattern to achieve better security.
- **Health Endpoint Monitoring pattern**: A load balancer need to be cognizant of the health of all Microservice instances it is serving. Health monitoring is a recommended strategy to monitor health of the virtual machines.
- **Throttling pattern**: Helps ensure scalability of the service by throttling request based on the capacity of the costed services.

Use cases

Following are few use cases where this pattern will be a right fit:

- **Near real-time systems**: Latency optimized load balancing is best suited for environments which are very dynamic in terms of the load they encounter and require high performance in terms of turnaround time for requests.
- **Geo-dispersed deployments**: This pattern is highly recommended for Geo-dispersed deployments of Microservices which caters to consumers around the world. Optimizing the routing logic helps improve the turnaround time for responses thereby providing a better performance.
- **Highly available systems**: Apart from optimizing the route, latency optimized load balancer can also be used to enable an automatic failover strategy. The service will start routing the request to a different Geo-location if it sees the performance degrading in the preferred location.

Queue Driven Decomposing Strategy

Problem

One of the biggest challenges in the Microservice architecture is to decompose services into reusable standalone services which can execute in isolation. The traditional monolithic architecture often contains inseparable redundant implementation of modules which minimizes the opportunities of reuse. With modules tightly coupled, maintaining it, in terms of upgrading, scaling, or troubleshooting it without affecting the whole application becomes impossible:

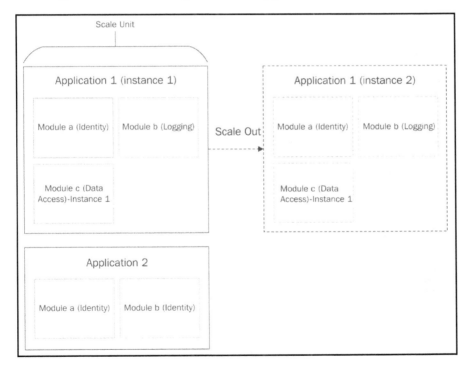

Queue driven decomposing strategy (Problem)

Solution

Decomposing tasks in to discrete sub tasks which can be encapsulated as standalone services is the fundamental concept behind the Microservice based architecture. These standalone services or Microservices are best reused if their inputs and outputs are standardized. A system comprising of Microservices will have the flexibility to independently scale at the level of each Microservice. This introduces the complexity of balancing load among multiple instances of the Microservice which is easily solved by introducing queues to level the load. A collection of Microservices couples with queues together form a pipeline to implement a business functionality:

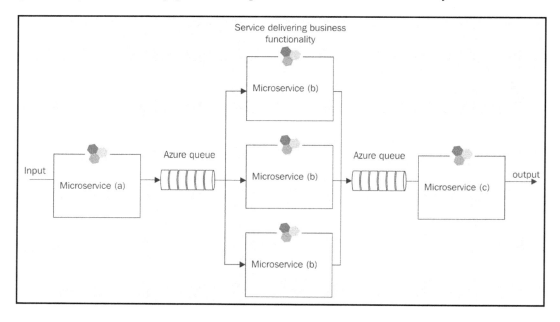

Queue driven decomposing strategy (Solution)

Microsoft Azure Service Bus queues or Azure Storage Queues can be used as a buffer between Microservices deployed on Microsoft Azure Service Fabric to implement this design pattern with minimal plumbing work.

Considerations

The following considerations should be taken into account while implementing this pattern:

- **Increase in Complexity**: Decomposing an application in to Microservices, introduces the complexity of managing these services discretely. Also, the communication between the processes becomes less deterministic as they are asynchronous by nature. It is important to account for the overheard in management effort while implementing this pattern.
- **Poison messages**: There is a chance that an instance of a Microservice in a pipeline fails to process a message pipe as it causes an unexpected fault. In this case, the Microservice will retry processing this message for few times and then discards it. These messages usually end up in a dead letter queue which then needs to be handled separately.
- **Transactions**: Incase an end-to-end processing of a pipeline fails in between, the state changes which are committed as a part of the current transaction must be reversed to preserve the integrity of the system.

Related patterns

Following are the related cloud design patterns which can be used in conjunction with this pattern:

- **Retry pattern**: Defines a recommended way of implementing retry logic to handle transient faults
- **Compensating Transaction pattern**: This pattern can be used to reverse state changes caused by a faulty transaction
- **Queue-Based Load Leveling pattern**: Pipes are best implemented using queues. Apart from providing a reliable delivery channel queues can also help in load balancing
- **Pipes and Filters pattern**: A similar pattern recommended for cloud deployed services

Use cases

Following are few use cases where this pattern will be a right fit:

- **Enterprise workflows**: This pattern is highly recommended for implementing workflows on top of a Microservice deployment to ensure reliability. Apart from acting as a channel to couple two Microservices, queues also act like a buffer for persisting workflow state.
- **Uneven scalability requirements**: Systems which have requirements around scaling a specific Microservice separately based on variable workload. The Microservices participating in a pipeline can be scaled out/in at every level thereby improving the capability of the system in being elastic.

Circuit Breaker

Problem

In a Microservice based system, individual services may fail at any point of time. If a client calls a service frequently, then each call would need to wait for a timeout before failing the operation. Making frequent calls to a failing service and waiting for response wastes system resources and slows down the whole application:

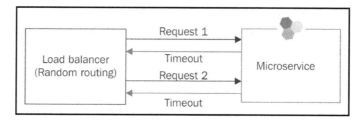

Circuit Breaker(Problem)

Solution

The circuit breaker pattern prevents calls to be made to a failing resource once the number of failures cross a particular threshold. To implement the circuit breaker pattern, wrap calls made to a service in a circuit breaker object. The circuit breaker monitors the failures attempts made to the service. Once the number of failed attempts to invoke a service exceeds a threshold value, the circuit trips for that service and any further calls to the service are short-circuited. The circuit breaker may keep the count of failed requests made to the service in a shared cache so that the count may be shared across all instances of the application. This setup ensures that application does not waste resources in waiting for response from a failing service. A fallback logic maybe implemented that gets invoked when the circuit breaker trips while the connection is still open which may return a value to the client application:

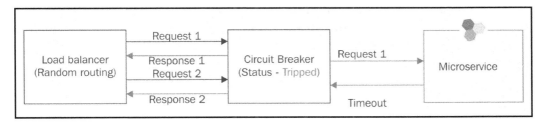

Circuit Breaker (Solution)

Considerations

The following considerations should be taken into account while implementing this pattern:

- **Performance**: Using circuit breaker has a performance implication depending on the type of cache used to store the failed request count.
- **Reacting to failures**: Clients using the circuit breaker pattern should implement fallback logic in case of failures. The client may either fail the operation or carry out a workaround such as saving the request in a queue that would be processed later.

- **Concurrency**: A large number of concurrent instances of an application may access the same circuit breaker object. The implementation of the circuit breaker should not block concurrent requests or add excessive overhead to each call to an operation.
- **Types of exceptions**: The type of exceptions that trip the circuit breaker should be carefully considered. A logical exception should not cause the circuit breaker to trip and short-circuit calls made to the underlying service.

Related patterns

Following are the related cloud design patterns which can be used in conjunction with this pattern:

- **Retry pattern**: Retry pattern works together with the Circuit Breaker pattern. The retry pattern is best used for transient fault handling which should be anticipated for cloud deployment of Microservices.
- **Health Endpoint Monitoring pattern**: Employing agents (external processes) to verify that applications and services are performing correctly.

Use cases

Following are few use cases where this pattern will be a right fit:

- If an operation to invoke a remote service or access a shared resource is highly likely to fail then the circuit breaker actively prevents it.
- Circuit breaker is not a substitute for handling exceptions in the business logic of your applications.

Message Broker for Communication

Problem

A Microservices based system is composed of a number of services. Integration of these services is a challenge because point-to-point integration between services requires many connections between them. Many connections usually translate into many interfaces. Change in interfaces of communication of service may lead to changes in all the services to which it is connected. Also, in several scenarios point-to-point communication is not possible because the various services in a Microservice based solution could be deployed to different security realms:

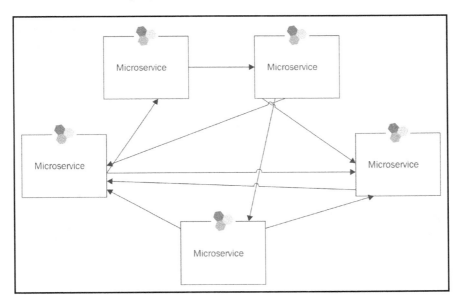

Message Broker for Communication (Problem)

Solution

The various services in a Microservice based application can communicate with each other via a message broker. A message broker is a physical component that handles the communication between services. Instead of communicating with each other, services communicate only with the message broker. An application sends a message to the message broker, providing the logical name of the receivers. The message broker looks up the services registered under the logical name and then passes the message to them:

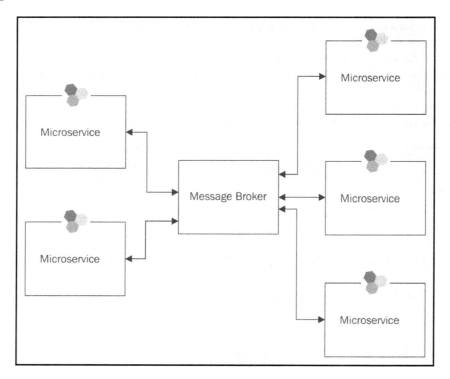

Message Broker for communication(Solution)

Such a service in Azure may be realized by using Azure Service Bus Topics and Subscriptions. Each service may publish messages on the topic and specify a set of properties of the message that identify the receiver this message should reach to. The services may create a number of subscriptions on the topic to receive messages addressed to them.

Considerations

The following considerations should be taken into account while implementing this pattern:

- **Performance**: The message broker pattern adds another component to your system and therefore the involved services will experience additional latency in communication. Point-to-point communication has lower latency than communicating via a broker.
- **Increased agility**: This pattern helps isolate change to individual services. Due to loose coupling of services, this pattern facilitates changes in the application.
- **High scalability**: Due to loose coupling of services, each service can be individually scaled. This gives the application administrators fine-grained control of scaling the services.
- **Ease of development**: Since each functionality is isolated to its own service, developing a service or functionality will not affect the other services and functionalities.
- **Load balancing**: The services in a Microservice based application may get scaled at different rates. The messages broker queues requests waiting to be processed by the services which helps the services consume the messages at their own rates.
- **Increased complexity**: Communicating with message broker is more complex than point-to-point communication.

Related patterns

Following are the related cloud design patterns which can be used in conjunction with this pattern:

- **Pipes and Filters**: This pattern helps perform complex processing on a message while maintaining independence and flexibility
- **Message Router**: This pattern helps decouple individual processing steps so that messages can be passed to different filters based on a set of conditions
- **Publish/Subscribe pattern**: This pattern helps broadcast an event to all interested subscribers
- **Point-to-Point Channel**: This pattern helps the caller be sure that exactly one receiver will receive the message or perform the call

Use cases

Following are few use cases where this pattern will be a right fit:

- **Reduced coupling**: The message broker decouples the senders and the receivers. The senders and receivers communicate only with the message broker.
- **Improved integrability**: The services that communicate with the message broker do not need to have the same interface. The message broker can also act as a bridge between services that are from different security realms.
- **Improved modifiability**: The message broker shields the services of the solution from changes in individual services.
- **Improved security**: Communication between applications involves only the sender, the broker, and the receivers. Other applications do not receive the messages that these three exchange. Unlike bus-based integration, applications communicate directly in a manner that protects the information without the use of encryption.
- **Improved testability**: The message broker provides a single point for mocking. Mocking facilitates the testing of individual applications as well as of the interaction between them.

Compensating Transaction

Problem

Transactions becomes complex in Microservices based system. This is because data owned by each Microservice is private to that Microservice and can only be accessed by the API exposed by the service. There is added complexity in Microservice based systems due to their polyglot persistence approach.

Although a partitioned and polyglot-persistent architecture has several benefits, this makes implementing transactions difficult:

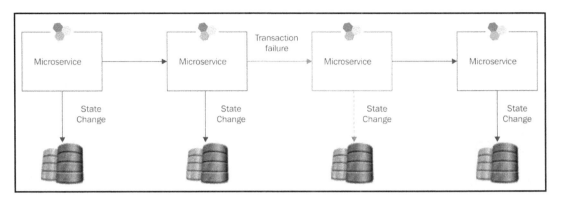

Compensating transaction (Problem)

Solution

For many Microservices based applications, the solution to achieve transactions is to use an event-driven architecture wherein state change is captured as events and published. Other services subscribe to these events and change their own data, which might lead to more events being published. Although Azure services such as Azure Service Bus Topics can be used to publish events, there are several other challenges with the approach such as how to atomically update state and publish events. Some of the approaches for maintaining atomicity are using the database as a message queue, transaction log mining, and event sourcing which are difficult to implement.

Eventual consistency of data may be achieved easily by the compensating transaction pattern. A common approach to realize this pattern is to use a workflow. A transactional operation should be designed as chain of separate work-steps that form a chain. If the operation fails at any point, the workflow rewinds back through the work-steps it has completed and reverses the work by using the compensator of each work-step.

The following diagram depicts work-steps and compensation steps in a multi-step workflow:

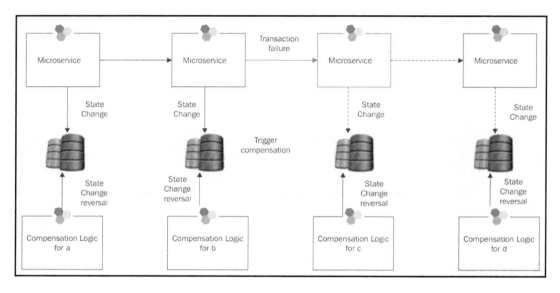

Compensating Transaction (Solution)

Using Azure Service Bus Queues auto forwarding property, such a workflow can be built easily. A working prototype of this pattern is available at Clemens Vasters' blog: `https://github.com/Azure-Samples/azure-servicebus-messaging-samples/tree/master/AtomicTransactions`.

Considerations

The following considerations should be taken into account while implementing this pattern:

- **Time-out scenarios**: An operation may not fail immediately but could block the operation. Time-outs must be considered while implementing this pattern.
- **Idempotency**: A work-step and its corresponding compensator should be idempotent which means that the compensator should not alter the state of work-step in a manner that it can be operated on again.

- **Data sufficiency**: A compensator should get sufficient data from the previous step to roll back the operation.
- **Retries**: Consider using retries in work-step before failing the operation.

Related patterns

Following are the related cloud design patterns which can be used in conjunction with this pattern:

- **Sagas**: Create workflows for Microservice based applications.
- **Retry pattern**: Use retry patter together with compensating transactions so that compensating logic doesn't get triggered on transient failures.

Use cases

Following are few use cases where this pattern will be a right fit:

- **Transactions**: In several scenarios such as travel bookings, the booking operations must be undone in case of failure. This pattern is useful for reversing operations in such scenarios.

Rate Limiter

Problem

Individual services in Microservice architecture have different **Quality of Service (QoS)** guarantees. If the processing requirements of the system exceed the capacity of the resources that are available, it will suffer from poor performance and may even fail. The system may be obliged to meet an agreed level of service, and such failure could be unacceptable.

Using auto-scaling pattern helps provision more resources with an increase in demand. This pattern not only consistently meets user demand, but also optimizes running costs. However, auto-scaling is not the optimal solution in the following scenarios:

- The backend service or data store has throttling limits which affect the limit of scale the application can achieve.
- There might be resource deficit in the window of time when resource provisioning is still going on:

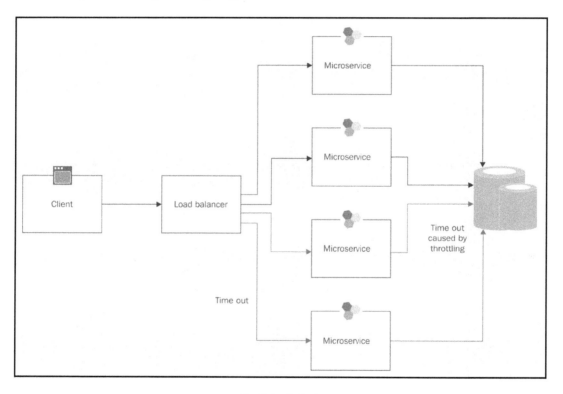

Rate Limiter (Problem)

Solution

A solution to overcome the above mentioned issues is to allow applications to use resources only up to a threshold limit and throttle the requests received after the limit is reached. The throttling limits may be applied to each user of the application or across users depending on the desired SLAs and QoS. Some of the throttling strategies that can be applied are:

- Rejecting requests from a client tagged with a particular key who has already accessed the APIs more than a particular number of times in a particular time duration
- Rejecting requests from a particular IP address after a particular number of requests have been made in a particular time duration
- Deferring operations performed by lower priority clients if the resources are nearing exhaustion

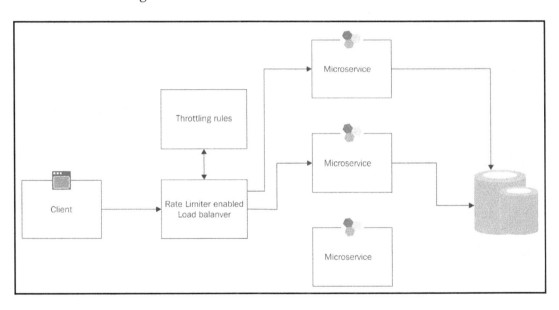

Rate Limiter (Solution)

Azure API Management has advanced throttling techniques that can be used to protect services and apply throttling limits on them.

Considerations

The following considerations should be applied while using this pattern:

- **Planning**: Decision to throttle requests affects the design of system. Throttling strategy and resources that need to be throttled should be decided on before implementation because it is difficult to add throttling after the system has been implemented.
- **Response**: A clear response indicating that user request has been throttled should be sent back to the client. This would help the client retry an operation after some time.
- **Auto-scale versus Throttle**: If there is a temporary spike in application load, then only throttling may be used instead of scaling the application.

Related patterns

Following are the related cloud design patterns which can be used in conjunction with this pattern:

- **Auto-scale**: Throttling can be used as an interim measure while a system auto-scales, or to remove the need for a system to auto-scale.
- **Queue-based Load Leveling pattern**: Queue-based load leveling is a commonly used mechanism for implementing throttling. A queue can act as a buffer that helps to even out the rate at which requests sent by an application are delivered to a service.

- **Priority Queue pattern**: A system can use priority queuing as part of its throttling strategy to maintain performance for critical or higher value applications, while reducing the performance of less important applications.

Use cases

Following are few use cases where this pattern will be a right fit:

- To ensure that a system continues to meet service level agreements
- To prevent a single tenant from monopolizing the resources provided by an application
- To handle bursts in activity
- To help cost-optimize a system by limiting the maximum resource levels needed to keep it functioning

Sagas

Problem

In a distributed system, messages sent by the services might not be controlled. As the system grows and more services are added, the system starts becoming unmaintainable. In a large distributed system, it becomes hard to track which message goes where.

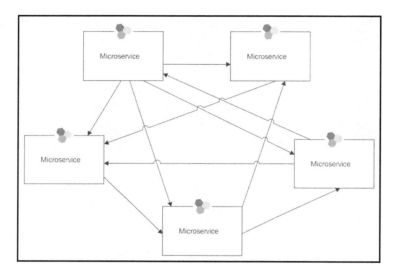

Sagas (Problem)

Another problem that Microservices-based system encounters is that there is no single source of truth that can be used by all the services. For instance, in an e-commerce application, when a customer places an order a message containing order details is sent to the procurement service. Once the order service responds, another message containing delivery details is sent to the delivery service. This leads to there being no single source of truth that contains the entire customer order data.

Solution

Using sagas, workflows can be implemented in a Microservice application. Sagas are state machines that model a workflow with steps to be executed. Sagas treat the various Microservices as implementations of workflow.

In a Microservice system, there is no central truth as the various Microservices each have a part of data stored in their database. Sagas can store the actual truth and each Microservice can get part of data it needs.

Saga maintains state in the form of object you define until saga finishes. A saga can coordinate message flow in the way you implement. You can instruct what message should be sent to a Microservice and what response should be expected from it and how the response should be used to send messages to other Microservices. A saga can persist its state in a durable storage which makes the sagas resistant to failures:

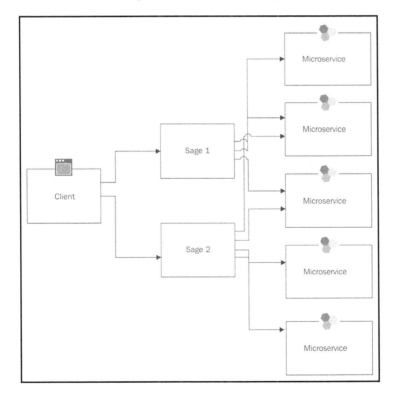

Sagas (Solution)

Although sagas can be implemented through several mechanisms, NHibernate provides an easy to use interface to build workflows and persist state in Azure storage.

Considerations

The following considerations should be applied while using this pattern:

- **Coordinate only**: Sagas are designed to coordinate the message flow. They make decisions through business logic. The actual work is delegated to the Microservices using the messages.
- **Message starting the Saga**: There might be more than one message that can start the saga.
- **Message order**: A delay in service response may result in messages arriving out of order. So, design the saga with fallacies of distributed computing in mind.

Related patterns

Following is the related cloud design patterns which can be used in conjunction with this pattern:

- **Compensating Transactions**: Sagas can be used to model compensating transactions so that messages are routed to compensators if work-step failed.

Use cases

Following are few use cases where this pattern will be a right fit:

- **Process with multiple message roundtrips**: Any Microservice application that involves modeling a workflow involving processes that require interaction among several Microservices can benefit from this pattern.
- **Time related process requirements**: Designing Microservices that start processing once a certain period of time has lapsed, for example delay in approval.

Master Data Management

Problem

In a Microservice-based architecture, services are modeled as isolated units that manage independent activities. However, fully functional systems rely on the cooperation and integration of Microservices. Data sharing in a Microservice architecture has its own sets of problems such as:

- Handling big volumes of data
- Consistency guarantees while reducing data-access contention using simple locks
- Whether to share database for master data

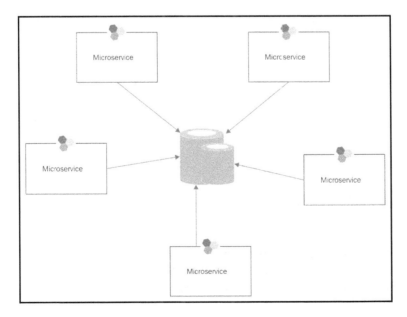

Master Data Management (Problem)

Solution

Large scale Microservice based applications such as Netflix use different databases for each Microservice. This approach helps the services stay independent of each other. A schema change in one of the service databases does not impact the rest of the services. This approach increases the complexity of data management as the systems may get out of sync or become inconsistent.

A custom or ready-made **Master Data Management** (**MDM**) tool should be used that operates in background to fix any inconsistencies. For example, an MDM tool can be used to find inconsistencies in customer ID across databases:

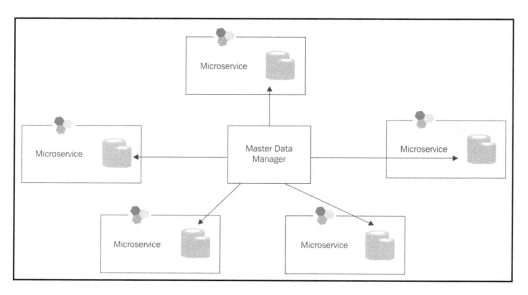

Master Data Management (Solution)

Considerations

The following considerations should be applied while using this pattern:

- **Eventual consistency**: Since MDM tools work in the background, only eventual consistency can be guaranteed by the system.
- **Conflict management**: In case inconsistency is found between records a conflict management strategy needs to be decided that would fix the inconsistent records.

- **Time constraint**: MDM Hub database needs to be loaded with data from various databases to detect inconsistencies.
- **Maintenance**: MDM implementation must incorporate tools, processes, and people to maintain the quality of the data. All data must have a data steward who is responsible for ensuring the quality of the master data.

Related patterns

Following is the related cloud design patterns which can be used in conjunction with this pattern:

- **ETL**: ETL is a type of data movement with possibly a complex acquisition from heterogeneous sources, and/or a complex manipulation with aggregation and cleansing, but always a simple write by overwriting any changes on the target.
- **Data Replication**: This pattern presents a special type of data movement (replication) with a simple acquisition and manipulation of the data, but possibly a complex write. The complexity of the write generally arises from the need to update both source and target and to eventually exchange the changes to the counterpart.

Use cases

Following are few use cases where this pattern will be a right fit:

- **Manage master data**: Inconsistency in shared data such as customer address may have a high business impact.
- **Merge other applications to an existing system**: In case of application mergers, data from other system needs to be merged into existing system. There might be cases where the same data is tagged with different identifiers in the individual application databases. An MDM implementation can help resolve these differences.

CQRS – Command Query Responsibility Segregation

Problem

State data in traditional applications is represented through a set of entities. The entities are stored in a single data repository against which two types of operations can take place.

- **Commands**: Operations that modify state
- **Queries**: Operations that read state

An operation cannot both update state and return data. This distinction of operations helps simplify understanding the system. The segregation of operations into commands and queries is called the **Command Query Separation (CQS)** pattern. The CQS pattern requires the commands to have void return type and the queries to be idempotent.

If a relational database such as SQL Server is used for storing state, the entities may represent a subset of rows in one or more tables in the database.

A common problem that arises in these systems is that both the commands and queries are applied to the same set of entities. For example, to update the contact details of a customer in a traditional e-commerce application, the customer entity is retrieved from the database and presented on the screen, which is a query operation. The entity is then modified and saved in the database through the data access layer (DAL), which is a command operation.

Although, this model works well for applications that have a limited set of business logic, this approach has certain disadvantages:

- There is a mismatch between the read and write representations of the data. While reading data, applications typically retrieve larger amount of data compared to writing that should affect one aggregate only.

- Reading data is a more frequent operation than writing. Since traditional applications use a single data repository, you can't scale read and write operations independently.
- Security and permissions are more cumbersome to manage in traditional applications because each entity is subject to both read and write operations, which might inadvertently expose data in the wrong context.
- Coupled representation of read and write models in traditional applications impede agility since changes in functionality result in high friction and incurs cost and time.

Solution

The CQRS pattern is like the CQS pattern with one major distinction – CQS pattern defines commands and queries as different methods within a type, whereas, the CQRS pattern defines commands and queries on different objects.

What this distinction means is that you can implement CQS in your applications by separating commands and queries as separate methods in a class, while retaining the same processing model to process both the models. CQRS, on the other hand completely separates the processing of commands and queries. Thus, the two patterns vary in scopes. The scope of the CQRS pattern is a bounded context, while the scope of CQS is a single class:

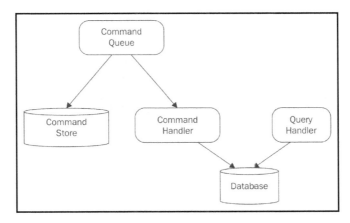

Structure of CQRS system

The preceding diagram presents the structure of a CQRS system. Users can submit commands to system which are stored in the command store and receive immediate feedback from the system. A user can check the status of progress of his commands through the user interface. A process will asynchronously move commands from the command store to the command queue, from where they will be picked by appropriate command handlers that will process the record and update the current state of data in the database.

Although not necessary, a CQRS system typically uses two separate physical databases for reads and writes so that they can be scaled independently. The read and write databases need not even have the same structure, for example, your application may write to a relational database such as SQL server whereas the reads operations are served through a document database such as MongoDB or Azure Cosmos DB. There are several approaches that can help synchronize the data in the read database and the write database. In case, the two databases have different structure, in case of failure of the read database, the state may be restored by replaying commands from the command store.

Responsibility of data validations is an important part of the CQRS pattern. The user interface should only be responsible for basic validations such as numeric values in phone number field, the business validations should be part of the domain logic and should be handled by the command handler.

Microservices in CQRS

The CQRS pattern can be realized through Microservices:

- The command store and command queue can be built through a Reliable Stateful Microservice. The service can forward the commands to appropriate command handlers. The command store can also be modelled as a Azure SQL database or as a Cosmos DB, whereas the command queue can be modelled as an Azure storage queue, a service bus queue or as a topic with a stateless reliable service acting as a broker between the two storages.
- The command handlers can be a separate Microservice. Each Microservices can handle the commands with its own logic.

- The query handler can be modelled as a separate Microservices. The command handler induces changes in the storage that the query handler queries on. These changes can be written to the read database by replicating the data written by the commands to the write database or by raising events using the Event Sourcing pattern.

Advantages

Following are a few of the advantages of this pattern:

- Splitting read operations and write operations to their own, Microservices help reduce its size. This in turn reduces the complexity of systems and helps improve scalability as you can scale the reads and writes independently.
- The read and write models can vary without affecting each other. This can help improve performance of read operations as you can denormalize the data or perform other operations to make read operations faster.
- You can run multiple versions of command handlers in parallel. This helps support deployment of new versions of Microservices.

Considerations

The following considerations should be applied while using this pattern:

- Transactions comprising read and write operations are hard to implement. Usually such operations are contained to an individual Microservice or require the use of other transaction mechanisms such as **2 Phase Commits** (**2PC**) or compensating transactions.
- CQRS is asynchronous by nature, therefore it is hard to ensure consistency across the various Microservices at any point of time.
- CQRS pattern might lead to higher development and infrastructure costs as multiple services need to be developed and deployed.

Related patterns

Following is the related cloud design patterns which can be used in conjunction with this pattern:

- **Event Sourcing**: This pattern describes in more detail how Event Sourcing can be used with the CQRS pattern to simplify tasks in complex domains; improve performance, scalability, and responsiveness; provide consistency for transactional data; and maintain full audit trails and history that may enable compensating actions.
- **Compensating Transaction**: This pattern can be used to reverse state changes caused by a faulty transaction.

Use cases

Following are few use cases where this pattern will be a right fit:

- **Collaborative data and complex business rules**: CQRS allows you to define commands with a sufficient granularity to minimize merge conflicts at the domain level. You can alter commands or queries independently of each other because their models are separate.
- **High performance reads and writes that can be tuned**: Scenarios where performance of data reads must be fine-tuned separately from performance of data writes, especially when the read/write ratio is very high, and when horizontal scaling is required.
- **Simplify business logic**: CQRS can be very helpful when you have difficult business logic. CQRS forces you to not mix domain logic and infrastructural operations.
- **Integration with other systems**: Especially in combination with Event Sourcing, where the temporal failure of one subsystem should not affect the availability of the others.

Event Sourcing

Problem

Traditional applications typically maintain the state of data by continuously updating the data as the user interacts with the application and keeps modifying the data. Continuous updates often involve transactions that lock the data under operation. Some of the problems with traditional applications are:

- Performing CRUD (Create, Read, Update, and Delete) operations directly against a data store impacts performance and responsiveness due to high processing overhead involved.
- In a collaborative domain, parallel updates on a single item of data may lead to conflicts.
- Traditional applications, in general, do not preserve history of operations performed on data and therefore there are no audit logs available unless maintained separately.

Solution

Event Sourcing models every change in the state of an application as an event object. The events are recorded in an append-only store. Application generates a series of events that capture the change that it has applied on data and these events are durably stored in sequence they were applied. The state itself is not saved in events, but it can be reconstructed by replaying the events.

The events are persisted in an event store that acts as the source of truth or system of record (the authoritative data source for a given data element or piece of information) about the current state of the data. The event store typically publishes these events so that consumers can be notified and can handle them if needed. Consumers could, for example, initiate tasks that apply the operations in the events to other systems, or perform any other associated action that is required to complete the operation. Notice that the application code that generates the events is decoupled from the systems that subscribe to the events.

Event Sourcing is like CQRS in approach. However, unlike commands in CQRS which define what is to be changed in an object, events contain data about a change that has been applied on state. Generally, CQRS and Event Sourcing work together. A command can change the data and the change can generate events to which other components of system can react. A practical example of this pattern is bank account statements, in which you can see the modification of account balance (state) by various transactions (events). Another practical example of application of this pattern is version control systems such as Git:

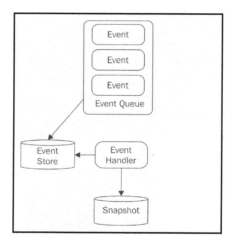

Event Sourcing (Problem)

The preceding diagram presents a high-level architecture of Event Sourcing pattern. The Event Queue can be implemented with messaging oriented middleware, which is a software or hardware infrastructure supporting the sending and receiving of messages between distributed systems. The Event Queue can receive events and send it to the Event Store.

The Event Store is an append-only store that receives all events from the Event Queue and appends them to the existing list of events. The event store can be used to reconstruct the state in case of failure or when you want to replay the events leading up to a desired state.

The Event Store can publish the saved events to which one or more Event Handlers can subscribe. The Event Handlers contain business logic which reacts to events. They can invoke commands that can make changes to the state. For example, a seat booking event handler can reserve seats in a scheduled flight and decrements the number of available seats.

Replaying events from beginning every time can lead to slow performance. Therefore, application can maintain Snapshots which contain the current state. Periodically the data in snapshot can be updated to stay in line with the new events. However, snapshot is an optional feature and may not be implemented if the application does not generate a lot of events.

To apply Event Sourcing pattern, look out for scenarios that involve auditing, reconstruction of historical state, or following a series of events such as bookings to an account.

Event Sourcing works well in concert with CQRS pattern. To implement this pattern through Microservices, it is recommended that your Microservices are built using the **Event Driven Architecture (EDA)**.

EDA models the communication between Microservices through events. In this architecture, each service is an event receiver and an event publisher. A Microservice that is interested in the processing outcome of another service can register to receive events from that service. This allows for loose coupling between services and easy modification of the workflow without affecting multiple Microservices. For example, for an e-commerce, this architecture would model the workflow as follows:

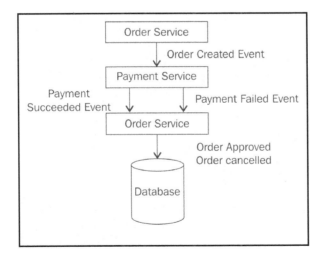

Event-driven architecture

- The Order Service creates an Order in a pending state and publishes an OrderCreated event.

- The Payment Service receives the event and attempts to charge payment instrument for the order received. It then publishes either a PaymentSucceeded event or a PaymentFailed event.
- The Order Service receives the event from the Payment Service and changes the state of the order to either approved or cancelled.

Following is a diagram of how CQRS and Event Sourcing patterns can be combined:

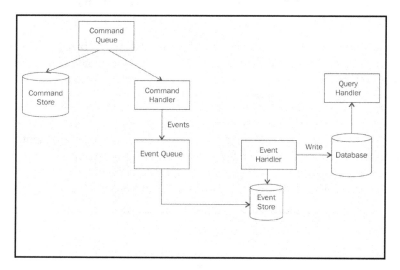

Event Sourcing with CQRS

Considerations

The following considerations should be taken into account while implementing this pattern:

- A common problem faced with this pattern is concurrency. If more than one event arrives concurrently and are processed by different event handlers, then optimistic locking should be used to ensure that the state is consistent. To implement optimistic locking, the following flow should be followed for handling a request. To understand the mechanism in detail let's consider a flight seat reservation scenario:
    1. The user interface raises a command to reserve two seats. A command handler handles the command raises the BookSeats event which gets loaded in the Event Queue and saved in Event Store.

2. The seat availability aggregate is populated by either querying all events in the Event Store. This aggregate is given a version identifier say X.

3. The aggregate performs its domain logic and raises the SeatsReserved event.

4. Before saving the SeatsReserved event, the event store verifies the version of the aggregate that raised the event. In case of concurrency, the version of the aggregate in store would be higher than the version of current aggregate.

Thus, you can avoid double booking by checking for versions before committing changes.

- Events cannot be changed. To correct the state appropriate events must be raised that compensate for the change in state.
- Event Sourcing pattern is based on domain driven design principles and therefore should follow terminology of the Ubiquitous Language. The names of events should be sensible in business context.
- Since events are basically messages, you need to keep standard messaging issues in consideration:
    - **Duplicate Messages**: Your command handlers should be idempotent to handle duplicate messages so that they don't affect the consistency of data.
    - **Out of Order Messages**: Choose FIFO message stores such as Service Bus Queues or Service Fabric Reliable Queue Collection to store events if you require messages to get stored in sequence.
    - **Poison Messages**: Messages that repeatedly cause failure should be marked as failed and sent to a dead-letter queue for further investigation.

Related patterns

Following is the related cloud design patterns which can be used in conjunction with this pattern:

- **CQRS**: Event Sourcing generally works in conjunction with CQRS pattern.
- **Message Broker for Communication**: Event Sourcing involves heavy communication between event store and event handlers which requires the use of a distributed messaging infrastructure.

Use cases

Following are few use cases where this pattern will be a right fit:

- **Event Driven Applications (EDA)**: Applications that use events to communicate with each other are a good fit for Event Sourcing.
- **Auditing**: Event Sourcing supports the feature of auditing without requiring any changes to be made in the application to support it.
- **Derive business value from event history**: Certain applications such as banking applications need to preserve history of events to determine the existing state. Preserving events can help answer historical questions from the business about the system.

Remindable Actors

Problem

An Actor based application may need to send several messages to an Actor instance. For example, an e-commerce application may require an Actor instance to update the user shopping cart. The Actor instance might be busy completing the process of adding a previous item to the cart. Since, the Actor operations are single threaded, the application will need to wait for the Actor to finish its previous operation to proceed with the next one.

The wait to complete operations degrades performance of application and affects user experience:

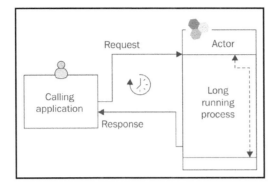

Remindable Actor (Problem)

Solution

All Actors in the system should message themselves when they receive a request. In the above example, the shopping cart Actor can accept the request to add more items to the shopping cart and send a message to itself with the details of item to add to the shopping cart. Once the Actor instance is done processing the previous request, it can consume a message from the queue and add the item to the shopping cart:

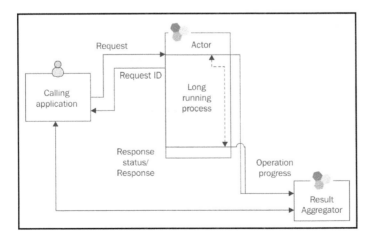

Remindable Actor (Solution)

Considerations

The following considerations should be taken into account while implementing this pattern:

- The Actors should be fault tolerant and be able to remove poison messages from the queue.
- The Actor operations should be idempotent.
- Reminders are not an alternative to scaling and partitioning. A single Actor instance with a lot of pending messages to process can't benefit from additional compute.

Related patterns

Following is the related cloud design patterns which can be used in conjunction with this pattern:

- **Compensating Transaction Pattern**: If an Actor is unable to complete operation, the supervisor Actor may message other subordinates to undo any work that they have previously performed.
- **Circuit Breaker Pattern**: An Actor can use this pattern to handle faults that may take a variable amount of time to rectify when connecting to a remote service or resource.

Use cases

Following are few use cases where this pattern will be a right fit:

- For releasing the application to invoke other Actors or perform other operations while an Actor instance is busy completing the previous operations.
- To improve efficiency of distributed systems that communicates via messaging.

Managed Actors

Problem

A task in an application composed of Microservices can comprise of several steps. The individual steps may be independent of each other but they are orchestrated by application logic that implements the task.

Application should ensure that all tasks related to an operation run to completion. This may involve resolving intermittent failures such as interrupted communication, temporary unavailability of remote resource and so on. In case of permanent failures; the application should restore the system to a consistent state and ensure integrity of end-to-end operation.

Solution

In the Actor programming model, an Actor can spawn other Actors. In such a scenario, the parent Actors are known as the supervisor and the Actors that it spawns are called subordinates. The subordinates carry out individual tasks of an operation that the supervisor is assigned to perform. The hierarchy may extend to deeper levels, that is, a subordinate may further delegate tasks to its subordinates and itself act as supervisor for those subordinates:

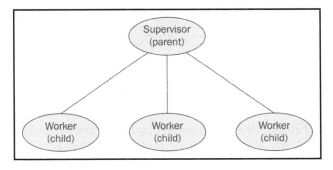

Managed Actors (Solution)

The role of supervisor is to aggregate the responses of the subordinates and report it to its parent, which may be the application itself or another supervisor.

In case of failures of one of the subordinates, the subordinate suspends its operations and reports the failure to its supervisor. The supervisor is responsible for managing failures. Based on the type of failure message, the supervisor can try to spawn the Actor again or message other Actors to rollback their operations.

The obvious benefit of this pattern is performance. Since the subordinates run concurrently, the over-all time it takes for the slowest subordinate to respond drives the performance of the system.

Another benefit of the pattern is the low cost of adding tasks to an operation. For example, to add a new task to an operation, you can add an independent subordinate to the hierarchy. The addition of new subordinate will not add latency to the system as the overall response time is still the response time of the slowest subordinate. You can find this pattern used widely in Netflix and LinkedIn.

Combining this pattern with Remindable Actors pattern can add resiliency and fault tolerance to your application.

The supervisor after sending a message to a subordinate can send a scheduled timeout reminder message to itself. If the subordinate responds before the message appears, then the message is discarded. If the response is not received or received after the timeout message appears, the missing information is either ignored or substituted with a default value. Thus, a failing service or a slow responding service will not break the application.

Considerations

The following considerations should be taken into account while implementing this pattern:

- The implementation of the pattern is complex and requires testing multiple failure scenarios.
- In case of failures, the supervisor may execute the Actors more than once. The logic of each of the subordinates should be idempotent.
- To recover from failure, the supervisor may ask the subordinates to reverse their operations. This may be a complex objective to achieve.

Related patterns

Following are the related cloud design patterns which can be used in conjunction with this pattern:

- **Compensating Transaction pattern**: If a subordinate is unable to complete operation, the supervisor Actor may message other subordinates to undo any work that they have previously performed.
- **Remindable Actors pattern**: A supervisor can request subordinate instances to queue tasks to be performed by them by messaging the task to themselves. This frees the supervisor to allocate tasks to other subordinates. This pattern also helps supervisor monitor latency of subordinates as previously discussed.
- **Circuit Breaker pattern**: A subordinate can use this pattern to handle faults that may take a variable amount of time to rectify when connecting to a remote service or resource.

Use cases

Following are few use cases where this pattern will be a right fit:

- For tasks that can operate in parallel without requiring input from previous tasks
- To improve efficiency of distributed systems that communicate via messaging

Summary

In this chapter we went through several patterns addressing problems related to challenges such as Optimization, Operation, and Implementation of enterprise grade Microservices.

19
Securing and Managing Your Microservices

Security is an integral part of your Microservices architecture. Due to many services at play in a Microservices application, the exploitable surface area of the application is higher than traditional applications. It is necessary that organizations developing Microservices adopt the Microsoft **Security Development Lifecycle (SDL)**.

Using the SDL process, developers can reduce the number of vulnerabilities in software while shipping it using agile methods. At its core, SDL defines tasks which can be mapped to the agile development process. Since SDL tasks do not realize functional objectives, they don't require a lot of documentation.

To implement SDL in conjunction with agile methodology, it is recommended that SDL tasks be divided into three categories:

1. **Every sprint requirements**: The SDL tasks in this category are important to implement therefore they need to be completed in every sprint. If these tasks are not completed, then the sprint is not deemed complete and the product cannot ship in that sprint. A few examples of such tasks include:
     - Run analysis tools daily or per build
     - Threat model all new features
     - Ensure that each project member has completed at least one security training course in the past year

2. **Bucket requirements**: The SDL tasks in this category are not required to be completed in every sprint. The tasks in this category are categorized into multiple buckets, and tasks from each bucket may be scheduled and completed across sprints. An example of such a classification is as follows:

- **Verification tasks**: This category includes mostly fuzzers and other analytics tools and may include tasks such as BinScope analysis, ActiveX fuzzing, and so on
- **Design review tasks**: This category includes tasks such as privacy reviews, cryptography design reviews, and so on
- **Response planning**: This category includes tasks such as defining the security bug bar, creating privacy support documents, and so on

Note that the number of tasks in the various categories may vary across projects and therefore need to be uniquely tailored for each project that is undertaken.

3. **One-time requirements**: These requirements need to be met only once in the lifetime of the project. These requirements are generally easy and quick to complete and are generally carried out at the beginning of the project. Even though these requirements are short and easy to accomplish, it may not be feasible to complete the requirements within an agile sprint as the team needs to deliver on functional requirements as well. Therefore, a grace period is assigned to each task in this category within which each task must be completed, which may vary depending on the complexity and size of the requirement. A few tasks that this category includes are adding or updating privacy scenarios in the test plan, creating or updating the network down plan, defining or updating the security bug bar, and so on.

 You can read more about SDL by visiting the following link: https://www.microsoft.com/en-us/SDL.
SDL-Agile, which is an extension of SDL, is documented at: https://www.microsoft.com/en-us/SDL/Discover/sdlagile.aspx.

Securing the communication channels

Your Service Fabric application is deployed on the Service Fabric cluster, which is a set of federated nodes that talk to each other over the network.

The generic structure of your Service Fabric cluster looks like the following:

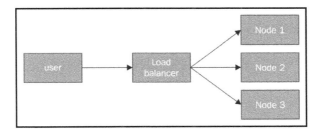

Generic structure of Service Fabric cluster

As you can see, there are two types of communication channels that are used by the Service Fabric:

- Channel to enable communication between cluster nodes (node-node)
- Channel to enable communication between clients and nodes (client-node)

Although you can choose not to secure the communication channels, by using open channels anonymous users can connect to the cluster and perform management operations on it and alter the cluster. Security cannot be an afterthought of implementation as an unsecured Service Fabric cluster cannot be secured later. Therefore, you should consider security of your cluster prudently.

Inter-node communication

Inter-node security ensures that only the authorized nodes can join a cluster and host applications. The nodes in a cluster running on Windows Server can be secured using either certificate security or Windows security. Let's discuss how we can secure a cluster using certificates so that only authorized nodes can join the cluster and only authorized cluster management commands can execute against the cluster.

While deploying the earlier examples, you must have noticed that we used to omit cluster security settings to simplify development. However, at this step you can specify the X.509 certificate that Service Fabric should use to secure communication between nodes. You can specify the certificate to use through any medium you wish to create your Service Fabric cluster, that is the Azure Portal, ARM template, or standalone JSON template. Also, you can specify up to two certificates in the configurations, one of which is the primary certificate used to secure the cluster, and the second certificate is an optional secondary certificate that can be used for certificate rollovers.

For the walkthrough, we will use a self-signed certificate; however, use of a certificate from a trusted **certificate authority (CA)** is advised for production workloads:

1. Create a new self-signed certificate. You can use PowerShell, tools such as OpenSSL, or any other tool that you personally prefer for the purpose. I will use PowerShell to generate a new self-signed certificate and save it on my desktop:

```
$certificatePassword = ConvertTo-SecureString
 -String [plain text password] -AsPlainText -Force
  New-SelfSignedCertificate -CertStoreLocation
Cert:\CurrentUser\My -DnsName [your cluster DNS name]
-Provider 'Microsoft Enhanced Cryptographic Provider v1.0' |
Export-PfxCertificate -FilePath
([Environment]::GetFolderPath('Desktop')+
 '/ClusterCertificate.pfx') -Password $certificatePassword
```

2. In the next step, we will sign in to our Azure subscription to perform the remaining operations:

```
Login-AzureRmAccount
Get-AzureRmSubscription
Set-AzureRmContext -SubscriptionId [azure subscription id]
```

3. Now let's create a resource group for our Service Fabric cluster and other resources that we will use:

```
New-AzureRmResourceGroup -Name [resource group name]
   -Location [resource group location]
```

4. We will use a cloud-based certificate store to store our certificate and provide it to our Service Fabric cluster. **Azure Key Vault** is a service that manages keys and passwords in the cloud. Key Vault helps decouple sensitive information such as passwords and certificates from applications. You may use an existing Key Vault but ideally, your Key Vault should reside in the same region and resource group for easy manageability and performance. The certificate added to the Key Vault will be installed on all the nodes in the cluster later through a configuration, as illustrated by the following diagram. This action can be accomplished through an ARM template, or by using a combination of PowerShell and Management Portal as we are doing currently:

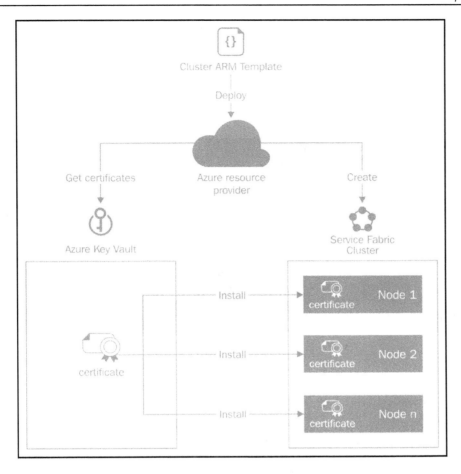

Applying security certificate on Service Fabric cluster from Key Vault

The following command will create a new Key Vault instance for you:

```
New-AzureRmKeyVault -VaultName [name of key vault]
  -ResourceGroupName [name of resource group]
  -Location [key vault location] -EnabledForDeployment
```

5. The execution of the preceding command will generate a summary of the generated Key Vault instance. You can copy the `ResourceId` of the generated instance to apply it on Service Fabric cluster configuration later. It is of the following format `/subscriptions/[subscription id]/resourceGroups/[resource group name]/providers/Microsoft.KeyVault/vaults/[key vault name]`:

```
VaultUri                      : https://microserviceskeyvault.vault.azure.net
TenantId                      : 8be3e297-afa5-4bb8-8e0d-13c7929a37eb
TenantName                    : 8be3e297-afa5-4bb8-8e0d-13c7929a37eb
Sku                           : Standard
EnabledForDeployment          : True
EnabledForTemplateDeployment  : False
EnabledForDiskEncryption      : False
AccessPolicies                : {8be3e297-afa5-4bb8-8e0d-13c7929a37eb}
AccessPoliciesText            :
                                Tenant ID                     : 8be3e297-afa5-4bb8-8e0d-13c7929a37eb
                                Object ID                     : 02f58afe-52c9-43c6-affb-35125d15aba9
                                Application ID                :
                                Display Name                  :
                                Permissions to Keys           : get, create, delete, list, update, import, backup, restore
                                Permissions to Secrets        : all
                                Permissions to Certificates   : all

OriginalVault                 : Microsoft.Azure.Management.KeyVault.Models.Vault
ResourceId                    : /subscriptions/                              /resourceGroups/microservices-rg/providers/Mi
                                ault
VaultName                     : microserviceskeyvault
ResourceGroupName             : microservices-rg
Location                      : southcentral us
Tags                          : {}
TagsTable                     :
```

Resource ID of KeyVault instance

6. We will now upload our certificate that we previously stored on the desktop to our Key Vault instance:

```
$cer = Add-AzureKeyVaultKey -VaultName [name of key vault]
   -Name [key name] -KeyFilePath
([Environment]::GetFolderPath('Desktop')+
'/ClusterCertificate.pfx') -KeyFilePassword $certificatePassword
```

7. You will now need to create a secret based on the certificate. For this purpose, we will create a JSON payload using the contents of the `.pfx` file:

```
$bytes = [System.IO.File]::ReadAllBytes(([Environment]:
          :GetFolderPath('Desktop')+'/ClusterCertificate.pfx'))
$base64 = [System.Convert]::ToBase64String($bytes)
$jsonBlob = @{
   data = $base64
   dataType = 'pfx'
   password = $password
   } | ConvertTo-Json
$contentbytes = [System.Text.Encoding]::UTF8.GetBytes($jsonBlob)
$content = [System.Convert]::ToBase64String($contentbytes)
$secretValue = ConvertTo-SecureString -String $content
```

```
 -AsPlainText -Force
Set-AzureKeyVaultSecret -VaultName [name of key vault]
-Name [key name] -SecretValue $secretValue
```

8. The `Set-AzureKeyVaultSecret` command returns a summary of the generated secret. From the summary, copy the ID of the secret:

```
SecretValue      : System.Security.SecureString
SecretValueText  : ewOKICAgICJkYXRhIjogICJNSU1LbXdJQkF6QONDbGNHQ1NxR1NJYjNEUUVIQWFDQQNrZ0VnZ3BFTU1JS1FEQONCZzRHQ1NxR1NJYjNEUUVIQWFD(
                   NEUUVNQ2dFQ29JSUUvakNDQlBvd0hBWUtLb1pJaHZjTkFRdOJBekFPQkFqSEVvZDdGM1NOS1FJQOI5QUvnZ1RZVHEzTDRwRUVham8vSj8ZL3d6WV
                   eHJoVOFCeTMxMXdMVxZ6dEJKZzkwVGhPNUwwb1VtVWxTd1JyL0zOWktEVUVWcUEyeEk5ZDBJb3NhO2UVHNONWRKVnROYzdaL2FUVitYQ3EyU0Fa
                   9wSnFxSnhiV21USnFmRkthRzFNbEVOTOtNaV1qd1FRU1BzYTNzdWJrQXJDQTVRY2g2RmMOQ1BmRXJmNE9NTkJVeVVZRFEzRzJZWWhieTk5MmNlbE5
                   anZhbUVtTk80dm1HYjZBRON2N1dLeEthSmhvMlVtLzdhcVNpeUpxQjFVOHNzam9tTFFA1NkkyUmdnZXNN1FewRYcGNKM0JxR3pIZERHK2hRNUlX
                   1HQ1NxR1NJYjNEUUVKR1RFROJBUUJBQUFBTUNJRONpcOdBUVFFZC2pUkEwY3hGGQVFTVwdCQkFFZOFWUUJNQUMWQVVBQkRBQUFBFTURzdOh6QUhCZ1
                   SjkvczRXZDRFRkROWTRDSFB0WXhWVGhppRW5Za2p0WTJQU1d4RkFnSUgwQT09IiwNCiAgICAiZGF0YVR5cGUiOiAgInBmeCIsDQogICAgInBhc3N3
Attributes       : Microsoft.Azure.Commands.KeyVault.Models.SecretAttributes
VaultName        : microserviceskeyvault
Name             : clustercertificate
Version          : 6cff4e1d4f02411db71c6a68b5d419a8
Id               : https://microserviceskeyvault.vault.azure.net:443/secrets/clustercertificate/6cff4e1d4f02411db71c6a68b5d419a8
```

Id of Secret in KeyVault

9. You will also need the thumbprint of the certificate that you used. You can copy it from the certificate properties or use the following PowerShell command for the purpose:

```
$clusterCertificate = new-object
 System.Security.Cryptography.X509Certificates.
 X509Certificate2 ([Environment]::GetFolderPath('Desktop')+
 '/ClusterCertificate.pfx'),
 $certificatePassword
$clusterCertificate.Thumbprint
```

10. Now, let's move to the Management Portal and create a new Service Fabric cluster. Populate the basic configuration options as before until you reach the security configuration step.

In the **Security** section, set the **Security mode** to **Secure**:

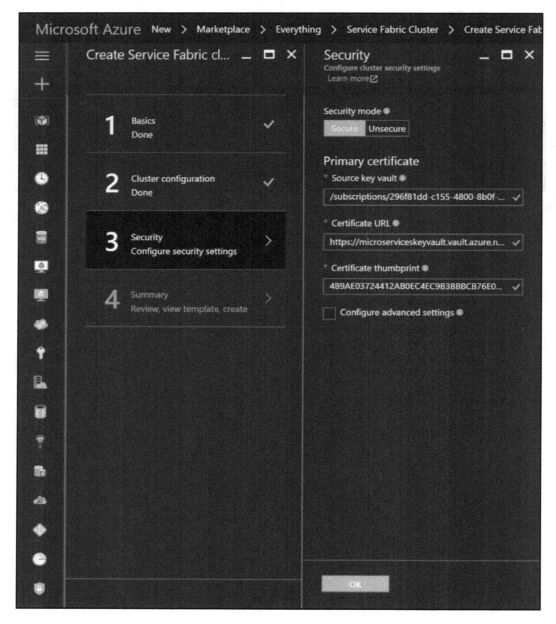

Service Fabric cluster security blade

11. You will not be asked to provide certificate details. Let's start populating the details one by one:
    - In the **Primary certificate** details section, set the value of **Source key vault** to the text that you generated in *step 5*
    - In the **Certificate URL** field, set the value to the secret ID that you copied in *step 8*
    - In the **Certificate thumbprint** field, set the value to the certificate thumbprint that you generated or copied from the PowerShell command output in *step 9*

12. By now, you have successfully applied the security settings on the cluster. Proceed to complete the remaining settings and allow the cluster to provision.

After you have applied a certificate on a Service Fabric cluster, it can only be accessed over HTTPS. You will only be able to navigate to your application on the cluster over HTTPS, which might raise untrusted certificate warnings as we have used a self-signed certificate for this example. You can add the certificate to the **Trusted Root Certificate Authority** of the local computer store to make the warnings go away.

To connect to your Service Fabric cluster, you would need to use the following command that adds the certificate to your request:

```
Connect-ServiceFabricCluster -ConnectionEndpoint ([your cluster DNS
name] + ':19000')  -X509Credential -ServerCertThumbprint
4b9ae03724412ab0ec4ec9b3bbbcb76e0d5374a9 -FindType FindByThumbprint -
FindValue 4b9ae03724412ab0ec4ec9b3bbbcb76e0d5374a9 -StoreLocation
CurrentUser -StoreName My
```

This command will present you with a summary of the cluster as follows:

```
ConnectionEndpoint     : {microserviceswithazure.southcentralus.cloudapp.azure.com:19000}
FabricClientSettings   : {
                         ClientFriendlyName                       : PowerShell-e6467898-1827-413c-863a-c9d679217881
                         PartitionLocationCacheLimit              : 100000
                         PartitionLocationCacheBucketCount        : 1024
                         ServiceChangePollInterval                : 00:02:00
                         ConnectionInitializationTimeout          : 00:00:02
                         KeepAliveInterval                        : 00:00:20
                         ConnectionIdleTimeout                    : 00:00:00
                         HealthOperationTimeout                   : 00:02:00
                         HealthReportSendInterval                 : 00:00:00
                         HealthReportRetrySendInterval            : 00:00:30
                         NotificationGatewayConnectionTimeout     : 00:00:30
                         NotificationCacheUpdateTimeout           : 00:00:30
                         AuthTokenBufferSize                      : 4096
                         }
GatewayInformation     : {
                         NodeAddress                              : 10.0.0.7:19000
                         NodeId                                   : 2eaf3840b9d1f36edd674699cf18489d
                         NodeInstanceId                           : 131266825585838911
                         NodeName                                 : _web_3
                         }
```

Summary of Service Fabric cluster

As you can see, now only authenticated clients can connect to your cluster; but additionally, you may want only authorized clients to make structural changes to your cluster, such as stopping nodes.

Let's discuss how we can authorize clients to perform operations on our cluster.

 You can secure the inter node communication channel on a standalone Windows cluster using Windows security. You can read more about it at: https://docs.microsoft.com/en-us/azure/service-fabric/service-fabric-windows-cluster-windows-security.

Client to node security

Previously, we talked about securing the communication between nodes of a Service Fabric cluster. To truly secure all the communication channels of Service Fabric, we need to secure.

Certificate security

Using X.509 certificates, you can configure your Service Fabric cluster to allow only authorized clients to execute management commands. You can set up certificates for two types of clients – the **admin client** which can perform administrative operations on your cluster, and the **read only client** which can perform only read operations on your cluster.

To specify the client certificate to use, you can use either the certificate thumbprint or the subject name of the certificate, which also requires the issuer thumbnail. To configure the client certificate, log on to the Management Portal and select your Service Fabric instance. Select the **Security** option and click on the **Authentication** button in the **Security** blade. Next, enter the details of the client certificate and allow the cluster updates to propagate:

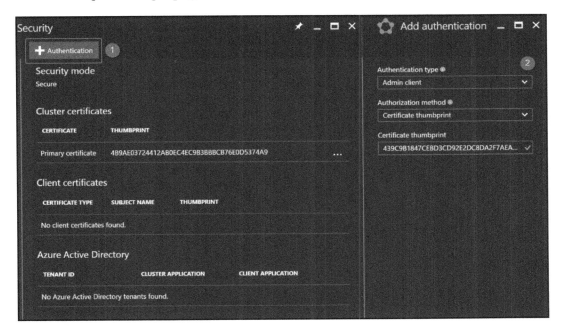

Cluster authentication steps

Once the cluster finishes updating, you can connect to the cluster without using the cluster certificate:

```
Connect-ServiceFabricCluster
 -ConnectionEndpoint ([your cluster dns name] + ':19000') `
    -KeepAliveIntervalInSec 10 `
    -X509Credential -ServerCertThumbprint [cluster
        certificate thumbprint] `
    -FindType FindByThumbprint -FindValue [client
        certificate] `
    -StoreLocation CurrentUser -StoreName My
```

Note that since in the preceding step we provisioned the client certificate for an Admin client, the clients with this certificate will have full management capabilities of the cluster.

Azure Active Directory security

Clusters running on Azure can also secure access to the management endpoints using **Azure Active Directory (AAD)**. For this purpose, you would need to create two AAD applications, one web application to enable authorized access to the web-based Service Fabric Explorer and one native application to enable authorized access to management functionalities through Visual Studio.

After provisioning these two applications, you can revisit the **Security** options of your cluster and add the tenant and application details in the **Authentication** blade.

Publishing an application to a secured cluster

To publish an application from Visual Studio, you only need to have the cluster security certificate added to Cert:\Current User\My store or Cert:\Local Machine\My store. Visual Studio automatically adds the following configuration to the published profile of your application:

```
<?xml version="1.0" encoding="utf-8"?>
<PublishProfile xmlns =" http:// schemas.microsoft.com/ 2015/ 05/
fabrictools" >
  <ClusterConnectionParameters
    ConnectionEndpoint ="[your cluster dns name]:19000"
    X509Credential =" true"
```

```
ServerCertThumbprint =" [cluster certificate thumbprint]"
FindType =" FindByThumbprint"
FindValue =" [cluster certificate thumbprint]"
StoreLocation =" CurrentUser"
StoreName =" My" />
  <ApplicationParameterFile Path ="..\ ApplicationParameters\
Cloud.xml" />
</PublishProfile >
```

Managing Service Fabric clusters with Windows PowerShell

Microsoft Service Fabric is a distributed systems platform engineered for hosting hyperscale Microservices. The addressed challenges around managing Microservices are packaging, deployment, scaling, upgrading, and so on. Apart from the rich graphical user interface exposed through Azure Portal and the management APIs, Service Fabric clusters can also be managed using Windows PowerShell cmdlets. This is the preferred mechanism for automating the management process.

Prerequisites

Service Fabric supports automation of most of its application lifecycle management tasks. These tasks include deploying, upgrading, removing, and testing Azure Service Fabric applications. Following are the steps to prepare your machine to execute Windows PowerShell cmdlets to manage a Service Fabric cluster:

1. Install the Service Fabric SDK, runtime, and tools which include the PowerShell modules. The SDK currently supports Windows 7, Windows 8/8.1, Windows Server 2012 R2, and Windows 10 operating systems. Microsoft Web Platform Installer can be used to download and install Service Fabric SDK.

2. After the installation is complete, modify the execution policy to enable PowerShell to deploy to a local cluster. This can be done by running the following command from PowerShell in administrator mode:

```
Set-ExecutionPolicy -ExecutionPolicy Unrestricted
-Force -Scope CurrentUser
```

3. Start a new PowerShell window as an administrator. Then, execute the cluster setup script. This script can be found in the following folder inside the SDK:

```
& "$ENV:ProgramFiles\Microsoft SDKs\Service
Fabric\ClusterSetup\DevClusterSetup.ps1"
```

4. Use the following PowerShell cmdlet to connect to the local Service Fabric cluster:

```
Connect-ServiceFabricCluster localhost:19000
```

This completes the setup for PowerShell to manage your local Service Fabric cluster. Now we can explore deploying, upgrading, testing, and removing applications to this cluster.

Deploying Service Fabric applications

After an application is built, it needs to be packaged for it to be deployed on a Service Fabric cluster. This task can be easily achieved using Visual Studio. The packaged application should be uploaded and registered before the Service Fabric cluster manager can instantiate the application. Following are the steps involved:

1. **Uploading an application**: This task is required as it places the application packages in a shared location from which the Service Fabric components can access it. An application package typically contains the following:
   - Application manifests
   - Service manifests
   - Code
   - Configuration
   - Data packages

   The following cmdlet can be used to upload an application package for deployment:

   ```
   Copy-ServiceFabricApplicationPackage <Source package folder>
   -ImageStoreConnectionString file:<Local image store path>
   -ApplicationPackagePathInImageStore <Application package name>
   ```

2. **Registering the application package**: Package registration makes the application type and version declared in the manifest available for use. Service Fabric reads the registered package, verifies it, and moves the package to an internal store for further processing. Application packages can be registered using the following cmdlet:

```
Register-ServiceFabricApplicationType <Application name>
```

All registered packages in the cluster can be listed using the following cmdlet:

```
Get-ServiceFabricApplicationType
```

3. **Instantiating the application**: The `New-ServiceFabricApplication` cmdlet can be used to instantiate a specific version of a registered application type. The application name should be declared at the deploy time using the following scheme:

```
Fabric:<Application name>
```

- The following usage of the preceding cmdlet can be used to create a new application instance:

```
New-ServiceFabricApplication fabric:/<Application name>
<Application type> <Application version>
```

- The following cmdlet can be used to list all the application instances which are successfully created in a cluster:

```
Get-ServiceFabricApplication
```

- The preceding command can be used along with the `Get-ServiceFabricService` cmdlet to list the services running under each application instance. Following is the usage:

```
Get-ServiceFabricApplication | Get-ServiceFabricService
```

Upgrading Service Fabric applications

To perform the upgrade, Service Fabric performs a comparison of the old and the new application manifest. The application is upgraded only if there is a change in version number. The following flowchart explains the application upgrade process:

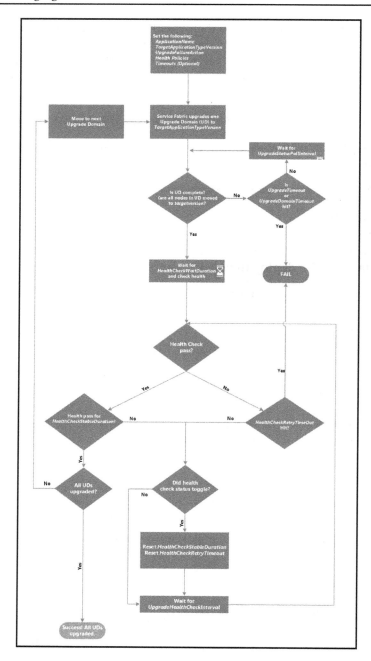

Application upgrade process

An already deployed Service Fabric can be upgraded to a newer version using PowerShell cmdlets. Following are the steps to be performed to upgrade a Service Fabric application:

1. **Package the application**: The first step for upgrading is to package the newer version of the application. This can be done using Visual Studio.

2. **Upload package**: Once packaged, the package needs to be uploaded into the Service Fabric image store. The following PowerShell cmdlet can be used to perform this operation:

```
Copy-ServiceFabricApplicationPackage <Package folder path>
-ImageStoreConnectionString file:<Local image store path>
-ApplicationPackagePathInImageStore <Application package name>
```

The parameter `ApplicationPackagePathInImageStore` informs the Service Fabric orchestrator about the location of the application package.

3. **Register the updated application**: The uploaded package now should be registered for Service Fabric to use it. This can be done using the `Register-ServiceFabricApplicationType` cmdlet:

```
Register-ServiceFabricApplicationType <Application name>
```

4. **Perform the upgrade**: Upgrading the application without downtime and handling failures gracefully is a key feature of Service Fabric. This process operates on various configurations set by the user such as timeouts, health criteria, and so on Parameters like `HealthCheckStableDuration`, `UpgradeDomainTimeout`, and `UpgradeTimeout` need to be set for Service Fabric to perform the upgrade. The `UpgradeFailureAction` also should be set by the user so that Service Fabric knows what to do if an upgrade operation fails. Once these parameters are decided, the upgrade process can be kicked off by using the `Start-ServiceFabricApplicationUpgrade` cmdlet:

```
Start-ServiceFabricApplicationUpgrade -ApplicationName
fabric:/<Application name>-ApplicationTypeVersion <New app
version>
-HealthCheckStableDurationSec <Duration>
-UpgradeDomainTimeoutSec <Timeout>
-UpgradeTimeout <Timeout> -FailureAction <Action> -Monitored
```

The application name in the preceding command must match the one specified for the already deployed application, as Service Fabric uses this name to identify the application.

5. **Check upgrade**: Service Fabric Explorer can be used to monitor the upgrade process for applications. The `Get-ServiceFabricApplicationUpgrade` cmdlet can also be used for this purpose:

```
Get-ServiceFabricApplicationUpgrade fabric:/<Application
Name>
```

Removing Service Fabric applications

Service Fabric supports removing an application instance of a deployed application, removing the application itself, and clearing the application package from the image store for permanent deletion.

Following are the steps to be performed to completely remove the application from a Service Fabric cluster:

1. **Removing application instances**: The following cmdlet can be used to remove application instances:

```
Remove-ServiceFabricApplication fabric:/<Application name>
```

2. **Unregistering the application**: The `Unregister-ServiceFabricApplicationType` cmdlet can be used to unregister an application type. Following is the usage:

```
Unregister-ServiceFabricApplicationType <Application name>
   <version number>
```

3. **Removing the application package**: The `Remove-ServiceFabricApplicationPackage` cmdlet can be used to remove an application package from the image store:

```
Remove-ServiceFabricApplicationPackage
-ImageStoreConnectionString file:<Image store path>
-ApplicationPackagePathInImageStore <Application Name>
```

Summary

We started off this chapter by detailing how the security of applications starts with **Secure Development Lifecycle** (**SDL**). We then went on to discuss the channel and node security of a Service Fabric cluster and how you can configure those using PowerShell and the Azure Management Portal. We later walked through the steps of deploying an application on a secure cluster.

20
Diagnostics and Monitoring

In an enterprise-scale Microservice deployment, your efficiency in managing services depends upon your ability to respond to outages and incidents. This in turn is heavily dependent on your ability to detect and diagnose issues quickly. The answer to the problem is to have an efficient monitoring and diagnostics solution in place. The fact that your services are hosted on commodity hardware, which is prone to failures, adds significant weight to the importance of having an efficient monitoring solution.

Service Fabric provides rich features to effectively monitor and manage the health of the Microservices deployed on its cluster. These features are capable of reporting near-real-time status of the cluster and the services running on it. Service Fabric employs a dedicated subsystem called the **health subsystem** to encapsulate all the monitoring and diagnostics features. To familiarize ourselves with this subsystem, let's explore the components within this subsystem, their roles, and responsibilities.

Health entities

Health entities, in the context of Service Fabric, can be considered as logical entities used by the runtime. These entities form a logical hierarchy based on the dependencies and interactions among them.

Service Fabric uses a *health store* to persist the hierarchy of its health entities and their health information. To ensure high availability, health store is implemented as a stateful service within the Service Fabric cluster and is instantiated with when the cluster starts.

The health subsystem leverages the health entities and hierarchy to effectively report, debugg, and monitor. The following diagram illustrates the hierarchy of health entities:

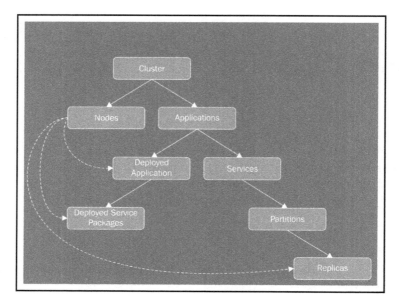

Hierarchy of health entities

You may notice that the health entities match the Service Fabric deployment entities discussed earlier in this book. Let's dive deeper to understand each of these entities and the parent-child relationships illustrated in the preceding figure.

The root node, **Cluster** represents the health of Service Fabric cluster. This is an aggregation of conditions that affects the entire cluster and its components. The first child of the cluster, **Node** represents the health of a Service Fabric node. Health information such as resource usages and connections for a node is captured within this health entity. **Applications**, the second child of the **Cluster**, represents a Service Fabric application. The health of all running instances of services in the scope of an application is aggregated into this entity. The **Services** entity represents all partitions of an application service deployed on the cluster. This entity can be further drilled down to **Partitions** which represents service partitions and **Replicas** which represents the replicas of each partition. The **Deployed Application** and **Deployed Service Packages** are entities which capture the application and services in scope of a specific node.

This granularity in the hierarchy makes it easy to identify a fault and fix is easily. For example, the cluster will appear unhealthy if one of its application is unhealthy. We can then drill down into the **Applications** sub tree to detect the service which is unhealthy and then to the partition and so on.

Service Fabric may use internal or external watchdog services to monitor a specific component. At any given point, the state of the health entities will represent near-real-time state of the cluster. A property called health state associated with each entity is used to identify the health of that entity.

Health state

Following are the four possible states for the health of a Service Fabric entity:

- **OK**: The entity and its children are healthy as of the current reports.
- **Warning**: This state informs us that there may be some potential issue on this entity of any of its children. A warning state does not mean that the entity is unhealthy. Delay in communication or reporting can also cause this state. A warning state will usually recover or degrade down to an error within some time. It is normal to see this state on your cluster while you are updating the application, service, or the cluster itself.
- **Error**: The entity has an error reported on it. A fix for this will be required to ensure correct functioning of this entity.
- **Unknown**: This state usually shows up when the reported entity is absent in the health store. This may be because of clean up or delay in the setup.

Health policies

Health store uses policies to determine the state of an entity. These policies are called **health policies**. Service Fabric, by default sets a set of health policies for the cluster based on parent-child relationships in the entity hierarchy. This means that a parent is marked as unhealthy if any of its children are reported as unhealthy. Apart from the default policies, custom health policies can be set for a Service Fabric deployment in the cluster or application manifest.

Cluster health policy

The health state of the cluster and the nodes deployed within the cluster is evaluated based on the cluster health policies. Custom cluster health policies can be set in the cluster manifest file under the `FabricSettings` section. The following is an example:

```
<FabricSettings>
  <Section Name="HealthManager/ClusterHealthPolicy">
    <Parameter Name="ConsiderWarningAsError" Value="False" />
    <Parameter Name="MaxPercentUnhealthyApplications" Value="20" />
    <Parameter Name="MaxPercentUnhealthyNodes" Value="20" />
    <Parameter Name="ApplicationTypeMaxPercentUnhealthyApplications-
               ControlApplicationType" Value="0" />
  </Section>
</FabricSettings>
```

Let's now understand what each of these parameters listed in the preceding policy is used for:

- `ConsiderWarningAsError`: This parameter specifies weather or not to treat warning reported by the health monitors as errors. This parameter is set to `false` by default.

- `MaxPercentUnhealthyApplications`: This parameter decides the threshold for marking the cluster entity as unhealthy based on the number of applications which can afford to be unhealthy at a given point of time. The default value for this entity is `0`.

- `MaxPercentUnhealthyNodes`: This is the threshold for marking the cluster as unhealthy based on the number of unhealthy nodes at that given point of time. This parameter helps us accommodate for nodes which are undergoing maintenance.

- `ApplicationTypeHealthPolicyMap`: This parameter helps qualify special applications with specific rules. In the preceding example the parameter is used to specify a tolerance threshold for applications of the type `ControlApplicationType` to 0. This feature helps specify significance of some applications over other in terms of their expected availability.

Application health policy

Application health policy defines the rules for evaluating and aggregating the health status for the application entity and its children entities. The custom application health policy can be configured in the application manifest by using the following parameters:

- `ConsiderWarningAsError`: Similar to the parameter in the cluster health policy. This will specify whether a warning will be treated as an error during health reporting
- `MaxPercentUnhealthyDeployedApplications`: This parameter specifies the threshold for the application entity to be marked unhealthy based on the number of unhealthy deployed applications in the cluster
- `DefaultServiceTypeHealthPolicy`: This parameter specifies the default service type health policy
- `ServiceTypeHealthPolicyMap`: This parameter specifies the service health policies map for each service type

Service type health policy

Service type health policy defines the rules to aggregate the health status of services deployed in a cluster on to the service health entity. This policy can be configured in the application manifest file. The following is an example:

```
<Policies>
    <HealthPolicy ConsiderWarningAsError="true"
        MaxPercentUnhealthyDeployedApplications="20">
        <DefaultServiceTypeHealthPolicy
                MaxPercentUnhealthyServices="0"
                MaxPercentUnhealthyPartitionsPerService="10"
                MaxPercentUnhealthyReplicasPerPartition="0"/>
        <ServiceTypeHealthPolicy
            ServiceTypeName="FrontEndServiceType"
                MaxPercentUnhealthyServices="0"
                MaxPercentUnhealthyPartitionsPerService="20"
                MaxPercentUnhealthyReplicasPerPartition="0"/>
        <ServiceTypeHealthPolicy
            ServiceTypeName="BackEndServiceType"
                MaxPercentUnhealthyServices="20"
                MaxPercentUnhealthyPartitionsPerService="0"
                MaxPercentUnhealthyReplicasPerPartition="0">
        </ServiceTypeHealthPolicy>
    </HealthPolicy>
```

```
</Policies>
```

This policy uses the following parameters to specify the tolerance levels:

- `MaxPercentUnhealthyPartitionsPerService`: The threshold for unhealthy partitions before marking a service entity as unhealthy
- `MaxPercentUnhealthyReplicasPerPartition`: The threshold for unhealthy replicas before marking a partition entity as unhealthy
- `MaxPercentUnhealthyServices`: The threshold for unhealthy services before marking an application entity as unhealthy

The default value for all the three preceding listed parameters is zero.

Health evaluation

Health evaluation can be performed manually by a user or by automated services employed to report on the system health. Health policies are used to evaluate and report the health of an entity which is then aggregated at a parent level in the entity hierarchy. This process cascades up to the root element of the hierarchy which is the **Cluster**. The following diagram illustrates this process of cascading aggregations:

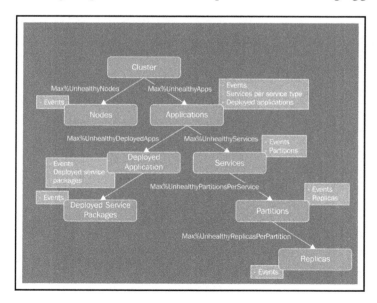

Cascading aggregations

After the health of child elements are evaluated, the health sub-system evaluates the health of a parent entity based on the maximum percentage of unhealthy children configured at a specific level.

Health reporting

The health sub-system used internal and external watchdogs to report the health of an entity. Watchdogs are background processes which are tasked to repeatedly perform a background tasks at pre-configured intervals. The watchdogs constantly monitor the health entities and generate health reports. A health report will have the following properties:

- `SourceId`: A unique identifier for this instance of the health report.
- `Entity identifier`: Used to identify the health entity on which the report is being generated. This can be any entity in the health hierarchy such as cluster, node, application, and likewise.
- `Property`: A string holding the metadata around which property of the health entity is being reported on.
- `Description`: A custom description.
- `HealthState`: One of the possible health states.
- `TimeToLive`: The time span specifying the validity of this health report.
- `RemoveWhenExpired`: A Boolean flag to specify if the report should be removed from the health store on expiry.
- `SequenceNumber`: An incrementing sequence number to identify the order in which the health reports were generated.

These reports are then transformed in to *health events* and stored in the health store after appending additional information such as UTC time stamps and *last modified* information.

PowerShell commands can be used to generate health reports and to view them. The following is an example:

```
PS C:\> Send-ServiceFabricApplicationHealthReport -ApplicationName
fabric:/<Application name> -SourceId <Report source> -HealthProperty
<Health property> -HealthState <Health state>

PS C:\> Get-ServiceFabricApplicationHealth fabric:/<Application name>
```

Now that we understand the health subsystem and the process how health is evaluation, let's explore the technologies which can be used to monitor a Service Fabric cluster.

Centralized logging

A Microservices application running on distributed platform such as Service Fabric is particularly hard to debug. You cannot debug the application by attaching a debugger to spot and fix the issue. Logging is a commonly used mechanism to track application behavior.

All the processes and applications running on distributed systems generate logs. The logs are usually written to files on local disk. However, since there are multiple hosts in a distributed system, managing and accessing the logs can become cumbersome. To solve this problem, a centralized logging solution is required so that multiple logs can be aggregated in a central location.

For your Service Fabric applications, you can enable collection of logs from each cluster node using Azure **Diagnostics** extension, which uploads logs to Azure Storage. Once you have aggregated the logs, you can use products such as Elastic Search, Azure Operations Management Suite, and so on, to derive useful information from it.

Collecting logs

There are two types of logs sources that you should stream to log storage:

- **Service Fabric logs**: Service Fabric platform emits logs to **Event Tracing for Windows** (**ETW**) and `EventSource` channels. Service Fabric logs include events emitted from Service Fabric platform such as creation and application, state change of nodes, and so on. These logs also contain information emitted from the Reliable Actors and Reliable Services programming models.
- **Application Logs**: These logs are generated from the code of your service. You can use the `EventSource` helper class available in Visual Studio templates to write logs from your application.

Diagnostic extension

Distributed systems collect logs using agents deployed on the nodes in the cluster. In Service Fabric, the Azure **Diagnostics** extension provides the monitoring and diagnostics capabilities on a Windows based Azure Service Fabric nodes. The **Diagnostics** extension collects logs on each VM and uploads them to the storage account that you specify. You can use the Azure Management Portal or Azure Resource Manager to enable **Diagnostics** extension on cluster nodes.

Deploying the Diagnostics extension

To deploy the **Diagnostics** extension during cluster creation, as shown in the following image, use the **Diagnostics** settings panel. To enable Reliable Actors or Reliable Services event collection, ensure that **Diagnostics** setting is set to **On**. After you create the cluster, you can't change these settings by using the portal:

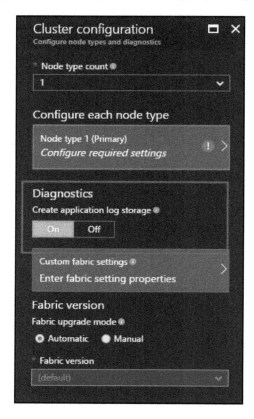

Set the Diagnostics setting of the cluster

Resource Manager templates can be used to enable diagnostics on an existing cluster or to update the configurations of an existing cluster.

 You can read more about the templates used to modify an existing cluster here: https://docs.microsoft.com/en-us/azure/service-fabric/service-fabric-diagnostics-how-to-setup-wad.

After setting up diagnostics on your Service Fabric cluster, you can connect the log data storage to services such as **Operations Management Suit** (**OMS**), Elastic Search, and so on. You can also use Application Insights SDK to send telemetry data to application insights so that you can monitor your application and respond to errors.

 You can read more about how you can configure OMS to retrieve data from diagnostics storage and display it in the OMS portal here: https://docs.microsoft.com/en-us/azure/log-analytics/log-analytics-service-fabric.

Summary

In this chapter, we explored the health monitoring system of Service Fabric which includes the health entities and health states. We also looked at health evaluation and reporting techniques used by Service Fabric.

Towards the end of the chapter we looked at installing the **Diagnostics** extension on the Service Fabric cluster.

21
Continuous Integration and Continuous Deployment

Continuous Integration (**CI**) and **Continuous Delivery** (**CD**) are two inevitable patterns for an agile software development team. These patterns become more relevant for an application development teams driven by Microservices due to the number of teams working on a project and their diverse release cycles. Continuous Integration can be defined as the process of merging developer code to a source depot after successfully building the project. Continuous Delivery then takes care of running the unit tests and deploying the application to a target environment.

Continuous Integration

Microsoft recommends the use of **Visual Studio Team Services** (**VSTS**) to continuously integrate your code into a source depot. The first step for setting up Continuous Integration is to set up a build definition. Following are the steps to be followed for creating a build definition from existing build templates:

1. Browse to the VSTS portal and navigate to the **Builds** tab.

2. Click on the **New** button to create a new build definition:

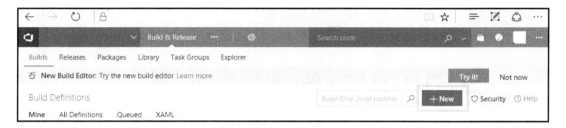

Create new build definition

3. Select **Azure Service Fabric Application** within the **Build** template category and click **Next**:

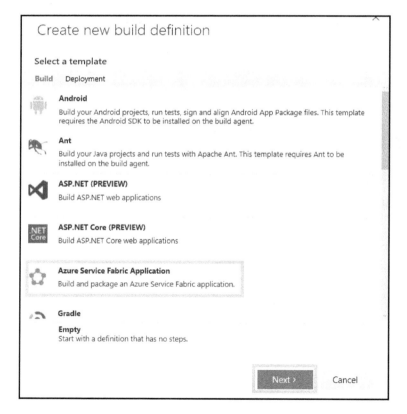

Select Service Fabric build definition template

4. Select the source control repository for the Service Fabric application and click **Create**:

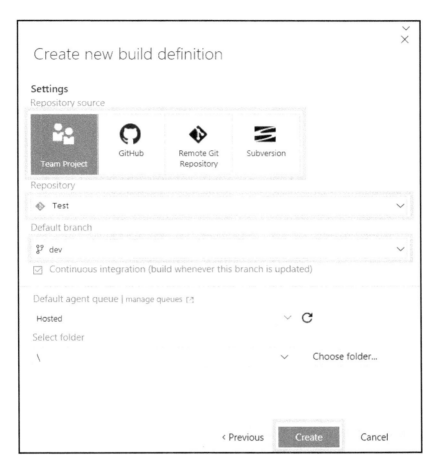

Create new build definition

5. Save the build definition with a name.

The following build steps are added to the build template as a part of this template:

1. Restore all NuGet packages referred to in this solution.
2. Build the entire solution.
3. Generate the Service Fabric application package.

4. Update the Service Fabric application version.
5. Copy the publish profile and application parameters files to the build's artifacts to be consumed for deployment.
6. Publish the build's artifacts.

A build can now be queued to test the build definition.

Continuous Delivery

Once we have a successful build, we can move ahead to create a release definition to automate Continuous Delivery. A VSTS release definition can be used to define the tasks which should be executed sequentially to deploy a packages Service Fabric application to a cluster. Following are the steps to be followed to create a release definition:

1. Browse to the VSTS portal and navigate to the **Releases** tab.
2. Select the **Create release definition** menu item:

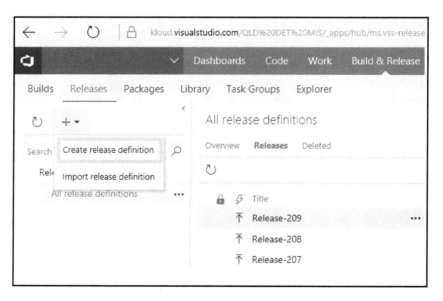

Create release definition

3. Select **Azure Service Fabric Deployment** within the **Deployment** template category and click **Next**:

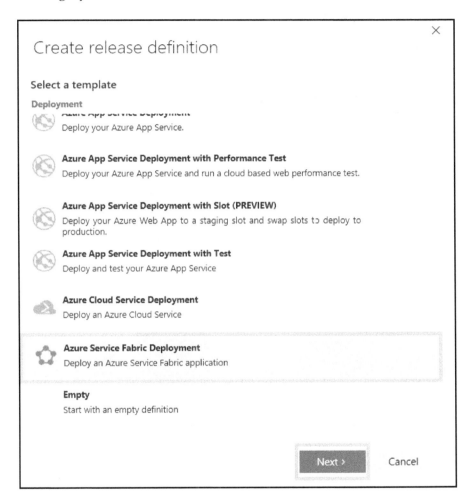

Select Azure Service Fabric template

4. Select the already created build definition from the drop-down list, click on the check box to enable Continuous Deployment and click on **Create**:

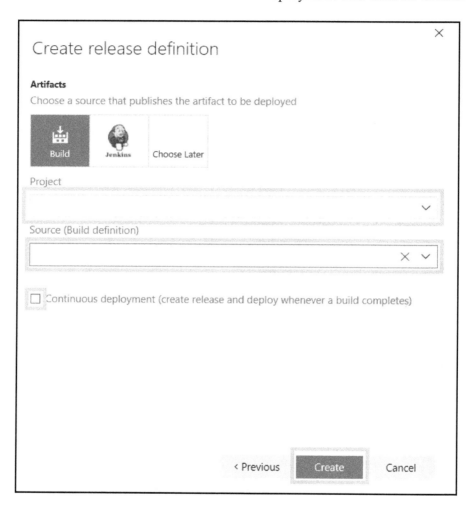

Select project and build definition

5. Add the **Cluster Connection** configuration:

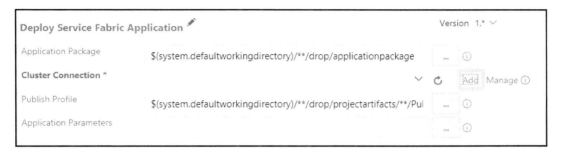

Setting application package path and publish profile

6. In the dialogue, give the cluster connection a name and add the **Cluster Endpoint** and click **OK**:

Add new Service Fabric connection

A release can now be triggered from the **Releases** tab manually to test the newly created release definition.

Now that we have explored a method of managing Continuous Deployment of application on Azure Service Fabric cluster, let's look into the options of running Microservices on other hosting platforms.

Deploying Service Fabric application on a standalone cluster

It is common for an enterprise application to be hybrid by nature in terms of its deployment strategy. Factors like strict enterprise policies around data storage and requirement of integrating with legacy systems usually forces an application to span across multiple data centers and hosting platforms.

A Service Fabric cluster can be created with machines running Windows Server on any hosting platform. These machines can be hosted on Azure, on a private on-premises data center, on **AWS** (**Amazon Web Services**), Google Cloud Platform, or any other similar platforms.

An installation package for Service Fabric can be downloaded from the Microsoft website which will contain the required files to setup a standalone cluster. It is advisable to enable internet access on the host machines to enable real-time downloading of files required for the Service Fabric runtime. Offline versions of these files are also available as an alternative.

The following link details the steps to create and configure a standalone cluster using Windows Server machines: `https://docs.microsoft.com/en-us/azure/service-fabric/service-fabric-cluster-creation-for-windows-server`.

Deploying the application

Once the cluster is created, PowerShell cmdlets can be used to deploy and manage applications on the standalone cluster. The first step would be connecting to the cluster. The following command can be used to connect to an existing Service Fabric cluster:

```
Connect-ServiceFabricCluster -ConnectionEndpoint
<*IPAddressofaMachine*>:<Client connection end point port>
```

Once connected, we should be able to launch the Service Fabric explorer remotely by browsing to the following
URL: `http://<IPAddressofaMachine>:19080/Explorer/index.html`.

The next step will be to upload the application package. The cmdlet for uploading the package is part of the Service Fabric SDK PowerShell module which should be imported before performing the upload.

The connection string for the local image store where the package has to be uploaded can be retrieved using the `Get-ImageStoreConnectionStringFromClusterManifest` cmdlet. `Copy-ServiceFabricApplicationPackage` cmdlet can then be used to copy the application package to the image store. Following is an example for the same:

```
PS C:\> Copy-ServiceFabricApplicationPackage -ApplicationPackagePath
<path> -ApplicationPackagePathInImageStore <application name> -
ImageStoreConnectionString (Get-
ImageStoreConnectionStringFromClusterManifest(Get-
ServiceFabricClusterManifest)) -TimeoutSec <timeout>
```

Once the package is copied to the image store the application can be registered using the following PowerShell cmdlet:

```
PS C:\> Register-ServiceFabricApplicationType <Application name>
```

Registry of an application can be verified using the `Get-ServiceFabricApplicationType` cmdlet:

```
PS C:\> Get-ServiceFabricApplicationType
```

After the application is registered, the next step is to create an instance of this application on the Service Fabric cluster. This can be achieved using the following cmdlet:

```
PS C:\> New-ServiceFabricApplication fabric:/<application name>
<application type> <version>
```

A deployed application can be verified using the `Get-ServiceFabricApplication` and the `Get-ServiceFabricService` cmdlets:

```
PS C:\> Get-ServiceFabricApplication
PS C:\> Get-ServiceFabricApplication | Get-ServiceFabricService
```

A Service Fabric cluster can also be deployed on Linux machines.

Details about setting up a Linux cluster can be found at the following link: `https://docs.microsoft.com/en-us/azure/service-fabric/service-fabric-linux-overview`.

Summary

In this chapter, we discussed how Visual Studio Team Services can be used to continuously integrate code to a centralized source repository and to continuously deploy Microservices on Azure Service Fabric cluster.

22
Serverless Microservices

Until recently, every code development was accompanied with overheads of maintaining orchestrations, deployments, and so on. With the evolution in IT, developers desire to eliminate waste and focus on specific business objectives.

In a serverless environment, developers only stay concerned with solutions and the monitoring of usage. The business saves on costs by paying for computation cycles consumed and not for the idle time of system. A serverless system lowers the total cost of maintaining your apps, enabling you to build more logic faster. In a serverless computing model, the cloud provider manages starting and stopping of the container of the service as necessary to serve requests and the business need not pay for the virtual machines on which the services execute.

The growing requirement of developing Microservices that are much smaller and highly focused has given rise to a new breed of services called Nanoservices. Nanoservices can either be triggered by specific events, or be configured to run behind an API management platform to expose it as a REST API endpoint.

Nanoservices share certain commonalities with Microservices which also form the definition boundary of Nanoservices:

- Nanoservices generally run in a lesser isolation than Microservices, which means that they can be more densely packaged than Microservices. However, Nanoservices are independently deployable just like Microservices are.
- Nanoservices are more finely grained than Microservices. A Nanoservice may contain just a few lines of code, which perform a very specific task for example, send an email on successful registration of a user.
- The execution environment of Nanoservices is more efficient than that of Microservices. The Nanoservices execution environment is cognizant of activation and deactivation of Nanoservices and its resource consumption and can therefore dynamically allocate and deallocate resources.

The smaller size of Nanoservices affects the architecture of solution. Nanoservices decrease the deployment risk due to smaller size of deployment units and can help deliver even more understandable and replaceable services. On the other hand, the complexity of deployment increases significantly as a bounded context, which earlier used to contain one or a couple of Microservices will now contain many Nanoservices each of which implement a very narrow functionality.

Isolation is not a clear demarcation between Microservices and Nanoservices as Microservices can be configured to share the same virtual machine while Nanoservices can be configured to run on independent virtual machines. Therefore, Microservices can be said to be a coarser form of Nanoservices.

Just like isolation, minimum size is also not a clear demarcation between Microservices and Nanoservices. For instance, in order to implement **Command Query Responsibility Segregation (CQRS)** in a solution, a Microservice may only be responsible for writing a certain type of data and another Microservice may be responsible for reading the same type of data, leading to Microservices have a small scope just like Nanoservices.

Before committing to Nanoservices

Nanoservices live within the sizing constraints of Microservices. Smaller size of modules enables the service to maintain and change. Therefore, a system composed of Nanoservices can be easily extended.

In a typical domain driven system, each class and function can be modelled as a separate Nanoservice. This leads to an increase in infrastructure costs such as that of application servers and monitoring solutions. Since implementing a complete business solution using Nanoservices might involve deploying several hundreds to a couple of thousands of Nanoservices, the infrastructure costs on the desired cloud platform need to be as low as possible. In addition, Nanoservices should not be long running or resource intensive.

Nanoservices require a lot of communication among themselves. This may lead to degraded performance. On certain platforms, Nanoservices may share a process, which may cause resource starvation and take away technological freedom. This approach however, can reduce the overhead of inter-service communication.

Before you plan to commit to a platform for hosting Nanoservices, the following objectives should be considered:

- Cost of infrastructure for hosting Nanoservices should be low. The platform should support rapid deployment and monitoring of Nanoservices.
- The Nanoservices platform should support dense deployment of Nanoservices.
- Inter-service communication will degrade performance. A highly reliable and efficient means of communication would ensure that the performance remains within acceptable limits.
- Nanoservices should be independently deployable and the platform should ensure that failures are not propagated between Nanoservices.
- Nanoservices are limited in terms of choice of programming language, platforms, and frameworks. You should study technical feasibility of building Nanoservices on a platform before committing to it.

Building Nanoservices with Azure Functions

Azure Functions allow developers to write serverless applications, meaning that developers or operations do not have to worry about the infrastructure on which the application executes. In many scenarios, application or business needs require a small piece of logic to be reused by other services for some small task to be performed based on an event such as sending a notification to user when a message is sent to a queue.

Such tasks were previously handled by WebJobs or scripts, which are difficult to reuse and connect in a flow of logic. Azure Functions give developers the ability to wrap the logic in a Nanoservice that can connect and communicate with other services to carry out the logic flow.

Azure Functions is part of web and mobile suite of services in Azure. In addition to Visual Studio tooling, you can design and manage Azure Functions from a dedicated portal at: `https://functions.azure.com`.

Currently you can create functions in JavaScript, C#, Python, and PHP as well as with scripting languages such as Bash, Batch, and PowerShell. The functions can be triggered by virtually any event in an on cloud or on-premise system or a third-party service.

Let's head over to `https://functions.azure.com` to explore Azure Functions in greater detail:

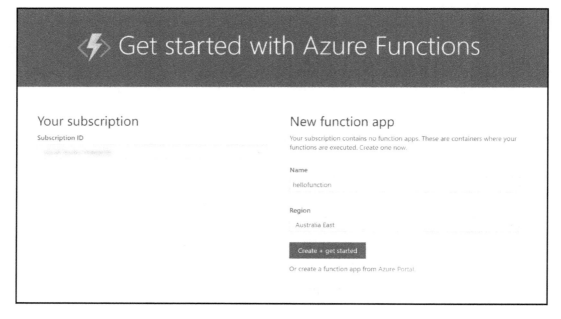

Azure Functions landing page

In the function area, you will notice that you can select a subscription where you want to create your function and assign a **Name** and **Region** to your function. Assign a name to your function and click the **Create + get started** button.

Once your function gets provisioned, you will be redirected to the Management Portal, on which you will be able to compose and manage your function:

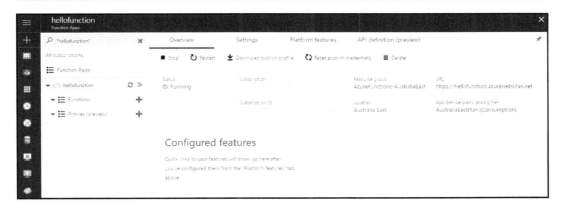

Azure Functions in Azure Management Portal

To add a function to your application, click on the + sign next to the **Functions** menu to bring up the quick start panel:

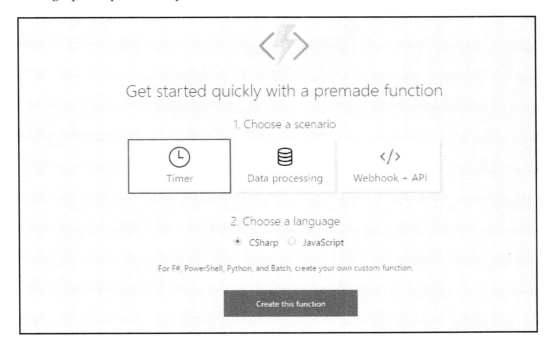

Azure Functions quick start panel

Select the **Timer** scenario, which will configure your function to get executed based on a configurable schedule. Set the language preference to compose the function as C# and click on **Create this function** button.

The previous steps will create a function that write a message to log every five minutes. You can view the log output in the window below the editor console:

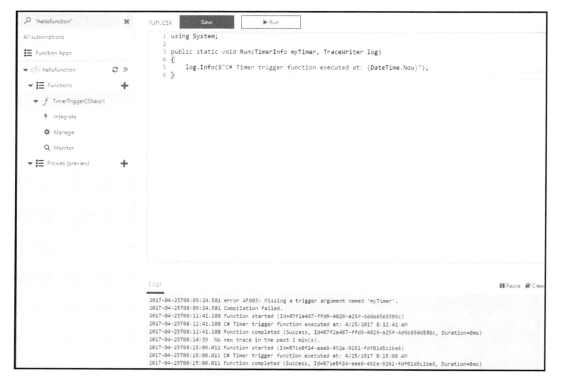

Azure Function

Let's change the logging frequency of this function, so that we can see more messages in the console. Click on the **Integrate** option under the **Functions** menu:

Change timer frequency

In the integration pane, change the **Schedule** CRON expression to six stars (* * * * * *), which means that function will execute every second, and click on **Save**.

Once the settings are saved, go back to the editor view where you will now find that new messages are logged every second. Click on **Manage** menu item and click on the **Delete** button to delete the function.

Function app templates

Although not necessary, function templates can help speed up development of functions. You can view the list of templates available to you by selecting **create your own custom function** in the function creation quick start panel:

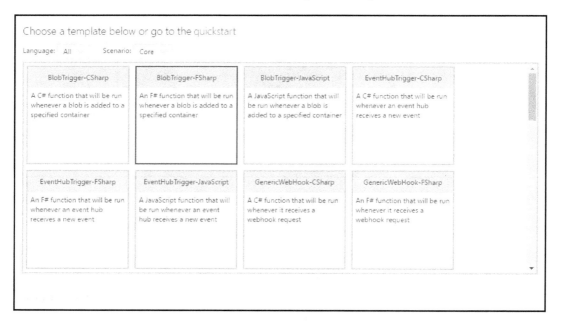

Azure Function quick start templates

Even if you are creating custom functions from scratch, it is helpful to look at the parameters that get passed to functions and their values from the templates. Let us next study the categories of functions that we can create today.

Timer function apps

The timer function apps run at configurable intervals. The time at which the function should execute is defined through a CRON expression. The CRON expression is composed of six fields: `{second} {minute} {hour} {day} {month} {day of the week}`. These fields, separated by white space, can contain any of the allowed values with various combinations of the allowed characters for that field. For example, to trigger your function every 15 minutes, your scheduling CRON expression should be set to: `0 */15 * * * *`.

Timer function apps are generally used to send information to other systems. They don't generally return information and write the progress of the operation to logs. This category of functions is typically built to clean up or manage reconcile or manage data at regular intervals. Timer functions are also used for checking the health of other services by pinging them at regular intervals. Just like any other category of functions, these functions can be combined with other functions to develop a complex scenario.

Data processing function apps

Most of the systems built in organizations today are data processing systems. A typical data processing system can perform one or a combination of the following tasks:

- Conversion of data from one format to another
- Targeting of input data to appropriate storage
- Validation and clean-up of data
- Sorting of data
- Summarization of data
- Aggregation of data from multiple sources
- Statistical analysis of existing or new data
- Generating reports that list a summary or details of computed information

Data processing function apps can be used to build Nanoservices that can be aggregated to form data processing systems. Data processing function apps are always triggered by a data event. A data event is raised when state of data changes in a linked resource for example an item being added to a table, a queue, a container, and so on.

A data processing function has a set of in parameters which contain the data coming in for processing. Some of the scenarios where data processing functions are commonly used are:

- **Responding to CRUD operations**: Scenarios which require performing an action whenever state of data in a data store changes for example sending an email whenever a new use signs up.
- **Perform CRUD operations**: Scenarios in which data needs to be created or updated in another data store in response to data being added or updated in a data store.

- **Moving content between data stores**: Scenarios which require moving content between data stores for example moving a file to a temporary location for approval before moving it to a discoverable location. Such data transfer tasks can be carried out through a data processing Nanoservice.
- **Access data across services**: Scenarios which require pulling data from data stores such as blobs, queues, tables, and so on, and perform operations on them. The Nanoservice that accesses data from the stores can be integrated with other applications or Nanoservices that wish to reuse the workflow of the Nanoservice.

Webhook and API function apps

The webhook and API functions get triggered by events in external services such as GitHub, TFS, Office 365, OneDrive, and Microsoft PowerApps.

With the webhook and API functions, you can build notification Nanoservices that can perform custom operations whenever they receive a message on a configured webhook. For example, you can use webhooks with OneDrive that notifies your Nanoservice whenever a file gets uploaded to a folder.

Webhook and API functions accept a request and return a response. They mimic the web API or web service flows. These functions generally require some **CORS (Cross-Origin Resource Sharing)** settings to be managed. While developing the Nanoservices you can use an asterisk wildcard so they are wide open. However, you need to be aware that to invoke these Nanoservices from other services, you would need to set the cross-origin information in your function app settings.

These types of functions are generally used for exposing functionality to other apps and services. Other systems and clients can make web calls using HTTP protocols to them and expect a response. These Nanoservices are generally integrated with logic apps to form a workflow.

Summary

In this chapter, we looked at the definition of Nanoservices and how we can build Nanoservices using Azure Functions. We experimented with a simple Azure Function and customized a few of its attributes.

We looked at the various types of Azure Functions and what is the use of each one of them.

Other Books You May Enjoy

If you enjoyed this book, you may be interested in these other books by Packt:

Implementing Azure Cloud Design Patterns
Oliver Michalski, Stefano Demiliani

ISBN: 978-1-78839-336-2

- Learn to organize Azure access
- Design the core areas of the Azure Execution Model
- Work with storage and data management
- Create a health endpoint monitoring pattern
- Automate early detection of anomalies
- Identify and secure Azure features

Beginning Serverless Architectures with Microsoft Azure
Daniel Bass

ISBN: 978-1-78953-704-8

- Identify the key advantages and disadvantages of serverless development
- Build a fully-functioning serverless application and utilize a wide variety of Azure services
- Create, deploy, and manage your own Azure Functions in the cloud
- Implement core design principles for writing effective serverless code

Leave a review - let other readers know what you think

Please share your thoughts on this book with others by leaving a review on the site that you bought it from. If you purchased the book from Amazon, please leave us an honest review on this book's Amazon page. This is vital so that other potential readers can see and use your unbiased opinion to make purchasing decisions, we can understand what our customers think about our products, and our authors can see your feedback on the title that they have worked with Packt to create. It will only take a few minutes of your time, but is valuable to other potential customers, our authors, and Packt. Thank you!

Index